S0-FJB-702

THE

PUBLICATIONS

OF THE

PIPE ROLL SOCIETY

VOLUME XCVII

NEW SERIES – VOLUME LIX

ISBN 0 901134 57 0

NORMAN CHARTERS FROM ENGLISH SOURCES: ANTIQUARIES, ARCHIVES AND THE REDISCOVERY OF THE ANGLO-NORMAN PAST

BY

NICHOLAS VINCENT

LONDON

PRINTED FOR THE PIPE ROLL SOCIETY BY

FLEXPRESS LIMITED, LEICESTER

2013

THE PUBLICATION OF THIS WORK HAS BEEN FACILITATED BY A GRANT FROM THE STENTON FUND COMMITTEE OF THE BRITISH ACADEMY

For Matthew

TABLE OF CONTENTS

PREFACE BY GENERAL EDITORS

Next year, 2014, will see the 800th anniversary of the defeat of King John's allies at the Battle of Bouvines, a defeat that is widely regarded as a watershed in John's troubled reign. Not only did it frustrate the king in his ambitions to recover his former Continental dominions, but it also left him with reduced resources and vulnerable to his political opponents in England. In this volume, the 59th volume in the New Series and the 97th to be published by the Society, Professor Nicholas Vincent illuminates the wealth of charters from ducal Normandy that are preserved in English archives and celebrates the achievements of the antiquaries of the nineteenth century, and of Thomas Stapleton, in particular, in bringing to light evidences of the Anglo-Norman past. The Society is, once again, grateful to the Stenton Fund of the British Academy for a generous grant towards the cost of publishing this volume. As general editors, we would also like to extend our warm thanks to Ron Naylor and his team at Flexpress Limited for their assistance in seeing this volume through to publication.

PAUL DRYBURGH
York

LOUISE WILKINSON
Canterbury

ACKNOWLEDGMENTS

The present study grew out of a paper, first presented at the The National Archives (the former Public Record Office) in the summer of 2004, to a conference organized by David Crook under the auspices of the Pipe Roll Society, intended to commemorate the 800th anniversary of King John's loss of Normandy. The article was already a long one. By the time that I came to work up the proceedings of the 2004 conference for publication, it had quite outgrown its original purpose. What had begun as an essay, sparked by a desire to find out slightly more than was disclosed by the *Dictionary of National Biography* of the life of Thomas Stapleton, first editor of the Norman Pipe Rolls, now demanded reworking into a book. Such books, being accidental rather than pre-planned, do not necessarily make for the most fluent or coherent of reading, although I hope that in the introduction below some sort of story emerges from the haphazard assembly of facts. In particular, I hope that Stapleton's achievements at last obtain the recognition that they deserve. For help in establishing the provenance of various manuscripts now in the British Library, I am indebted to Claire Breay, Justin Clegg and Julian Harrison. Peter Meadows served as an expert guide to the Gage archive in Cambridge. Richard Gameson and Patrick Zutshi helped me with various of Stapleton's references to Norman and Italian manuscripts, John Charmley with political intrigue, Carole Rawcliffe with an expert medico-historical opinion, and Juliet Tyson with all manner of things, not least with the interpretation of various rude remarks in French. For assistance, well beyond the call of duty, in uncovering and transcribing the correspondence between Stapleton and Sir Thomas Phillipps, I am grateful to Hugh Doherty. Lord Gerald Fitzalan Howard and Susan Fitzalan Howard, John Martin Robinson and Mrs Pat Meanwell facilitated my access to Stapleton's surviving books and notebooks at Carlton Towers. Judy Burg at Hull spent a deal of time searching for a lost box of Stapleton's papers which eventually re-emerged just as this book was going to press, thanks to the detective work of Tim Gates. David Knights and Josephine Hutchings assisted with enquiries at Stonyhurst and Lincoln's Inn, Julian Pooley with others of Stapleton's letters. As always, I have benefited enormously from the wisdom and assistance of Christopher Brooke, David Carpenter, David Crouch, Judith Everard, Daniel Power and Nigel Ramsay. David Crouch and Daniel Power, in particular, proved ideal sounding boards and suppliers of significant information. Without help from the staff of the Canterbury Cathedral Archives, and in particular from Mark Page and Cressida Williams, joint authors of the magnificent new online catalogue of the Chartae Antiquae, the Canterbury section of what follows would have been a great deal more difficult to assemble. This book is dedicated to the eldest of my children, thanks to whom, and to a system of national education a great deal better than anything currently available in the United Kingdom, I have now spent something approaching three thousand hours (more than four months solid), sitting on the Eurostar between Paris and London. In Normandy, Paris and elsewhere, I wish to express particular gratitude to the ever-helpful archivists and library staffs at Evreux and Rouen, to the late Michel Nortier, to Jean-François Nieus and Thérèse de Hemptinne, to Ghislain Brunel at the Archives nationales, and to Florent Lenegre at Rouen. I wish that I could express similar gratitude to the former archivist of the Archives de Calvados at Caen.

Nicholas Vincent

LIST OF ABBREVIATED REFERENCES

Acta Henry II	*The Letters and Charters of King Henry II (1154–1189)*, ed. N. Vincent and others (Oxford forthcoming)
Actes Philippe Auguste	*Recueil des actes de Philippe Auguste, roi de France*, ed. H.–F. Delaborde, M. Nortier and others, 6 vols (Paris 1916–)
AD	Archives départementales
AN	Paris, Archives nationales de France
ANS	*Anglo-Norman Studies*
Archbp	Archbishop
BEC	*Bibliothèque de l'Ecole des Chartes*
BIHR	*Bulletin of the Institute of Historical Research*
BL	London, The British Library
Bnf	Paris, Bibliothèque nationale de France
Book of Fees	*Liber Feodorum. The Book of Fees Commonly Called Testa de Nevill*, 3 vols (London 1920–31)
Bp	Bishop
Cal. Chart. R.	*Calendar of Charter Rolls*, 6 vols (London 1903–27)
CCA	Canterbury Cathedral Archives
CFR	*Calendar of Fine Rolls of the Reign of Henry III*, ed. D. Carpenter, P. Dryburgh and B. Hartland (Woodbridge 2007–)
Close Rolls	*Close Rolls of the Reign of Henry III*, 14 vols (London 1902–38)
CLR	*Calendar of the Liberate Rolls*, 6 vols (London 1916–64)
CN	*Cartulaire Normand de Philippe-Auguste, Louis VIII, Saint-Louis et Philippe-le-Hardi*, ed. L. Delisle (Caen 1882)

Cottineau

L.H. Cottineau, *Répertoire topo-bibliographique des abbayes et des prieurés*, 3 vols (Mâcon 1935–70)

CP

The Complete Peerage, ed. G.E. Cockayne, revised by V. Gibbs, H.E. Doubleday, Lord Howard de Walden and G.H. White, 12 vols in 13 (London 1910–57)

CPR

Calendar of Patent Rolls (London 1891–)

CRR

Curia Regis Rolls of the Reigns of Richard I, John and Henry III Preserved in the Public Record Office (London 1922–)

Delisle, *Recueil*

Recueil des Actes de Henri II roi d'Angleterre et duc de Normandie concernant les provinces françaises et les affaires de France, ed. L. Delisle and E. Berger, 4 vols (Paris 1909–27)

Diceto

Radulphi de Diceto Opera Historica. The Historical Works of Master Ralph de Diceto, Dean of London, ed. W. Stubbs, 2 vols, RS (London 1876)

EHR

English Historical Review

EYC

Early Yorkshire Charters, vols i–iii ed. W. Farrer (Edinburgh 1914–16), vols iv–xii, ed. C.T. Clay, Yorkshire Archaeological Society Record Series extra series (1935–65)

Fauroux, *Recueil*

Recueil des actes des ducs de Normandie (911–1066), ed. M. Fauroux, Mémoires de la Société des Antiquaires de Normandie xxxvi (Caen 1961)

Fleming

R. Fleming, 'Christchurch's Sisters and Brothers: An Edition and Discussion of the Canterbury Obituary Lists', *The Culture of Christendom: Essays in Medieval History in Commemoration of Denis L.T. Bethell*, ed. M.A. Meyer (London 1993), 114–53

Foedera

Foedera, Conventiones, Litterae etc., or Rymer's Foedera, 1066–1383, ed. A. Clarke et al., vol.1 part i (London 1816)

GC

Gallia Christiana in Provincias Ecclesiasticas distributa, 16 vols (Paris 1715–1865)

Gervase	*The Historical Works of Gervase of Canterbury*, ed. W. Stubbs, 2 vols, RS (London 1879–80)
Haskins, *Institutions*	C.H. Haskins, *Norman Institutions* (New York 1918)
Hatton's Seals	*Sir Christopher Hatton's Book of Seals*, ed. L.C. Loyd and D.M. Stenton (Oxford 1950)
HMC	Historical Manuscripts Commission
Howden, *Chronica*	*Chronica Rogeri de Houedene*, ed. W. Stubbs, 4 vols, RS (London 1868–71)
Howden, *Gesta*	*Gesta regis Henrici secundi et Ricardi primi*, ed. W. Stubbs, 2 vols, RS (London 1867)
J–L	*Regesta Pontificum Romanorum*, ed. P. Jaffé, revised edition by S. Loewenfeld and others, 2 vols (Leipzig 1885–8)
JSA	*Journal of the Society of Archivists*
Jugements	*Recueil de Jugements de l'Echiquier de Normandie au XIIIe siècle*, ed. L. Delisle (Paris 1864)
Landon, *Itinerary*	*The Itinerary of King Richard I*, ed. L. Landon, PRS new series xiii (1935)
Layettes	*Layettes du Trésor des Chartes*, ed. A. Teulet, H.–F. Delaborde and E Berger, 5 vols (Paris 1863–1909)
Léchaudé, *Extrait*	*Extrait des chartes et autres actes normands ou Anglo-normands qui se trouvent dans les archives de Calvados*, ed. Léchaudé d'Anisy, 2 vols (Caen 1834–5)
Lit. Cant.	*Literae Cantuarienses*, ed. J.B. Sheppard, 3 vols, Rolls Series (London 1887–9)
Loyd, *Origins*	L.C. Loyd, *The Origins of Some Anglo-Norman Families*, ed. C.T. Clay and D.C. Douglas, Harleian Society ciii (1951)
Memoranda Roll 1 John	*The Memoranda Roll for the Michaelmas Term of the First Year of the Reign of King John (1199–1200)*, ed. H.G. Richardson, Pipe Roll Society n.s. xxi (London 1943)

MGH	Monumenta Germaniae Historica
Monasticon	Sir William Dugdale and Roger Dodsworth, *Monasticon Anglicanum*, ed. J. Caley, H. Ellis and B. Bandinel, 6 vols in 8 (London 1846)
MRSN	*Magni Rotuli Scaccarii Normanniae sub regibus Angliae*, ed. T. Stapleton, 2 vols (London 1840–44)
MTB	*Materials for the History of Thomas Becket*, ed. J.C. Roberton and J.B. Sheppard, 7 vols, RS (1875–85)
ODNB	*The Oxford Dictionary of National Biography*, ed. H.C.G. Matthew and B. Harrison (Oxford 2004, here citing the electronic version at http://www.oxforddnb.com)
Orderic	*The Ecclesiastical History of Orderic Vitalis*, ed. M. Chibnall, 6 vols (Oxford 1969–80)
Patent Rolls	*Patent Rolls 1216-32*, 2 vols (London 1901–3)
Pouillés Rouen	*Pouillés de la province de Rouen*, ed. A. Longnon (Paris 1903)
Power, *Norman Frontier*	D. Power, *The Norman Frontier in the Twelfth and Early Thirteenth Centuries* (Cambridge 2004)
Powicke, *Loss*	F.M. Powicke, *The Loss of Normandy 1189–1204* (2nd ed., Manchester 1961)
PR	*Pipe Roll*, published, save where indicated below, by the Pipe Roll Society
PRO	The Public Record Office, London (The National Archives)
PRS	Pipe Roll Society
Red Book	*The Red Book of the Exchequer*, ed. H. Hall, 3 vols, RS (London 1896)
Regesta	*Regesta Regum Anglo-Normannorum*, ed. H.W.C. Davis, C. Johnson, H.A. Cronne and R.H.C. Davis, 4 vols (1913–69)

Registres	*Les Registres de Philippe–Auguste*, ed. J.W. Baldwin (Paris 1992)
RHF	*Recueil des historiens des Gaules et de la France*, ed. M. Bouquet and others, 24 vols in 25 (Paris 1738–1904)
RLC	*Rotuli Litterarum Clausarum*, ed. T.D. Hardy, 2 vols (London 1833–44)
RLP	*Rotuli Litterarum Patentium*, ed. T.D. Hardy (London 1835)
Rot. Chart.	*Rotuli Chartarum*, ed. T.D. Hardy (London 1837)
Rot. Lib.	*Rotuli de Liberate ac de misis et praestitis regnante Iohanne*, ed. T.D. Hardy (London 1844)
Rot. Norm.	*Rotuli Normanniae in Turri Londinensi asservati*, ed. T.D. Hardy (London 1835)
Rot. Ob.	*Rotuli de Oblatis et Finium*, ed. T.D. Hardy (London 1835)
Round, *Calendar*	*Calendar of Documents Preserved in France Illustrative of the History of Great Britain and Ireland*, ed. J.H. Round (London 1899)
RS	Rolls Series
Spear, *Personnel*	*The Personnel of the Norman Cathedrals During the Ducal Period, 911–1204*, ed. D.S. Spear (London 2006)
Stein	H. Stein, *Bibliographie générale des cartulaires français* (Paris 1907)
TNA	The National Archives of the United Kingdom
'Torigny'	The 'Chronicle' of Robert de Torigni, in *Chronicles of the Reigns of Stephen, Henry II and Richard I*, ed. R. Howlett, 4 vols, RS (London 1884–89), vol.1
VCH	*The Victoria County History*

INTRODUCTION

The study that follows is intended to draw attention to some of the more significant documentary sources for ducal Normandy to be found in English manuscript collections, in certain instances well-known to historians of the Anglo-Norman realm, in others more obscure. In searching for such records, I have had of necessity to recreate the fascinating, but to date neglected story of the earliest antiquaries, both English and French, whose exploration of Norman archives helps to explain why so many Anglo-Norman antiquities are today to be found in England rather than France. Anyone who has ventured into the departmental archives of Normandy, the Bibliothèque nationale, or the Archives nationales in Paris, will be aware of the extent of the contribution that French documentary resources have still to make to the study of the Anglo-Norman realm. In terms of the vast numbers of single sheet charters surviving in the collections at Rouen, Caen, or amongst the Templar and Savigny charters in the Archives nationales, Normandy and Paris boast resources, for the most part still unpublished and in many cases virtually uncatalogued, that dwarf the relatively sparse evidences for Normandy that survive on the other side of the Channel. Nonetheless, England's archives are not entirely bereft of significance to the study of ducal Normandy. Just as the history of Normandy, from the death of Robert of Torigny if not before, has to be written using chronicles that are for the most part English rather than Norman in authorship – Norman historical writing drying up in a most startling fashion after the 1180s – so the documentary resources now preserved in England have a vital role to play in our understanding of ducal Normandy, not only at the very end of the Anglo-Norman realm, immediately before 1204, but throughout the period of Norman ascendancy, from the eleventh century onwards.[1]

In what follows, I shall restrict myself for the most part to evidences that were issued in Normandy for Norman lands, which directly involve Norman institutions or which concern the Plantagenet administration of Normandy. Even here, however, the distinction between Norman and Anglo-Norman evidence is not an easy, nor necessarily a helpful distinction to draw. Domesday Book is in many ways a very 'English' record, and yet without it we would be deprived of most of what we know of the landholding elite of eleventh-century Normandy. Charters issued for monasteries in Yorkshire or Wales can be just as important for establishing the descent of Norman families or the retinues of Norman lords as they are for understanding conditions on the English side of the Channel. Indeed, working from evidences that were as much English as Norman, Lewis

---

[1] For the feebleness of the later ducal chronicle tradition, see D. Power, 'Angevin Normandy', *A Companion to the Anglo-Norman World*, ed. C. Harper-Bill and E. van Houts (Woodbridge 2003), 63–4.

Loyd has taught us more about the prosopography of eleventh and twelfth-century Normandy than is to be found in many a study that restricts its focus to Normandy alone.[2]

My introductory survey is itself divided into four parts. In the first, I shall consider the principal classes of medieval evidences preserved in the royal, subsequently the Public records, beginning with the so-called Norman Pipe and chancery rolls, before looking beyond these to the scattered fragments of Norman charter or administrative material still to be found amongst the other classes of The National Archives. In the second part of this survey, I shall turn from the documents themselves to their editors, and in particular to the activities of two men, Thomas Stapleton (1806–1849) and Amédée Louis Léchaudé d'Anisy (1772–1857), whose endeavours can be used both to illustrate the emergence of 'Anglo-Norman' history as a distinct subdiscipline of medieval scholarship and to explain why so many of the more interesting documentary evidences for twelfth and thirteenth-century Normandy are today to be found not in Normandy itself but in The National Archives, the British Library, and on occasion, in collections scattered across not only England but the English-speaking world. In a third section, I outline a group of more than sixty Norman or Anglo-Norman charters, gathered from the various documentary collections thus far considered, intended to illustrate the importance of these English collections and the degree to which they still contain significant and in many cases untapped evidence for the history of medieval Normandy. The introduction concludes with a survey of a further forty-five charters from northern France, by no means all of them 'Norman' although in several instances of significance for the history of the barons of the Norman frontier, still preserved amongst the archives of Canterbury Cathedral: perhaps the most important cache of such documents preserved in any English archive since the Middle Ages, and for the most part previously unpublished. The one hundred and twenty-one documents outlined in sections three and four of the introduction are thereafter edited in the main body of the text.

This is by no means a comprehensive survey, either of the archives or of the antiquaries who have worked on them. The history of Anglo-Norman scholarship in England has yet to be written. But, as a foretaste of some of the stories still to be told, I hope that the present investigation may serve at least to whet the appetite.

---

[2]   See in particular Loyd, *Origins*, and the immensely learned notes to *Hatton's Seals*.

1. THE NATIONAL ARCHIVES AND THEIR MEDIEVAL NORMAN EVIDENCES

Historians have long been aware of the existence of two bodies of evidence in The National Archives, fundamental to our knowledge of medieval Normandy: the so-called Norman 'Pipe' Rolls, recording the accounting process of the Norman Exchequer, and the equally important but somewhat inappropriately named 'Norman Rolls' of the royal chancery, now classes E 373 and C 64.[3]

The actual contents of the Norman Exchequer Rolls (E 373) I shall leave for future detailed description by Vincent Moss, the acknowledged expert charged with the responsibility of re-editing these documents.[4] Here I shall restrict myself to their most obvious features. But for the Norman Exchequer Rolls, the first surviving from the account taken at Michaelmas 1180, the last from the account taken at Michaelmas 1203, our knowledge both of Norman ducal finance and of ducal administration would be as derisory as our knowledge of the finance and administration of the more southerly parts of the Plantagenet dominion, regions for which we lack any financial accounts, at least before the thirteenth century. Without the Norman Exchequer accounts we might be tempted to suppose that the kings of England derived little or no financial advantage from their lands in Normandy, and that the duchy itself was peripheral to the Plantagenets' concerns: suppositions which, as the Norman accounts make plain, would be entirely false. This supplies a salutary reminder that we should not necessarily discount the financial significance of other regions, such as Poitou or Gascony, to Henry II and his sons merely because no financial accounts survive for these regions. The physical format of the Norman Exchequer Rolls corresponds closely to that of the English Pipe Rolls, save that the 'rotulets' of the Norman rolls are slightly narrower and are sewn together into considerably shorter membranes than those used at the

---

[3] For a brief introduction to the Norman chancery rolls, with more detailed consideration of the Norman 'Pipe' Rolls, see H. Jenkinson, 'Financial Records of the Reign of King John', *Magna Carta Commemoration Essays*, ed. H.E. Malden (London 1917), 262–3, 265–6, 270–3, 285–9.

[4] Pending the publication of a full study, see *Pipe Rolls of the Exchequer of Normandy*, ed. V. Moss, PRS n.s. liii (2004), with further volumes still in press; V. Moss, 'Normandy and England in 1180: The Pipe Roll Evidence', *England and Normandy in the Middle Ages*, ed. D. Bates and A. Curry (London 1994), 185–95; idem, "The Defence of Normandy 1195–1198', *ANS*, xxiv (2002), 145–61; idem, 'Reprise et innovations: les rôles normands et anglais de l'année 1194–1195 et la perte de la Normandie', *La Normandie et l'Angleterre au Moyen-Age*, ed. P. Bouet and V. Gazeau (Caen 2003), 89–98. There is an excellent introduction to the 18 rolls and accounts in TNA class E 373 by David Crook, available as introduction to the typescript TNA calendar to E 373. I would nonetheless dispute Dr Crook's suggestion that a reference to a twenty-year farm in the earliest of the Norman Pipe Rolls (*MRSN*, i, 12) necessarily proves the existence of such rolls as early as the 1160s.

Westminster Exchequer.[5] The writing of both the Norman and English rolls is strikingly similar. As yet, it is impossible to say whether the Norman rolls are equivalent to the English Pipe Rolls in the circumstances of their writing: were they drawn up and annotated as an integral aspect of the process of account each year, marked up as the account proceeded, with the details of sums paid or not paid by the accounting officers being entered on the roll as these officers rendered their accounts? Or are they instead fair copies of accounts already rendered?[6] A number of the documents stored in the main Norman Pipe Rolls series are in fact not Pipe Rolls at all but foreign accounts, dealing with income or expenditure by particular local officials.[7] The earliest of the Norman Exchequer Rolls may well be 'Pipe Rolls' integral to the process of account, although certainty here is difficult to achieve.[8] Were it not for the fact that the *Dialogue of the Exchequer* tells us that the Chancellor's Roll was maintained as a fair copy made from the Treasurer's Pipe Roll, the writing and format of the surviving English Chancellors' Rolls would not necessarily permit us to distinguish them from those of the Exchequer. A comparison of the writing and format of the three surviving Exchequer Rolls from 1180 – the Norman Pipe Roll, and the English Pipe and Chancellor's Rolls – reveals, at least superficially, as many similarities as differences.[9] Only later, with the Norman account rolls for the reign of King John, do we appear to enter the realm, not of 'Pipe Rolls' proper, used in the process of account, but that of 'counter rolls' or fair copies, on occasion surviving in duplicate, of accounts already rendered by the various individual bailiffs accounting each year at the Caen Exchequer. As such, these later Norman Exchequer Rolls differ fundamentally from their English counterparts, and become closer both in function and physical appearance to other such 'counter-rolls', including the so-called 'Pipe Rolls' of the bishopric of Winchester, surviving from 1208 onwards.[10]

---

[5] Compare, for example, the sewn-up rotulets of TNA E 373/10 (Norman Pipe Roll 1180), which are approximately 295mm. wide and 500mm. long, with those of the equivalent English Pipe Roll, TNA E 372/26, which are 400mm. across and up to 1400mm. long. Both rolls are ruled into approximately 7mm. line spaces. Similar distinctions continue to apply into the 1190s and beyond.

[6] For the processes here, see M. Hagger, 'Theory and Practice in the Making of Twelfth-Century Pipe Rolls', *Records, Administration and Aristocratic Society in the Anglo-Norman Realm*, ed. N. Vincent (Woodbridge 2009), 45–74.

[7] As noted by Jenkinson, 'Financial Records', 270–3.

[8] The rolls of 1180 (TNA E 373/10), 1184 (E 373/1, incomplete) and 1198 (E 373/2) could well be 'Pipe Rolls'. The roll for 1195 (E 373/18) is perhaps a counter roll. A great deal more work is required before the mysteries that underline the process of account in Normandy are fully solved.

[9] Thus, I would question whether a casual observer could easily distinguish the circumstances of the making of the Chancellor's Roll 26 Henry II (TNA E 352/13, Michaelmas 1180) from those of the Treasurer's Pipe Roll (TNA E 372/26).

[10] See here the forthcoming work of Vincent Moss, and meanwhile, for the bishopric of Winchester account rolls and the 'counter roll' form in general, see N. Vincent, 'The Origins of the Winchester Pipe Rolls', *Archives*, xxi (1994), 25–42.

The Norman Exchequer Rolls have long been recognised as a source of fundamental significance to the history of ducal Normandy. However, even today historians remain in many cases readier to celebrate than to use them. This peculiar state of affairs results not from any inadequacy of the rolls themselves but from the way in which they were published: a story that I shall tell in detail in the second part of this essay and that is of fundamental significance if we are to understand not only how English scholars first came into contact with the documentary resources of Normandy, but why, even today, these resources remain less than fully exploited. For the moment we need merely note that Thomas Stapleton, first editor of the Norman Pipe Rolls, never completed his edition, published in two volumes in 1840 and 1844 but left without an index to persons and places. The index volume, which he had always intended, may not even have been begun by the time of Stapleton's premature death in 1849.[11] As a result, short of trawling through 575 pages of densely spaced Latin text, it remains impossible to use Stapleton's edition with any ease. The vast majority of persons or places went unlisted by Stapleton, let alone properly identified. His interest in particular Norman families was pursued at the expense of any real concern for the vast numbers of lesser knights and royal servants whose careers could be traced from the accounts, whilst his knowledge of Norman topography, though remarkable for an Englishman, predated by many years the publication of the Norman topographical dictionaries which, though neither comprehensive nor especially easy to use, must be considered essential to any modern historian of the duchy. Moreover, given the chaotic state in which Stapleton found the Norman Exchequer records, he failed to note the existence of various fragments and additions which have more recently come to light. An index appended to the inaccurate French reprinting of Stapleton's edition, undertaken between 1845 and 1852, and a card index to Stapleton's edition, compiled under the guidance of Sir James Holt – now, thanks to Daniel Power, circulating in a revised digital form – go some way towards opening up the rolls to more detailed enquiry.[12] But not until the publication and indexing of Dr Moss's edition, still some years from completion, will the rolls themselves be usable in the way that the

---

[11] According to the anonymous obituarist in *The Gentleman's Magazine* (1850), part 1, 323, the index volume was held back 'more from the deficiency of funds for its production than any disinclination on the part of the editor'.

[12] For the principal edition, see *Magni Rotuli Scaccarii Normanniae sub regibus Angliae*, ed. T. Stapleton, 2 vols (London 1840–44), printing most of the records now assembled as TNA E 373/1–18. Various fragments, including estreats and memoranda, now TNA E 101/152/1, E 101/349/1A and E 101/505/4, recovered since Stapleton's time, were printed by H. Legras, 'Un fragment de rôle normand inédit de Jean sans Terre', *Bulletin de la Société des Antiquaires de Normandie*, xxix (1914), 21–31, and as *Miscellaneous Records of the Norman Exchequer 1199–1204*, ed. S.R. Packard, Smith College Studies in History xii nos 1-4 (Northampton Mass. 1926–7). Dr Moss's forthcoming edition is intended to replace both Stapleton and Packard. Stapleton's edition was very swiftly disseminated in France via its reprinting by Léchaudé d'Anisy: *Grands rôles des échiquiers de Normandie*, and *Magni Rotuli Scaccarii Normanniae*, ed. A. Léchaudé d'Anisy and A. Charma, Société des Antiquaires de Normandie, xv–xvi (new series v–vi) (1845–52). It is this French reprinting which is the only one to be supplied with a published index. The digital index can be supplied to anyone who cares to apply to me for it by email.

English Pipe Rolls have been used for a century or more. Only when they are at last properly indexed will the full glory of the Norman Exchequer Rolls become apparent. They will in due course yield up an extraordinary multitude of references for genealogists, for the historians of building and landscape, for economic historians, as well as for the wider history of the duchy's politics. For the moment, Thomas Stapleton's endeavours must serve as an illustration both of the heroic nature of archival research, and of its potential perils. We shall encounter Stapleton again in due course, but for the moment let us pass from the Norman Exchequer rolls to the other chief class of Norman records to be found in The National Archives: records whose editing represented a relatively modest achievement compared to the heroic labours of Stapleton.

By contrast to the records of the Norman Exchequer, by the early nineteenth century most of the so-called Norman Rolls of the chancery had long been identified and classified, used widely by Thomas Madox if by few other English historians.[13] Since at least the early eighteenth century, French historians had been keen to gain access to the Norman, Gascon and French rolls stored at the Tower of London, precisely because it was hoped that they might supply a complete picture of English administration and landholding in France comparable to that supplied for England itself by the English chancery rolls. It was with such ends in mind that Thomas Carte, as early as 1743, published an incomplete catalogue of various of the entries in these rolls, and that in the 1760s Louis Bréquigny travelled to London to make more extensive transcripts. The full publication of the earliest of the chancery's Norman Rolls in 1835, carried out under the direction of Thomas Duffus Hardy for the Record Commissioners, brought with it great expectations. 'When the whole of this important body of evidence is published', Hardy wrote, 'there is scarcely a city or town in Normandy, Gascony, or such of the other provinces of France as were formerly subject to England, which will not be able to find its charter of incorporation, augmentations of its privileges, or confirmations of its franchises': a statement that must be accounted one of the more outrageously optimistic ever to have been committed to writing by an English scholar.[14] By publishing a full edition of the six surviving Norman rolls of John's reign, together with a single, much later Norman Roll for the reign of Henry V, Hardy in fact revealed what French scholars had already discovered: that the rolls themselves were extremely diverse in nature, and that they could in no way live up to the great expectations that had once been entertained of them in France. This in itself may explain why publication thereafter ceased.[15] None of the remaining Norman Rolls of the reign of Henry V has

---

[13] T. Madox, *The History and the Antiquities of the Exchequer of the Kings of England,* first published 1711, here quoting from the 2nd ed., 2 vols (London 1769), i, 156–7, 170–7, 516–25, quoting extensively from the Norman Fine, Charter and Contrabrevia rolls for the year 2 John (1200-01).

[14] *Rot. Norm.,* p.iii.

[15] Hardy's edition, *Rot. Norm.,* carries what was to prove the over optimistic title 'Vol.1 de annis 1200–1205, necnon de anno 1417'. It was reprinted, not entirely accurately, by Léchaudé

since been published, and although, in a rare example of Anglo-French co-operation, the thirteenth-century Gascon Rolls (C 61) did eventually appear in print, no attempt whatsoever has been made as yet to publish the 120 or so Gascon Rolls after 1318, or the later, so-called French Rolls (now reclassified amongst the Treaty Rolls, C 76) dating from the reign of Edward III and his successors.[16] The only printed guides to the fifteenth-century Norman Rolls remain entirely inadequate: the highly selective index by Thomas Carte, published in 1743, supplemented by a series of equally jejune abstracts published in the Public Record Office Deputy Keeper's Reports for 1880–1.[17] As we shall see, the effect of this has been to deprive historians of access to what is in reality an extremely valuable source for ducal Normandy both before and after 1204.

The series of Norman Rolls begins with six such rolls compiled in the reign of King John. It was apparent even to Hardy, their editor, that these six rolls were far from uniform in nature.[18] If we sort them into their various classes, we find that the first is a roll of seven membranes, with an elaborate contemporary title: 'Roll of Norman charters and cyrographs, made in the time of Guarin de Glapion seneschal of Normandy, in the second year of the reign of King John, with Samson abbot of Caen and Ralph l'Abbé then serving at the Exchequer, Peter de Lions serving as the King's clerk'.[19] This title, however, is misleading, since the 43 charters recorded here span the period from the 1150s through to John's reign. All of them relate to Normandy. Nineteen are private charters, the majority described as concords or final concords made at the Exchequer at Caen, most of them apparently, and two of them certainly, issued in the second year of John's reign, but at least one having been made in the presence of the previous seneschal of Normandy, William fitz Ralph, and another dated at Caen in 1202, the

---

d'Anisy as part of his re-edition of *Grands rôles des échiquiers de Normandie* (1845), 89–136.

[16] Two volumes of *Treaty Rolls* have been published, ed. P. Chaplais and J. Ferguson (London 1955–72), extending to 1339. For the Gascon Rolls, published variously by Charles Bémont and others, and yet continued to 1317, see the listing in *Gascon Rolls Preserved in the Public Record Office 1307–1317*, ed. Y. Renouard and R. Fawtier (London 1962), pp.i–ii. A project led by Dr Malcolm Vale of Oxford and Dr Paul Booth of Liverpool to publish the remaining Gascon Rolls is in progress. For details, see www.gascon.rolls.org.

[17] T. Carte, *Catalogue des rolles gascons, normans et françois*, 2 vols (Paris/London 1743); appendices to the 41st and 42nd *Report of the Deputy Keeper of the Public Records* (London 1880–1), at respectively pp.671–810 and pp.313–472. These English 'Norman Rolls' are not to be confused with the later chancery registers of Henry VI for his French possessions, now AN JJ172–5, whence the extensive extracts relating to Normandy, *Actes de la chancellerie d'Henri VI concernant la Normandie sous la domination anglaise (1422–1435)*, ed. P. le Cacheux, 2 vols (Rouen/Paris 1907–8).

[18] To date, the best guide to the Norman 'chancery' rolls remains that by Jenkinson, 'Financial Records of the Reign of King John', 263, 285–8.

[19] TNA C 64/3 m.7: *Hic est rotulus cartarum et cyrographorum Normann(ie) factus tempore Guar(ini) de Glapion tunc senesc(alli) Normann(ie) anno secundo regni reg(is) Iohannis, assistentibus ad scac(carium) Sansone abbate Cadom' et Rad(ulfo) Labe, Petro de Lions clerico domini regis.* This is written throughout in a fine chancery-style hand, on sheets approximately 260mm wide. Apparently complete, since there is a great deal of parchment left blank and unruled at the end of m.1. Printed in full in *Rot. Norm.*, 1–22.

third year of John's reign.[20] The remaining twenty-four charters are royal, two of them of Henry II, three of Richard, and no less than nineteen of King John. The vast majority of the royal as of the private charters have been abbreviated and in the process deprived of their dating clauses and witness lists. However, of the nineteen charters of John, two are dated not to the King's second but to his third year, 25 November 1201 and 1 April 1202.[21] Of the remaining sixteen charters of John, all of them undated, no less than seven are also to be found enrolled in the main series of chancery Charter Rolls (C 53), covering England as well as France and preserving complete witness lists and dates. Four of the seven are to be found on the Charter Roll 2 John, two are preserved in the Charter Roll for the year 1 John, and another in the Charter Roll 5 John, the dating range of all nineteen charters extending from 4 January 1200 to 1 July 1203.[22] What we have here, therefore, seems not to be a distinct Norman Charter Roll independent of the principal chancery roll of charters, nor an annual summary of charters recited before the Exchequer in the year 2 John (May 1200–1), but a much more miscellaneous collection of documents, in some ways analogous to the English Cartae Antiquae Rolls (C 52), preserving some but not all of the charters and records shown at the Caen Exchequer between 1200 and 1203. In the normal run of events, the King's charters to Norman beneficiaries, together with those issued to beneficiaries in England, Ireland and the rest of France, were enrolled on the chancery Charter Rolls (C 53), the earliest such roll surviving for the year 1 John (1199–1200).[23] The Norman 'Charter Roll', however, is of particular significance, both for its preservation of records from those years, the third and fourth of King John's reign (May 1201–3), for which the chancery Charter Rolls no longer survive, and for its preservation of much more miscellaneous instruments and final concords.

What this roll of charters and cyrographs represents, I would suggest, is the continuation of a process, painstakingly traced by Daniel Power, by which some, though perhaps not all final concords made before the Norman Exchequer were being enrolled, certainly by 1190 and quite possibly as early as Michaelmas 1186.[24] The enrolments were not in the same form as the writ or charter rolls of the English royal chancery, but were rolls maintained at the Norman Exchequer as a record of miscellaneous business transacted before the Exchequer, perhaps for the lack in Normandy of

---

[20] *Rot. Norm.*, 6–7, 12–17.

[21] *Rot. Norm.*, 17–19.

[22] *Rot. Chart.*, 32b (*Rot. Norm.*, 20, to William Piculf, at Bonneville-sur-Touques, 4 January 1200), 35 (*Rot. Norm.*, 16, to Ardenne, at Barfleur, 6 February 1200), 65 (*Rot. Norm.*, 11, to Simon de Foumouchon, at La Roche-d'Orival, 26 May 1200), 69b (*Rot. Norm.*, 2–3, 15, to Walter archbp of Rouen and to the abbey of Ardenne, both at Argentan, 7 June 1200), 91b (*Rot. Norm.*, to John de Sackville, at Canterbury, 25 March 1201), 109b (*Rot. Norm.*, 21–2, to Robert de Lisieux, at Rouen, 1 July 1203).

[23] TNA C 53/1 et seq, printed in *Rot. Chart.*, pp.xl–i, 1ff.

[24] D. Power, 'En Quête de sécurité juridique dans la Normandie angevine: concorde finale et inscription au rouleau', *BEC*, clxviii (2010), 327–71, esp. pp.346–52, citing key evidences from L. Valin, *Le Duc de Normandie et sa cour (912–1204)* (Paris 1910), 278–9; Round, *Calendar*, no.461.

anything analogous to the feet of fines, or third part of tripartite cyrographs, maintained for judicial business in England from July 1195 onwards. The closest analogy to the lost series of Norman Rolls, of which C 64/3 stands as sole reminder, may lie in the English Exchequer's Cartae Antiquae Rolls and in such semi-private 'cartulary' rolls as the so-called 'Chester Domesday': a roll of fines and charters made before the Exchequer of the earldom of Chester from the 1190s onwards.[25]

We can deal fairly rapidly with the next two rolls printed by Hardy. The first is a roll entitled 'rotulus Norm(annie) inceptus die Ascensionis Domini de oblat(is) recept(is) anno regni reg(is) I(ohannis) secundo', of four membranes, preserving 51 entries relating to fines made with the King for property and rights in Normandy, Anjou (3 entries), Poitou (2 entries) and on both sides of the Channel (at least 2 entries relating to land in Normandy and England).[26] The roll is clearly the counterpart to the Oblata or Fine Roll 2 John for the King's English and Irish dominions,[27] but in this instance covering not only Normandy but all the King's French lands north and south of the Loire. Such rolls were an essential feature of Exchequer practice from the very beginning, and must have existed from the time of the very earliest Exchequer Pipe Rolls, being indispensable to the compilation of entries on the Pipe Rolls for new fines and offerings.[28] In this particular instance, we lack the Norman Exchequer accounts taken at Michaelmas 1200 or Michaelmas 1201, and hence cannot easily check off the entries on the Norman Oblata Roll against the Norman accounts. Even so, fines recorded in the Oblata Roll are still to be found at Michaelmas 1203, being cleared in the next surviving Norman Exchequer Roll.[29] Like the equivalent English/Irish Oblata Roll for the year 2 John, entries on the Norman Oblata Roll are marked up according to the particular bailiwick in which the fine would be entered on the Norman Exchequer Roll, although with what appears to be less regularity or clarity than in England. Assuming the Norman Oblata Roll to be complete, its four membranes and

---

[25] R. Stewart-Brown, 'The "Domesday" Roll of Chester', *EHR*, xxxvii (1922), 481–500. The Chester roll appears to have dated from the time of earl Ranulph (1181–1232), being introduced at some time between 1194 and 1208.

[26] TNA C 64/2, again written in a 'chancery' hand, but less neatly than the Norman roll of charters C 64/3, the membranes measuring approximately 250mm. at their widest, printed in full in *Rot. Norm.*, 37–44.

[27] TNA C 60/1B, printed in *Rot. Ob.*, 76–143.

[28] See here the remarks by David Carpenter on the early Fine and Originalia Rolls implied by the processes involved in the making of the English Pipe Roll, at least as early as 1130: D. Carpenter, ' "In Testimonium Factorum Brevium": The Beginnings of the English Chancery Rolls', *Records, Administration and Aristocratic Society in the Anglo-Norman Realm*, ed. N. Vincent (Woodbridge 2009).

[29] See, for example, William de Pirou's offer of 1200 livres angevin for the Norman lands of William de Tracy (*Rot. Norm.*, 38, with marginal notation 'Constant' et Vire'), of which just over 430 livres is recorded as still owing in the Norman Exchequer account taken at Michaelmas 1203 (*MRSN*, ii, 529, duly entered in the account for the Cotentin), or Peter de St-Hilaire's fine of 200 livres and a horse for the land of 'Leges' (*Rot. Norm.*, 39, with marginal notation 'Moret'), still entirely unpaid in 1203 (*MRSN*, ii, 545, in the account for the bailliage of Mortain).

51 entries can be compared to the 22 membranes and 421 entries on the English/Irish roll of this year, to supply some idea of the relative volume of fines negotiated with the King's English or French subjects. Particularly notable is the feeble rate of fines recorded from Anjou or Poitou (a mere five entries), which may suggest either that the King's southern subjects had less cause to make offerings to the King for lands or privileges, or, more plausibly, that such offerings were for the most part negotiated not with the King himself but with his southern officers, whose records are now entirely lost.[30]

Hardy also published a roll of valuations, in four membranes, recording the values of English lands held by Norman landowners. The majority of these entries concern southern England, apparently being taken on sworn inquest, and concern ecclesiastical corporations as well as secular Norman landowners. As Hardy himself was aware, the roll supplies only a limited survey of English lands held by Normans in 1204, and in many instances relates to estates that long after 1204 remained in the hands of alien, Norman abbeys and priories.[31] It is nonetheless extremely significant, being our only contemporary survey of part, though by no means all, of the 'Terre Normannnorum' confiscated by King John in 1204.[32]

The three remaining Norman Rolls of the reign constitute a chronological series of writ-rolls. Unlike the charter or valuation roll, but in company with the Oblata Roll, they seem to have issued from the itinerant royal chancery rather than the Exchequer. In two cases they carry contemporary titles, the first entitled simply 'A roll of contrabrevia of the 2nd year in Normandy', made up of six membranes of writs dated between 17 May 1200 and 9 April 1201, the second entitled 'A roll of lands released and of contrabrevia for Normandy, Anjou and Poitou begun at Ascension Day, 23 May in the 4th year of the reign of King John' and continuing with eleven membranes of writs dated between 25 May 1202 and 12 May 1203. The third roll lacks a heading and is clearly incomplete, but preserves four membranes of writs very similar to those on the contrabrevia rolls 2 and 4 John, in this instance covering part of the year 5 John, for the period July– 6 December 1203.[33] The specific mention of contrabrevia might suggest that all three rolls, although prepared in the chancery, were intended for the use of the Norman Exchequer, and reminds us of Richard fitz Nigel's statement that as early as the 1170s, the chancery of Henry II was compiling contrabrevia for the use of the English Exchequer, recording all financial writs issued from the itinerant royal chancery for which account would in

---

[30] During the period in question, May 1200 – May 1201, the King was in Normandy in May, Anjou in June, Poitou and Gascony in July-August, returned to Normandy in September and thence to England in October, where he remained until the following year.

[31] TNA C 64/7, printed in *Rot. Norm.*, 122–43, with commentary by Hardy at p.xxi.

[32] See now T.K. Moore, 'The Loss of Normandy and the Invention of "Terre Normannorum", 1204', *EHR*, cxxv (2010), 1071–1109.

[33] See table below p.13.

due course have to be made before the Exchequer barons.[34] None of the Norman Contrabrevia Rolls, however, is exclusively given over to Norman Exchequer business. Although virtually all of their writs are financial in nature, or at least relate to grants of land for which accounts might be owing or excused, a large number of them relate not to Normandy but to Anjou and Poitou, for which it is generally assumed no accounts were rendered at the Norman Exchequer. Various of the southern writs nonetheless assume a forthcoming account, as for example on 25 June 1200, when William des Roches, seneschal of Anjou, was sent a writ of 'computate', to cover 25 livres spent by the prévôt of Chinon on (siege) machines being made by Master Urric, the King's engineer, or when the seneschal of Poitou was commanded on 1 September to pay Savaric de Mauléon 200 livres angevin of his money fee 'at our Exchequer' ('ad scaccarium nostrum').[35] In addition, both rolls preserve copies of writs that should rightly have been presented not to the Norman, Angevin or Poitevin Exchequers but to the Exchequers of England or Ireland. A writ of 10 October 1200, for example, entered on the Norman 'Contrabrevia' Roll 2 John, ordering the treasurer and chamberlain of the English Exchequer to pay the wages of two clerks who had sung the 'Cristus Vincit', is duly re-entered, in its proper place, in the roll of contrabrevia preserved for England and Ireland, known today as the earliest of the Liberate Rolls, for the year 2 John.[36] A writ of 13 February 1203, entered on the Norman Contrabrevia Roll 4 John, ordering the justiciar of Ireland to pay an annual pension to Richard de Thwit, is marked with a note that it should be (re)written in the roll for England ('et notandum quod debuit scribi in rotulo Angl'), presumably in the now lost English 'Contrabrevia/Liberate' Roll 4 John.[37]

If we compare the three Norman Contrabrevia Rolls to the equivalent rolls for England, various significant features emerge. The earliest English Contrabrevia or Liberate Roll survives only in fragments for the period May 1200–April 1201, and like its successors, today surviving for the years 3 and 5 John, includes writs relating to Ireland as well as England.[38] Just as English or Irish writs entered by mistake on the Norman Contrabrevia Roll appear to have been recopied onto the appropriate English roll, so when Norman writs were mistakenly entered on the English rolls they were marked for cancellation, on occasion with a note that they should be included instead in the roll for Normandy.[39] A Norman writ, begun on the English/Irish Liberate Roll 2 John, was never completed, but is entered

---

[34] *The Course of the Exchequer by Richard Son of Nigel*, ed. C. Johnson (London 1950), 32–4, especially p.34, referring to the duty of the clerk of the constabulary sent to the Exchequer *cum contrabreuibus ... de hiis tantum que ad curiam fiunt*.

[35] *Rot. Norm.*, 27–8.

[36] *Rot. Norm.*, 34; *Rot. Lib.*, 1. Here and in what follows, I have checked the printed editions against the surviving rolls in TNA.

[37] *Rot. Norm.*, 77, and cf. the three writs to Geoffrey fitz Peter justiciar of England enrolled at p.92, which likewise belong properly to the roll for England rather than Normandy.

[38] TNA C 62/1, with various parts wrongly filed with C 64/1, printed, from the various fragments, in *Rot. Lib.*, 1–11; *Memoranda Roll 1 John*, 88–97.

[39] *Rot. Lib.*, 15–16, 67–8, 72.

in full and in correct chronological sequence on the equivalent Norman Contrabrevia Roll.[40] In one instance from the roll 5 John, a writ of 18 October 1203 ordering Peter of Stokes to restore a fee to the bishop of Lisieux, the copy of this writ mistakenly entered on the English roll is not only marked for removal to the Norman roll ('debent inrotulari in rotulo Norm'), but the copy, in this instance a mere abstract, subsequently made in the Norman roll appears with a marginal note stating that the writ was also to be found in the English roll ('in rotulo Angl' totum breue').[41] Since in the Norman roll this abstract is once again entered in more or less correct chronological sequence, between two writs dated 16 October 1203, we can assume that the Norman and the English rolls were compiled simultaneously, probably by the same group of chancery scribes, enrolling writs as and when they were issued from the chancery, but dividing the enrolment between English and Norman rolls depending upon whether the business in question related to the King's English and Irish, or to his Norman, Angevin and Poitevin dominions. In much the same way, a writ to Hugh de Neville and the bailiffs of Marlborough in Wiltshire, mistakenly commenced on the Norman Roll amongst business of November 1203, is cancelled incomplete, but can be found entire in the corresponding position on the English Liberate Roll.[42]

---

[40] *Memoranda Roll 1 John*, 90; *Rot. Norm.*, 27, to Guérin de Glapion concerning a quittance of debt to William de Laste.

[41] *Rot. Lib.*, 67–8; *Rot. Norm.*, 107.

[42] *Rot. Norm.*, 112; *Rot. Lib.*, 73.

SUMMARY LIST OF
CONTRABREVIA/LIBERATE ROLLS 2–5 JOHN (1200–1204)

2 John (1200–1)

Normandy/Anjou/Poitou (17 May 1200–9 April 1201) (C 64/4, printed
Rot. Norm., 22–37, headed 'Rotulus de contrabreuibus anno ii. in
Norm(annia)') (106 entries, of which 76 for Normandy, 21 for Anjou,
8 for Poitou, 1 for England)
England/Ireland (26 May 1200–27 April 1201) (C 62/1 and C 64/1, printed
Rot. Lib., 1–11; *Memoranda Roll 1 John*, 89–97, no contemporary
heading) (135 entries, of which 133 for England, 1 for Ireland, 1 for
Normandy)

3 John (1201–2)

Normandy/Anjou/Poitou (Missing)
England/Ireland (3 May 1201–22 May 1202) (C 62/2, printed *Rot. Lib.*,
11–33, no contemporary heading) (127 entries, of which 121 for
England, 3 for Normandy, 2 for Ireland, 1 for Anjou)

4 John (1202–3)

Normandy/Anjou/Poitou (23 May 1202–12 May 1203) (C 64/5, printed *Rot.
Norm.*, 45–98, headed 'Rotulus terrarum liberatarum et contrabreuium
de Norm(annia), Andeg(auia) et Pict(auia) inceptus die Ascensionis
Domini xxiii. die Maii anno regni illustris regis Ioh(ann)is iiii.') (424
entries, of which 374 for Normandy, 27 for Anjou, 19 for Poitou, 3 for
England, 1 for Ireland)
England/Ireland (Missing)

5 John (1203–4)

Normandy/Anjou/Poitou (25 June–5 December 1203) (C 64/6, printed
Rot. Norm., 98–122; *Memoranda Roll 1 John*, 98–9, no contemporary
heading) (210 entries, of which 208 for Normandy, 2 for Anjou, the
whole now badly rubbed, stained and repaired)
England/Ireland (16 May 1203–29 May 1204) (C 62/3, printed *Rot. Lib.*,
34–108, headed: 'Rotulus terrarum et denariorum liberatarum in Anglia
anno regni domini regis Iohannis quinto') (368 entries, of which 353
for England, 10 for Ireland, 5 for Normandy)

The King crossed from England to France in June 1199, from France to
England in February 1200, from England to France in April 1200, from
France to England in October 1200, from England to France May 1201,
and remained in France until his last crossing from Normandy to England
around 6 December 1203.

This division into separate English/Irish and Norman/French series is significant. However, it tells us more of the King's perception of his various dominions, divided by the Channel, than it does of the precise purposes to which the rolls themselves were put. Richard fitz Nigel's description of contrabrevia implies copies of writs abstracted specifically for the purposes of account at the King's Exchequer. But this is a description that does not sit easily with either of the surviving series of enrolments, for Normandy/France or for England/Ireland. The Norman Contrabrevia Rolls – unless we are to assume, somewhat implausibly, that they were sent in turn to the various accounting agencies in Normandy, Anjou and Poitou – appear to represent the abstraction of financial writs and mandates relating to the King's continental lands which would nonetheless have had to be further abstracted into originalia rolls in order to be used specifically for the accounting procedures at the Exchequers of Caen, Angers or elsewhere. In the same way, the English/Irish Liberate Rolls would have to be further abstracted to assist accounts at the Exchequers of Westminster or Dublin.[43] To this extent, the enrolments represent an intermediate stage of the recording process: chancery records that have not yet reached the final stage in which they could have been used in the King's various Exchequers. To this extent, I am happy to endorse the opinion of David Carpenter: that the earliest of the writ rolls, today known as 'Liberate Rolls' or rolls of 'contrabrevia' for Normandy and England are in fact better regarded as part of the same series as the Close Rolls which emerge after 1205. The business that they record is more extensive than simply the writs of 'liberate', 'computate' and quittance which were implied by the Exchequer's insistence upon 'contrabrevia' copies of financial writs issued by the itinerant chancery. Instead, they appear to mark progress towards much fuller enrolment of the chancery's outgoing letters close.[44] Whilst I remain unconvinced by Carpenter's suggestion that these Close Rolls, let alone the Charter or Patent Rolls, had been in existence for many years before John's accession as King, they undoubtedly bear testimony to the sophistication of the chancery's record-keeping after 1199.

As I hope will be apparent, the picture that emerges from these rolls is significant for our understanding of the entire phenomenon of enrolment in the royal chancery. It suggests that the writ rolls preserved today are not to be identified with the contrabrevia of which Richard fitz Nigel wrote, and hence that Fitz Nigel's reference to contrabrevia does not necessarily

---

[43] In one instance from John's reign, we have both a so-called Fine or Oblata Roll (TNA C 60/3A, printed in *Rot. Ob.*, 287–371) and a supposed Originalia Roll (C 60/3B), for the one year 7 John. The Originalia Roll, however, is no more than a duplicate Fine Roll. Its fragmentary state of preservation prevents us from establishing whether the few Irish entries on the Oblata Roll were omitted from the duplicate, but nonetheless there are no indications of cancellation, collation or correction to suggest that in this instance the co-called Originalia Roll served any different function from the chancery Oblata Roll. For the earliest surviving Originalia Roll, for part of the year 7 Richard I (1195–6), stored amongst the Exchequer rather than the chancery records and clearly collated against entries on the Pipe Roll, see E 163/1/3, printed with commentary in *Memoranda Roll 1 John*, pp.xxi, 85–8.

[44] Carpenter, ' "In Testimonium Factorum Brevium" '.

imply that full enrolments of the chancery's financial writs were already being made as early as the 1170s. Fitz Nigel's *contrabrevia* could have been, indeed most likely were, mere memoranda rather than enrolments in the form familiar from the surviving chancery rolls. I have argued elsewhere that full-blown enrolment of writs and charters did not begin until the first year of King John, and that the earliest rolls that survive today are in many instances the very first such rolls to be compiled, not merely the first survivors from a much more ancient series, itself now lost.[45] The very first chancery enrolment of John's reign survives today as the Charter Roll 1 John, begun shortly after the King's coronation in May 1199.[46] Thereafter, the two writ rolls for Normandy and England are the only other rolls of writs or charters, apart from the Charter Roll itself, to survive for John's second year, 1200–1. Significantly, although the writ rolls were checked off against one another, to ensure that English writs on the Norman roll were transferred to the equivalent English roll, no such indications are to be found of collation between these writ rolls and any other rolls. In particular, although letters patent are occasionally copied into the writ rolls, there is never any suggestion that such letters would be better enrolled elsewhere.[47] This is highly significant, since it suggests that the earliest surviving Patent Roll, for the year 3 John (1201–2), is not merely the first such roll to survive, but in all probability the very first such roll of letters patent ever compiled.[48] Nor is this the only conclusion to be drawn. Of the 106 entries on the earliest Norman Roll, 92 were made during the first half of the year between May and October 1200 when the King was in France, and only fourteen thereafter, during the seven months between October 1200 and April 1201 when the King was in England. The fourteen Norman writs of October to April are vastly outnumbered by the 55 English and Irish writs recorded in the English roll for the single month October–November 1200. We might conclude from this firstly, that the regularity with which the King communicated with the Exchequers of Normandy and England varied enormously depending upon on which side of the Channel the King was established, and secondly, that it was

---

[45] N. Vincent, 'Why 1199? Bureaucracy and Enrolment under John and his Contemporaries', *English Government in the Thirteenth Century*, ed. A. Jobson (Woodbridge 2004), 17–48, esp. 22–4, 39–43.

[46] *Rot. Chart.*, pp.xl, 1ff. Various charters issued in the first few weeks of the reign were either never enrolled or are lost from the damaged opening membranes of the roll. For examples here, dated between 7 and 17 June 1199, see *Foedera*, 75–6; BL ms. Additional Charter 33597.

[47] See the various entries on the Norman writ roll 2 John marked in the margin, apparently in the same hand as (and as an integral part of) the writing of the roll, *Lit(tere) pat(entes)*, *Lit(tere) patentes. In Norm(annia)*, or *Lit(tere) pat(entes) Andeg(auie)*: *Rot. Norm.*, 22–3, 25–6, 28, 32–3. In one instance (*Rot. Norm.*, 33) a letter is marked 'letters close', *claus' lit(tere)*, all of these entries apparently being internal memoranda rather than notes for correction or transfer to another set of enrolments. Neither of the two entries on the Norman writ roll 4 John, marked in the margin *Pat(entes)* (*Rot. Norm.*, 64, 86) is enrolled on the equivalent Patent Roll 4 John. An entry on the English/Irish Liberate/Close Roll for November 1203 is marked *debent inrotulari inter litteras patentes* (*Rot. Lib.*, 72), although I can find no such entry in the equivalent Patent Roll 5 John.

[48] TNA C 66/1, printed in *RLP*, 1–11.

the very fact that the King controlled a cross-Channel dominion, whose various offices of account were established as permanent institutions, distant from the itinerant chancery, that contributed to the decision to begin enrolment in the first place. Had John lost his Norman lands in 1199 rather than in 1204, it is possible that the chancery rolls would never have had to be invented. As it was, once begun, the writ rolls for Normandy and England were amalgamated and expanded after 1204 into the first of the much more extensive rolls of letters close, recording not just financial but vast numbers of administrative writs for all parts of the King's dominion, covering England, Ireland and France.[49]

As a source for the history of ducal Normandy, the six surviving Norman chancery rolls are of vital significance. Without them, we would be deprived of many of the finer details of our picture of how Plantagenet government in Normandy functioned and in due course collapsed. Albeit for a brief few years, at the very end of the duchy's independent history, the clouds part and we are able to glimpse the machinary of ducal administration laid bare. Accounting by writ was a feature of the Norman Exchequer at least as early as 1180, and the drawing up of Norman Exchequer Rolls was itself a phenomenon almost certainly older than the first surviving account roll, though perhaps not much older than the 1170s. The first surviving Norman account roll, for 1180, refers to no account roll, as opposed to account, earlier than Michaelmas 1176, suggesting that the introduction of account rolls to the Norman Exchequer is a phenomenon to be associated with the period during which Richard of Ilchester, bishop of Winchester and a major figure at the English Exchequer, served as *de facto* seneschal of Normandy.[50] References to an earlier series of Norman Rolls, noticed by Léopold Delisle and thence cited by most subsequent commentators, on investigation depend upon the entirely unreliable testimony of the eighteenth-century jurist, Guillaume de la Foy, who claimed not only to have seen a roll of accounts for 1136 but another 'roll', made at the Norman Exchequer in 1061, a date that seems impossibly early. De la Foy had a vested interest here, as a Norman on the eve of the French Revolution, in establishing the immemorial antiquity of Norman institutions in order that the independence of Norman legal custom might be established and recognised.[51] The chancery Norman Rolls supply no proof that the chancery

[49] *RLC*, i, 1–33.
[50] *MRSN*, i, 69: *sicut continetur in rotulo anni mclxxvi*. For a reference, as early as the 1160s, to obligations and privileges of the men of Fécamp recorded *secundum quod recognitum est et in rotulo meo scriptum*, see Delisle, *Recueil,* i, 482–3 no.338. The roll here could well be a master roll of farms, such as must have existed even before full scale annual account rolls were introduced to the Norman Exchequer. For Richard of Ilchester as the author of reforms in Normandy after 1176, see Haskins, *Institutions*, 174–8, 327–8. Even before the Pipe Roll form was introduced to royal or private Exchequers, accounts would nonetheless have had to be taken, though one assumes in a less sophisticated and less extensively documented form. See here N. Vincent, 'The Origins of the Winchester Pipe Rolls', 25–42.
[51] For what appears to be a reference to the Norman Exchequer itself, as early as the time of King Henry I, see J.H. Round, 'Bernard the King's Scribe', *EHR*, xiv (1899), 425–8. Delisle's remarks (*Magni Rotuli Scaccarii Normanniae*, ed. Léchaudé d'Anisy and Charma (1852), pp.xxx–i, whence Haskins, *Institutions*, 105 n.87), are derived from the testimony of G. de la Foy, *De la*

was enrolling Norman writs or charters before the first or second year of King John. There may have been an earlier series of such rolls, now lost, but the evidence, as for the enrolment of writs and charters in England, suggests on the contrary that regular enrolment of charters, as opposed to the irregular copying in the Exchequer of fines and charters, was an innovation of the reign of King John.

Both the Norman Exchequer and chancery rolls, we must assume, were evacuated to England at the time of John's flight from Normandy in 1203, a command being issued to the bailiffs of Shoreham on 21 May 1204 to allow Peter de Lions, the King's clerk and previously a leading official of the Exchequer of Normandy, carriage and safe conduct in bringing rolls and charters from Caen to London.[52] In the process of evacuation, and amidst the subsequent disorders of the royal archive, much, we must assume, was lost. The survival of a fragment of a Norman Exchequer Roll for 1184, today preserved amongst the records of the Templars in Paris, and the preservation in France of copies of the 1172 inquest into knights' fees, copied before 1208 into the chancery registers of the victorious Philip Augustus, suggest that part at least of the Exchequer archive was abandoned in France.[53] Perhaps only a small part, however, since after 1204 there is little to suggest continuity in the procedures of the Exchequer at

---

constitution du duché ou état souverain de Normandie (1789), 233: 'J'ai eu en ma possession un ancien rôle de l'échiquier tenu en l'an 1136, contenant des résultats de comptes rendus pour le pays de Caux, touchant les revenus des tenements du duc assis en Monstrevilliers, et il doit exister de pareils rôles dans plusieurs chartriers d'anciennes maisons', but previously noting at p.232 a 'rôle', said by De la Foy to have been made before the Exchequer at Rouen in 1061, to which reference had recently been made in Jean-Baptiste-Gabriel-Marie de Milicent's (revolutionary) *Journal de Normandie*, no.52 (Saturday 28 June 1788), 209. Here, De Milicent merely reports the announcement by Avoyne de Chantereyne, perpetual secretary of the Société académique at Cherbourg, 20 June 1788, that a copy had been made in 1766 by the antiquary Thomas le Marchant from an inquest ordered by Thomas Leighton, governor of Guernsey, 15 July 1597, which itself claimed to cite 'un extrait d'un rôle de l'Echiquier de Rouen', dated 19 October 1061, by which Duke William had granted equal moieties of the island of Guernsey to the monks of Mont-St-Michel and to Samson d'Anneville the duke's squire ('ecuyer'), in the latter case in return for perpetual service by Samson and his heirs as squires of the body whenever the duke should come to Guernsey, later compounded for an annual rent of 10 livres tournois. The misunderstanding here could have arisen from a misreading of a copy of Fauroux, *Recueil*, no.111 or no.141, or even *Regesta Regum Anglo-Normannorum. The Acta of William I (1066–1087)*, ed. D. Bates (Oxford 1998), no.212, but even so would be sufficiently grave to invalidate any other claims that De la Foy has to make about chronology. More likely it was based upon a sixteenth-century forgery, as noted by Fauroux, *Recueil*, p.29 n.47 (with references to numerous subsequent citations of the forged charter).

52 *Rot. Lib.*, 102–3, and for the expense incurred here, a fairly meagre 4s. 6d., see *PR 6 John*, 99.
53 For the fragment of the 1184 roll, see L. Delisle 'Observations sur un fragment des rôles de l'échiquier de Normandie relatif à l'année 1184', published variously in *Magni Rotuli Scaccarii Normanniae*, ed. Léchaudé d'Anisy and Charma (1852), pp.v–xxxii, 109–113; separately by Delisle as *Magni Rotuli Scaccarii Normanniae de anno domini ut videtur MCLXXXIV fragmentum* (Caen 1851, with a dedication to the Society of Antiquaries in memory of the work of Thomas Stapleton), and in Delisle's *Introduction* to Delisle *Recueil*, 334–44. A further fragment of Norman memoranda, printed by H. Legras, 'Un Fragment de rôle normand inédit de Jean sans Terre', *Bulletin de la Société des Antiquaires de Normandie* xxix (1914), 21–31, is taken from the Exchequer miscellanea in TNA rather than from a source surviving in France.

Caen. Although the Caen Exchequer continued to function, and although valuable records survive from the early thirteenth century onwards of judicial and other decisions made there, the Pipe Roll form appears to have been abandoned immediately or very shortly after 1204.[54] Deprived of its archive, it seems that the Caen Exchequer adopted less laborious methods of account than those followed during the period of Norman and Plantagenet rule.

The Norman Exchequer and chancery rolls of King John's reign are undoubtedly the most significant sources for ducal Normandy now housed in The National Archives. They are not, however, the only surviving Norman rolls. After a gap of more than 200 years, the chancery series begun and ended under John resumes with the English reconquest of Normandy under Henry V, and continues as rolls of letters patent bearing upon Norman affairs from the year 5 to the year 10 Henry V (C 64/8–17). Much of the material preserved in these later Norman Rolls is of strictly fifteenth-century interest and relates to the administration and occupation of Normandy by Henry V.[55] Vital as it is to the study of the Hundred Years' War, it has never been published in full. However, Norman monasteries after 1415 were anxious to obtain renewal of earlier privileges granted by the kings and barons of the old Anglo-Norman realm, and the inspeximus charters by which Henry V renewed such earlier privileges are preserved in large numbers amongst the later Norman Rolls. As a result, these fifteenth-century rolls rank as an important resource for the study of Normandy before 1204. This was appreciated as long ago as the time of William Dugdale, who made extensive use of the Norman Rolls of Henry V's reign in compiling the entries for the alien priories in his great *Monasticon.*[56] After Dugdale, the rolls were used by a number of French antiquaries of the eighteenth century, including Bréquigny and Lenoir.[57] Thereafter,

---

[54]   *Recueil de Jugements de l'Echiquier de Normandie au XIIIe siécle*, ed. L. Delisle (Paris 1864); E. Perrot, *Arresta communia scacarii... 1276–1294* (Caen 1910). Further Exchequer memoranda in French, for the years 1246–50, are preserved in a fourteenth-century copy of the 'Coutumier de Normandie', now BL ms. Additional 25003 fos.98r–99v, acquired from the library of Sir Francis Palgrave in 1862, and cf. F. Joüon des Longrais, 'Le Manuscrit de Berlin Hamilton 192 et ses arrêts de l'Echiquier', *Travaux de la semaine d'histoire du droit normand tenue à Guernesey du 8 au 13 juin 1938* (Caen 1939), 319–47, esp. 337–47.

[55]   A statement that applies to virtually all of the contents of the only one of these late rolls to have been published in full: TNA C 64/8, printed in *Rot. Norm.*, 145–385. Likewise there seem to be no early charters recited in either of the Norman Rolls for the year 6 Henry V, C 64/9–10, and only one (of Henry II, known to Delisle, *Recueil,* i, no.340, but not from this source) in the roll 7 Henry V part 1 (C 64/11 m.7).

[56]   *Monasticon*, vi, 1061–1119.

[57]   Extracts by Bréquigny and others in Bnf mss. Moreau 630–1, 665–79; AN ms. M39 no.6/20, and by Bréquigny and De la Rue at Caen AD Calvados 386 Edt 1–2 (Archives de la ville de Falaise), the majority of the early inspeximuses being preserved here in Moreau 630–1. Much more extensive extracts by Lenoir, though apparently after Bréquigny, are to be found in Lenoir ms.69, now held by the Marquis de Mathan at the Château de Semilly (of which microfilms can be consulted both in the AN (104Mi69) and at Rouen in the Archives départementales). For the Norman-born Louis-Georges-Oudart Feudrix de Bréquigny (1714–95), and for his tour of English archives in 1764–5, resulting in various of the transcripts now in Bnf mss. Moreau 623–733, see R. Poupardin, *Catalogue des manuscrits*

however, they were largely ignored by Norman historians, who appear to have assumed that all their important contents had already been sifted and fully disclosed. Neither Léopold Delisle nor, more remarkably, Marie Fauroux, appear to have used the Henry V Norman Rolls directly, although both scholars were aware of their existence and to some extent of their importance. As a result, Delisle, for one, missed a number of charters of King Henry II for Norman beneficiaries which are preserved in the Henry V rolls but nowhere else.[58] Nor is it only English royal charters that are preserved in the Henry V enrolments. Besides charters of the pre-Conquest counts and dukes of Normandy, from Richard II through to William the Bastard,[59] we find charters of the Kings of France, from Louis VII and Louis IX through to Philip IV,[60] of the eleventh and twelfth-century bishops of Rouen and Bayeux,[61] of the great feudal landowners such as the counts of Meulan, and of a number of lesser Norman barons both before and after 1204.[62] Some of these charters have been published from this or from other sources. Many are still either unpublished or entirely unknown. A representative selection, but by no means an exhaustive survey, is printed below in the appendix of documents.

Beyond those rolls of the chancery and Exchequer specifically devoted to Norman affairs, there are few classes of thirteenth-century enrolment in The National Archives from which the affairs or the memory of Normandy is wholly absent. The Charter Rolls of King John (C 53), beginning in 1199, record grants to Norman beneficiaries for the first five years of the reign, through to 1204, and thereafter, like the Close and Patent Rolls (C 54 and C 66), record a regular stream of Norman business, including

---

des collections Duchesne et Bréquigny (Paris 1905), pp.xxii–iii; H. Omont, *Inventaire des manuscrits de la collection Moreau* (Paris 1891), pp.viii–ix, 224. For the Norman Maurist Dom Jacques-Nicolas Lenoir (1720–92), see M. Le Pesant, 'Les manuscrits de Dom Lenoir sur l'histoire de Normandie', *Bulletin de la Société des Antiquaries de Normandie*, 1 (1949), 125–51; idem, 'Répertoire des informations analysées par Dom Lenoir', *Cahiers Léopold Delise*, xvi fasc.1–2 (1967), 3–48.

[58] For example, Henry II to the abbey of La Trinité-du-Mont at Rouen: TNA C 64/15 (Norman Roll 8 Henry V part 3) m.16, of which there is a copy by Lenoir in Lenoir ms.69 p.439, and in Bnf ms. Moreau 631 fos.61v–62r. Henry II to La Noë, printed from an unknown source by Delisle, *Recueil*, ii, no.710, but clearly derived from TNA C 64/12 (Norman Roll 7 Henry V part 2) m.18, of which there is a copy in Lenoir ms.69 p.418.

[59] See, for example, TNA C 64/12 (Norman Roll 7 Henry V part 2) mm.7–8, 34–5, 37, Dukes Richard II to St-Wandrille (1024) and Robert to St-Amand Rouen (1030) and Cerisy (1032), printed by Fauroux, *Recueil*, 114 no.27, 188 no.62, 193 no.64, either failing to note the Norman Rolls as source or citing them only at second hand.

[60] For charters of Louis VII, see TNA C 64/13 m.26. For Louis VIII, see C 64/17 m.13. For Louis IX, see C 64/12 mm.11, 22, 33; C 64/13 mm.1, 5; C 64/15 mm.4, 6, 13, 14, 21; C 64/16 mm.12–13; C 64/17 mm.3, 5, 17. For Philip IV, see C 64/13 mm.8, 13; C 64/14 m.7; C 64/15 m.23; C 64/16 m.11; C 64/17 mm.5, 6, 17.

[61] For charters of archbps Robert and Hugh of Rouen to Rouen cathedral, Bec and the monks of Gournay, see TNA C 64/13 m.21; C 64/15 m.10; C 64/17 m.3. For charters of the bps of Bayeux to St-Amand at Rouen, see TNA C 64/12 m.37.

[62] For charters of Robert and Waleran counts of Meulan to St-Wandrille, Jumièges, Notre-Dame de Gournay, Bec and Grandmont, see TNA C 64/12 m.7; C 64/13 mm.21, 25; C 64/14 m.7; C 64/15 m.10. There is a particularly rich collection of private charters to Bec referred to or inspected in C 64/13 m.21.

the confirmation of earlier charters long into the thirteenth century and beyond.[63] The series of Charter Rolls is marred by a succession of gaps during the reign of King John, so that although we have surviving rolls for the years 1, 2 and 5 John (May 1199–1201, and May 1203–4), the rolls for 3 and 4 John (May 1201–1203), crucial years in the history of Normandy, have vanished without trace, almost certainly not long after they were compiled. Even for those years which are covered by the surviving Charter Rolls, by no means all royal charters were properly enrolled in chancery, so that on occasion we find originals, even of King John, that should have been enrolled but were not. Two of these have recently attracted the notice of Professor Daniel Power and throw new light upon the rebellion of Robert count of Sèes: one of the key events that paved the way for the Capetian conquest of Normandy in 1204.[64] Various twelfth-century charters are copied into the so-called Cartae Antiquae Rolls (C 52), apparently first drawn up for the use of the Exchequer rather than the chancery.[65] There is some Norman business in the Fine Rolls (C 60), the later English Pipe Rolls (E 372) and the Liberate Rolls (C 62), for the most part concerning the English lands of the Norman monasteries,[66] and even the so-called Curia Regis Rolls of Henry III's reign (KB 26) are crucial sources for the history of the alien priories, of the lands of Normans confiscated in England after 1204, and on occasion, as with their recital of final concords, preserve material directly relevant to the history of Plantagenet Normandy from before 1204.[67] Even in such as yet uncleared thickets of The National Archives as the Exchequer Memoranda Rolls (E 159 and E 368), we find the occasional Norman charter, including, as late as the fifteenth century, a long and important bull of Pope Alexander III confirming the possessions of the nuns of Almenêches.[68]

---

[63] *Rot. Chart.*, continued in calendar form through to the sixteenth century as *Cal. Chart. R.* For these, and for the other chief series of published or calendared enrolments, including the Close and Patent Rolls, see the lists in E.L.C. Mullins, *Texts and Calendars. An Analytical Guide to Serial Publications* (London 1958), 3–36.

[64] D. Power, 'The End of Angevin Normandy: The Revolt at Alençon (1203)', *Historical Research*, lxxiv (2001), 444–64.

[65] The first 20 of these rolls are published as *The Cartae Antiquae Rolls*, ed. L. Landon and J. Conway Davies, PRS n.s. 17, 33 (1939–60). Thereafter, the rolls have to be consulted in the original.

[66] The Fine Rolls are published to the end of the reign of King John as *Rot. Ob.* Thereafter, the project to publish these rolls through to the end of the reign of Henry III has so far produced three volumes of printed calendar, *CFR*, with a major site online at http://www. finerollshenry3.org.uk. The so-called Fines of the Month on this site include several articles related to Normandy. The Pipe Rolls to the year 8 Henry III (1224) are printed in a series of volumes by the Pipe Roll Society. The Liberate Rolls to 1272 are calendared as *CLR*.

[67] Printed as *CRR*. For specifically Norman charters preserved in these rolls, see for example *CRR*, vi, 273, also printed (probably with the assistance of Thomas Stapleton) by D. Gurney, *The Record of the House of Gournay*, 4 vols (London 1848–58), i, 215, whence Delisle, *Recueil*, no.325. For charters of Henry I to Notre-Dame-du-Pré at Rouen, one of them calendared from other sources in *Regesta*, ii, no.1290, the other (a writ to the sheriff of Berkshire) apparently not in the *Regesta*, see *CRR*, xiii, nos 418, 2669; TNA KB 27/181 (Coram Rege Plea Roll Trinity term 33 Edward I) m.54d.

[68] TNA E 159/180 (KR Memoranda Roll 5 Henry IV, Michaelmas 1403–Trinity 1404), Communia Recorda section, un-numbered membrane of the Hilary term, in an inspeximus by Geoffrey bp of Sées, John abbot of St-Martin Sées, Michael abbot of Silly and John abbot of

Our search for Norman evidences in The National Archives by no means ends with the principal chancery and Exchequer enrolments. Indeed, the deeper we delve in the records, the more National Archives classes we find in which Norman documents still lurk. We might begin here with single-sheet charters and writs, and with the main series of Exchequer Ancient Deeds (E 40, E 326 and so forth), assembled from a variety of sources but for the most part consisting of single sheet charters that entered the Exchequer Augmentation Office or the Treasury of the Receipt after the Reformation, following the crown's dissolution of the monasteries. A substantial number of charters in these collections concern the lands of alien priories, and hence involve gifts of English land to or by the monasteries of Normandy, including St-Martin de Sées, Fécamp, St-Evroul, St-Fromond, Lire, Cormeilles, Conches and Clairuissel.[69] Compared to charters such as this, which are as much or more concerned with lands or monasteries in England, there are, perhaps not surprisingly, few charters amongst the Ancient Deeds which directly concern lands in Normandy itself before 1204. One such, a grant by Robert de Port-Mort to Hamelin earl of Warenne of a fee at Louvetot (Seine-Maritime, cant. Bellencombre, com. Grigneuseville), was nonetheless published by Charles Clay in his *Early Yorkshire Charters*.[70]

The Exchequer Ancient Deeds series were formed so long after the events of 1204 that it is not surprising that they contain few charters directly relating to pre-1204 Norman lands. Fortunately, there is one class of deeds (now divided into three) in The National Archives – those of the Duchy of Lancaster (DL 25, DL 26, DL 27) – formed much earlier, from the 1260s onwards, which gathers together the charters of families that almost within living memory had held lands across the Channel. The Duchy of Lancaster deeds are comparatively rich in Norman evidences. Some of the plums here, including an important charter of Hugh archbishop of Rouen for the monks of St-Evroul and their priory established at Neuf-Marché-en-Lions,

---

St-André-en-Gouffern, May 1248. The bull, dated 7 October 1178, is printed from this source in *Monasticon*, vi, 1032–3, whence J–L no.13107, which is perhaps distinct from an original, and a later copy, which survive at Alençon AD Orne H3357; H5535, supposedly dated 4 October 1172, for which see *Papsturkunden in Frankreich. Neue Folge 2. Band: Normandie*, ed. J. Ramackers, Abhandlungen der Gesellschaft der Wissenschaften zu Göttingen Philologisch-Historische Klasse 3 Folge 21 (Göttingen 1937), 46.

[69] Many thousands of the various Ancient Deeds series are catalogued in *A Descriptive Catalogue of Ancient Deeds in the Public Record Office*, 6 vols (London 1890–1915). From those portions as yet uncatalogued in print, for English properties of St-Martin de Sées, see TNA E 210/9419; E 326/7525, 8918, 9295, 9298–9300, 9401, 11550, 11609, 12550; E 329/140, 181, 202. Fécamp: E 326/13281. St-Evroul: E 326/5303, 8609, 8771. St-Fromond: E 326/8009, 8078, 8780, 8781–3. Lire: E 211/705a; E 326/8881–2, 8885, 8889. Cormeilles: E 326/11192; E 329/192. Conches: E 329/186. Clairuissel: E 40/14533, 14958.

[70] TNA E 40/5923, whence *EYC*, viii, 125–6 no.83, noting a further copy in BL ms. Cotton Vespasian F xv (Lewes Cartulary) fo.31r.

and a charter of the Cantiloupe family relating to their estate at Pissy
(Seine-Maritime, cant. Notre-Dame-de-Bondeville, com. Pissy-Pôville),
have long been printed.[71] Two charters involving William du Hommet,
constable of Normandy, and the Anglo-Norman estate of the lords of
Fougères have been employed elsewhere to illustrate the complicated
history of the Fougères lands in England and Normandy, both before and
after 1204.[72] Others, concerning an exchange of lands in the Roumare fee
in both England and Normandy, were published by Stenton and Cazel.[73]
Nonetheless, there are many other deeds here that would richly repay
study.[74] Once again, only a representative selection is printed below.

Beyond the Ancient Deeds series, historians of Anglo-Norman relations
after 1204 cannot afford to ignore the considerable number of Norman
letters, petitions and alien priory accounts preserved in The National
Archives series of Ancient Correspondence (SC 1), Ministers Accounts (SC
6), Papal Bulls (SC 7) and Ancient Petitions (SC 8).[75] All of these classes
are well indexed, and in certain cases (most notably SC 8) fully searchable
online. The two papal bulls in SC 7 relating to Normandy before 1204 both
concern the Norman benefices held by Peter de Lions, chief clerk of the Caen
Exchequer before the fall of Normandy, and appear to have been brought to
England at the same time that Peter took responsibility for evacuating the
Exchequer archive from Caen.[76] Ancient Petitions (SC 8) includes several
letters from the Norman religious concerning estates in England, or, as in
the case of Beaubec, their daughter house in Ireland.[77] The more important
early Norman items from Ancient Correspondence (SC 1) were noticed

---

[71] TNA DL 27/22, printed in *Ancient Charters Royal and Private Prior to AD 1200*, ed. J.H.
    Round, PRS x (1888), 31–2 no.18. DL 25/3076, printed by F.A. Cazel, 'Norman and Wessex
    Charters of the Roumare Family', *A Medieval Miscellany for Doris Mary Stenton*, ed. P.M.
    Barnes and C.F. Slade, PRS n.s. xxxvi (1962), 82–3, 88 no.7.
[72] TNA DL 27/26–7, printed by N. Vincent, 'Twyford Under the Bretons 1066–1250',
    Nottingham Medieval Studies xli (1997), 80–99, at pp.96, 98.
[73] TNA DL 25/2372, whence *Documents Illustrative of the Social and Economic History of
    the Danelaw from Various Collections*, ed. F.M. Stenton (London 1920), 377–8 no.520; DL
    25/37, whence Cazel, 'Norman and Wessex Charters', 82, 86 no.3, and cf, 86–7 no.4.
[74] For examples, see below pp.86–9.
[75] The accounts in TNA SC 6/1125–7 are particularly valuable in identifying the English estates
    of alien priories. A new and superb online catalogue of the series SC 8 is available online via
    the main National Archives site: www.nationalarchives.gov.uk. Papal bulls are calendared
    in the *List of Diplomatic Documents, Scottish Documents and Papal Bulls Preserved
    in the Public Record Office*, PRO Lists and Indexes xlix (London 1923). The Ancient
    Correspondence is calendared by P.M. Barnes, with a two volume index, in the *List of Ancient
    Correspondence of the Chancery and Exchequer Preserved in the Public Record Office*, PRO
    Lists and Indexes xv (revised edition, 3 vols, New York 1968).
[76] TNA SC 7/19/13 and SC 7/35/7, concerning the church of Gonneville-sur-Mer, and the chapel
    of Vesqueville belonging to Peter's church of Villy (Calvados), calendared by J.E. Sayers,
    *Original Papal Documents in England and Wales from the Accession of Pope Innocent III to
    the Death of Pope Benedict XI (1198–1304)* (Oxford 1999), 14 nos 25–6, and for Peter see
    above p.17.
[77] See, for example TNA SC 8/87 no.4312; SC 8/174 no.868; SC 8/227 no.11337, concerning
    the English estates of the cathedral of Rouen and the monks of Fécamp and St-Georges-de-
    Boscherville. For petitions and inquests relating to the Irish lands of Beaubec, shortly after
    1300, see SC 8/271 nos 13505–10.

by Pierre Chaplais in his edition of *Diplomatic Documents*, including a justly famous letter of *c.*1227, written by a burgess of Caen, expiating on the reasons why John had lost Normandy and suggesting means by which Henry III could win back the duchy's allegiance to the Plantagenets.[78]

All told, from the enrolments to the original deeds, there are few medieval holdings in The National Archives that do not in some way, however tangentially, touch upon the history of Normandy. Here, however, rather than search for further needles amidst haystacks, I wish to pass on to a much later, but nonetheless crucial group of sources, that are not as widely used as they merit. Thus far we have considered the principal bodies of evidence surviving in The National Archives relating to ducal Normandy. Our focus must now shift from The National Archives to other English archives, and in particular to those that were enriched, for the most part in the nineteenth century, by the first generations of antiquaries who became interested in Anglo-Norman antiquities. Amongst these scholars and collectors, one man, who we have already encountered, stands supreme: Thomas Stapleton, editor of the Norman Pipe Rolls, genealogist, collector and Anglo-Norman antiquary *sans pareil*.

---

[78] *Diplomatic Documents Preserved in the Public Record Office*, ed. P. Chaplais (London 1964), esp. 139–40 no.206, from TNA SC 1/55 no.3, and for commentary on the letter of the burgess of Caen, see J.C. Holt, 'The End of the Anglo-Norman Realm', in Holt, *Magna Carta and Medieval Government* (London 1985), 64–5.

2. THE ANTIQUARIES AND THE REDISCOVERY OF THE ANGLO-NORMAN PAST

With the exception of the publication of Domesday Book – a source whose importance to the history of ducal Normandy surely requires no emphasis here – English antiquaries of the seventeenth and eighteenth centuries had made only half-hearted attempts to engage with the Norman as opposed to the insular, Anglo-Norman dimension of English history after 1066.[79] William Dugdale (1605–1686), it is true, had corresponded with the heirs of the great André Duchesne (1584–1640), from whom he acquired transcripts of Norman charters for the abbey of Lire, used in the section on alien priories that Dugdale appended to his *Monasticon Anglicanum*.[80] Some years earlier, via William Camden (1551–1623), Duchesne himself had come into possession of the Cotton manuscript of William of Poitiers' *Gesta Guillelmi*, which seems subsequently to have returned to London and to have been burned in the Cotton fire of 1731.[81] Richard Zouche, an Oxford jurist, as early as 1629 had attempted to compare the English law of land tenure with Norman custom.[82] Humfrey Wanley (1672–1726) is to be found, in the 1720s, purchasing for the Harleian Library a small collection of Norman charters (relating to the abbey of La Noë, the Templars and the vicars choral of Evreux cathedral), ultimately from a source in Evreux.[83] It was not, however, until the 1750s that any real advances were made in the English appreciation of the Norman past. In 1752, the Norman-born but Eton and Oxford-educated Andrew Ducarel (1713–1785), made a tour of his homeland that was to prove crucial in the scholarly rediscovery of

---

[79] For a brief introduction to the themes considered below, see D.J.A. Matthew, 'The English Cultivation of Norman History', *England and Normandy in the Middle Ages*, ed. D. Bates and A. Curry (London 1994), 1–18, at p.6 noting William Camden's *Anglica Normannica Hibernica Cambrica a veteribus scripta* (Frankfurt 1602), printing of part of Orderic Vitalis' chronicle, misattributed to William of Malmesbury.

[80] For Duchesne's transcripts, supplied to Dugdale in July 1648, including evidences from the cartularies of Lire and Cluny, see Oxford, Bodleian Library ms. Dugdale 11.

[81] R.H.C. Davis, 'William of Poitiers and his History of William the Conqueror', in Davis, *From Alfred the Great to Stephen* (London 1991), 123–8, reprised in *The Gesta Guillelmi of William of Poitiers*, ed. R.H.C. Davis and M. Chibnall (Oxford 1998), pp.xliii–v, and cf. E.M.C. Van Houts, 'Camden, Cotton and the Chronicles of the Norman Conquest of England', *Sir Robert Cotton as Collector*, ed. C.J. Wright (London 1997), 238–52; Matthew, 'English Cultivation of Norman History', 6, noting that Camden also obtained a manuscript of the *Encomium Emmae* for Duchesne.

[82] R. Zouche, *Elementa iurisprudentiae definitionibus regulis* (Oxford 1629), noticed by Matthew, 'English Cultivation of Norman History', 7.

[83] N. Vincent, 'Early Norman Charters in the British Library: The Cotton Charters for La Noë, St-Etienne de Renneville and Evreux Cathedral', *Tabularia* (forthcoming).

that greatest of Anglo-Norman monuments, the Bayeux Tapestry.[84] In 1767, in collaboration with another Anglo-French antiquary, Smart Lethieullier (1701–1760), Ducarel published an account of his discoveries together with an edition of the 1172 inquest into Norman knights' fees preserved in the Red Book of the Exchequer (today TNA E 164/2 fos.160r–162r).[85] Having secured the election of dom Jean Bourget, monk and historian of Bec, as an honorary member of the Society of Antiquaries, Ducarel oversaw the publication of an English translation of Bourget's history of the abbey, embellished with transcripts of various English charters.[86] He also, in continuation of the work of Dugdale, published a long, though less than entirely reliable, account of alien priories.[87]

In the decades before the Revolution of 1789, French scholars such as Lenoir and Bréquigny had travelled to London to search out what could be found of Norman or French history in the records at the Tower, whilst some years earlier, investigating materials for a new edition of De Thou's *Histoire universelle*, the Jacobite Thomas Carte (1684–1754) had done important work in both the Parisian and the municipal archives of France.[88]

---

[84] For Ducarel, see the article by R. Myers in *ODNB*; A.C. Ducarel, *A Tour Through Normandy in a Letter to a Friend* (London 1754).

[85] A.C. Ducarel, *Anglo-Norman Architecture Considered in a Tour Through Part of Normandy* (London 1767); R. Myers, 'Dr Andrew Coltée Ducarel (1713–1785): A Pioneer of Anglo-Norman Studies', *Antiquaries, Book Collectors and the Circles of Learning*, ed. R. Myers and M. Harris (Winchester 1996), 45–70; R. Myers, 'Dr Andrew Coltée Ducarel, Lambeth Librarian, Civilian and Keeper of the Public Records', *The Library*, 6th series xxi (1999), 199–222; Matthew, 'English Cultivation of Norman History', 11–12. For the 1172 inquest, the standard edition is now that in *Red Book*, ii, 624–47, with commentary at pp.ccxxx–vi, pointing out that Ducarel had clearly corrected the Red Book copy by reference to a further copy in the Register B of Philip Augustus. Related inquests, for Mont-St-Michel and for the Avranchin, are preserved only in copies from Mont-St-Michel and from the lost cartulary of La Lucerne, for which see Delisle, *Recueil*, i (Introduction), 332–3, 345–7; C.H. Haskins, 'The Inquest of 1171 in the Avranchin', *EHR*, xxvi (1911), 326–8. The fact that further copies of the inquest preserved in the Red Book were inserted into Registers A, B and C of Philip Augustus, in a version updated at some point between 1204 and 1208, suggests that the French royal chancery acquired a copy left behind in Normandy at the time of the Plantagenet evacuation of Normandy: an important indication that by no means all of the records of Plantagenet administration were dispatched to England in 1204. For the most recent edition of the French Register copies, see *Registres*, 267–76.

[86] J. Bourget, *The History of the Royal Abbey of Bec near Rouen in Normandy* (London 1779), esp. pp.vi–vii for Bourget's election to the Antiquaries (10 January 1765) and his meetings with Ducarel.

[87] A.C. Durcarel and T. Warburton, *Some Account of the Alien Priories and of Such Lands as They are Known to have Possessed in England and Wales*, 2 vols (London 1778). An attempt to list the English lands of Bec had already appeared in Ducarel's translation of Bourget's *History of Bec*, 134ff.

[88] For Carte, see *A Summary Catalogue of Western Manuscripts in the Bodleian Library at Oxford*, iii, ed. F. Madan (Oxford 1895), 113ff. Ironically, Carte's searches were undertaken only after the initial printing of Rymer's *Foedera* (1704–1717) which was supposed to cover all treaties negotiated between England and France, several of them recorded only in French archives (cf. M.M. Condon and E.M. Hallam, 'Government Printing of the Public Records in the Eighteenth Century', *JSA*, vii (1982–5), 349–59). Carte's manuscripts, now in the Bodleian Library at Oxford, include an important sixteenth-century municipal cartulary for the vill of Angers: ms. Carte 91 (SC 10537), containing charters of the Plantagenet kings, not noticed in the standard guide to French cartularies by Stein, and cf. mss. Carte 89–90, 92.

For the most part, however, English and Norman antiquaries had worked independently of one another, with only scant regard for the documentary riches that might be found on opposing sides of the Channel. As a result, the great series of French transcripts of early charters, made in the seventeenth and eighteenth centuries by the likes of Duchesne, Baluze and Moreau, today housed in the Bibliothèque nationale, are almost as poorly supplied with materials gathered from England as the collections of Glover, Dugdale or Dodsworth are devoid of genealogical proofs from Normandy or northern France, and this despite the fact that for a period of 150 years after 1066 the very barons and knights whose early history both Duchesne and Dugdale sought to elucidate were as likely to have been found issuing charters at Rouen or Caen as at Westminster or Warwick.[89]

THOMAS STAPLETON

The principal author of a change in attitudes here, Thomas Stapleton (1806–1849), was, in the words of his memorialist, a master of 'calm, patient, scrupulous, truth-loving perserverance in research'.[90] His brief (and woefully under-researched) entry in the old *Dictionary of National Biography*, rehashed virtually unchanged for the new, gives the impression of a dull and uneventful life lived by an antiquary of little intrinsic significance. No doubt, the hard-pressed *Dictionary* writer (whose entry on Stapleton is one of over 400 such entries for which this particular contributor was responsible) took his cue from the obituarist who in 1849 had remarked, with fine condescension, that 'Mr Stapleton devoted himself most enthusiastically to the dry elaboration of historical and genealogical details [...] No literary drudgery seemed to come amiss to him; from the unravelling of an intricate line of succession to the collation of monotonous records and the compilation

---

[89]　For Brécquigny's transcripts from England, now in the Moreau collection, see above n.57.
[90]　John Bruce, introduction to *Chronicon Petroburgense*, ed. T. Stapleton, Camden Society (1849), p.v. Stapleton has attracted surprisingly little attention from his successors. With the exception of Bruce's memoir and a brief obituary notice in the *Proceedings of the Society of Antiquaries of London* ii (1853), 72, the anonymous memoir in *The Gentleman's Magazine*, cxx (1850), part 1, 322–4, provides virtually the only source for the entry in the old *Dictionary of National Biography* (*sub* Stapleton, Thomas), which itself was barely changed for the new *ODNB*. The old *Dictionary of National Biography* gave Stapleton's birth date as 1805. He was in fact born, as the second of nine children of Thomas Stapleton of Carlton near Goole in Yorkshire (1778–1839), on 16 October 1806: Burke's *Peerage and Baronetage*, 75th edition (London 1913), 209–10. His papers are not listed in the otherwise extremely valuable handlist of *Papers of British Antiquaries and Historians*, HMC Guides to the Sources for British History xii (2003). A catalogue of his books and manuscripts at Wilton Place, compiled after his death, still survives amongst the Stapleton papers in Hull History Centre, University Archives mss. DDCA3/10/1. Two files of Stapleton's working notes have recently resurfaced at Hull (Ibid. DDCA/33/28 and 54/98), thanks to the detective work of Tim Gates. Other letters from or relating to Stapleton were drawn to my attention by Julian Pooley from amongst the mostly uncatalogued papers of the antiquary John Gough Nichols, for which, see http://www.le.ac.uk/el/resources/nichols/links.html. For a letter from Stapleton to Madden, written on mourning paper (following the death of Stapleton's father) from 13 Wilton Place, Belgravia, 17 December 1839, with jocular comments on a manuscript history of St-Martin-des-Champs Paris, see BL ms. Egerton 2842 fo.142. For more extensive correspondence with Sir Thomas Phillipps and John Gage, see below.

of minute and voluminous indexes'.[91] In reality, Stapleton was a great deal more interesting and a great deal more influential than the drudge that his previous biographers have portrayed. He was also a great deal more peculiar. The edition of the Norman Exchequer Rolls that he published between 1840 and 1844, although neither entirely comprehensive nor wholly free from error, remains a remarkably accurate one.[92] Above all it was extraordinarily precocious, being the outcome of a proposal first broached in 1830 by Henry Petrie (1768–1842), a one-time dancing master turned antiquary and Keeper of the Records in the Tower of London.[93]

The Norman Exchequer accounts themselves went unnoticed until the early eighteenth century, when a fragment of the account taken at Michaelmas 1184 was discovered amongst the unsorted jumble in the White Tower of the Tower of London, being brought thereafter to the attention of Thomas Madox (1666–1727), the greatest of Exchequer historians.[94] Madox knew of the 1184 fragment, and of the survival of the Norman chancery rolls (C 64, considered above). He seems, nonetheless, to have remained entirely unaware of the survival of other, more extensive Norman Exchequer accounts. Petrie appears to have shared in this ignorance when, in 1830, he printed his prospectus edition of the 1184 Norman Pipe Roll, apparently as part of the wider proposals then being aired for the publication of the early English Exchequer Pipe Rolls. However, Petrie's 1830 edition, soon republished in Normandy, led directly to the discovery of further and much more extensive documentary evidences of the Norman Exchequer.[95]

---

[91] Anonymous obituary in *The Gentleman's Magazine*, cxx (1850), part 1, 322, noting that 'The absorbing interest of a favourite subject may in some men become a more powerful incentive to laborious study than any desire of emolument or even any appetite of fame can produce in more sordid or more ambitious minds ... Indeed, it is too certain that (Stapleton's) health was prematurely sacrificed to his close and painful application'. According to the online *ODNB* site, Thompson Cooper wrote 415 entries for the original *Dictionary of National Biography*. The reviser of his article on Stapleton for the *ODNB*, Elizabeth Baigent, is credited with an even more remarkable 439.

[92] *MRSN*, printing most of the records now assembled as TNA E 373/1–18. Various fragments, including estreats and memoranda now E 101/349/1A and E 101/505/4, recovered since Stapleton's time, were printed as *Miscellaneous Records*, ed. Packard. Dr Moss's forthcoming edition is intended to replace both Stapleton and Packard. Stapleton's edition was very swiftly disseminated in France via its reprinting by Léchaudé d'Anisy: *Grands rôles des échiquiers de Normandie*, and *Magni Rotuli Scaccarii Normanniae*, ed. A. Léchaudé d'Anisy and A. Charma, Société des Antiquaires de Normandie, xv–xvi (new series v–vi) (1845–52).

[93] For Petrie, see D. Knowles, *Great Historical Enterprises* (London 1963), 101; J.D. Cantwell, *The Public Record Office 1838–1958* (London 1991), and the somewhat acerbic memoir by Joseph Hunter in BL ms. Additional 36527 fo.172r. For Petrie's edition, see *Magni Rotuli Scaccarii Normanniae de anno ab incarnatione domini MCLXXXIIII* (London 1830) (iv + 12pp.), printed on paper and in at least one instance on vellum (as in BL printed books 13653, presented to Thomas Grenville). This, the work of Petrie, is wrongly attributed to Stapleton in the TNA catalogue entry for series E 373.

[94] Madox, *Exchequer* (1769), i, 165–9, with extensive extracts, attributing the fragment's rediscovery to a Mr Holmes, working in the time of Queen Anne, hence 1702 X 1711.

[95] In reprinting Petrie's fragment in his *Extrait des chartes et autres actes normands ou Anglo-normands qui se trouvent dans les archives de Calvados*, 2 vols (Caen 1834–5), ii, 349–65, the Norman antiquary Léchaudé d'Anisy correctly identifies Petrie as author, although stating that the 1830 edition was published at Caen rather than London.

The credit for bringing these discoveries before a wider public belongs to Thomas Stapleton, in 1830 aged twenty-four, the second son of a Yorkshire landholder whose family had keen antiquarian concerns, being themselves claimants to a peerage in abeyance since 1507 but pursued from at least 1789 by Thomas' great-uncle (d.1821) and eventually revived in favour of Thomas' elder brother Miles (1805–1854), summoned by writ to the House of Lords in 1840 as 8th Baron Beaumont.[96] Besides being immensely well connected – Thomas' grandmother Mary (d.1826) was a daughter of the 3rd earl of Abingdon, and his mother Maria (d.1827) a daughter of Sir Robert Gerard, 9th baronet, claiming descent from the Irish FitzGerald companions of Richard Strongbow – the Stapletons were rich, with a stately home at Carlton Towers near Goole in Yorkshire, later remodelled by Edward Welby son of the more famous Augustus Welby Pugin, and a landed income in the 1880s estimated, one suspects more than a little optimistically, in excess of £25,000. Their Catholicism had excluded the Stapletons from public office since the Reformation, and was so staunchly English and Cisalpine that in 1850, Thomas' brother, Miles, preferred to join the Church of England rather than accept the restoration of the ultramontane Catholic hierarchy.[97] Miles' son Henry, the 9th Baron, did not reconvert to Catholicism until 1869, becoming an ardent protagonist of the Carlist cause in Spain, rebuilding Carlton Towers in the most lavish neo-Gothic style, fighting in the Zulu war of 1879–80 and, in 1888, taking for his bride Violet, daughter of the fashionable West-End milliner Madame Elise and her husband Frederick Wootton Isaacson (1836–98). The latter, from 1886 Conservative M.P. for Stepney, was probably neither a Catholic nor an Anglican by birth, but was rich enough to settle £6,000 a year and a lump sum of £100,000 on his daughter at the time of her marriage.[98] The 9th baron died childless in 1892, aged only 43, and was succeeded by his younger brother, Miles the 10th Lord Beaumont, another soldier and a Catholic since 1880, who himself died in September 1895, at the age of only 45, when his gun discharged as he was crossing a stile. The fact that this 'accident' occurred after lunch on the same day that Lord Beaumont had drafted his last will and testament did not go unremarked by contemporaries. The Stapletons had become a short-lived family, at least

---

[96] Correspondence, draft petitions and pedigrees relating to the family's claim to the barony, from 1789 onwards, are preserved in Hull History Centre, University Archives DDCA2/49.

[97] By the time of his death in 1854, although declared by his widow to have died an Anglican, the 8th Baron Beaumont himself declared that 'his religion was that of the rationalists of Germany'. See here letters of his younger brother, Gilbert Stapleton, to their sister, Catherine, 19 and 22 August 1854: Hull History Centre, University Archives ms. DDCA2/52/22, the first of these letters declaring that 'all is over for the true faith in the head of our family after so many centuries'. In the aftermath, and despite the determination of his widow to raise her surviving son as an Anglican, Cardinal Wiseman attempted to intervene, pointing out that he had baptized the heir a Catholic, and that just as Catholic guardians were on occasion forced to give up their charges to be raised as Protestants, so in this instance, legal counsel should be sought as to whether a Protestant guardian might not be obliged to give up a child for Catholic education: Ibid. DDCA2/52/23, letters of 23 September 1854.

[98] For genealogical notes on the Isaacson family, preserved amongst the Stapleton family papers, see Hull History Centre, University Archives DDCA2/54/1, apparently made in an attempt to prove descent from one or other of the English families of this name.

in the male line. In 1896, following the death of the 10th baron and the posthumous birth of a second daughter, the peerage was permitted, under special privilege, to pass to his elder daughter, recognised as Baroness Beaumont in her own right. In 1914, she married the 3rd Lord Howard of Glossop. Their son, Miles Francis Stapleton Fitzalan Howard succeeded a kinsman in 1975 as 17th Duke of Norfolk.[99]

Thomas Stapleton, the younger brother of the 8th Baron Beaumont, was schooled at Stonyhurst, the Jesuit school recently transferred to Lancashire from Flanders where it had been established from penal times until the French revolutionary wars of the 1790s forced its closure.[100] He bore the same name as the sixteenth-century Thomas Stapleton (1535–98), recusant priest, theologian, and biographer of both Thomas Becket and Thomas More, professor at Douai and Louvain, with whom the Stapletons of Yorkshire claimed kinship.[101] It is unclear how the younger Thomas honed his historical and palaeographical skills, though in the 1820s it is unlikely that his progress in these disciplines would have been hindered by the fact that, as a Catholic, he was disbarred from admission to either Oxford or Cambridge (neither of which university was prepared to admit Catholics until 1895). His family's peerage claim was derived from the 1st Baron, Henry de Beaumont (d.1340), descended both from the lords of

---

[99] For all of this, Burke's *Peerage and Baronetage*, here using the 75th edition of 1913, is indispensible, with further details supplied from *CP*, ii, 59–67, at 66n. noting that, in 1910, the three widows of the 8th, 9th and 10th barons Beaumont were all still living, the widow of the 8th baron having married her husband, Thomas Stapleton's brother, as long ago as 1844. A copy of the will of Thomas Stapleton the elder (d.1839), father of Thomas the antiquary, is preserved at Hull History Centre, University Archives ms. DDCA2/49/111 (15 March 1833, leaving Thomas the younger a life interest in an estate at Easby, and naming in all seven sons then still living: Miles, Thomas, Gilbert, Henry, John, Brian and Richard fitz Alan). The only brother of Miles and Thomas to have bucked the family trend towards an early death, John Stapleton (1816–1891), barrister and MP for Berwick, converted and remained an Anglican, married in his mid 40s and fathered at least four sons who themselves had issue. For Henry, 9th Baron Beaumont, see M. Bence-Jones, *The Catholic Families* (London 1992), 171, 204–5, 217–21. For a copy of the will of the 10th Baron, dated 16 September 1895, see Hull History Centre, University Archives ms. DDCA3/13/4. See also H.E. Chetwynd-Stapylton, *Chronicles of the Yorkshire Family of Stapleton* (London 1884); J.M. Robinson, *Carlton Towers. The Yorkshire Home of the Duke of Norfolk* (Derby 1991). For an engraving of Carlton Hall before its remodelling in 1840 by the architect John Chessell Buckler (1793–1894), see N. Waugh, 'Dame Etheldreda Stapleton: Her Home and Kindred, 1624–1668', *Downside Review*, xxviii (1919), 79–99, esp. pp.84, 99. For the involvement of Lord Salisbury in the petitioning to allow the 10th baron's daughter to assume the peerage, see letters of December 1895 to the dowager Lady Beaumont, in Hull History Centre, University Archives mss. DDCA2/52/9 (9 December 1895); DDCA2/49/54, and DDCA2/49/144 (Letters Patent of Queen Victoria declaring Mona Josephine Tempest Stapleton to be Baroness Beaumont, 1 June 1896).

[100] I owe to the school archivist my knowledge that Thomas Stapleton entered Stonyhurst on 6 September 1817 and left on 29 July 1824, attending the school from just before his eleventh to just before his eighteenth birthday. His elder brother, Miles, and three other brothers were also schooled there. For the early history of the school, see H. Chadwick, *St Omers to Stonyhurst* (London 1962).

[101] For Thomas Stapleton, author of numerous theological counterblasts to Protestantism as well as of the *Tres Thomae seu res gestae S. Thomae apostoli, S. Thomae archiepiscopi Cantuariensis et martyris, Thomae Mori Angliae quondam cancellarii*, first edition (Douai 1588), reprinted (Cologne 1612), see *ODNB*.

Beaumont in Maine and from John de Brienne, titular King of Jerusalem.[102] This, together with the Gothic splendours of Stonyhurst and the school's strong connections to the tradition of Catholic exile in France, may have contributed to Thomas' own fascination not only with the feudal past, but specifically with Anglo-Norman genealogy. Certainly, it was the Beaumont peerage claim, and Stapleton's desire to prove his family's descent both from the Beaumonts and from Henry fitz Ailwin, first mayor of London, that underlay the extraordinary and for the most part absurdly irrelevant detail with which he traced the descendants of Fitz Ailwin in the introduction to his edition of the London chronicle, the so-called *De Antiquis Legibus Liber*, published in 1846.[103] The absurdities here were in fact more significant than his readers may have supposed, since they give clear signs of the mental collapse that, within a short time, was to overtake Stapleton, darkening the final years of his life. Many of the details of Stapleton's career remain obscure to us. He nonetheless seems to have been a man possessed both of taste and of an infectious sense of humour. From Stonyhurst, he had proceeded not to the universities but to Lincoln's Inn, where he was admitted (aged 17) in February 1824, and from where he was called to the bar on 5 February 1830.[104] This may not imply any real study of the law, since it was common for gentlemen to obtain the qualifications of barrister without any intention of practicing. It is nonetheless conceivable that Stapleton would have been trained in the rudiments of conveyancing and property transfers: the basic knowledge necessary for an understanding of medieval charters. Certainly, the law was one of the few professions that were open to Stapleton as a practising Catholic. Surviving letters refer to his dining in fashionable society, to his attendance at the theatre (to which his elder brother Miles contributed the not entirely incompetent sub-Shakespearean verse-drama *Francesca di Faenza*),[105] and above all to his devotion to Anglo-Norman antiquities, themselves a thoroughly fashionable pursuit, entirely appropriate to a younger son of aristocratic descent. To this extent, there is considerable contrast between the Catholic, urbane and worldly-wise Stapleton and his close contemporary Rawdon Brown: Protestant, thin skinned and irritable explorer of the Venetian archives, whose Italian researches began at almost exactly the same time that Stapleton was making

---

[102] Burke's *Peerage and Baronetage* (75th edition, 1913), 209.

[103] *De Antiquis Legibus Liber. Cronica maiorum et vicecomitum Londoniarum*, ed. T. Stapleton, Camden Society xxxiv (1846), p.iii ff., concluding triumphantly at p.ccxxxiv: 'And thereby we acquire the certain knowledge that Miles-Thomas now Lord Beaumont, and Montagu now Earl of Abingdon, are, at the time of this publication, the lineal descendants and heirs of the body of Henry FitzAylwin, first Mayor of London'. For a more jaundiced view of the circumstances in which the Beaumont peerage was revived, see J.H. Round, *Studies in Peerage and Family History* (London 1901), 30–1.

[104] London, Lincoln's Inn Archives Admissions Register B1a19 fo.144r; Black Book A1a22 pp.34, 36. Stapleton left membership of the Inn on 13 January 1840 'having retired from the profession of the law': Ibid. Black Book A1a23 p.372. For these, and for further details, I am indebted to the Inn's archivist, Josephine Hutchings.

[105] Miles Stapleton, Lord Beaumont, *Francesca di Faenza: A Tragedy* (London 1843), with what were surely impossible demands for a complete change of scene for the closing two-line tableau, but with verse that sits firmly within the tradition of Italian-Gothic created by Byron and Shelley, later taken up by Browning and Poe.

his own first forays into the archives of Normandy.[106] In 1828, only a year after attaining his majority, Stapleton was already seeking admission to the Society of Antiquaries, and by the mid 1830s he was hard at work in the investigation of the Anglo-Norman past, eagerly encouraging the search for further Norman evidences in the Tower, contributing to the deliberations of learned societies, and above all drawing attention to important Norman charters preserved in the Norman provincial archives in France.[107]

Stapleton worked at a time of fundamental change in English historical scholarship, when the dilettantism of the eighteenth century was gradually

---

[106] See here the splendid set of essays collected as *Rawdon Brown and the Anglo-Venetian Relationship*, ed. R.A. Griffiths and J.E. Law (Stroud 2005). Brown first 'discovered' Venice in 1833, at a time when Stapleton himself was in Italy.

[107] He was elected a fellow of the Society of Antiquaries in 1829: London, Society of Antiquaries, ms. Minute Book 1823–30, entries for 27 November 1828 (anonymous testimonial submitted on behalf of Thomas Stapleton Esq. of Lincoln's Inn), 15 January 1829 (elected), 5 February 1829 (admitted). It is perhaps revealing that amongst his own papers, virtually the only 'private' correspondence that his family chose to preserve was the letter from the Antiquaries, 16 January 1829, announcing his election: Hull History Centre, University Archives ms. DDCA/33/28. He first appears as a member of the Society's Council in May 1835, shortly before his proposal to publish the Norman accounts: Society of Antiquaries, ms. Council Book 1829–47, entry for 5 May 1835. John Gage also supported his election to the Athenaeum in an undated letter from the Nichols papers, drawn to my attention by Julian Pooley. Of the various charters cited in Stapleton's articles at this time, the majority appear to be taken from printed sources. However, as early as 1835 Stapleton was exhibiting transcripts of charters from Normandy to his fellow antiquaries (*The Gentleman's Magazine*, cvi (1836), part 1, p.648), and he was undoubtedly in contact with Norman scholars, including Achille Deville and the Abbé de la Rue (for whom see below). For his printing of charters in 1836 from the collection of Deville and from the Mont-St-Michel cartulary at Avranches, see T. Stapleton, 'Ancient Charters Relating to Property in Normandy', *Archaeologia or Miscellaneous Tracts Relating to Antiquity*, xxvii (1838), 21–8, and see also the various Warenne charters printed by Stapleton from unidentified but almost certainly Norman sources, in 'Observations in Disproof of the Pretended Marriage of William de Warren', *Archaeological Journal*, iii (1846), 9–26. For others of Stapleton's articles including charters from the departmental archives at Rouen and Tours, see 'Observations on the History of Adeliza, Sister of William the Conqueror', *Archaeologia*, xxvi (1836), 349–60; 'Observations upon the Succession to the Barony of William of Arques in the County of Kent', *Archaeologia*, xxxi (1846), 216–37; 'Holy Trinity Priory, York', *Memoirs Illustrative of the History and Antiquities of the County and City of York Communicated to the Annual Meeting of the Archaeological Institute of Great Britain and Ireland held at York, July 1846* (1848); *Historical Memoirs of the House of Vernon* (privately printed 1855). In the late 1830s he published an extensive series of deeds relating to Marrick Priory in Yorkshire, from the collections of Martin Farquhar Tupper of Lincoln's Inn (1810–1889), the Victorian best-selling author and perhaps a contact from Stapleton's time of residence in the same Inn of court: *Collectanea Topographica et Genealogica*, v (1838), 100–24, 221–59, from original charters most of which thereafter 'remained' in Stapleton's possession, being today amongst his family's papers in Hull History Centre, University Archives DDCA2/29/1–131, with a few strays in Leeds University, Brotherton Library, and cf. *Western Manuscripts and Miniatures*, Sotheby's Sale Catalogue (London, 11 December 1979), lot no.17; BL ms. Egerton Charter 406 (information courtesy of Tim Gates and Nigel Ramsay), the most important of the early royal charters for Marrick having been sold together with others of Stapleton's collections, now BL ms. Additional Charter 75053 (Henry II), and cf. Manchester, John Rylands Library ms. Beaumont Charter 91 (priory rental of 1435). Of the French departmental archives from which Stapleton undoubtedly derived materials for publication, those at Caen appear to preserve no details of researchers before the twentieth century, and those at Rouen (AD Seine-Maritime ms. 3T) preserve only fragmentary records of readers before 1860 (3T71–9).

yielding place to a more critical approach. Above all, the Record Commission charged with the publication of official state papers, and from 1838 the establishment of the Public Record Office as a repository for all state archives, previously scattered across half a dozen offices in London and Westminster, had encouraged a new emphasis upon documentary, as opposed to chronicle or literary sources in the writing of English history. In an age of Gothic revival, in which the novels of Sir Walter Scott and the architecture of Sir Charles Barry vied for the attention of men and ladies of fashion, it is not surprising that it was upon the Middle Ages, and particularly upon the period between 1066 and 1350, that much of the new interest in documents tended to focus. It was in this period that eighteenth-century scholars had, somewhat reluctantly, agreed that the true origins of Parliament were to be located, and it was to this period that many of the greater landed families of England, amongst them the would-be barons Beaumont, sought to trace their origins. The central Middle Ages were therefore both fashionable and regarded as peculiarly significant, not least in explaining how England, with its Parliament, its peers and its unwritten but nonetheless ancient Constitution, had escaped the horrors of revolutionary and Buonapartist France.[108]

This revived interest in Anglo-Norman antiquities had been heralded in 1783 by the publication of Abraham Farley's edition of Domeday Book, paid for at considerable expense out of government funds and adding momentum to the calls for the establishment of an official Records Commission, expressed in July 1800 by an address by the House of Commons to King George III, in which the sovereign was warned that the nation's records lay 'exposed to erasure, alteration and embezzlement... lodged in places where they are daily perishing by damp or incurring a continual risk of destruction by fire', and answered in the King's letters patent of 19 July, empowering the principal secretaries of state not only to establish better means for the records' preservation and storage but 'to make exact calendars and indexes thereof, and to superintend the printing of such calendars and indexes and original records and papers as ye shall cause to be printed'.[109] The irony that this decision, so significant in the rediscovery of the Anglo-French past, should have been taken by a Hanoverian king, in the midst of a protracted war with France, cannot be allowed to pass unremarked.

---

[108] For much of this, including Robert Brady's demolition, as early as the 1690s, of the idea of the immemorial Saxon Parliament, see R.J. Smith, *The Gothic Bequest. Medieval Institutions in British Thought 1688–1863* (Cambridge 1987).

[109] Both the address and the letters patent are printed as introductory matter to the *Taxatio Angliae et Walliae auctoritate papae Nicholai IV*, ed. S. Ayscough and J. Caley (London 1802). For the various commissions that followed, see P. Walne, 'The Record Commissions, 1800–1837', *JSA*, ii (1960–4), 8–16; R.B. Pugh, 'Charles Abbot and the Public Records: The First Phase', *BIHR*, xxxix (1966), 69–85. For Farley's edition of Domesday, undertaken in the aftermath of schemes by the Society of Antiquaries from the 1750s onwards to prepare an edition, see Condon and Hallam, 'Government Printing of the Public Records', 348–88, esp. 373–83.

By contrast to the early employees of the Record Commission, Stapleton had the good fortune to work at a time of relative calm in Anglo-French relations, at a time moreover when the French themselves, fuelled in no small part by the flood of new peerage claims launched under the restored Bourbon and then the Orleanist monarchies, were once again beginning to take an interest in the feudal past.[110] Relations between France and England had entered a new and closer phase after Waterloo, and were entwined yet further by the July Revolution of 1830, if not on an entirely friendly, then certainly on a closely symbiotic basis. The late engagements with the Revolution and thereafter with Buonaparte, however much they may have entrenched the English in a stereotyped view of the French as the sworn enemies of Anglo-Saxon liberties and the rights of property, had once again drawn attention to the extent to which Anglo-French rivalry lay at the very core of English history. In France itself, historians had become obsessed with the English past, not least for the usefulness of the history of Charles I, Oliver Cromwell and the restoration of the Stuarts in plotting the possible future of the restored Bourbons and subsequently of the Anglomaniac Louis-Philippe. It is well worth remarking that, since 1520 and the meeting of the Field of the Cloth of Gold, the very first visit paid by a ruling English sovereign to a ruling king of France should have been that paid by Queen Victoria to Louis-Philippe in his Norman castle of Eu, in September 1843, just as Louis-Philippe's return visit to Victoria in 1844 was the first by a reigning French king since 1356 and Jean II's captivity in the aftermath of the battle of Poitiers. On a less happy note, it was to be from the Norman port of Le Havre, in March 1848, that Louis-Philippe and his family fled into exile in England, the King boarding ship disguised as an Englishman and speaking loudly and volubly in English so as to throw off any spies. It was in these same years, of the 1840s, that the very idea of an 'entente cordiale' was first coined.[111]

In light of this new Anglo-French rapprochement, even as early as the second decade of the nineteenth century and within a few years of Napoleon's defeat in 1815, antiquaries such as Hudson Gurney (1775–1864) and Dawson Turner (1775–1858) were entering into correspondence with the historians of Normandy, many of whom, most notably Charles Duhérissier de Gerville (1769–1853) and the abbé Gervase de la Rue (1751–1835), had found shelter in England in the aftermath of the revolution of 1789. In 1818, a year after the opening of Dawson Turner's correspondence, Thomas Dibdin made his 'bibliographical, antiquarian and picturesque tour' of Normandy, reporting on the published books and at least some of the manuscript treasures to be viewed in the new public libraries of Rouen, Caen and elsewhere, and encountering amongst other luminaries the 'great archaeological oracle of Normandy', the abbé de la Rue who, in exile

---

[110] For the great market in forged titles of nobility to which such claims gave rise, see R.–H. Bautier, 'La Collection des chartes de croisade dite "collection Courtois"', *Comptes Rendus des Séances de l'Academie des Inscriptions et Belles-Lettres* (1956), 382–6.
[111] For all of this, see M. Price, *The Perilous Crown: France Between Revolutions, 1814–1848* (London 2007), esp.313–19, 368.

after 1790, had been elected to the London Society of Antiquaries.[112] De Gerville, exiled after 1792 to the wilds of Humberside, had subsequently enlisted as a volunteer in the emigré regiment 'Loyal Emigrant'.[113] Dibdin's descriptions, and Gurney and Turner's correspondence with these men, and with the great historian of the Eure, Auguste Le Prévost (1787–1859), paved the way for the enterprise not only of historians such as Hudson Gurney's cousin, Daniel Gurney (1791–1880), author of a monumental history of the Anglo-Norman Gournay family, but for the various trips which Gurney and Turner financed after 1817 for the watercolourist John Sell Cotman (1782–1842), sent to record the surviving architectural antiquities of Normandy.[114] Dibdin, Turner and Cotman were followed into Normandy by other antiquaries and searchers after the Gothic and the picturesque, including Charles Stothard and his wife, who returned to England in 1818 with a famous series of illustrations from the Bayeux tapestry. Stothard also visited the great abbey of Fontevraud on the Loire, by this time converted into a prison. There, in 1816, he found the remains of the funeral monuments of the Plantagenet kings and queens (Henry II, Richard I, Eleanor of Aquitaine, and Isabella of Angoulême), mouldering in a cellar, under threat of destruction at the hands of prisoners who came there to draw water from a well. The architectural framework in which they had been placed since the sixteenth century had been destroyed during the Revolution, and in 1809 an attempt had been made to secure their removal to a projected Musée des Monuments français in Paris. Stothard now suggested that they be 'saved' for the British nation and re-established in Westminster Abbey, an idea taken up by the Prince Regent and still being discussed in 1819. Further efforts to remove them from Fontevraud were to be made in 1846, when it was suggested that they be sent to the Musée des Souverains at the Louvre, and again in 1867, when Napoleon III seriously entertained the possibility of gifting them to Queen Victoria: a proposal that led to outcry in the French press, and that was diplomatically declined by the British government, the Emperor instead dispatching plaster cast reproductions, today still amongst the collections of the Victoria and Albert Museum.[115] Meanwhile, as the Stothards' excursion to Fontevraud suggests,

---

[112] Elected 20 June 1793, information courtesy Society of Antiquaries. For Dibdin's meeting with him, see T.F. Dibdin, *A Bibliographical, Antiquarian and Picturesque Tour in France and Germany*, 3 vols (London 1821), i, 309.

[113] L. Delisle, *Notice sur la vie et les ouvrages de M. de Gerville* (Valognes 1853), pp.1–20, and cf. F. Lefèvre, *La Famille de Charles du Hérissier de Gerville* (St-Lô 1996), with further details recorded in a letter from Gerville to Dawson Turner: Cambridge, Trinity College, Archives, Dawson-Turner correspondence, 18 juillet 1844.

[114] Gurney, *Record of the House of Gournay*. For Hudson Gurney, and the genesis of Cotman's illustrations both to Dawson Turner's *Account of a Tour in Normandy*, 2 vols (London 1820) and to Cotman's own *Architectural Antiquities of Normandy*, 2 vols (London 1822), see M. Rajnai and M. Allthorpe-Guyton, *John Sell Cotman, Drawings of Normandy in Norwich Castle Museum* (Beccles 1975), quoting extensively from Dawson Turner's correspondence now at Trinity College, Cambridge. Cotman's letters are edited by K.H. Isherwood, 'John Sell Cotman's Letters from Normandy 1817–20', *The Walpole Society* xiv–xv (Oxford 1926–7). For Turner, see also *Dawson Turner: A Norfolk Antiquary and his Remarkable Family*, ed. N. Goodman (Chichester 2007).

[115] Mrs Charles Stothard, *Letters Written During a Tour through Normandy, Britanny, and Other*

the search for Anglo-Norman antiquities had begun to extend beyond the immediate vicinities or either Normandy or England. Henry Gally Knight (1786–1846), for example, followed up an architectural tour of Normandy in 1831 with some of the earliest attempts to trace the impact of 'Norman Gothic' architecture upon the churches of Sicily and southern Italy.[116]

As with Stapleton's education at Stonyhurst, itself the product of the revolutionary wars that had forced the Jesuits to flee Liège for Lancashire, it is important to remember how recently and to how great an extent the upheavals of the French Revolution had affected approaches to the Anglo-French past. In these new circumstances, the Middle Ages were laid bare not just to rediscovery but to plunder. This was true both of the architectural historians and of the genealogists. Just as the Gurneys had been motivated, at least in part, by a desire to hunt out the earliest records of their own Anglo-Norman family history, so in 1826, Jeremiah Holmes Wiffen (1792–1836) – Quaker, historian, translator of Tasso, and author of the verse 'Sensations under the Influence of Nitrous Oxide Described: Written Immediately after Inhaling it' – had embarked for Normandy to search out the earliest records of the Russell family, ancestors of his patron, the Duke of Bedford. Wiffen spent nearly four months in the archives at St-Lô and Caen, and at the end of this visit carried back with him to England not only an abiding memory of the welcome that had been afforded him, but a substantial number of original charters, 'liberated' from the archives at Caen.[117] Wiffen's memories are set down for us in a verse 'Farewell to Normandy', marked by more than a faint echo of the then fashionable poetry of Ossian and Sir Walter Scott.[118]

By coincidence, Scott himself was in Paris at precisely this time, and on successive nights, 30 and 31 October 1826, was able to attend performances at the Comédie Française of a play based upon the story

---

Parts of France in 1818, ed. A. E. Bray (London 1820), esp. pp.294–5,and for the Fontevraud tombs, see also P. Gourdin, 'Tentatives d'enlèvement des gisants des Plantagenêts, lettres, voeux et discours 1809–1864', *Société des Lettres, Sciences et Arts du Saumurois*, 89eme année no.147bis (October 1998), 131–73, esp. pp.132–9, 146–57, 165–6.

[116] H.G. Knight, *An Architectural Tour in Normandy with Some Remarks on Norman Architecture* (London 1836); Idem, *The Normans in Sicily, Being a Sequel to 'An Architectural Tour in Normandy'* (London 1838); Idem, *Saracenic and Norman Remains to Illustrate the 'Normans in Sicily'* (London 1840).

[117] I have told the story of Wiffen at greater length elsewhere: N. Vincent, 'A Collection of Early Norman Charters in the British Library: The Case of Jeremiah Holmes Wiffen', *Cahiers Léopold Delisle*, liii fasc.1–2 (2004), 21–45. Here, see J.H. Wiffen, *Historical Memoirs of the House of Russell from the Time of the Norman Conquest*, 2 vols (London 1833), esp. i, pp.xi–xii, 549, for the dates of his tour. For a brief biography of Wiffen by his daughter, and for his poetry, including the 'Sensations', see *The Brothers Wiffen: Memoirs and Miscellanies*, ed. S.R. Pattison (London 1880), esp. pp.223–4. For the subsequent fate of Wiffen's Norman charters, see below n.355.

[118] Wiffen, *Historical Memoirs*, i, 534–49 appendix 24, in 24 stanzas, supposedly written whilst travelling between Rouen and Mantes, 6 October 1826. Note that Wiffen supplies this date in what one might assume to be the distinctively 'Republican' form '10th month 6th, 1826'. Wiffen's patron, John 6th Duke of Bedford (1766–1839), had earlier championed the cause of the radical Whigs. The poem was published first in Paris as *Farewell to Normandy*, a single copy surviving as Bnf livres imprimés YK–95.

of Henry II and Fair Rosamond, and at the Odéon of an opera fashioned from his own *Ivanhoe*.[119] The degree to which post-Napoleonic Europe had adopted English literary heroes, from Shakespeare to Scott, is hardly to be exaggerated, and is reminiscent in many ways of the French lionization of Hollywood film stars after the liberation of 1944. These were the years of Berlioz's Shakespeare worship, culminating in the *Symphonie Fantastique* (1830) with his *hommage* to the actress Harriet Smithson, whose Ophelia he had first seen in September 1827. The same period brought to birth that long string of Italian operas by Donizetti, celebrating not only the literary creations of Scott, from *Il Castello di Kenilworth* (1829) to *Lucia di Lammermoor* (1835), but such solidly English heros and heroines as Alfred the Great (*Alfredo il Grande*, 1823) and the toponymically over-specific *Emilia di Liverpool* (1824).

Wiffen rather fancied himself a poet in the same mould as Scott. His ambition, however, was not equalled by his performance. In the hands of Edward Lear and his later and less polite imitators, the matching of English rhymes to foreign place-names was to become a minor art-form. As practised by Wiffen, it must be accounted less an art than a torture: 'How gaily did the moonbeams glance ... on thy cathedral spires, Coutances', and 'Safe be the antiquarian scrolls ... that fill thy storied tower, St-Loo' being typical of Wiffen's efforts.[120] Wiffen's verses nonetheless record the names of some of the more prominent Norman antiquaries who were already, as early as the 1820s, facilitating access to Norman archives by English scholars: 'learn'd De la Rue', 'tasteful' Léchaudé d'Anisy, 'hail-worthy' Le Prévost and perhaps above all 'learned' de Gerville.[121] It was de Gerville who had already inspired the warmest of friendly feelings from Gurney and Cotman. Cotman, who spoke virtually no French, and who had been criticised for his linguistic shortcomings by no less an authority than Le Prévost, could nonetheless declare that 'I must say if I ever loved a man, 'tis De Gerville'.[122] In Wiffen's reminiscence, it is likewise de Gerville, the future mentor of the young Léopold Delisle, who receives the most rapturous of thanks.

---

[119] *The Journals of Sir Walter Scott*, ed. W.E.K. Anderson (Oxford 1972, here citing the new edition Edinburgh 1998), 256–8, at p.259n. noting that Scott's own command of French was slight and owed more to Froissart than to the nineteenth century.

[120] Wiffen, *Historical Memoirs*, i, 541–2.

[121] Ibid., 543–5.

[122] Rajnai and Allthorpe-Guyton, *John Sell Cotman*, 4, 33. That Cotman's sentiments were amply reciprocated by de Gerville is apparent from de Gerville's extensive correspondence (1820–1849) with Dawson Turner, now preserved in Cambridge, Trinity College archives, much of it taken up with requests for news of Cotman and his state of health. See especially letters from de Gerville to Turner of 4 February 1820 ('Dites lui (Cotman), je vous prie, que je l'aime de tout mon coeur'), 2 June 1823 ('depuis que je l'ai vu la premiére fois, mon attachement pour lui (Cotman) a été constant').

'De Gerville! In thy lettered home
Days melted into hours; with thee
To guide, 'twas luxury to roam
Around the healthy crags of Brix'.[123]

Working from printed sources and occasional visits to the archives, de Gerville had in 1820 distributed, both in France and in England, a long series of 'Notes sur le berceau de quelques unes des familles etabliés en Angleterre': in effect, the very earliest attempt to compile a prosopographical dictionary of the Anglo-Norman baronage, more than a century in advance of the later enterprises of Lewis Loyd and Katharine Keats-Rohan.[124] De Gerville's efforts were admittedly primitive, and remained unpublished. They were, however, informed by considerable knowledge of the printed English sources, most notably Dugdale's *Monasticon* and the county histories, and were early drawn to the attention of John Gage Rokewode (1786–1842), a close friend of Thomas Stapleton, through whose good offices de Gerville was in 1832 elected a corresponding member of the London Society of Antiquaries, an honour which he seems greatly to have coveted.[125] De Gerville, it should be noted, like Le Prévost and many others of his compatriots, spoke and wrote an English far better than the French commanded by his correspondents across the Channel.[126] A direct comparison might be drawn between this generation of Norman antiquaries, at work after 1800, and the much earlier group of English antiquaries, at work after 1600. Both groups consisted for the most part of men of independent means, struggling to rescue the archival remnants of a past that was rapidly disappearing, in England as a result of the Dissolution of the monasteries, in Normandy as a result of the revolution of 1789. Albeit on a far more limited scale than Sir Robert Cotton or Sir William Dugdale, Norman antiquaries such as de Gerville, Le Prévost and de la Rue not only transcribed but collected medieval manuscripts, many of which, despite the establishment of provincial archives for the reception of the remnants of the monastic and feudal past, were still orphaned or

---

[123] Wiffen, *Historical Memoirs*, i, 543. For a more extensive description of just such an excursion arranged by de Gerville on behalf of Cotman in September 1820, see letters from de Gerville to Dawson Turner: Cambridge, Trinity College archives, Dawson Turner correspondence, 15 September 1820. For proof that de Gerville corresponded with Wiffen for at least a year after Wiffen's departure from Normandy, see Caen AD Calvados F5803 fol. 281r (118r), where, next to transcripts of charters of Henry the Young King and of William du Hommet, de Gerville has appended a note 'Copie de ces actes et de la page suivante envoyée à M. Wiffen, Xbre (i.e. December) 1827' (reference courtesy of Daniel Power).

[124] A copy of this mémoire, in de Gerville's hand, liberally annotated by Le Prévost, survives at Evreux AD Eure 4F171, appended to a letter sent to Dawson Turner on 1 November 1820.

[125] Evreux AD Eure 5F33, letters from Le Prévost to de Gerville 2 July 1832, 15 January and 10 March 1833. Gerville's election, together with those of Monsieur de Caumont, president of the Société des Antiquaires de Normandie, and Monsieur Licquet, librarian at Rouen, was signalled on 6 December 1832: *The Gentleman's Magazine*, cii (July–December 1832), 561.

[126] De Gerville's perfect English is apparent throughout his correspondence, and was used in corresponding with Le Prévost as a code to mask sensitive remarks about their contemporaries. Le Prévost himself is to be found quoting from Hamlet in the original: Evreux AD Eure 5F33, letters of 23 November 1827, 1 June 1831.

homeless fifty years after their scattering to the revolutionary winds. What is distinctive about the Norman antiquaries working after 1815 is not so much their own, specifically Norman concerns, but the fact that, via the work of their English correspondents, not least Thomas Stapleton, they were able to communicate with a far wider audience and thus to address far wider, Anglo-Norman concerns than might otherwise have been the case. In all of this, Stapleton's Catholicism and his willingness to address European, not merely English themes, played a highly significant part.

Nor was this trade in evidence and ideas an entirely one-way process. In 1834, de la Rue published the opening lines of an poem, written in the old-French vernacular, that he had read in a manuscript at Oxford whilst in exile from the Revolution after 1789. This helped spark a quest, funded by the Anglophile minister of education, François Guizot. A year later, in July 1835, a young French philologist named Francisque Michel tracked de la Rue's manuscript to its resting place in the Bodleian Library. To students of French language and literature a discovery had been made as momentous as anything that could be claimed in the fields of Egyptian hieroglyphs or Babylonian cuneiform, themselves deciphered during this same period in highly publicized circumstances and as the result of co-operation, not just competition, between English and French experts. The Oxford manuscript contained the earliest known version of the *Chanson de Roland*, hereafter broadcast as the very first French epic, written in Anglo-Norman dialect and unearthed as a direct result of Anglo-French rapprochement.[127]

Gurney, Wiffen, Dibdin and Stothard, had already broadcast the antiquarian splendours and the natural beauties of Normandy by the time that Thomas Stapleton first developed his taste for Anglo-Norman history in the 1820s. Wiffen, indeed, had not only drawn attention to the fact that 'everything which revives our association with a country so intimately connected with our early baronage and history may be welcome to a large class of readers', but to some extent had spelled out Stapleton's future programme of research, noting that amongst the Norman archives 'every bundle which I opened disclosed some note or memorial of the surnames most renowned

---

[127] A. Taylor, 'Was There a Song of Roland?', *Speculum*, lxxvi (2001), 28–65, esp. pp.28–33.
The first correct publication of hieroglyphs was made in 1822 by Jean-François Champollion, following earlier transcriptions by the English polymath, Thomas Young, from the Rosetta Stone, itself housed in the British Museum since its seizure from the French in 1802.
The cuneiform alphabet was first correctly identified by Eugène Burnouf, in 1836, with full decipherment thereafter led by the Englishman, Henry Rawlinson. There is a direct connection here to the rediscovery of the Anglo-Norman past, since in 1857, Burnouf's daughter, Laure, married the great Léopold Delisle, remaining his principal secretary and amanuensis through to her death in 1905. At his own death, in 1910, Delisle willed the sum of 4000 marks to the Académie des Inscriptions et Belles-Lettres, in part to ensure the Académie's perpetual maintenance of the 'modeste tombe' in Père-Lachaise housing the remains of Burnouf and his wife and of Léopold and Laure Delisle: *Comptes-rendus des séances de l'Académie des Inscriptions et Belles-Lettres*, liv (1910), 439–40, and cf. N. Vincent, 'Léopold Delisle, l'Angleterre et le Recueil des Actes de Henri II', *Léopold Delisle: Colloque de Cerisy-la-Salle (8–10 octobre 2004)*, ed. F. Vielliard and G. Désiré dit Gosset (St-Lô 2007), 231–57.

in Norman or in English story – Cliffords, Percies, Clintons, Byrons, Mortimers and Bruces'.[128] Stapleton nonetheless deserves credit as one of the very first English historians not only to appreciate, but to possess sufficient scientific expertise to exploit the all too obvious fact that the barons of post-Conquest England were for the most part French, with vast and as yet untapped archival evidences to be found in France.

Working in the 1830s, Stapleton was again fortunate to coincide with the first true opening up of the Norman provincial archives to scholarly research. The huge mountains of parchment and paper confiscated from the suppressed religious corporations after the Revolution, in Normandy dating back to the eleventh century or beyond, represented a resource whose depth even the likes of Duchesne and Baluze had barely begun to sound. Carted off to the newly established préfectures after 1790, and thereafter subjected to all manner of hazards and indignities, not least by those who feared that such archives were a dangerous reminder of the feudal past, or of England's domination in France, it was not until the 1820s that the medieval charters of Normandy, now housed in the newly-established departmental archives, were reopened to research. Meanwhile, at Lisieux, the entire local archive was burned, a celebration that elsewhere formed part of the prescribed activities of the revolutionary weekday 'décadi', set aside for public instruction and the correction of morals.[129] Further south, although still within the former Plantagenet dominion, at Saintes, on 10 August 1793, the townspeople had formed a circle to dance around the bonfire made of their archives, embracing each other with 'la plus étroite fraternité' before singing the Marseillaise.[130] Nor was it only the mob that burned records. At Coutances, we are told, the cathedral's canons spent three days burning an enormous quantity of parchment, pretending that the documents themselves were rotted, but in reality, one suspects, because of anxiety over their politically inflammatory nature.[131] 1900 portfolios ('liasses') of archives were selected for destruction, between July 1795 and October 1796, by the Commission de Triage appointed to weed the 3000 'liasses' housing the medieval archives of the estates of Brittany, and the contents of the Breton Trésor des Chartes at Nantes were only saved because the doorway leading to the cupboards and wooden boxes made for these records in the reign of Anne of Brittany (1488–1514) was hidden behind barrels of coin.[132] Even the newly formed departmental archives

---

[128] Wiffen, *Historical Memoirs*, pp.xi–xii, 534.

[129] For the law of 7 Messidor (25 June 1794), actually not so disastrous as supposed by Round, see H. Bordier, *Les Archives de la France* (Paris 1855), esp. pp.7–11, 383–9. For the deliberate destruction of archives, including those of Lisieux, see pp.332–4. For the subsequent revival of professional history in France in the 1820s and 30s, see the splendid survey by Pim den Boer, *History as a Profession. The Study of History in France 1818–1914*, trans. A.J. Pomerans (Princeton 1998).

[130] L. Audiat, *Saint Eutrope et son prieuré* (Saintes/Paris 1877), pp.ii–iii.

[131] See the memoir by Léchaudé d'Anisy in TNA PRO 31/8/140B part 1 p.122, whence the introduction to Round, *Calendar*, p.xxxi.

[132] M. Jones, '"Membra disjecta" of the Breton "Chambre des Comptes" in the Late Middle Ages: Treasures Revisited and Rediscovered', *War, Government and Power in Late Medieval*

were not immune from disaster, brought on as much by incompetence as by deliberate malice. There is, for example, the terrible story of the Norman charters of Marmoutier, gathered together after 1790 in the archives départementales at Tours. At some point in the 1790s, a decision was taken to disperse these documents amongst the archives of each département in which Marmoutier's dependent priories had been situated. In this way, the charters of the priories of Bohon, Héauville, Sacey and Mortain were posted off from Tours to the archives de la Manche at St-Lô. The functionary to whom they were addressed, however, refused to pay the cost of the postage, so that an entire dossier of eleventh and twelfth-century Norman charters vanished into the French postal system, perhaps never again to be seen.[133] In the meantime, under separate instructions issued in 1798, the Minister of the Interior, François de Neufchâteau, had ordered that all cartularies were to be removed from local archives and sent to the new central library established in Paris, the future Bibliothèque nationale. Such manuscripts, 'fruits des siècles barbares', were judged to be too important in testifying to the criminality of the religious institutions of the Ancien Régime to be entrusted to merely local keeping.[134] In reality, although this order was invoked and obeyed in some localities, elsewhere it sowed confusion and led to yet further dispersal of already scattered archives.

By the 1830s, half a century after the Revolution, the worst of the horrors had been wrought. From time to time, even so, the urge to destroy was not entirely laid to rest. In February 1831, a mob protesting against the legitimist sympathies of the archbishop of Paris seized the entire archiepiscopal library and dumped it into the Seine.[135] Shortly before this, a unique manuscript of Herbert of Bosham's 'Liber Melorum', preserved in the Bibliothèque Municipale at Arras, was deliberately mutilated by the local librarian to spite the town authorities with whom he was in dispute, every tenth leaf of the book being sold as scrap parchment to a local tailor for use as measuring tape.[136] Neglect or accident, however, rather than deliberate destruction

---

France, ed. C. Allmand (Liverpool 2000), 211.

[133] As recounted by Delisle, *Recueil*, i (Introduction), p.23, citing the official report of the archivist at Tours. For evidence suggesting that at least part of Marmoutier's Norman archive came into the possession of the English manuscript collector, Sir Thomas Phillipps, see below p.78 n.277.

[134] Order of 1er nivôse an VII (21 December 1798), reprised in *Chartes de l'abbaye de Jumièges (v.825 à 1204)*, ed. J.–J. Vernier, 2 vols (Rouen/Paris 1916), i, pp.ix–x: 'Ces titres, fruits des siècles barbares, se lient trop essentiellement à leur histoire pour pouvoir en être distraits. Il faut qu'ils attestent à la postérité ce que l'ambition et l'artifice des corporations privilégiées ont obtenu de la crédule ignorance de nos pères, et qu'ils lui faissent apprécier l'heureuse révolution qui s'est faite dans l'esprit humain'.

[135] P. Thureau-Dangin, *Histoire de la monarchie de juillet*, 7 vols (Paris 1884–92), i, 188–94.

[136] *The Diary and Memoirs of John Allen Giles*, ed. D. Bromwich, Somerset Record Society lxxxvi (2000), 245, 254–6, reporting the subsequent purchase of the mutilated leaves by Sir Thomas Phillipps. As a former Phillipps manuscript (Phillipps 16865), they were exported to the United States in 1977 (whence the microfilm copy in BL Microfilm R.P. 1517 part iii), but then returned to London for sale, with a particularly detailed description and history in the Sotheby's Sale Catalogue (*Western Manuscripts and Miniatures*) (London 1 December 1998), pp.56–60 lot 79, incidentally revealing that more than 1300 other such leaves, deliberately cut from Arras manuscripts, left behind in France by Phillipps in the 1820s, in 1885 recovered on

were now the principal threat. Into the 1840s, unquantifiably vast numbers of medieval charters taken from northern French municipalities continued to be used as wadding in the cannons of the artillery school at Metz.[137] In 1835, Jules Michelet (1798–1874) reported disgraceful neglect amongst the departmental archives of south-western France, where some archives were entirely unstaffed, others were housed in leaky attics infested with rats and mice, and still others were at risk of being sold off piecemeal to amateur manuscript collectors.[138] Michelet's tour of the archives came less than a year after his first visit to England, undertaken in July-August 1834. There, he had gone at least twice to the records in the Tower of London, meeting Petrie and the young Thomas Duffus Hardy (1804–1878), viewing the vast series of rolls in their oak presses and admiring the fact that the records were stored free from damp or humidity. After a frantic tour in which he took in the sights of both Ireland and Scotland and, as a devotee of Sir Walter Scott, passed by but lacked the courage to call upon Scott's house at Abbotsford, Michelet returned to London and the British Museum where he admired the ordered calm and where he inspected a charter of David King of Scotland, as much for the fact that David was mentioned in the preface to Scott's *Sir Tristrem* as for the charter's intrinsic historical interest. The English themselves Michelet found fat and arrogant, their much-vaunted countryside nothing more than one vast meat factory suited to a nation of butchers. Their records, by contrast, were kept in far better conditions than those of France.[139]

The happy, if misleading, impression of English archival efficiency that Michelet carried away with him can be explained by the revival of the English Record Commission, the first Commission having lapsed upon the death of George IV in 1830. Thanks to what in the early 1830s were the remarkably buoyant finances of the second Record Commission, at almost the precise moment that Stapleton began work and that Michelet prepared to cross to England, the first of a series of calls had been broadcast to French scholars to collect evidences of the English past from French provincial archives – a call answered in Normandy by such antiquaries as Achille Deville and Léchaudé d'Anisy, and in Paris by various of the pupils of the newly-established Ecole des Chartes. Such researchers were prepared to transcribe large numbers of Anglo-Norman charters in return for money so generously

---

behalf of the Arras library, were destroyed by an incendiary bomb in July 1915, before they had been reunited with the manuscripts from which they had been removed.

[137] Known because of the willingness of local historians to recover some ten kilograms (just under 400 charters) of such materials in exchange for blank modern parchment purchased at ten francs the kilo: C. Brunel, 'Les Parchemins de la collection Salis aux archives historiques de la ville de Metz', *BEC*, lxxv (1914), 351–2.

[138] J. Michelet, *Oeuvres complètes*, ed. P. Vialleneix (Paris 1971–), iii, 539–64, cited by Den Boer, *History as a Profession*, 87, and cf. J. Michelet, *Journal: tome 1 (1828–1848)*, ed. P. Viallaneix (Paris 1959), 183, 201, 209.

[139] Michelet, *Journal*, 123–60, esp.128, 154 (visits to the Tower), 131 (English countryside), 142–3, 146 (Scott), 156 (visit to the British Museum).

and so unexpectedly disbursed from English public funds.[140] The author of these appeals, Charles Cooper (1793–1873), secretary to the second Record Commission from 1831, dreamed of establishing the study of government records upon new scientific foundations, and even of endowing an English rival to France's Ecole des Chartes. In the immediate term, and despite disbursing something over £400,000 in public funds, Cooper bequeathed very little to his successors save for a debt of £24,000 and the controversy which, after 1836, caused the collapse of the Record Commission. In the longer term, from Cooper's fecklessness and extravagance were born not only the principal publications of the chancery rolls of the reign of King John – the *Rotuli Chartarum*, *Rotuli Litterarum Patentium* and *Rotuli Litterarum Clausarum*, published in splendid folios under the editorial oversight of Thomas Duffus Hardy and all proclaiming themselves to be *in Turri Londinensi asservati* – but the very idea of a centralized Public Record Office, itself from the beginning embellished with the volumes of transcripts of charters from Normandy paid for from Cooper's funds.[141] I shall return to these transcripts in due course, and in much greater detail. For the moment, let it be noted that, even without setting foot on Norman soil, Thomas Stapleton and his fellow antiquaries were by the 1830s in a position to gain access to documentary treasures in England that until then had lain in a state of benign but near-total neglect.

Nonetheless, for all of these advantages, Stapleton worked as a true pioneer. Until very recently, the question of which Norman or French archives he visited, and precisely when, remained unanswerable. Thanks to the rediscovery and cataloguing of the papers of his intimate friend, John Gage Rokewode, we can now employ more than thirty surviving letters from Stapleton to construct a very clear picture of his progress through the Norman and French archives. The correspondence begins in March 1831, when Stapleton was twenty-four and Gage (as Stapleton called him, and we should too, since he adopted the name Rokewode only very late in life) in his mid 40s.[142] Gage was well connected, being the younger son of a Suffolk baronet, with access to the highest Whig circles. In the 1830s, for example, when working on

---

[140] For the initial circular, sent out by the Commission's secretary Charles Cooper in December 1833, requesting amongst other things information on the survival of further records of the Norman Exchequer, see *Revue Anglo-Française*, ii (1834), 421–33, iii (1835) 130–1. The *Revue* itself bears testimony both to the new spirit of Anglo-French co-operation under the July monarchy, and to the fashion for all things British, not least in light of the success of the novels of Scott.

[141] For Cooper, see the brief biography by J.A. Hamilton in the *ODNB*, with remarks on his desire to establish an English Ecole des Chartes by Walne, 'The Record Commissions', 12, 14–15; J. Cantwell, 'The 1838 Public Record Office Act and its Aftermath: A New Perspective', *JSA*, vii (1982–5), 277–86, esp. 277–8. A file of correspondence concerning Cooper's appeal for transcriptions from France, including a number of letters from French researchers that are frankly extortionate in their calls upon the Commission's funds, is preserved in TNA PRO 30/10/28, and cf. below pp.67–72.

[142] Cambridge University Library mss. Hengrave Hall 21/3–13 (Gage correspondence 1831–1841), as drawn to my attention by Peter Meadows. For the first of the surviving letters, dated at The Grove, 6 March 1831, reporting Stapleton's visit to Bolton Hall and his transcription of the original contract for building Bolton Castle, see Ibid. 21/3/22.

the Benedictional of St Aethelwold, he seems simply to have borrowed the manuscript, already regarded as priceless, from the Duke of Devonshire, in order that he might have an engraver make up plates.[143] We should nonetheless beware of exaggerating the grandeur of Gage's position: Thackeray, a close contemporary, has one of his characters, a peer's daughter, remark that marriage to 'a gentleman who was but the younger son of a Suffolk baronet' was, in itself evidence for a lack of 'pride'.[144] Just as significant as his family's baronetcy was the fact that Gage was a member of a distinguished Catholic line, educated by the Jesuits of Stonyhurst, a decade or so before Stapleton's arrival at that school, and thereafter trained up in the law at Lincoln's Inn, in the chambers of the leading Catholic barrister, Charles Butler (1750–1832), according to much the same pattern as Stapleton a decade later.[145]

Until his inheritance of the Rokewode estate from his elder brother Robert, in 1838, which led him to change his name, John Gage acted in effect as steward of his family's estates in Suffolk. From his rooms in Lincoln's Inn, he conducted the affairs of Hengrave Hall near Bury St Edmunds, ensuring that annuities were paid to his sister-in-law and his two young nephews, including Sir Thomas Gage (born in 1810) who had inherited the baronetcy, but who spent most of the 1830s on a very rackety grand tour, being joined in Italy by his mother, the widowed Lady Mary Anne, herself the daughter of an Irish peer. Lady Mary Anne's letters to John Gage are typified by a plangent snobbery, in which enquiries about the transfer of funds mingle with complaints about the extravagence of her sons, and with the gossip and goings on of the English Catholic community in Rome. When considered in the context of the great pile of bonds, mortgages and begging letters that characterizes the rest of Gage's business correspondence, they suggest that, until his change of fortunes and name in 1838, Gage himself was far from

---

[143] As noted by T.A. Birrell, 'The Circle of John Gage (1786–1842), Director of the Society of Antiquaries, and the Bibliography of Medievalism', *Antiquaries, Book Collectors and the Circles of Learning*, ed. R. Myers and M. Harris (Winchester 1996), 75.

[144] *Henry Esmond* (1852), preface 'The Esmonds of Virginia'. George Warrington, best friend of *Pendennis* (1849), is an earlier representative of the breed.

[145] For the general background to Gage's friendship with Stapleton, see Birrell, 'The Circle of John Gage', 71–82. Gage was enrolled at Stonyhurst from 24 September 1798 until 26 December 1804: information that I owe to the Stonyhurst archivist, Mr David Knight. His elder brothers, Thomas and Robert, were amongst the band of scholars evacuated from Flanders in 1794, as the founding generation of boys brought to England and thence to Stonyhurst itself: Chadwick, *St Omers to Stonyhurst*, 391. For Butler, schooled at Douai in the 1760s, later to make use of antiquarian studies in the pursuit of Catholic causes, see N.L. Abercrombie, 'The Early Life of Charles Butler', *Recusant History*, xiv (1977–8), 281–92. For evidence that Gage and Stapleton were already friends by the time of Stapleton's call to the bar in 1830, see Lincoln's Inn Archives ms. Bar Book B2a3 fo.27r, where Gage served as surety to the official record of the signature of Thomas Stapleton.

comfortably established.[146] On occasion during the 1830s, we find Stapleton offering to defray Gage's travelling expenses.[147]

By the time of his first encounter with Stapleton, Gage was a published author. In 1829 – the same year, coincidentally, that an Act for Catholic Emancipation was passed – he had been elected Director of the Society of Antiquaries, in effect as keeper of the Society's collections and overseer of its literary ventures, with considerable patronage to distribute amongst the printers and engravers of London. As has been noted by previous commentators, the fact that this position came to Gage despite his Catholicism, is no small testimony to his own personal charms and his ability to avoid religious controversy.[148] In this, he was a fit mentor for Thomas Stapleton, whose Catholicism seems to have been as sincere as it was discreet. In Normandy and elsewhere on the continent, their religion undoubtedly opened doors to Gage and Stapleton that might otherwise have remained closed. We find, for example, the Norman antiquary de Gerville not only reminiscing to Gage about the Catholic families that he had visited during his English exile of the 1790s, but openly congratulating him on his rise to so prominent a position in the Society of Antiquaries, given the notorious anti-Catholic prejudices of the English.[149] By the time that their correspondence opens, Gage had been friends with Stapleton for at least a year: in August 1830 they were planning to visit Ely together, to examine manuscripts.[150] No doubt their shared sense of distinction, as well-born Catholics, and their mutual experience of schooling in the surroundings of Stonyhurst – a school, if ever there was one, calculated to induce either love or loathing for the Gothic past – contributed to what was clearly a very close friendship. As members of Lincoln's Inn – Gage under the protection of Charles Butler, Stapleton under the protection of Gage – they followed in a proud tradition of Catholic lawyers, able to deploy the records of the feudal past in pursuit of present concerns, not least the repeal of England's still oppressive Penal Laws. Although Stapleton himself seems never to have practised as a lawyer, his brother Miles, Lord Beaumont, was to play no small part in the eventual repeal of much of this deadweight of

---

[146] Gage's estate papers are today in Bury St Edmunds, Suffolk Record Office, with particularly illuminating evidences, relating both to the Gage estates and to the absentee Lady Mary Anne and her sons, preserved in the bundles of correspondence, mss. 449/5/15 esp. 449/5/15/14, 17–18. The letters of Lady Mary Anne to John Gage, and the occasional, frequently illegible palimpsests sent by the young Sir Thomas, recording his triumphs in Rome, Greece, Constantinople and Vienna, would richly merit study in their own right.

[147] For example, in letters of 22 December 1833 and 15 July 1834, noting a loan to Gage of £50 prior to their joint tour of Normandy that summer: Cambridge University Library ms. Hengrave Hall 21/5/190; 21/6/144.

[148] Birrell, 'The Circle of John Gage', 72–3, 75–6.

[149] Cambridge University Library ms. Hengrave Hall 21/6/90, Gerville to Gage, 7 May 1834, including memories of Gerville's time at Colchester *c.*1798, of Lord Euston (later Duke of Grafton) and of the Catholic chapel at Gifford's Hall.

[150] See Oxford, Bodleian Library ms. Phillipps-Robinson c.623 fo.122r–v, with Sir Thomas Phillipps asking them to seek access to the Ely cathedral library, to search out topographical manuscripts and the Ely cartularies and charters.

anti-Catholic legislation.[151] Meanwhile, their Catholicism not only opened doors on the continent, but rendered Gage and Stapleton themselves open to continental and cosmopolitan influences. In the still far from tolerant 1830s, their joint role as leaders of opinion in the Society of Antiquaries appears all the more remarkable, not least because, as Gage's most recent biographer has suggested, the programme of research that Gage pursued was so innovative: nothing less than a 'cultural-anthropological approach to the religious life of the Middle Ages'.[152] Not only genealogy but liturgy, not only Gothic taste but a sense of the still-living traditions of monasticism informed their ventures. The generation of seventeenth-century gentlemen who had first sought to uncover England's monastic and medieval past, could claim closer proximity to the Middle Ages, both in chronological and socio-political terms. Their Protestantism, nonetheless, rendered them hostile or indifferent to much that was of importance. Gage and Stapleton, although writing a full two hundred years later, amidst the warm after-glow of the Gothic revival, in an England of railways and parliamentary reform, could nonetheless, through their high-bred Catholicism, comprehend aspects of the medieval past that the seventeenth-century antiquaries had found antipathetic. Their friendship was to have significant consequences, not least upon the literary career of the distinctly un-Catholic Thomas Carlyle. By collaborating together, later in the 1840s, on their Camden Society edition of the chronicle of Jocelin of Brakelond, Gage and Stapleton made no mean contribution to English letters, being directly responsible for Carlyle's decision to employ abbot Samson of Bury in his *Past and Present*. Here Samson served as a model of all that was good about the twelfth-century past, and all that was most rotten about the industrialised and socially polarized England of the 1840s.[153]

By the late 1820s, Gage had already travelled widely on the continent. On 18 June 1815, during a brief excursion to Holland, he had been in Utrecht on the same fateful day that, unbeknown to him, the French were defeated at Waterloo; just over a week later, he visited the battlefield to assist a Suffolk neighbour in recovering the body of his son, killed in the fighting at Hougemont farm.[154] He made a tour of Italy in 1826–7, visiting Naples and Rome, and in the summer of 1830, he was contemplating a tour of Normandy, soliciting letters of introduction to de Gerville from Dawson Turner.[155] In

---

[151] For the role of Miles Stapleton, in 1844 acting with the convert barrister, Thomas Anstey, to petition Parliament for the repeal of a mass of redundant penal legislation, see B. Ward, *The Sequel to Catholic Emancipation*, 2 vols (London 1915), i, 272–6.

[152] Birrell, 'The Circle of John Gage', 80.

[153] *Chronica Jocelini de Brakelonda de rebus gestis Samsonis abbatis monasterii sancti Edmundi*, ed. J.G. Rokewood, Camden Society xiii (1840). For Stapleton's role in the formation of the Camden Society in 1838, see A. and J.I. Freeman, *John Payne Collier. Scholarship and Forgery in the Nineteenth Century*, 2 vols (New Haven 2004), i, 317.

[154] Gage's delightful memoir of this visit is now Cambridge University Library ms. Hengrave Hall 42, with extensive extracts printed by T.A. Birrell, '"A Sentimental Journey" Through Holland and Flanders by John Gage', *Across the Narrow Seas: Studies in the History and Bibliography of Britain and the Low Countries Presented to Anna E.C. Simoni*, ed. S. Roach (London 1991), 197–205.

[155] A selection of his excerpts and comments 'On reading Virgil during a tour in Italy in 1827' is

the event, this visit seems to have been postponed until the following year, when Gage was undoubtedly at Rouen, making contact with de Gerville, Le Prévost and various of the more prominent antiquaries of Normandy for whom he arranged election as corresponding members of the London Society of Antiquaries: an honour for which the Normans expressed almost pathetic gratitude.[156] It should not be forgotten here that in the 1830s, France was a recently conquered nation. Its elite, and especially its Catholic elite, was only too aware that England was militarily and economically the dominant power. This dominance was attributed both to England's immunity from the revolutionary spirit of 1789 or 1830, and to the survival of an aristocracy, well represented by the young Thomas Stapleton, that had prospered whilst the French aristocracy had succumbed to self-indulgent hubris whence the nemesis of the guillotine. At much the same time that Gage and Stapleton were touring Normandy, the young Alexis Clérel, comte de Tocqueville, born in 1805 and hence an almost exact contemporary of Stapleton, was exploring the causes of the fall of the Ancien Régime and in the process drawing a mordant contrast between his own fellow aristocrats in Normandy and the more open, tax-paying, entrepreneurial English elite to which both Gage and Stapleton belonged. De Tocqueville's first visit to England took place in 1833, at precisely the time that Stapleton was first exploring the archives of Normandy. With his town house at Valognes, and his elected office as député for the département of Manche, Tocqueville was both a close neighbour and constitutional representative of the antiquary and Anglophile, de Gerville.[157] Auguste Le Prévost, besides being the distinguished editor of Orderic Vitalis, was himself député for the neighbouring department of the Eure. Just as Tocqueville explored America and England for democratic alternatives to French autocracy, so Le Prévost had a love of English

---

preserved as Cambridge University Library ms. Hengrave Hall 42, and for letters addressed to him 'poste restante' at Naples and Brussels in January and August 1827, see Bury St Edmunds, Suffolk Record Office 449/5/15/7. For Dawson Turner, in letters of 27 July 1830, regretting that 'It is not, I am sorry to say, in my power to furnish you with a letter of introduction to M(onsieur) de Gerville, but on the other hand, it gives me pleasure to add that you certainly will not want it, for he is one of the most obliging men alive and your introducing yourself to him as an antiquary will be all that is needed', referring to Turner's correspondence with de Gerville, to differences that had arisen over Cotman's illustrations, and to the possibility that Gage might visit Lisieux and Bayeux as well as Rouen, see Cambridge University Library ms. Hengrave Hall 21/2/167.

[156] Cf. Cambridge University Library ms. Hengrave Hall 21/6/146, where, in letters of 17 July 1834, Stapleton refers to an earlier visit paid by Gage to Fécamp and Upper Normandy. Gage's visit of 1831 was to lead directly to the election of the antiquaries de Gerville, Le Prévost, Licquet, Deville and Langlois as corresponding members of the Society of Antiquaries: Ibid. 21/4/21, 26, 175, and cf. 21/5/47 (where Le Prévost, following doubts about the suitability of adding the antiquary de Caumont, emphasises, in English and by underscoring, that de Caumont is a 'gentleman'). For the French side of this correspondence, see Evreux AD Eure 5F33, letters of Auguste Le Prévost to de Gerville, 2 July 1832, 15 January and 10 March 1833. On their first meeting, Gage appears to have met with an uncharacteristically frosty reception from de Gerville, normally the most urbane of hosts: Cambridge, Trinity College archives, Dawson Turner correspondence, letters from de Gerville to Dawson Turner 18 July 1844 and 27 December 1849.

[157] In general here, see H. Brogan, *Alexis de Tocqueville* (London 2006), esp. 241–52, for Tocqueville's 1833 visit to England, itself strongly influenced by a reading of Sir Walter Scott.

poetry, of Shakespeare and of more recent authors, exhibited in the English quotations scattered across his correspondence, albeit that in his essay *Sur la poésie romantique* (1825), he took a chauvinistically 'French' view of romanticism, championing Châteaubriand and Madame de Staël as the just heirs to the French parnassus of Racine and the century of Louis XIV, without a moment's glance at Coleridge or Wordsworth, let alone at Byron, Shelley or Scott.

The correspondence between Stapleton and Gage commences in earnest in July 1831, by which time Stapleton was in Rouen, at the start of a European tour that was to last more than three years. Thereafter, it supplies both a delightful and an extremely significant insight into Stapleton's methods and achievements. We might suppose that the world of Gage and Stapleton was a far from happy one, mired in religious controversy. Surely we are about to embark upon that dolorous route of backbiting, penny-pinching and pedantry that characterizes so much of antiquarian, and perhaps especially of Catholic antiquarian endeavour. In fact, nothing could be further from the truth. Both Gage and his younger disciple, Thomas Stapleton, in so far as their correspondence allows for an accurate psychological assessment, were of a sunny and humorous disposition, at least until Gage's death in 1842, at the age of 56, of a sudden stroke, whilst out shooting. Schooled amidst memories of penal and later revolutionary persecution; surrounded at Stonyhurst by the relics, many of them hideously gruesome, of the Jesuit past, Gage and Stapleton might be supposed to have imbibed something of the 'gloomth' of Horace Walpole combined with the conspiratorial high seriousness of Lord Acton. On the contrary, the world that they inhabited seems to have had been far more that of *Pendennis* than of *The Castle of Otranto*. There are as few outbreaks of Actonian angst to be found in Stapleton's letters as there are glad reminiscences of girls, gaiety and field sports to be found in the later correspondence of Lord Acton and Professor Döllinger. About the only thing that Gage and Acton seem to have shared in common, besides their Catholicism, was the fact that their private papers were preserved in glorious abundance. If the determination to preserve letters be a Catholic trait, then Gage and Acton were the most devout of Catholics. It is all the more ironic that their papers, in the one case radiating sweetness and light, in the other stale with disappointed obsession, should be preserved side by side in Cambridge, in the library of a university itself famed more for its Puritanism than its Catholicism.

And so to Stapleton's letters. At Rouen, in July 1831, during what may perhaps have been his first visit to the city, Stapleton spent time in the Bibliothèque Municipale transcribing letters of Robert of Jumièges, eleventh-century bishop of London, in an attempt to assist Gage with his researches on the Benedictional of St Aethelwold.[158] Although he presented

---

[158] Cambridge University Library ms. Hengrave Hall 21/3/58, 17 July 1831. For the so-called 'missal' (actually a sacramentary) of Robert of Jumièges, with Robert's donation inscription (Rouen, Bibliothèque Municipale ms. Y.6), see *The Missal of Robert of Jumièges*, ed. H.A. Wilson, Henry Bradshaw Society xi (1896), 316. Gage had in February 1832 presented

an introduction to the librarian, Monsieur Licquet, from Henry Petrie, together with a copy of Petrie's edition of the 1184 Norman Pipe Roll, there is little at this stage to suggest any profound acquaintance with Anglo-Norman antiquities.[159] Rather, Stapleton's tastes seem to have been broad and to have extended to all aspects of the 'Gothic' past. Moreover, Rouen was merely the first stopping point on a grand tour which took him via Châteaudun, Chartres, Blois, Poitiers and Bordeaux, down to Pau and the Pyrenees and thence via Marseille to Rome. The antiquities of all of these places were of interest to Stapleton, and were immediately communicated to Gage. There are hints here that Stapleton's previous reputation was as a valetudinarian or invalid. From Bordeaux, in August 1831, he wrote, despite 'my usual good health', of 'harassing colds', and from Marseilles he boasted that Gage 'would have been impressed to see the debilitated invalid of Burlington Quay walking fifteen miles a day, scaling mountains near 10,000 feet high'.[160] In Rome, where he was established throughout 1832, he was granted access to the papal archives with permission to examine the papal registers. Somewhat disappointed, he reported that the registers began only in the thirteenth century, and that their contents relating to England, in so far as the 'miserable indexes' would allow, had already been transcribed by the archivist, Monsignor Marini, who had recently sent his transcripts to England.[161] There may be an element of

---

the Antiquaries with a paper on the so-called Benedictional of Archbishop Robert (Rouen, Bibliothèque Municipale ms. Y.7), published as an appendix to his 'A Dissertation on St. Aethelwold's Benedictional', *Archaeologia*, xxiv (1832), 118–36, at p.136 acknowledging the assistance of Messieurs Licquet and Langlois at Rouen, and cf. *The Benedictional of Archbishop Robert*, ed. H.A. Wilson, Henry Bradshaw Society xxiv (1903). I am indebted to Richard Gameson for his assistance here.

[159] Cambridge University Library ms. Hengrave Hall 21/3/63, Stapleton to Petrie, dated at Châteaudun, 24 July 1831. Théodore (François-Isidore) Licquet (1787–1832).

[160] Ibid. 21/3/70, 73, letters dated at Bordeaux and Marseilles, 10 August and 29 September 1831. Burlington Quay was a fashionable seaside resort, now absorbed into Bridlington, East Yorkshire.

[161] Ibid. 21/4/139; 21/5/27, letters dated at Rome, 28 April 1832 and 27 February 1833, *inter alia* reporting a meeting with Gage's nephew 'but he is rather too green for me to get on any great footing of intimacy with him'. The nephew, Sir Thomas Gage, and his mother Lady Mary Anne were in Rome, Naples or Sicily for much of 1832–3. I have found only one reference to Stapleton in their correspondence: Bury St Edmunds, Suffolk Record Office ms. 449/5/15/14, in letters of Lady Mary Anne to John Gage, dated at Rome, 11 April 1833, reporting the return of the young Sir Thomas Gage from Naples and remarking 'I very seldom see your friend Mr Stapleton'. For the Vatican archives, in the 1830s only recently returned from captivity in Paris, see O. Chadwick, *Catholicism and History: The Opening of the Vatican Archives* (Cambridge 1978), 22–5, 146 n.16. For the later history of English exploration of the papal registers, see J. Sayers, 'The Vatican Archives, the Papal Registers and Great Britain and Ireland: The Foundations of Historical Research', *The Foundations of Medieval English Ecclesiastical History. Studies Presented to David Smith*, ed. P. Hoskin and others (Woodbridge 2005), 194–209 and P. Zutshi, 'The Publication of Entries in the Papal Registers Concerning Great Britain and Ireland', *Friedensnobelpreis und historische Grundlagenforschung: Ludwig Quidde und die Erschließung der kurialen Registerüberlieferung*, ed. M. Matheus, Bibliothek des Deutschen Historisches Instituts in Rom cxxiv (Berlin 2012), 585–601, noting Stapleton's letter to Gage at pp.587–8. For the 48 volumes of transcripts, for the most part from papal registers, made under the supervision of the Vatican Prefect, Monsignor Marino Marini, sent to the State Papers Office in 1829 and thence transferred to the British Museum in 1845, see BL mss. Additional 15351–15400.

exaggeration to these claims: in all probability, Stapleton never set foot inside the archives themselves, to which entry was forbidden under the most dire penalty of excommunication, and the Marini transcripts had been dispatched to London at least three years before 1832, a great deal less recently than Stapleton's letter leads us to suppose. All of this suggests an understandable desire by a younger man, Stapleton, to impress a much older and more distinguished mentor, Gage. Merely for his visit to the archives, however, Stapleton deserves recognition as a pioneer: as perhaps the first English antiquary of modern times even to have glimpsed the early papal registers, forty years in advance of Joseph Stevenson, W.H. Bliss and their successors. In the Vatican Library, and here pointing towards his own later mastery of the Anglo-Norman past, he undoubtedly consulted an important early manuscript of Orderic Vitalis.[162] At Orvieto, in the Cathedral archives, he transcribed a bull of Pope Gregory X relating to the murder, in 1271, of Henry of Almain, nephew of King Henry III nephew of King Henry III, an incident all the more famous for its inclusion in Dante's *Inferno*.[163] In retrospect, this emerges as a momentous period in Anglo-Roman relations.

Besides Stapleton, other distinguished British visitors were in Rome in 1832–3. The ubiquitous Sir Walter Scott was there at Easter 1832, at the very end of his long career. At the very beginning of his, so was W.E. Gladstone. It was in St Peter's Basilica, in March 1832, according to his biographer, Lord Morley, that Gladstone experienced his first conception of unity in the Church and with it the 'pain and shame of schism which separates us from Rome'.[164] A year later, at Easter 1833, the city was visited by two young fellows of Oriel College Oxford: Richard Hurrell Froude and John Henry Newman. Froude was hoping to see a manuscript of Thomas Becket's letters in the Vatican library, crucial to his rediscovery, soon shared by Newman, of a community of interest between medieval English catholicism and modern Anglicanism. Dr (the later Cardinal) Wiseman, then rector of the English College in Rome and one of Stapleton's contacts, promised Froude assistance in the Vatican collections where Wiseman himself had been appointed keeper of Arabic manuscripts. From such contacts and experiences was the Oxford Movement born.[165]

For much of his time in Italy, Stapleton did not travel alone. His companion is not identified in his letters, but was undoubtedly his elder brother, Miles, who was still with him on the continent in the following year. An otherwise

---

[162] As noticed in letters to Gage of 22 December 1833: Cambridge University Library ms. Hengrave Hall 21/5/190, and for the manuscript, Vatican Reginensis Latina 703, see *Orderic*, i, 121.

[163] Cambridge University Library ms. Hengrave Hall 21/7/214, proposed in a letter to Gage, 8 December 1835, as suitable subject for a paper to the Antiquaries.

[164] J. Morley, *The Life of William Ewart Gladstone*, 2 vols (London 1908), i, 64, and cf. A. Isba, *Gladstone and Dante* (Woodbridge 2006), 47. For Scott, see Scott's *Journals*, ed. Anderson, 798–801.

[165] *The Letters and Diaries of John Henry Newman: III (New Beginnings)*, ed. I. Kerr and T. Gornall (Oxford 1979), 228–84; L.I. Guiney, *Hurrell Froude: Memoranda and Comments* (London 1904), 98, 179; N. Vincent, *Becket and the Victorians* (forthcoming).

cryptic remark in a letter sent by Stapleton from Rome on 28 April 1832, leads to a remarkable discovery about their continental odyssey. 'The death of Mrs Nevill', Thomas Stapleton writes 'and consequent return to England together with the melancholy duel by my brother, cast rather a gloom over my stay here'.[166] A search of contemporary newspapers reveals that, in February 1832, Miles Stapleton had been challenged to a duel by a much older man, Major General Sir Lorenzo Moore (d.1837), an army officer with a distinguished record of service in the West Indies. Stapleton had been engaged to marry Moore's daughter, but when she herself broke off the engagement, had penned a satirical poem on the subject. This had somehow come into the father's hands. Verse, of a not entirely amateur order, was one of Miles Stapleton's pursuits: his *Godesberg Castle* (1829) is a highly romanticized and bloodthirsty exploration, somewhat after the school of Scott, of the remorse attending the last hours of an apostate archbishop of Cologne converted to Lutheranism in order that he might marry his true love. The poem on Teresina Moore led her father to call Stapleton out. In the ensuing duel, fought on Wimbledon Common on 13 February, Stapleton refused to fire. Moore discharged his pistol, seriously wounding Stapleton, and as a result of witnesses having observed the shots from a passing coach, was committed to Guildford gaol, being released on recognizances of £4000, once Stapleton himself showed signs of recovering from his wounds.[167]

Miles Stapleton's novel, *Paynell, or the Disappointed Man*, published in two volumes in 1837, is an odd blend of the exoticism of Beckford and the romantic 'Bildungsroman' strain of Bulwer Lytton's *Ernest Maltravers* (published that same year). Here chivalry, opium, divorce, Catholicism, gambling and Mediterranean travel all rub shoulders with only a vague semblance of a plot and amidst an overriding assumption that anyone below the dignity of a peer must be either an unspeakable tuft-hunter or an unmentionable drudge. The book's anti-hero, Lord Paynell (named, of course, after the medieval barons who had preceded the Stapletons as lords of Drax), enjoys a rather different fate, shooting dead his opponent, De Wroth, in a duel fought over a lady's honour. There was an aftermath to the real-life duel, which sheds further light on Thomas Stapleton's antiquarian interests. Having jilted Miles Stapleton, Teresina Moore went on to marry, on 1 January 1834, the Reverend Samuel Lysons (1806–1877) of Hempsted Court, Gloucestershire, himself the son of the antiquary Daniel Lysons (1762–1834) and nephew of Samuel Lysons (1763–1819), antiquary and topographer who from 1804 had served as predecessor to Henry Petrie as

---

[166] Cambridge University Library ms. Hengrave Hall 21/4/139.

[167] For Moore and the duel, see the obituary of Moore in *The Gentleman's Magazine*, n.s. vii (June 1837), 658–9, noting that Moore had entered the army in 1787 which would suggest that he was at least thirty years older than Miles Stapleton; J.G. Millingen, *The History of Duelling* (London 1841), ii, 321–3; J. Loose, *Duels and Duelling. Affairs of Honour around the Wandsworth Area* (Wandsworth 1983), 15 (which contains the only account of the cause of the dispute yet found, but unreferenced). The Stapleton affair of 1832 came less than three years after the notorious duel between the Duke of Wellington and Lord Winchilsea fought in 1829.

Keeper of the Records in the Tower of London.[168] Teresina's decision to jilt a Catholic, Miles Stapleton, in order to marry an Anglican priest, might suggest a religious dimension to the affair. What is beyond doubt is that, via his elder brother's engagement and subsequent duel, Thomas Stapleton enjoyed yet another link, albeit a scandalously unexpected one, to the inner circles of the Society of Antiquaries and to that well-connected group of dilettantes who, over the previous few decades, had done so much to revive historical research in England. When Miles Stapleton did eventually marry, in 1844, his bride was herself not a Catholic but an Anglican, Isabella Anne Browne, daughter of the 3rd Lord Kilmaine. Writing to his sister to announce the engagement, Lord Beaumont laid great stress upon the distinction of the Browne family descent, but made no mention at all of his bride's religion. As for his brother, he declared that he would have written to Thomas to inform him were he sure of the postal service, but 'I do not think he will regret my determination as he is very comfortably off and a determined bachelor'.[169]

Although in general a supporter of the Reform Act, whilst abroad Stapleton was prompted by reports of a 'foolish' speech by Lord Shrewsbury to hope that Reform's 'too democratical elements can be modified'. He was nonetheless shocked by the taxation imposed by the Roman church and by the raising of the duty on salt which 'grinds the lower orders'.[170] There are symptoms here of that dissatisfaction with papal rule that was to lead Stapleton's brother to break with the Church, and in the late 1840s to attack not only the 'degrading despotism of an ecclesiastical government' but the entire principle by which central Italy was subjected to Pius IX and his combined spiritual and temporal rule.[171] In Rome, Stapleton conferred with Dr (the future Cardinal) Wiseman, studied Vitruvius and considered the possibility, having already toured the Abruzzi and having visited Naples and Sicily, of extending his horizons to Greece, where King Otto had

---

[168] For biographies of Samuel (d.1877), known as 'Canon Lysons', and of his father and uncle, see *ODNB*. Teresina was christened Eliza Sophia, but seems to have been known only by her third name. Besides the Lysons' antiquarian manuscripts, now in the BL (noted in *ODNB*), there is a substantial correspondence collected by their family, now at Gloucester, Gloucestershire Record Office D8460.

[169] Hull History Centre, University Archives ms. DDCA2/52/21, Lord Beaumont to his sister Catherine, 20 August 1844. The marriage settlement is dated 7 September 1844: Ibid. DDCA3/12/1. For the religious difficulties that were to arise after Lord Beaumont's death in 1854, see above p.28.

[170] For remarks on Reform and on the perilous state of Roman finances presided over by the 'odious Bernetti' (Tommaso Bernetti (1779–1852), reactionary Secretary of State to Pope Gregory XVI), see Cambridge University Library ms. Hengrave Hall 21/3/28; 21/4/139; 21/5/27, letters of 18 March 1831, 28 April 1832 and 27 February 1833.

[171] See here the published remarks of Miles Stapleton, Lord Beaumont, *Austria and Central Italy* (London 1849), at p.22 commenting, in the aftermath of the revolutions of 1848, on a Pope (Pio Nono) who 'mixes so much comedy with tragedy, that it is a question whether, even in the Catholic world, more will not laugh than weep over it'. It was his outspoken criticism of the use of force on behalf of the papacy that led to the rejection of Prince Albert's proposals that Miles Stapleton be appointed special go-between with Rome: J.P. Flint, *Great Britain and the Holy See: The Diplomatic Relations Question, 1846–1852* (Washington D.C. 2003), 160, 265 n.204.

recently been crowned, less than a decade after the Greek adventures of
Lord Byron.[172] In the event, he returned, via the distinctly less adventurous
pleasure-gardens of Baden, to Paris, where he was established by September
1833. By this time, his sights clearly were set upon a detailed enquiry into
Anglo-Norman history, to which end he obtained letters of introduction
to Auguste Le Prévost from the antiquary and continental traveller Lord
Arundell (1785–1834). In Paris, he is to be found reading the *Memoirs
of the House of Russell* by Wiffen, who 'holds out a most encouraging
prospect to all who follow in the same track'.[173] By 9 October he was at
Rouen, determined at this stage to complete a history of the manor of
Drax in Yorkshire, for which it was essential that he trace evidences of the
Norman family of Painel of Hambye and Drax.[174] Drax (now the site of one
of the largest and ugliest power stations in northern Europe), lies within
a bowshot of the Stapleton house at Carlton. It was from Rouen, on 2
December 1833, that Stapleton sent by far the longest and most interesting
of his reports to Gage. For six weeks he had toured the archives of Lower
Normandy, copying deeds of the Painel family and of the Gournays, 'to add
a page to my friend, Daniel Gurney's apocryphal book' (i.e. to Gurney's
Record of the House of Gournay, of which publication did not in fact begin
for a further fifteen years).[175] He had stayed with de Gerville at Valognes
and had been allowed to make extracts from the cartularies of Savigny and
St-Sauveur-le-Vicomte and from a 'bad copy' of the Painel charters from
the lost cartulary of Hambye.[176] His report of this visit to de Gerville is
worth quoting *in extenso*:

> 'M(onsieur) de G(erville) is one of the most hospitable and
> kindest of men, but so irritable that he cannot endure the slightest
> contradiction, and obstinate in error. The great merit is his
> topographical knowledge. He knows almost every acre of ground
> in the department … He has a few English works in his library, and
> blindly follows their dictums'.

It is interesting to compare this judgement with de Gerville's own, much
kinder opinion of Stapleton, forwarded to Gage in 1835, after all three men
had at last met.[177] Gerville was as much charmed as annoyed by Stapleton's
youth and opinions, and extremely impressed with him both as a scholar
and as an authority on Latin charters:

---

[172] Cambridge University Library ms. Hengrave Hall 21/5/27.

[173] Ibid. 21/5/147, letters dated at Paris, 15 September 1833. His copy of Wiffen's *Memoirs* is still in the library at Carlton Towers.

[174] Ibid. 21/5/156, 'I employ my leisure here in exploring the cartularies in the library, noting down everything relating to England and the early Anglo-Norman barons'.

[175] Ibid. 21/5/179, for this and what follows.

[176] Various of his transcripts from Gerville's copy of Hambye evidences are still preserved in his Norman note-book at Carlton Towers. See also letters of de Gerville to Gage, 13 February 1835, Ibid. 21/7/35, reporting de Gerville's recent acquisition of a cartulary of the leper hospital of the Hôtel-Dieu at La Haye-Pesnel 'bien moins important et bien moins volumineux que ceux dont Mr Stapleton a fait des extraits chez moi'.

[177] Ibid. 21/7/35, de Gerville to Gage, 13 February 1835.

'Notre compagnon de voyage, M(onsieur) Stapleton, a passé probablement le tem(p)s des élections au sein de sa famille. Je ne sais pas s'il a le projet de revenir en France. Il est difficile d'avoir plus d'habiléte qu'il n'en a pour explorer les anciennes chartres (*sic*) et ce qu'il y a de plus précieux, c'est qu'il a une grande habitude de lire avec des yeux excellents. Il joint l'amour du travail et la persèverance à une sagacité et une mémoire parfaites (*sic*). Si quelquefois il visait trop à l'infaillibilité, ce qui arrive trop souvent a son age, il n'aurait besoin que d'un guide comme vous pour devenir parfait. Depuis quelques années les personnes qui sont dans l'age le plus agréable de tous, le printemps de la vie, se persuadent trop facilement qu'ils peuvent porter en même tem(p)s les fruits. C'en est trop a la fois. S'il y a quelques personnes auxquelles cela arrive ce sont des exceptions rares, des 'pauci quos aequus amavit Jupiter aut ardens evexit ad aethera virtus';[178] avec vous, M(onsieur) Stapleton peut y arriver. D'ailleurs, il va bientôt arriver insensiblement à la saison. Ici, en faisant place aux fruits, les fleurs n'ont pas encore tout a fait disparu'.

Stapleton might aim too much and too hastily at perfection, but in de Gerville's opinion, with Gage's guidance, he would master his materials before ever losing the first flush of youth. The generosity of this testimonial, from a man whose memory stretched back long before the Revolution of 1789, gives some indication of de Gerville's charm and his importance as a mentor, of Cotman in the 1820s as of the young Léopold Delisle, the greatest of his protégés, two decades later.

At Cherbourg in 1833, Stapleton found no manuscripts worthy of notice, but at St-Lô, 'I litterally (*sic*) dug out of the disorderly masses of papers several valuable charters relating to the Paynells, a seal of Paynell impaling Bertram (unique) and the cartulary of the English priory of Lodres, dependent upon Montbourg, which I copied nearly all'. At Bayeux, where he had 'the richest treat' – the cathedral cartulary (now known as the 'Livre Noir') – he was able to make use of his family connections. The cathedral library and its treasures, including the cartularies of Bayeux, Longues, Cordillon and Mondaye, was 'strictly private and extremely difficult of access'. The bishop, however, had been in England, at Old Hall Green, where he had worked under Stapleton's uncle, Bishop Gregory Stapleton, at the Catholic college of St Edmund established in Hertfordshire following its evacuation from Douai, after 1793.[179] As a result all doors were opened; the librarian, the Abbé Guerin, allowed Stapleton free run of the library, and Stapleton stayed for fifteen days. It was at this juncture that he was first introduced to the Abbé de la Rue. Contrary to the reports of other Englishmen, and contrary to his own less than flattering opinion of the

---

[178] Virgil, *Aeneid* VI.129–31.
[179] Gregory Stapleton (1748–1802), Vicar Apostolic of the Midland District of England and titular bp of Hierocaesarea from 1800 until his death.

much more accommodating de Gerville, Stapleton was entirely charmed by the old abbé:

'I got acquainted with that literary giant of Caen. Though past his 80th year, his memory is of yesterday, his knowledge of the chroniclers and bards of the Middle Ages perfectly astounding, his collections immense. In fine, to sum up all, I learnt more from him during the few hours I conversed with him at the Château of Cambes than I have been able to glean from the other antiquaries in days and weeks. Unfortunately, age has made the Abbé extremely suspicious – those that have suffered under the lash of his satire accuse him of purloining from the public archives. This accusation, I am afraid in some measure true, has caused him to seal up his vast collections from the eyes of the world. He told me himself that he possessed the cartularies of St Etienne, St Barbe Desert, the "parvum cartularium" of Bayeux and a copy by Langevin himself of the MSS. I have spoken of above [the cathedral customal]. Add to this innumerable loose charters and the collections of Dom. Lenoir in eighty cartoons (*recte* cartons), copies of documents long since swept away by the whirlwind of the Revolution. He, however, obligingly transcribed from the originals two Paynell charters, one of the utmost importance as it is the only document which identifies the Paynells of Fontenay-Paisnel and Moutiers Hubert with the Paynells of West Rasen in Lincolnshire, which you may remember our visiting together'.

In the library and the archives at Caen, Stapleton was assisted by another local antiquary significant in the history of Anglo-Norman scholarship, Léchaudé d'Anisy, but expressed his suspicion that poor Latin would undermine whatever merits Léchaudé's *Extrait* from the archives of Calvados, then passing through the press, might possess. Léchaudé was by this time chiefly engaged in transcribing Anglo-Norman evidences for the English Record Commission. Stapleton meanwhile was considering a history of the Domesday tenants in chief: 'I have, since my late excursions, vast materials for such a history – but Drax must have precedence'.[180] Re-established in Rouen, he read the cartularies of St-Georges-de-Boscherville and of the hospital of St-Gilles de Pont-Audemer, both in the municipal library at Rouen. In the St-Gilles cartulary, he came across an early Anglo-Norman translation of Magna Carta, whose significance he drew to the attention both of Gage and of the local antiquary, Achille Deville.[181] He had, indeed, stumbled across a most important document, whose publication was to be delayed a further 140 years until J.C. Holt edited it for the *English Historical Review* in 1974.[182] He copied further Gournay charters

[180] Ibid. 21/5/179. Throughout, this letter has been scribbled over with pencil notes and 'et ceteras' by Gage, replacing the more controversial passages, perhaps with a thought to publishing it, suitably censored, for the Antiquaries.
[181] Ibid. 21/5/190, letters from Rouen, 22 December 1833.
[182] J.C. Holt, 'A Vernacular-French Text of Magna Carta, 1215', *EHR*, lxxxix (1974), 346–56, reprinted in Holt, *Magna Carta and Medieval Government* (London 1985).

in the Rouen archives, for Daniel Gurney, from the fonds of Beaubec and Clairuissel, and expressed a desire to contribute to the newly initiated *Collectanea Topographica et Genealogica* from his collection of Norman transcripts 'which regard England and which is fast swelling to thousands'. At the recommendation of Le Prévost, he was also preparing to ask the Marquis de Blosseville's permission to make copies from the cartulary of St-Pierre-de-Préaux, then still in private hands. Two other cartularies, of Fécamp, were reported to be in private custody, but of these we hear no more. The discovery of so many Gournay deeds with a connection to Beauvais inspired Stapleton to seek an introduction so that he might consult the archives départementales de l'Oise. As he wrote to Gage, 'My antiquarian mania absorbs me quite'.[183] In February the following year, he returned to Paris, lodging in the most fashionable part of town, at 7 rue de la Paix. From here, he set out on forays to the Bibliothèque du roi (now the Bibliothèque nationale), to take transcripts from the registers of Philip Augustus (themselves not as yet transferred to the Archives nationales), from various Norman manuscripts, including the cartulary of La Trinité at Caen, and from Gaignières' transcripts of Mont-St-Michel charters.[184] Not all was drudgery – 'I cannot <?deliver> myself from temptation and I lead rather a dissipated life, playing whist etc half the night'[185] – but, by April, he had also penetrated the Archives nationales, exploring the seals in the Trésor des Chartes and, again with great precocity, noting their significance as evidence for the early emergence of heraldry.[186] A plan by his father to visit Paris had to be abandoned, and for the future of the Orleanist monarchy he was less than optimistic, predicting 'the French population are too well versed in the trade of arms to be long quiet – here every shop-boy knows how to handle a musket'.[187] By July, however, now established with his brother, Miles, and his cousin, Lord William Fitzgerald, at Dieppe, he could look forward to a meeting with Gage, who at last had agreed upon a joint tour of Norman antiquities.[188] The tour itself was planned with

---

[183] The foregoing entirely from letters dated at Rouen, 22 December 1833: Cambridge University Library ms. Hengrave Hall 21/5/190, *inter alia* requesting that Gage send a copy of Stacey Grimaldi's edition of the *Rotuli de Dominabus* (London 1830) for Le Prévost, and the obituary of Mr Brunel, 'the engineer', for the distinguished Norman antiquary Eustache-Hyacinthe Langlois (1777–1837).

[184] Ibid. 21/6/43; 21/6/65, letters of 5 March and 13 April 1834.

[185] Ibid. 21/6/43, also expressing thanks to Gage for Stapleton's election to the Athenaeum 'and for the diplomatic skill with which you wheedled the governor (Stapleton's father) into paying the entrance fees. I have written to him to express my deep sense of his kindness. I trust we shall have many a snug dinner together there to discuss our Norman tour'.

[186] Ibid. 21/6/65, 80, 97, 126, letters of 13 and 30 April, 18 May and 18 June 1834, reporting, *inter alia*, on negotiations to procure copies of Britannia medals in the Bibliothèque royale and on a seal of Arthur of Brittany, at that time the romantic hero of the black legend of King John. For seals as an early source for the history of heraldry, see A. Ailes, 'Heraldry in Twelfth-Century England: The Evidence', *England in the Twelfth Century*, ed. D. Williams (Woodbridge 1990), 1–16.

[187] Ibid. 21/6/80, Stapleton to Gage, 30 April 1834, less than two years after the Parisian uprising of June 1832 that forms the climax of Victor Hugo's *Les Misérables*.

[188] Ibid. 21/6/144, letters of 15 July 1834. As early as May, de Gerville was anticipating a visit from Gage: Ibid. 21/6/90, letters of 7 May 1834 including de Gerville's memories of his time in Suffolk as an emigré during the 1790s, and cf. 21/7/189, Gage to de Gerville, 20 October

meticulous care, and was intended to take in an extraordinary number of places and archives, from Rouen, via Pont-Audemer, Bec, Lisieux, Moutiers-Hubert ('berceau' of the Painel family of Drax), Falaise, Caen, Bayeux, Carentan, Valognes (to stay with de Gerville, who could arrange excursions to Briquebec, Cherbourg and Barfleur), St-Lô, Coutances, Hambye, Avranches, Mont-St-Michel, Mortain, Domfront, Alençon, Sées, Verneuil, Evreux, Vernon, returning to Rouen via Château-Gaillard.[189] For anyone who in the late twentieth or early twenty-first century has made their own exploration of the Norman past via Norman archives, Stapleton's enthusiasm and stamina are not only remarkable but touching reminders that we tread a path long trod. In the summer of 1834, less than fifty years after the great Norman monasteries, chief source of our archival and archaeological evidences, welcomed their last visitors, Stapleton and Gage embarked upon their great excursion. They undoubtedly visited de Gerville at Valognes, de la Rue at Caen, and by early October were in Rouen.[190] At some point they met Auguste Le Prévost, who in the following year is to be found not only seeking the remembrance of 'notre infatigable ami, Monsieur Stapleton', but recommending to Gage the young Prosper Mérimée, appointed Inspecteur général des Monuments historiques, and recently returned from the first of his famous 'Voyages' in which he set out to record the scandalously neglected architectural antiquities of France.[191] Unfortunately, so far as our knowledge of Stapleton is concerned, the reunion between Stapleton and Gage, and Stapleton's return to England, where he was established by December 1834, put an end to any more lengthy correspondence.[192] Absence not only makes the heart grow fonder but the pen run more easily. Proximity, by contrast, has an annoying tendency to stifle the written word.

Thus far, there is nothing to suggest that Stapleton had any particular intention of editing Norman Pipe Rolls. Rather his interests appear to have embraced all aspects of the Anglo-Norman past. His one surviving

---

1834, disputing de Gerville's reliance upon the notes of an antiquary for details of Coutances cathedral that were still to be seen.

[189] Itinerary proposed by Stapleton in letters of 17 July 1834: Ibid. 21/6/146, noting that Gage had already visited Fécamp and Upper Normandy.

[190] Ibid. 21/6/111, Gerville to Gage, 2 October, clearly 1835, although filed together with correspondence of the previous year. For their visit to de la Rue, see letters of de la Rue to Gage, 13 October and 21 November 1834, referring to presentation copies of de la Rue's recent work, entrusted for presentation to Lord Aberdeen and the Duke of Bedford: Ibid. 21/6/187, 194.

[191] Ibid. 21/7/107, Le Prévost to Gage, 9 May 1835, recommending Mérimée as bearer of the present letters, 'l'un de nos jeunes savants les plus distingués et les plus zélés'. For Mérimée's 'Voyages', the first undertaken to the Midi between August and December 1834, followed by a brief visit to London in May 1835, see Prosper Mérimée, *Notes de voyages*, ed. P.–M. Auzas (Dijon-Quetigny 2003).

[192] Cambridge University Library ms. Hengrave Hall 21/6/215, letters sent from The Grove, 23 December 1834, *inter alia* reporting Stapleton's access to a Wardrobe account for the year 14 Edward II, then in private hands, subsequently published by Stapleton, from the collection of Joseph Hunton of Richmond, as 'A Brief Summary of the Wardrobe Accounts of the Tenth, Eleventh and Fourteenth Years of King Edward the Second', *Archaeologia*, xxvi (1836), 318–45.

Norman note-book, today preserved in his family home of Carlton Towers, together with his extraordinary collection of printed books, still constituting the bulk of the Carlton Towers library, testifies to an interest in the family histories of the Anglo-Norman baronage rather than to any narrow specialization in the Norman Pipe Rolls.[193] Beginning with transcripts from the cartularies of Préaux and Fontevraud, which he had borrowed as early as 1830 from Sir Thomas Phillipps, the surviving note-book (which can represent only a tiny fraction of the evidences which Stapleton transcribed) is divided thereafter into a series of entries, for the most part arranged parish by parish for lower Normandy, detailing the families who had held these lands after 1066, often with extensive transcripts from Norman charters, in some cases from familiar sources, in others from manuscripts, including original deeds at St-Lô, that have long since disappeared.[194] Phillipps, of course, had for many years been travelling on the continent in search of manuscripts, occasionally printing items from his collection.[195] Indeed it may even have been Phillipps who, unwittingly, inspired Stapleton's decision to edit the Norman Pipe Rolls, since it was from Phillipps, apparently in August 1830, that Stapleton seems first to have borrowed Petrie's privately printed edition of the Pipe Roll fragment of 1184.[196] As we have seen, Stapleton was employing

---

[193] The library of several thousand printed books, including most of the standard antiquarian and historical reference works for Anglo-Norman history published before 1850, often with presentation inscriptions from fellow antiquaries, is the object of a valuable though necessarily skeletal typescript catalogue by Clive and Jane Wainwright, John Martin Robinson and others, compiled in the 1990s. I am indebted to Lord Gerald Fitzalan Howard and to his Estate Administrator, Mrs Pat Meanwell, for my access to the library at Carlton Towers and for much other assistance.

[194] Carlton Towers Library mss. Notebooks (library reference 2J), one of four notebooks in large octavo, the other three being dedicated to Yorkshire transcripts, with a further notebook of Anglo-Norman pedigrees, small octavo (library reference 19D). For Phillipps' loan of the cartularies of Préaux, Fontevraud and St-Florent-lès-Saumur in January-February 1830, see Oxford, Bodleian Library ms. Phillipps-Robinson e.471 (Middle Hill Loan Book) fo.84r–v. These cartularies are today all in the Bnf, mss. nouv.acq.latines 1929 (Préaux), 1930 (St-Florent) and 2414 (Fontevraud) (Stein nos 1390, 3084, 3404). For their acquisition by Phillipps and their eventual return to Paris, see below p.78.

[195] See, for example, the anonymous Kentish antiquary who in 1836, inspired by Sir Thomas Phillipps' printing of various early charters from St-Bertin's purchased at Calais, 'at once started for St Omer in the hopes of discovering further traces of these treasures', returning with extensive copies from the St-Bertin's transcripts in the local Bibliothèque Municipale: 'Notes from the Chartulary of the Abbey of St Bertin', *Archaeologia Cantiana*, iv (1861), 203–19, inspired by Phillipps' paper, first read to the Antiquaries in 1832, recounting his recent purchase at Calais of three early St Bertin's deeds, including an original bull of Adrian IV for St Omer, March 1157: T. Phillipps, 'Charters Relative to the Priory of Trulegh in Kent', *Archaeologia*, xxi (1834), 146–50. The bull (J–L 10133, formerly Phillipps ms. 35828) is today Manchester, John Rylands Library ms. Philllipps Charter 24. The other originals printed in 1834 remain untraced.

[196] Oxford, Bodleian Library ms. Phillipps-Robinson c.623 fo.122r–v, Stapleton to Phillipps, thanking him for the loan of Baker's *Northamptonshire*, and continuing 'I would thank you to lend me Petrie's *Rot. Normannorum* to look at, if you are not occupied with it', followed by a note from Phillipps 'Sent the Norman Roll printed by Petrie who gave it to me'. The letter is dated Tuesday 24 August, without specifying the year. However, within the possible span of dates, 24 August fell on a Tuesday only in 1830, 1841 and 1847. By 1841, Stapleton had already completely re-edited Petrie.

further copies of Petrie's edition as diplomatic gifts in Normandy, as early as July 1831.[197] The proposal that he himself edit Pipe Roll material was not, however, broached until December 1835, and its chief movers were not Phillipps or Stapleton but Gage and, rather surprisingly, Frederick Devon (1800–1858), clerk of the Chapter House at Westminster Abbey and inveterate opponent of Sir Francis Palgrave in the great convulsions that shook the Record Commission later in the 1830s.[198] Writing to Gage on 8 December that year, Stapleton set out his intention:

> 'In your letter, you mention that Mr Devon had asked you whether you thought I should be inclined to edit the Norman Pipe Roll. I conceive the duties of an editor would have this extent, viz. the writing of the preface, the collating of the text, footnotes and indexes. In the preface should be an account of the roll itself and of the Norman Exchequer, accurate details defining the modern limits of the ancient territorial divisions of Normandy, the bailiwicks, honours etc and notice how far the nature of the feudal tenures and services are exemplified by the roll and how far it is corroborative of the received opinions of the French writers, Brussel, La Roque, Houard;[199] a particularizing of the new facts, if any, learnt from the roll itself respecting persons and places of historic interest. The foot-notes should merely contain such contemporary notices as may serve to identify the individual named in the text as an active partizan or in official employ. In the index of names of places, the modern name when it can be ascertained should be appended, and the same will apply to local surnames. And perhaps as an appendix it would be advisable to print the "Feoda Normannia" from the original registers of Philip Augustus in the Bibliot(h)eque du Roi and of which I have a copy. The two documents would present a perfect view of the division of estates amongst the Anglo-Normans, and of the extent of the forfeitures consequent upon the conquest of P(hilip) Augustus. If this view is in accordance with Mr Devon's, I should have no objection to sacrifice my time to the advancement of my favorite object of enquiry, viz. the elucidation of the history of our Anglo-Norman baronage'.[200]

---

[197] Cambridge University Library ms. Hengrave Hall 21/3/63, Stapleton to Petrie, dated at Châteaudun, 24 July 1831.

[198] Frederick Devon, clerk of the Chapter House from 1819, having entered the service of the records together with his brother Charles, under the patronage of Caley and with support from the Treasury. Editor of Issue Rolls and Pell Rolls (1835–7), and author of a published letter of 1832 defending the Record Commissioners against charges laid by Francis Palgrave (Deputy Keeper of the Records 1838–61). Threatened with dismissal under the upheavals of 1838, but eventually promoted Assistant Keeper 1840–1858. For his career, see Cantwell, *Public Record Office*, esp. 22–3, 48–9, 80–1, 116–17, 124–5, 189–90, 572.

[199] Brussel, author of the *Nouvel examen de l'usage général des fiefs en France*, 2 vols (Paris 1727); Gilles-André de La Roque (1598–1686), author of the *Histoire généalogique de la maison de Harcourt*, 4 vols (Paris 1662), and David Houard (1725–1802), chief authority on the 'Coutume de Normandie'.

[200] Cambridge University Library ms. Hengrave Hall 21/7/214, letter of 8 December 1835.

The programme elucidated here, apart from the excerpts out of the registers of Philip Augustus, was almost precisely that which Stapleton brought to fruition a decade later. Clearly it met with the approval of the Society of Antiquaries, since on 20 December 1835, Stapleton wrote to Gage to express his delight at the Society's acceptance of his proposal.[201] At this stage, he can have had very little idea of the extent of the task to which he had committed himself. In particular, during these first exchanges he appears to have envisaged little more than an edition of one of the Pipe Rolls of Richard I's reign, to complement that of 1184 already printed by Petrie.[202] It was only as the exploration of the public records led to the discovery of further manuscripts that Stapleton began to appreciate the need to do rather more than edit one or two rolls. By February 1836, he was writing to Gage:

> 'As I am engaged in collating the Norman Pipe Roll, I am anxious to submit to the Council the propriety of printing at the same time the other rolls of the same description preserved in the Chapter House. I find from Sir Francis Palgrave that those of two of the years of Henry II are entire, and both together will not exceed the single one of Richard. There are also a few detached fragments of other rolls which it would be desirable to have preserved, so that the whole may appear together'.[203]

From 1835, Stapleton proceeded with dogged determination. In recovering what today still represents the vast majority of the surviving Norman Exchequer accounts, he was, as he himself confessed, put to great trouble. The Norman Exchequer evidences, like the national archives in general, were still for the most part unsorted, being physically divided between deposits still lodged at the Tower, at the Chapter House of Westminster Abbey and at the Pell Office under the custody of the Comptroller General of the Exchequer.[204] At the precise moment that Stapleton began work, the Records Commission experienced one of those budgetary convulsions to which public bodies are all too prone, succumbing at last to the extravagance of its Secretary, Charles Cooper, and to the pamphlet war to which Cooper's extravagance had given rise. The outcome here was the Public Record Office Act of 1838, and the first attempts both to centralize the records and to place them under a single management.[205] The chaos of

---

[201] Ibid. 21/7/221: 'I feel infinitely flattered at the prospect of my name appearing as the editor of so curious and valuable a document as the Norman Pipe Roll on behalf of so learned a society as that of the Antiquaries and I trust I shall not prove unequal to the task. I am glad you approve of my views as to the manner of editing it, but I presume that it will be subject of discussion at the Council when I return to town'.

[202] Publication of the Richard I Pipe Rolls is all that is envisaged in Le Prévost's notice of the scheme, in a letter to Gage, 6 March 1836, wishing Stapleton well and for the speedy recovery of his father from illness: Ibid. 21/8/32.

[203] Ibid. 21/8/21, letters of 27 February 1836.

[204] As noted by Stapleton, *MRSN*, i, pp.iv–v.

[205] The original Records Commission established in 1800 lapsed in 1830 on the death of George IV. Its successor, established in 1831, responsible for some of the most important work yet

this period, during which the records were only slowly and painfully being removed to the new Public Record Office, can still be recaptured from the correspondence of the Office's early keepers.[206] Here, amidst complaints of the indolence and low morals of a staff working in the aftermath of the poisonous personal disputes of 1836 and in conditions of such squalor that a single water-closet served the needs of the thirty-five inmates of Carlton Ride, we find that the records themselves were in constant peril from fire and theft. In 1843, just as the second volume of Stapleton's edition of Norman Pipe Rolls was passing through the press, an entire series of fourteenth and fifteenth-century English Exchequer Issue Rolls was put up for auction, having apparently been 'removed' from the Pell Office to Petrie's library and thence to the sale rooms after his death.[207] More disastrously still, in the late 1830s, Frederick Devon, clerk of the Chapter House at Westminster and chief instigator of the plan that Stapleton edit the Norman Rolls, became embroiled in scandal, when it was discovered that a London fishmonger had been permitted to buy up Exchequer records from Somerset House, carted off as waste at £8 the ton.[208]

From 1835 onwards, no doubt as a result of their regular personal reunions, the correspondence between Stapleton and Gage dwindles to a mere trickle, with virtually nothing recorded of progress on the Norman Rolls.[209] These were difficult years for Stapleton in more senses than one. His father seems to have entered a long period of invalidity, so that Thomas and his brothers were required to maintain permanent attendance on him, keeping watch over his consumption of wine and fearing for recurrent bouts of 'dangerous excitability', first at their house, The Grove, near Richmond, then at Carlton to which the family had returned by June 1839, only a few months before his father's death.[210] Not all was gloom. In December 1836, Stapleton

carried out on early chancery and Exchequer records, fell victim to a pamphlet war and in 1836 to the attentions of a Select Committee of the House of Commons, by which the commissioners were accused, often unfairly, of both shoddy work and excessive expense. For an overview here, and for various of the pamphlets and official reports, see Cantwell, 'The 1838 Public Record Office Act', 277–86; *Letters from Eminent Historical Writers Relating to the Publications of the Board of Commissioners on the Public Records* (London 1836, the BL copy, printed books T2098, bound up with much other related material); *Report from the Select Committee on the Record Commission* (London 1836); D.M. Stenton, 'The Pipe Rolls and the Historians, 1600–1883', *Cambridge Historical Journal*, x part 3 (1952), 271–92, esp. 288–92.

206 TNA PRO 1/1ff, used extensively by Cantwell, *Public Record Office.*

207 For the water-closet, see a letter of Henry Cole: TNA PRO 1/7 correspondence of 3 October 1843. For the sale of Issue Rolls by Fletcher's of Piccadilly, see Ibid. letters and insertions of 14 March 1843. For earlier losses, see TNA PRO 1/121/1.

208 Cantwell, *Public Record Office*, 48–9.

209 A brief exception here occurs in letters of 28 November 1836, where Stapleton asks Gage to forward transcripts from the 1180 Pipe Roll to de Gerville: Cambridge University Library ms. Hengrave Hall 21/8/169. In July 1835, Stapleton was looking forward to visits to Norfolk and then Bonn, according to a letter to John Gough Nichols, 18 July 1835, now in private hands, drawn to my attention by Julian Pooley.

210 For reports on his father's health, see Cambridge, University Library ms. Hengrave Hall, 21/7/221 (' ... the wine and other stimulants have not produced any dangerous excitability'); 21/8/17, 169, 179; 21/9/13 ('another stroke', 4 February 1839); 21/11/104. There is a portrait

reported hunting in Yorkshire: 'I was out with the hounds for the first time yesterday, and today I feel both stiff and sore, but I love the sport'.[211] In the same year, he was planning a trip to Worcester, where Joseph Hunter asked him to search out evidences of Shakespeare's grandmother.[212] In 1839 he reported a prolonged stay his brother Miles had made at Buxton, where he been forced into regular encounters with Mrs Fitzherbert (d. March 1837 *sic*), Catholic kinswoman of John Gage and wife/mistress to the late King George IV: 'He says she never uttered a wise or true thing the livelong day'.[213] Nonetheless, his forced exile in Yorkshire clearly dragged, with Stapleton admitting his desire to 'return to the antiquarian society, club dinners, lovely women etc of the big city'.[214] Again, in June 1839, there are touches of gallantry in his correspondence with Gage, his 'worthy mentor', who was reminded 'Should you ever meet my fair one in your rides, pray let me have a dispatch to tell me how she looks'.[215]

Later that year, Gage and Stapleton made a further joint expedition to France, their second since 1834, a visit to Normandy in the summer of 1836 having left few traces.[216] Their 1839 tour is recorded in a surviving pocket book kept by Gage.[217] Departing from Dover, on 9 August 1839, they travelled via Calais, Boulogne and Abbeville to Rouen, where:

> 'Monsieur Deville explained to us the finding of the statue of Richard I in the sanctuary of the cathedral and the heart of the king in a leaden sarcophagus let into the base of one of the columns. He also showed us some of the powder or dust of the heart which was wrapped in red silk of which some little portions remained'.

Leaving Rouen on 21 August, they travelled via Pont-Audemer and Honfleur to Caen, where they met Léchaudé d'Anisy, and from where they pressed on for Bayeux and Valognes, for a further visit to Monsieur de Gerville. Thence, via Lessay, Coutances and the Bibliothèque at Avranches,

---

of Thomas the elder (d.1839) still at Carlton Towers, showing a balding man in middle-age, apparently painted by no very distinguished hand. In the past this has sometimes been mistaken for Thomas the younger, the antiquary, of whom, in fact, no likeness seems to survive.

[211] Ibid. 21/8/179.
[212] Ibid. 21/8/46, Hunter to Stapleton, 30 March 1836.
[213] Ibid. 21/9/13, Stapleton to Gage, 4 February 1839. Mrs FitzHerbert was the widow of Thomas FitzHerbert of Swynnerton (d.1781) who, by a previous marriage, was father to Gage's mother.
[214] Ibid. 21/9/13.
[215] Ibid. 21/11/104, Stapleton to Gage, 12 June 1839, and for the address as 'mentor', see 21/8/179.
[216] For the 1836 tour, see letters of Achille Deville to Gage, 29 September 1836, regretting that he had not been in Rouen to greet Gage that summer and referring to transcripts of charters sent to Stapleton at Calais: Ibid. 21/8/160, and cf. Ibid. 21/8/169, 179, Stapleton to Gage 28 November and 15 December 1836, referring to recent discussions with de Gerville. It was almost certainly the 1836 tour which led to Stapleton's acquisition of his own collection of original Norman charters: below pp.79-83.
[217] Bury St Edmunds, Suffolk Record Office 449/5/18.

they passed into Brittany in early September, touring the province from east to west and visiting an extraordinary number of historical sites, including St-Malo, St-Brieuc, Morlaix, Brest, Quimper, Carnac, and the islands of the Morbihan. Their tour included both St-Gildas-de-Rhuys and Le Pallet, associated with the growing legend of Peter Abelard, and Gage expressed himself particularly impressed with the ruins of the abbey of Quimperlé, which perhaps helps to explain Stapleton's acquisition of the original manuscript of the Quimperlé cartulary. Leaving Nantes on 30 September, they travelled up the Loire to Angers, Saumur, Fontevraud (which they found being employed as the regional prison and where they were shown the Plantagenet tombs), Tours, Marmoutier, and thence to Blois, Orléans, Chartres and Paris, where they seem to have remained from mid-October until 11 November, working for part of the time in the Bibliothèque du roi. They reached Calais, en route for England, on 18 November, having in the previous week toured Brussels and, on 15 November, visited the battlefield of Waterloo (which Gage had first visited in 1815, only a few days after the battle itself). Gage's pocket book exhibits a particular concern with three themes: the travellers' regular attendance at Sunday mass, their financial arrangements, and above all their exploration of the physical remains of the Gothic, especially the monastic or ecclesiastical past. There is also some reference to women: to the Breton peasant girls, for example, who, like Thomas Hardy's *Woodlanders* (1887), came to market to sell their hair.

This is almost the last that we hear of Stapleton's dealings with Gage. Their correspondence dries up entirely in April 1841, after a final missive reporting the engraving of the map for Stapleton's Pipe Roll edition.[218] Gage's death, the following year, shuts off our chief insight into Stapleton's research. Meanwhile, a fragmentary correspondence between Stapleton and the great manuscript collector, Sir Thomas Phillipps, drawn to my attention by Hugh Doherty, throws further light on Stapleton's expedition of 1839, and in particular upon his visits to Tours, from where he sent Phillipps copies of various charters of Marmoutier, and to Caen, where he delivered books from Phillipps to the Norman antiquary, Léchaudé d'Anisy, in payment for various transcripts that Léchaudé d'Anisy had made from the archives at St-Lô. The books included Dawson Turner's *Account of a Tour in Normandy*, published in 1820, and itself amongst the earliest witnesses to the growing English taste for Norman antiquities, the more picturesque and 'feudal' the better.[219] In April 1840, Stapleton asked Phillipps for a loan

---

[218] Cambridge University Library ms. Hengrave Hall 21/13/44, Stapleton to Gage, 23 April 1841.
[219] Oxford, Bodleian Library ms. Phillipps-Robinson d.128 fos.156r–157r, referring amongst others to a charter of Geoffrey de Dinan (Round, *Calendar*, no.1181); Ibid. ms. Phillipps-Robinson d.225 fos.67r–8r, 70v–71v (Phillipps to Stapleton, December 1839–January 1840), referring to transactions with Léchaudé d'Anisy over his copy of the Loders cartulary (cf. ms. Phillips-Robinson c.471 fo.93r, Stapleton to Phillipps, 29 December 1839), sent by Stapleton to Phillipps on 12 January 1840 with a covering note from Stapleton (ms. Phillipps-Robinson d.128 fo.156r–7r) that 'some of the pieces are merely noted by the contents, nor is the worthy gentleman much of a Latin scholar, so you must eke out the text and correct the solecisms, and not lay them at the door of the monks. The transcriber fixes no price, but will be quite content to take in exchange any English work you may think would repay his manual labour,

of a copy of the cartulary of Préaux, to correct various of his earlier notes.[220] In August 1844, he was once again preparing to sail by packet boat from Southampton to Le Havre, to return a copy of a survey of the diocese of Rouen that he had borrowed from Auguste le Prévost, to deliver his own edition of Norman Pipe Rolls to the Bibliothèque Municipale at Rouen and to visit 'my other friends in that province'.[221] A few years later, in the summer of 1847, touring East Anglia, he made a special excursion to visit Dawson Turner, the doyen of Anglo-Norman antiquaries, at Yarmouth.[222]

Sir Thomas Phillipps, for all his later reputation as a rabid anti-Catholic, seems to have shown no particular prejudice against the Catholic Stapleton. Following a moderate speech on religious issues made in the House of Lords by Stapleton's brother, in August 1843 Phillipps wrote to Stapleton with his congratulations, stating, with quite extraordinary lack of self-awareness, 'I am not a bigotted Protestant and you are not a bigotted Catholic ... and consequently we feel, I trust, an approximation of sentiment':[223] this from a man whose canvassing of the electors of Grimsby (only just across the Humber from the Stapleton estates in the East Riding),

---

in the supposition that you had employed him to copy it at so much a folio'. As payment, Stapleton suggested a copy of Dawson Turner's *Account of a Tour in Normandy*, or Mrs Stothard's *Letters Written During a Tour in Normandy* (London, 1820), 'neatly bound'. A visit by Stapleton to St-Lô in December 1839 may be inferred from the fact that a copy of a charter of Richard de Redvers to Montebourg, still amongst Stapleton's papers (Manchester, John Rylands Library ms. Beaumont Charter 92) was made by François-Nicolas Dubosc, the archivist of St-Lô (1839–79), on 1 December 1839. Another charter from St-Lô, of John Painel to the abbey of La Lucerne (March 1277/8), was copied for Stapleton, again perhaps by Dubosc, no doubt because of its fine heraldic seal. Stapleton's copy, with facsimile seal impression in modern sealing wax, is today still amongst his family's papers at Hull History Centre, University Archives ms. DDCA/37/46 G, from an original at St-Lô, itself printed as *Cartulaire de la Luzerne*, ed. F.–N. Dubosc (St-Lô 1878), 113 no.13, perhaps the same seal 'of Paynell impaling Bertram' referred to in Stapleton's correspondence with Gage in 1833, above p.53, and cf. pp.52, 54 for other Painel charters copied for Stapleton in 1833 by de la Rue.

[220] Oxford, Bodleian Library mss. Phillipps-Robinson d.128 fo.158r–v (Stapleton to Phillipps, 9 April 1840).

[221] Oxford, Bodleian Library ms. Phillipps-Robinson d.132 fos.193r–4r (Stapleton to Phillipps, 6 August 1844), incidentally apologizing for his failure to attend on Phillipps for a meeting with the eminent German medievalist, Georg Pertz.

[222] Cambridge, Trinity College archives, Dawson Turner correspondence, letters from Stapleton to Turner, 5 and 7 August 1847, suggesting that the two men had only recently met through the good offices of Daniel Gurney. Stapleton's correspondence with Auguste le Prévost dated to at least as early as 1840, when 'notre savant correspondant Monsieur Stapleton' had advised Le Prévost on the identity of various of the Anglo-Norman landowners listed by Orderic Vitalis: Orderic Vitalis, *Historiae Ecclesiasticae*, ed. A. le Prévost, 5 vols (Paris 1838–55), ii, 166n., and cf. iii, 29–30, and the note by Léopold Delisle in *BEC*, xlii (1881), 250–3, referring to what seems to have been an extensive correspondence between Stapleton and Le Prévost, once in the possession of Delisle, assumed burned with others of Delisle's papers *c.*1905. Presentation copies by Le Prévost of the first three volumes of his edition of Orderic, addressed 'à monsieur Stapleton de la part de son devoué serviteur' and 'à monsieur Thomas Stapleton à Londres, hommage de la reconnaissance de l'editeur pour son travaillant concours' are still to be found amongst Stapleton's library at Carlton Towers (library shelf 17E).

[223] Oxford, Bodleian Library ms. Phillipps-Robinson e.375 fo.37r–v, Phillipps to Stapleton 26 August 1843.

even as early as 1826, had been supported by verses warning his potential constituents against:

> 'Popery! Detested name!
> Popery's malignant reign!
> See the Faggot, Smoke and Flame –
> Read your children's destiny ...'

What absence of bigotry was it, one wonders, that led Phillipps sincerely to believe that his mail was being intercepted by Jesuits, and that the Great Exhibition of 1851 was 'only a cloak, a Trojan Horse, to introduce thousands of our Catholic enemies into the heart of our country'?[224]

Anti-Catholicism and an obsession with the feudal past were shared passions of another notorious contemporary of Stapleton. Thirty miles across the Humber from the Stapleton house at Carlton, Charles Tennyson of Tealby, uncle of the poet and son of a successfully avaricious Market Rasen land agent, created a new name for himself, appropriating an entirely bogus Norman ancestry as Charles 'Tennyson D'Eyncourt'. With the name came a dream palace, Bayons Manor at Tealby, turretted and battlemented in each and every style from Norman romanesque to nineteenth-century 'railway Gothic'. So anxious was Charles Tennyson to prove his Norman descent that he bought up property in the commune of Aincourt (Val-d'Oise, cant. Magny-en-Vexin), supposedly the 'berceau' of his line, to which, in 1846, he encouraged his religiously fixated daughter (a jilted admirer of Bulwer Lytton) to retire, rather than confront the scandal of her entering a Catholic nunnery.[225]

Meanwhile, begun in 1836 under the auspices of the Society of Antiquaries, and with the active co-operation of the financially embarrassed Record Commission, which agreed to lend Stapleton not only the handwritten transcript of the 1184 roll made for Petrie but the 'record' type which Petrie's printer had used,[226] Stapleton's edition of the Norman Pipe Rolls took nearly a decade to reach the presses, even though specimen pages were being run off for him by the Antiquaries' Council as early as June 1836.[227] Thereafter, a certain mystery surrounds the printing costs of the two-volume edition. The first volume appeared in 1840. The second, published by the Antiquaries in 1844, was sold at 12 shillings to fellows

---

[224] For this and other examples of Phillipps the anti-Catholic, see A.N.L. Munby, *The Family Affairs of Sir Thomas Phillipps*, Phillipps Studies ii (Cambridge 1952), 64–72.

[225] R.B. Martin, *Tennyson: The Unquiet Heart* (Oxford 1983), 211–14, 299–300.

[226] London, Society of Antiquaries, ms. Council Book 1829–47, entries for 2 February 1836, 1 March 1836 (noting that it was Francis Palgrave who communicated the discovery of further Norman Exchequer accounts in the Pell Office, of which the Society requested transcripts), 19 April 1836. For the type, compare the 1830 edition by Petrie, *Magni Rotuli*, p.1, with *MRSN*, i, 109, showing that although the type was reused, the whole of Petrie's edition was reset and revised.

[227] London, Society of Antiquaries, ms. Council Book 1829–47, entry for 7 June 1836.

and 16 shillings to the general public.[228] There is no separate costing for either volume amongst the Antiquaries' accounts, whose printing expenses nonetheless soared in 1843 from an annual figure of approximately £700 or £800 to an unprecedented £1594.[229] This sudden rise seems to have had less to do with Stapleton's rolls than with the ongoing financial crisis associated with the Society's publication of Anglo-Saxon texts, abruptly terminated in 1844.[230] All told, we are left to speculate that Stapleton himself, as was certainly the case with others of his ventures, may have paid for, or at least subsidised, the publication of his edition out of his own resources.[231]

Stapleton's edition was prepared at much the same time, and to some extent in continuation of the work that the Reverend Joseph Hunter – a fellow Yorkshireman but a Yorkshireman of a very different stamp – had already carried out on the earliest of the English Exchequer Rolls: for the year 31 Henry I and 3 John, published by the Record Commission in 1833, and the rolls for 2–4 Henry II and 1 Richard I, transcribed by Hunter or on his behalf in the 1830s but, as a result of the Record Commission's financial difficulties, not published until 1844.[232] The precocious nature of this work is once again worth emphasising. Only in 1884, forty years after Stapleton and Hunter's work, did publication of the English Pipe rolls resume, no longer with government funds but through the newly formed Pipe Roll Society, dependent upon private subscriptions. Nonetheless, even in comparison with Hunter's work, Stapleton's remains supremely competent. The map of ducal Normandy in whose drawing Stapleton appears to have taken particular pride, was still being reprinted as the best available as

---

[228] *Proceedings of the Society of Antiquaries of London*, i (1849), 31.

[229] London, Society of Antiquaries, ms. Ledger Book 1815–52, accounts for artists' and publishers' costs 1839–45.

[230] J. Evans, *A History of the Society of Antiquaries* (Oxford 1956), 236–7.

[231] This runs contrary to the claims of the obituarist in *The Gentleman's Magazine*, cxx (1850), part 1, 322, who states that the Norman rolls were published at the expense of the Society of Antiquaries and, in respect to the non-appearance of an index, that Stapleton's labours here were 'prevented more from the deficiency of funds for its production, than any disinclination on the part of the Editor'.

[232] *Magnum Rotuli Scaccarii ... de anno tricesimo-primo regni Henrici primi*, ed. J. Hunter (London 1833); *Rotulus Cancellarii vel Antigraphum Magni Rotuli Pipae de tertio anno regni regis Johannis* (London 1833); *The Great Rolls of the Pipe for the Second, Third and Fourth Years of the Reign of King Henry the Second*, ed. J. Hunter (London 1844); *The Great Roll of the Pipe for the First Year of the Reign of King Richard the First*, ed. J. Hunter (London 1844). For correspondence between Hunter and Charles Trevelyan over the cost of editing and printing those rolls left in page proof or not yet set up in type at the demise of the Records Commission in 1836, see TNA PRO 1/7, letters of 13 November and 8 December 1843. Hunter requested and was paid £90 for his editorial work on the *Pipe Rolls 2–4 Henry II* (£30) and *1 Richard I* (£60). It is a sobering thought that, even including these fees, print runs of 500 copies were costed at £52 and £122 respectively. The most expensive of the volumes published in 1844, the second of Hardy's volumes of Close Rolls (*RLC*, ii, published in 1844), was costed at £221. For Hunter's often vituperative memoirs of his contemporaries, and for his correspondence, in which there is no indexed reference to Thomas Stapleton, see BL mss. Additional 24864–78, 36527. Hunter, however, was himself in correspondence with Norman antiquaries, as revealed by letters of Auguste Le Prévost to de Gerville, 19 October 1829: Evreux AD Eure 5F33, and cf. above p.61 for his attempts in 1836 to persuade Stapleton to search for evidences of the Shakespeare family.

late as the second edition of Sir Maurice Powicke's *Loss of Normandy* in 1961.[233] Stapleton seems to have learned here from the acknowledged topographical expertise of de Gerville, to the extent of investing heavily in topographical reference works; a complete set of several hundred very detailed maps of regional France, purchased in Paris, and the two-volume *Dictionnaire des postes aux lettres* (1835) still remain in the Carlton Towers library as testimony to his determination correctly to identify Norman place names. Above all, Stapleton's massive introductory 'observations', drawing in part upon the rolls themselves, in part upon notes compiled from cartularies both in England and in France, represent one of the first serious attempts to survey not only the history of Norman administration but of twelfth-century Norman genealogy, landholding and religious patronage. In compiling these 'observations', Stapleton worked with direct reference to the departmental archives of Normandy: an achievement that was more or less unique for an English antiquary of his generation. In the early 1840s indeed, Phillipps had expressed the hope that Stapleton would proceed from the Pipe Rolls to publish a full-scale Norman 'Baronage', 'A *Norman Dugdale*, to come down as late as the end of <the reign> of H(enry) 3 or to 1300'.[234] This was destined never to be. Shortly after the publication of his second volume of Norman Pipe Rolls, Stapleton suffered a nervous collapse.[235] He died at Cromwell Lodge, Brompton, on what was then the outskirts of London, on 3 December 1849, aged only 43. Ironically, and as a symbol of the death of that spirit of Anglo-French co-operation that had so enlivened the 1830s and 40s, at much the same time that Stapleton lay dying at Cromwell Lodge, François Guizot, historian of England and one-time prime-minister of France, was established in exile in the same suburb of Brompton, a mere three streets away, at 21 Pelham Crescent.[236] By his friends, Stapleton's condition was blamed directly upon over-work. His death certificate, however, attributes his demise to

---

[233] Stapleton, introduction to *MRSN*, i, p.vii; Powicke, *Loss*, endpapers, and see a letter from Phillipps to Stapleton, 6 June 1840, asking 'When are your Norman Rolls coming out? I long for the map in particular': Oxford, Bodleian Library ms. Phillipps-Robinson d.224 fo.84r.

[234] Oxford, Bodleian Library mss. Phillipps-Robinson e.379 fos.20v–21r (Phillipps to Stapleton, 4 August 1841); Phillipps-Robinson d.132 fos.195r–6r (Stapleton's reply, 16 September 1844, stating that 'I have a good many projects in hand as to editing archaeological works, with the aid of the different societies, but if I undertake a Norman Dugdale, as you suggest, I am afraid I should have to bear all expenses, without much prospect of a remunerating rule').

[235] Bruce, introduction to *Chronicon Petroburgense*, pp.v–vi, written in August 1849, after Stapleton's retirement but before his death: 'It has long been generally known that Mr Stapleton ... has been suffering under an affliction of the most melancholy kind', but allowing that 'If his health should ever be so far restored as that he should again take an interest in the affairs of the (Camden) Society ...'. As Vice-President of the Antiquaries since 1846, Stapleton last chaired a meeting of the Society on 18 May 1848, having in the previous winter contributed what appears to have been a long and distinctly rambling account of the career of a fourteenth-century Newcastle burgess: *Proceedings of the Society of Antiquaries of London*, i (1849), 219, 221–6, 265. Nigel Ramsay has suggested to me that Stapleton played some role in compiling the detailed genealogical tables and notes to Henry Drummond's lavish folio *Histories of Noble British Families*, 2 vols (London 1846). However, the genealogies reproduced there contain such a degree of mythology that it is difficult to believe that Stapleton could have lent them approval.

[236] Price, *The Perilous Crown*, 373.

'Monomania – Disease of the Brain – Certified', and states that his death was notified to the local registrar by Henry Greenslade, also of Cromwell Lodge, present at the death.[237] This suggests clinical insanity ('monomania' being a fashionable term, borrowed from the French 'monomanie', applied to all manner of psychological disturbances, from psychopathic through to suicidal delusions), followed by some degree of certified confinement, and the possibility of death from the final stages of a common but unnameable disease that would not have been specified on any gentleman's death certificate.[238]

LÉCHAUDÉ D'ANISY

From the tragedy of Stapleton's final years, we need now to return to the 1830s, and specifically to the most prolific of the Norman antiquaries whose work appeared in print at much the same time as that of Stapleton himself. As noted already, Thomas Stapleton in the 1830s was able to call upon the assistance of Norman antiquaries in his search for charter materials from the Norman archives. In doing so, he was merely following a lead set by the Record Commission itself, which after 1831 had sent an appeal for French researchers to assemble materials relevant to the history of England.[239] The results of this appeal are today to be found in the various groups of

---

[237] Death certificate, Kensington Registry Office volume 3 p.214 no.299, and note the date, 3 December, which corrects that (4 December) still given in the *ODNB*. There are no coroner's records for this division of Middlesex surviving in the London Metropolitan Archives, the keeping of such records at this date being little better than that reported of the coroner's court in Dickens' *Bleak House* (1853). A catalogue of Stapleton's books, manuscripts, maps and pedigrees at 13 Wilton Place, Knightsbridge (a family home), was made, presumably for probate purposes, 13–17 December 1849: Hull History Centre, University Archives ms. DDCA3/10/1, recording their subsequent delivery to Lord Beaumont, Thomas' brother, and incidentally recording that Thomas' will, of 30 January 1841, was proved in the prerogative courts of Canterbury 29 January 1850, and York 15 February 1850.

[238] For the concept of 'monomania' derived from the idea put into circulation by Pinel's student J. E. D. Esquirol (1772–1840) of morbid obsession with a single idea, and for its relation to suicidal impulses, see B. Bynum, 'Discarded Diagnoses: Monomania', *The Lancet*, ccclxii issue 9393 (25 October 2003), 1425; Auguste Gillet, 'Dissertation sur la Monomanie' thesis for doctorate of medicine (Strasbourg 7 August 1829) (including division into various classes including 'Erotomania' and 'Demonomania'); Francois Gout, 'Essai sur la monomanie suicide', thesis for doctorate of medicine (Paris 25 May 1832). In the contemporary short story 'The Farm-House, A Story of Monomania' by Charles Ollier (*Fallacy of Ghosts, Dreams, and Omens; with stories of Witchcraft, Life-in-Death, and Monomania* (London 1848), 229ff), a rich man, who 'derived from nature a mind of morbid sensitiveness', is driven mad after 1792 by fears of the French Revolution, and, having 'brooded over imaginary disasters until his faculties were overpowered' (p.249), ends by shooting himself.

[239] For the original appeal from Charles Cooper, acting as Secretary to the Commission, see above n.140. The appeal was sponsored in France both by Royer-Collard and by Guizot: TNA PRO 30/10/28, letters of 10 October 1834, 6 February, 23 June, 21 July and 4 November 1835. From the Commission archives, Cooper subsequently gave the British Museum a series of French manuscripts, including BL mss. Additional 9346 (Brief inventory of the 'Angleterre' files of the Layettes du Trésor des Chartes (AN J628–56), in what appears to be a s.xvii or s.xviii hand) and Additional 9383 (List of the English documents in the AN 'Cartons des rois' series K, by the archivist Daunou, 30 March 1832, with list of expenses at the end totalling 93 Francs), and cf. BL ms. Egerton 773 (Inventory of the Norman and Picard and Breton files of the Layettes du Trésor des Chartes, s.xviii).

foreign transcripts in The National Archive (TNA series PRO 31/8), the most important being five volumes of transcripts made in the mid-1830s by students of the École des Chartes (PRO 31/8/133–7),[240] a massive volume of transcripts made by Achille Deville in 1833–4 (PRO 31/8/140A) for the most part from the archives at Rouen, and the three volumes of transcripts, entitled the 'Cartulaire de Basse-Normandie' (PRO 31/8/140B parts 1–3), compiled in 1835–6 by Léchaudé d'Anisy from a wide variety of sources, including the departmental archives at Caen and St-Lô. The process by which the Record Commissioners came into possession of these transcripts, like most aspects of Anglo-French relations, was by no means untroubled. Surviving correspondence demonstrates that the Record Commissioners spent almost as much time in negotiating the expenses of their French amanuenses as in establishing scholarly priorities. One French agent alone, Adrien Berbrugger, requested and received a monthly retainer of 500 francs (roughly £240 per annum, at much the same time that the struggling, but comfortably bourgeois young composer, Hector Berlioz, was attempting to support himself in Paris on an annual allowance of just over 1000 francs or £40). The demand by Léchaudé d'Anisy, that the English government pay him the extraordinary sum of £1000 (roughly 25,000 Francs) for his three volumes of transcripts, very nearly ensured that his 'Cartulaire de Basse-Normandie', today one of the treasures of The National Archives, was returned unopened to France.[241] For a time, Thomas Stapleton himself

---

[240] Copied for the most part by the 'Chartistes' Eugène de Stadler and Adrien Berbrugger. For Stadler, later attached to the Archives impériales (now the AN), rising to become inspector-general of departmental archives, see Bordier, *Les Archives de France*, 86. Louis Adrien Berbrugger (1801–1869), whose somewhat wheedling letters to Cooper, Secretary of the Record Commission, represent our chief source of knowledge on the history of this venture, spent much of his subsequent career in French north Africa, publishing widely on the history and antiquities of Algeria, including an account of the library at Algiers in whose formation he played a distinguished part: L.A. Berbrugger, *Bibliothèque Musée d'Alger. Livret explicatif des collections diverses de ces deux établissements* (Algiers 1860); J. Charpy, 'Les Chartistes et l'Outre-Mer', *L'Ecole nationales des Chartes: Histoire de l'Ecole depuis 1821* (Woippy 1997), 294. He was in London in July 1834, where Michelet met him in the Tower records office, listened to his horrific stories of French atrocities in Algiers (only recently occupied by the French) and borrowed a book from him which he later returned to Duffus Hardy: Michelet, *Journal*, 128–9, 154. For a full list of those involved in the work of transcription from the archives of Paris, see TNA PRO 30/10/28 letters of 16 June, 23 July and 25 August 1835, listing the expenses, besides Berbrugger and Stadler, of MM. Lepescheux d'Herbinville, Castelnau and (the very distinguished) Alexandre Teulet at the AN, and of M. Lecabanne at the Bnf. Letters of 15 September 1835 show that Berbrugger recommended that Teulet replace him as chief agent, and report that the refusal of the Treasury to pay Lacabanne had resulted in Lacabanne witholding his services. Two years later, Teulet reported briefly (letters of 20 November 1837) on the dispatch to London of further transcripts, mostly of early-modern documents.

[241] For the correspondence here, chiefly from Berbrugger, see TNA PRO 30/10/28, including letters sent by Berbrugger between 31 December 1834 and 15 September 1835 when he resigned his stipend in order to take up a post as secretary to the French governor of Algeria. For financial demands, see especially letters of 17 January, 6 February, 1 May, 16 June, 5 July, 23 July, 25 August and 15 September 1835. For Léchaudé d'Anisy, whose transcripts are first mentioned in letters of Berbrugger of 6 February 1835, see letters of 25 January 1837, in which Léchaudé d'Anisy sets out his grievances over his treatment and lodges an appeal to the English Treasury, offering to negotiate over his original demand for £1000. It should be noted that concerns about the cost of obtaining copies were by no means restricted to those seeking materials from

considered bidding for the manuscript, should the Record Commissioners fail to pay Léchaudé's price.[242] Some idea of the Commissioners' liberality can be gauged from the fact that, as late as 1837, Charles Cooper, their Secretary, was still considering the purchase of French antiquities that had little or nothing to do with the Public Records, including collections of medals from the reigns of Louis XIV and Napoleon, valued respectively at 1423 and 1129 francs (*c*.£60 and £50).[243] Nonetheless, for all of these alarms, the importance for the history of medieval Normandy of the dozen or so volumes of transcripts that found their way to London was eventually, if somewhat belatedly, recognised. A brief list of the contents of the Deville volume were appended to the abstract of Rymer's *Foedera* published after 1869,[244] and Eyton used both the Deville and the Léchaudé d'Anisy transcripts widely in his *Itinerary of Henry II* published in 1878.[245] During the 1890s, it was with these same transcripts to serve as his guide that John Horace Round set out to compile his *Calendar of Documents Preserved in France*: an essential tool of reference, and still the first port of call for most Anglophone students seeking access to the resources of the French archives.[246] The tragi-comic story of Round's *Calendar* has been told elsewhere by Edmund King.[247] However, there is a dimension to this story which has never properly been unravelled. Round was, on the whole, most favourably impressed with the transcripts made by Léchaudé d'Anisy and Deville. In particular, he realised that many of the charters transcribed from private collections by Léchaudé d'Anisy were no longer to be found in Normandy or Paris, expressing his surprise at the generally low opinion of Léchaudé d'Anisy that he encountered from his colleagues – or as he

---

the French archives. Asked in the 1850s to advise on the best method of obtaining copies of documents from the Public Record Office in London, the great French archivist Teulet is said to have responded that there was only one way and that was 'de donner beaucoup d'argent': Evreux AD Eure 5F42, undated letter from Léopold Delisle to Thomas Bonnin.

[242] See here Cambridge University Library ms. Hengrave Hall 21/8/179, Stapleton to Gage, 15 December 1836, 'Poor d'Anisy you may indeed say, if such be the fact, try and learn the grounds of this proceeding. I fear his copies of charters were ill selected and ill copied, he was very deficient in the knowledge of the Basse Latinity. Should his collections be returned upon his hands, in our next excursion I may have a deal with him', and cf. Ibid. 21/9/13 (4 February 1839), 'I am anxious to have the particulars of d'Anisy's case'. As late as December 1841, Léchaudé was complaining that the Commissioners had failed to send him a complimentary copy of the *Rotuli Normanniae* and that his transcripts languished unpublished amongst the shelves of the Master of the Rolls' Library 'never destined to see the light': TNA HO 45/87 (letters of Edward Protheroe to the Home Secretary, Sir James Graham, 8 December 1841).

[243] TNA PRO 30/10/28, memorandum inserted between letters of 15 December 1837 and 26 January 1838.

[244] *Syllabus (in English) of the Documents Relating to England and other Kingdoms Contained in the Collection Known as 'Rymer's Foedera'*, ed. T.D. Hardy, 3 vols (London 1869–85), iii, appendix C, 143–57.

[245] R.W. Eyton, *Court, Household and Itinerary of King Henry II* (London 1878).

[246] Round, *Calendar*.

[247] E. King, 'John Horace Round and the "Calendar of Documents Preserved in France"', *ANS*, iv (1982), 93–103, with some sidelights by N. Vincent, 'Léopold Delisle, l'Angleterre et le Recueil des Actes de Henri II', *Léopold Delisle: Colloque de Cerisy-la-Salle (8–10 octobre 2004)*, ed. F. Vielliard and G. Désiré dit Gosset (St-Lô 2007), 231–57.

clearly regarded them, his rivals and inferiors – in France.[248] What he did not seem to realise, and what his French colleagues, with a discretion that is far from typical, seem to have concealed from him, was that it was precisely because Léchaudé d'Anisy had worked on these charters in the 1820s and 30s that so many of them were no longer to be found in the Norman public archives.

Amidst the archival chaos of early nineteenth-century Normandy, the magnificently named Amédée Louis Léchaudé d'Anisy (1772–1857) stands out as a figure of particular significance, heroic and sinister by turns. Born at Versailles, where his father Jules-Antoine L'Echaudé was employed as a royal carpenter, Amédée Louis entered the corps of engineers, assisting before 1789 with works on the park of the Petit Trianon. On the coming of revolution, he played a role, as ingénieur-géographe, in the division of France into départements, but in 1792, because of his previous association with the Ancien Régime, found it expedient to enlist in the 16th regiment of chasseurs à cheval, serving thereafter in the suppression of counter-revolution in Maine and Anjou and eventually in the wars in Italy, where he was wounded and discharged from active service. Following the Bourbon restoration, he served for two years, from 1816, as director of poor-relief for the département du Calvados, an office then established in the remains of the abbey of La Trinité at Caen. Married to a local heiress, with substantial properties both at Caen and at nearby Thaon (Calvados, cant. Creully), he settled down to the life of a gentleman scholar, pursuing his researches in the local archives and making only one further, and unsucessful bid for public office, following the July days of 1830.[249] At Caen he became one of the small band of Norman antiquaries fully to appreciate the perilous condition in which many thousands of medieval charters had survived the Revolution. Doggedly, and in the face of all manner of obstacles, he worked through vast mountains of uncatalogued and often rotting parchment, realising that an entire class of documentary sources stood on the verge of destruction.[250] It was Léchaudé d'Anisy who discovered, buried under piles of dust and refuse in the sous-préfecture at Mortain, the great series of several hundred twelfth-century charters for Savigny and the Abbaye-Blanche at Mortain that today constitutes one of the wonders of the Archives nationales in Paris.[251] With his engineer's training, it was Léchaudé d'Anisy

---

[248] Round, *Calendar*, p.xxix n., 'A somewhat low opinion of M. D'Anisy's scholarship is entertained in France'.

[249] For biographical notices, see R.-N. Sauvage, *Le Fonds de l'abbaye de Saint-Etienne de Caen aux archives du Calvados* (Caen 1911), pp.x–xii, esp. pp.x–xi note 7; R.-N. Sauvage, 'Manuscrits de la collection Mancel à Caen', *Catalogue général des manuscrits des bibliothèques publiques de France*, xliv (Paris 1911), 6–7.

[250] See, for example, his claim to have spent 'six années à exhumer de la poussière des archives plus de dix mille chartes, diplômes, bulles, lettres royaux et autres actes anglais et normands revêtus de 500 sceaux': Léchaudé, *Extrait*, i, 3.

[251] TNA PRO 31/8/140B part 3 pp.57–174, and cf. Round, *Calendar*, p.xxx. These documents seem first to have been drawn to the attention of English scholars in a brief communication apparently by the young Léopold Delisle: 'Documents Relative to the Abbey of Furness Extracted from the Archives of the Abbey of Savigny', *Journal of the British Archaeological Association*, vi (1851), 419–24. For those of the charters that were tranferred to Paris rather than

who, in March 1819, had helped excavate and then reseal the tomb of the Conqueror's Queen Matilda in the abbey of La Trinité at Caen.[252] Caen itself boasted a small but distinguished community of English expatriots, most prominently, from 1830 until his death ten years later (in the town asylum from 'general paralysis of the insane'), George 'Beau' Brummell, one-time leader of London fashion, now honorary Consul at Caen to His Britannic Majesty, King William IV.[253]

The various works that Léchaudé published between 1823 and 1852, including his two-volume calendar, or *Extrait*, from the medieval charters of the département du Calvados, and his re-edition for a French audience of the works of Ducarel on the Bayeux Tapestry and of Stapleton and Hardy on the Norman Exchequer and chancery rolls, although lacking in scholarly finesse, were nonetheless crucial in reviving interest in the history of ducal Normandy amongst the Normans themselves.[254] Unfortunately, having begun as an admirer and afficionado of all things documentary, Norman and medieval, Léchaudé d'Anisy could not resist the temptation to proceed from admiration to collection, and from collection to outright theft. By the 1850s, his private library was bulging with charters and manuscripts that he had 'removed' for safe-keeping from the archives, especially the archives départementales at Caen, and which he had somehow forgotten to return. The resulting scandal can be traced from the letters of Léopold Delisle, Léchaudé d'Anisy's one-time collaborator and affectionate admirer, and resulted in a police order of October 1853 commanding that Léchaudé d'Anisy's library be searched and many of its treasures restored to their rightful, public ownership.[255] In the process, however, it is clear that Léchaudé d'Anisy's collecting had been conducted on so massive a scale that by no means everything that he had 'removed' was still with him in 1853 or thereafter returned to the public archives. Amidst the massive series of his transcripts now housed in the Bibliothèque nationale at Paris, covering the religious houses of most parts of Normandy and apparently

---

being taken to St-Lô where they were destroyed in 1944, see AN mss. L966–80. Slightly earlier, in 1822, thanks to an investigation provoked by Auguste Le Prévost, the vast collection of charters for the abbeys of Jumièges and St-Wandrille, believed burned after the Revolution, had been rediscovered at the sous-préfecture of Yvetot, being transferred thence to the departmental archive at Rouen only in 1827: *Chartes de l'abbaye de Jumièges,* ed. Vernier, i, pp.ix–xiv.

[252] As reported by Léchaudé d'Anisy himself, in TNA PRO 31/8/140B part 3 pp.286–93.

[253] For Brummell's years in Caen, for the most part spent in the Hôtel d'Angleterre, rue Saint-Jean, and for his squalid syphilitic end, see I. Kelly, *Beau Brummell: The Ultimate Dandy* (London 2005), pp.xi–xiii, 381–463.

[254] Léchaudé d'Anisy, *Antiquitées anglo-normandes,* 2 vols (Caen 1823–5); *Examen littéraire d'un passage du livre ... du Ducarel* (Caen 1824); Léchaudé, *Extrait,* 2 vols (1834–5), with a *Recueil des sceaux normands et anglo-normands* (Caen 1834); *Grands rôles des échiquiers de Normandie,* and (with A. Charma) *Magni Rotuli Scaccarii Normanniae,* Mémoires de la Société des Antiquaires de Normandie, xv–xvi (1845–52); Léchaudé d'Anisy and M. de Sainte-Marie, *Recherches sur le Domesday ou Liber Censualis d'Angleterre* (Caen 1842).

[255] See, in particular, R.N. Sauvage, 'Lettres de Léopold Delisle à Antoine Charma', *Bulletin de la Société des Antiquaires de Normandie* xxxviii (1929), 378–9, Delisle suggesting that the police be kept out of the affair so far as was possible, remarking, with commendable sympathy, that 'Un vieillard qui a consacré sa vie à l'étude de notre histoire, a droit à quelques ménagements. Il a déjà bien chèrement expié les torts qu'il a à se reprocher'.

copied independently of the three volumes of his 'Cartulaire de Basse-Normandie' preserved in The National Archives at Kew, there are many dozens of seventeenth and eighteenth-century transcripts and even a few twelfth-century originals that one suspects Léchaudé d'Anisy 'borrowed' from the public archives at Caen and elsewhere, and which were still in his library at the time of his death.[256]

THE SCHOLAR COLLECTORS

Although conducted on a heroic scale, Léchaudé d'Anisy's 'borrowings' typified a long-standing tradition in France: a tradition, as the sale of Petrie's Issue Rolls demonstrates, to which the English public archives, as late as the 1840s, were themselves far from immune. From at least the time of Richelieu and Colbert, France could boast a flourishing trade in medieval antiquities including manuscripts and charters, that had led, even before the Revolution, to the dispersal of many of the greater treasures of the Norman monastic collections, some of which are to be found today preserved not in Normandy or even Paris but in the most unlikely and out-of-the-way places. The Revolution merely exacerbated this tendency, so that after 1789 ever greater quantities of charter material began to appear in the booksellers' catalogues. Emigrés, most famously the Abbé Gervais de la Rue (1751–1835), arrived in England in the 1790s with their bags stuffed full with medieval charters and seals.[257] We shall return to the Abbé very

---

[256] For the Léchaudé manuscripts that entered the Bnf in 1859, most significantly mss. Latin 10063–84 and 11036–51, see L. Delisle, *Le Cabinet des manuscrits de la Bibliothèque impériale*, 3 vols (Paris 1868–81), ii, 305–6; M. Nortier, 'Les Sources de l'histoire de la Normandie à la Bibliothèque nationale', *Cahiers Léopold Delisle*, xxix fasc.3–4 (1980), 19–26, 28. Half a dozen volumes of Léchaudé d'Anisy's transcripts from otherwise well-known sources entered the British Museum (now the BL) in 1862: BL mss. Additional 24919–23, perhaps acquired at the posthumous sale of what remained of Léchaudé's collection, for which see *Catalogue des livres rares et des manuscrits précieux composant la bibliothèque de feu M. Léchaudé d'Anisy* (Muffat of Paris, 1861), whilst others, including an extensive collection of papers relating to his own estate at Anisy, are now at Caen AD Calvados F4068–83. For original charters of the Empress Matilda and King Henry I, apparently 'collected' by Léchaudé d'Anisy from the Archives at Caen, see Bnf ms. Latin 10083 nos 3–4, whence *Regesta*, ii, no.1946, iii, no.567, and cf. Bnf ms. Latin 10065 fos.32–3 for originals of the abbess of Beaumont-lès-Tours (1229) and of William de Mowbray, tipped into another of Léchaudé's manuscripts. Two other originals, of Robert Rossel, 1222–3, are amongst Léchaudé's transcripts at Caen AD Calvados F4068 Liasse 1 nos 22, 24. A substantial correspondence between Léopold Delisle and the various functionaries of Caen, St-Lô and elsewhere, resulting from Delisle's attempts after 1853 to reassign the documents confiscated from Léchaudé d'Anisy's collection, is preserved in Bnf ms. nouv.acq.françaises 21848, listing (nos 339, 341) at least 200 charters restored to the archives départementales at Alençon, 600 to Caen, 84 to St-Lô and 58 originally taken from the préfecture at Mortain. For other documents abstracted from this source, see below appendix no.68.

[257] For De la Rue, royal Professor of History at Caen from 1786, deported to England in 1796, returned to France 1797 and restored to his post at the university of Caen after 1808, see the biographies by F. Vaultier, in De la Rue, *Nouveaux essais historiques sur la ville de Caen et son arrondissement*, 2 vols (Caen 1842), i, pp.i–lii; F. Galeron, 'Notice historique sur les travaux littéraires de l'abbé De la Rue et principalement sur ses manuscrits', *Mémoires de la Société des Antiquaires de Normandie* x (1837), 650–74. For an assessment of various

shortly. For the moment, we need merely notice that theft was common amongst the French archives, both before and after 1790, and that the chaotic state of the provincial archives through at least to the 1850s gave opportunity to amateurs and collectors, amongst them both Sir Thomas Phillipps and the ubiquitous Thomas Stapleton, to acquire entire boxloads of charters that by rights should never have left public ownership. Some of these treasures have since found their way back into public collections, in France and elsewhere.[258] Various early charters, for example, copied in Paris for the Record Commissioners in 1835, seem thereafter to have become 'dislodged', even from the Layettes du Trésor des Chartes, the holiest of holies in the French national archives, subsequently finding their way into the hands of Francis Moore, an English collector resident in Paris. Various of Moore's 'acquisitions' from the Trésor des Chartes were purchased, at auction in 1856, by the British Museum.[259] Many other such documents, looted either from central or from local departmental archives, continue to elude rediscovery, being hoarded away as guilty secrets or consigned to the market with understandable discretion.

To take particular examples, only a few years ago an extraordinarily important twelfth-century cartulary of St-Etienne Caen resurfaced in the archives départementales de Calvados, having been 'removed' by the Abbé de la Rue and thereafter housed in the library of the Marquis de Mathan at the château de Semilly. It appears to have been the state of the

---

of his less reputable activities in the Caen archives, and for the recovery of various of his 'borrowings' for the Mancel Collection and the Bibliothèque Municipale at Caen, see Sauvage, *Le Fonds de l'abbaye de Saint-Etienne*, p.x notes 4–5; Sauvage, 'Manuscrits de la collection Mancel', 4–6. Various letters and notes from De la Rue, chiefly relating to his studies of the troubadours and Wace, are preserved amongst the Douce collection in Oxford, Bodleian Library, and in BL mss. Royal 16.F.II fo.1v; Egerton 2840 fos.68, 251, 311 (Madden referring to 'the poor old man <who> always goes blundering on'); Additional *5017 (De la Rue on Wace). His abstracts from the later Norman chancery rolls then stored in the Tower of London are preserved at Caen AD Calvados 386 Edt 2 (Archives de la Ville de Falaise).

[258] For Phillipps in particular, see below p.78. For other Norman charters or cartularies, provenance unknown, see for examples of BL mss. Additional 15605, 17307, cartularies of Montebourg and Bolleville (Stein nos 513, 2524), the first acquired by the British Museum, 8 November 1845, by purchase from the bookseller Thomas Rodd, who himself had acquired it from the collection of a Monsieur Motteley in Paris, the second acquired by the Museum, 12 February 1848, by purchase from the bookseller William Boone. For a stray Norman charter of Henry II, see Princeton University Library, Manuscripts Division, Department of Rare Books and Special Collections ms. Scheide Collection Document no.6992, printed by J.R. Strayer as 'A Forged Charter of Henry II for Bival', *Speculum*, xxxiv (1959), 230–7, reprinted in Strayer, *Medieval Statecraft and the Perspectives of History* (Princeton 1971), 28–38.

[259] See here P. Chaplais, 'Chartes en déficit dans les cartons "Angleterre" du Trésor des Chartes', *BEC*, cix (1951), 96–103, reprinted in Chaplais, *Essays in Medieval Diplomacy and Administration* (London 1981), ch.12, from BL mss. Additional Charters 11293, 11297 etc, including several items seen in the Archives nationales in 1835 by Eugene de Stadler and Adrien Berbrugger, copied into their transcripts, now TNA PRO 31/ 8/133, but thereafter acquired by Moore. Another such 'dislodgement' from the Trésor des Chartes, formerly AN J190A no.1, a charter of Eleanor of Aquitaine for Fontevraud, found its way before 1834 into the possession of Achille Deville, who copied it for the Record Commissioners (TNA PRO 31/8/140A no.200) as if from his own collection, before giving it to the Bibliothèque nationale (Bnf ms. Latin 9230 no.8, cf. *Layettes*, i, 208 no.506).

château's roof that eventually forced the Marquis into selling his treasure, and even then it is supposed that there are other treasures in the Marquis' library, all of them products of the enterprise of Gervais de la Rue, that should ensure a watertight roof for many years to come.[260] In light of what we now know of the relations between de la Rue and the Marquis, it is ironic to find Jeremiah Wiffen, in 1826, commemorating their friendship in grandiloquent doggerel:

> 'Learned De la Rue! With Caen's gray towers,
> Hail and farewell! Time's hour-glass ran
> Pure gold in Cambes' delightful bowers,
> With thee and thy belov'd Mathan'.[261]

Even in his own lifetime, de la Rue did not always inspire the most friendly of feelings. Although an exile in England after 1789, he was later taken to task by the English for ingratitude. Writing to Dawson Turner from Caen in 1820, the Englishman John Spencer Smyth, then preparing a new edition of Ducarel's Anglo-Norman *Antiquities*, remarked upon de la Rue's refusal to make any reference to the hospitality that he had earlier received in England, drawing Turner's attention to an extraordinary sermon that de la Rue had preached in 1811, in which the abbé had stirred up his fellow countrymen of the national guard to emulate the actions of their great ancestor, William I, and, under the glorious leadership of Buonaparte, to lead a second Norman conquest of England. Smyth urged Turner to publish this sermon in full.[262] It was at much the same time as de la Rue's inflammatory sermon that the Bayeux tapestry had been removed from Bayeux to the Louvre (now rechristened the 'Musée Napoléon'), where it was exhibited as a blueprint for what was supposed to be Buonaparte's repetition of the success of William the Conqueror in crossing the Channel to defeat the perfidious English.[263] In Normandy, de la Rue enjoyed a reputation little better than that which he commanded in England. De Gerville, for example, writing to Dawson Turner, remarked that as custodian of the archives in Caen, de la Rue 'can sometimes be persuaded to provide assistance if he is cornered, but if one places any trust in him he will repay it merely with (empty) promises'.[264]

---

[260] The cartulary is now Caen AD Calvados J non coté. For other original charters of La Trinité at Caen still at Semilly, some as early as the reign of William I, see Bates, *Regesta William I*, 275 no. 59, 297–8 no. 64. The Abbé de la Rue was a close associate of the then Monsieur de Mathan during his period of exile under the Revolution.

[261] Wiffen, *Historical Memoirs*, i, 544. For a less flattering assessment of the abbé, as an 'odd character' notorious for 'his closeness of conduct', see Rajnai and Allthorpe-Guyton, *John Sell Cotman*, 32.

[262] Cambridge, Trinity College archives, Dawson Turner correspondence, letters of Smyth to Turner, 8 October 1820.

[263] C. Hicks, *The Bayeux Tapestry: The Life Story of a Masterpiece* (London 2005), 95–120, with brief reference to de la Rue at pp.131–2.

[264] Cambridge, Trinty College archives, Dawson Turner correspondence, letters of de Gerville to Turner, 4 February 1820: 'Mr Le Prévot eut pu tirer quelque chose de l'abbé de la Rue, dont on obtient quelquefois des renseignements quand on le tient à la gorge, mais dont on n'a que des promesses quand on se fie à lui', and see further letters of 10 January 1822 in

De la Rue and Léchaudé d'Anisy were by no means the only kleptomaniacs let loose in the Norman departmental archives. Amongst the original Norman charters of King Henry II of England recently assembled for publication by the British Academy, one at least entered the Bibliothèque nationale as late as 1910 via purchase from a bookseller of Caen.[265] Others, sold at auction in the nineteenth century, continue to emerge, sometimes in the most surprising of locations, from St Petersburg to New York.[266] A charter for St-Sauveur-le-Vicomte, acquired by Sir Thomas Phillipps source murky but unknown, is today in the library of Reading University, whilst, at the moment of writing, anyone with a few thousand dollars to spend can still acquire, from a bookdealer in New York, an original charter of Henry II for the priory of Le Plessis-Grimoult with sign manuals (including a purportedy unique 'signature' by Thomas Becket), which passed from public ownership to the abbè de la Rue, from de la Rue to Thomas Stapleton and thence, via Stapleton's descendants, to public auction.[267] Even The National Archives can boast at least one such escaped public treasure: an original charter of Henry II for the monks of Mont-St-Michel, presented to the Public Record Office in October 1873 by the Cornish antiquary John Jope Rogers, and acquired by Rogers in circumstances that are probably best left unprobed.[268]

There are important consequences here for the Norman transcripts series in The National Archives. Many of the transcripts made for the Record Commissioners, and in particular those by Léchaudé d'Anisy, prove, on examination, to be of charters that are preserved in no other form. Léchaudé d'Anisy worked for many weeks in the archives dèpartementales de la Manche at St-Lô. This archive, one of the greatest of all of the collections for medieval Normandy, was still for the most part uncatalogued in 1944 when destroyed by Allied bombing. The tragedy at St-Lô was all the greater for the fact that the documents themselves had been dispatched

which de Gerville reports de la Rue's disappointing and tardy response to Turner's request for information on various of the churches of Calvados. For equally disparaging remarks by Le Prévost about de la Rue, see Evreux AD Eure 5F33: letters from Le Prévost to de Gerville, 23 November 1827.
[265] Bnf ms. nouv.acq. françaises 21689 fo.5, purchased for the Bnf by Delisle, 31 May 1910, from Louis Jouan, bookseller of Caen. Printed by Delisle, *Recueil*, ii, no.608.
[266] See, for example, *Catalogue d'une importante collection de lettres autographes ... dont la vente aura lieu à Paris ... le Mardi 27 Novembre 1888* (Etienne Charavay, Paris 1888) p.17 lot no.82, an original charter of Henry II for St-Martin's Tours, untraced by Delisle. According to the marked copy of the sale catalogue in the Bnf (salon des manuscrits ref. CV2352), it was purchased in 1888 by the dealer Charavay himself. Printed by Delisle, *Recueil*, ii, no.475. In 2007, it was identified as amongst the archives of the St Petersburg Academy of Sciences.
[267] Reading University Library ms.1488, formerly Phillipps ms. 27727, purchased at Sotheby's 26 November 1975 lot no.819, printed from later copies by Delisle, *Recueil*, i, no.62. The charter for Plessis-Grimoult, once in the collection of Thomas Stapleton at Carlton Towers, sold again at Christie's 20 June 1990 lot.37, most recently bought-in at the sale of the stock of H.P. Kraus: *The Inventory of H.P. Kraus* (Sotheby's sale catalogue, New York 4–5 December 2003), 226 lot no.308. Printed from Léon Maître's transcript by Delisle, *Recueil*, i, no.75.
[268] TNA PRO 30/26/36, whence J.J. Rogers, 'Note on a Charter of Privileges Granted by King Henry the Second', *Journal of the Royal Institution of Cornwall*, v (1874–8), 23, the text printed, from two other duplicate originals later destroyed at St-Lô, by Delisle, *Recueil*, i, no.36.

for safe storage in the Massif Central, at the commencement of World War II. It was only the success of Anglo-American propaganda in convincing the local archivist that any Allied landing would come via Calais rather than Normandy that persuaded him, only a few weeks before the D-Day landings, to arrange for the transport back to St-Lô of some six or seven shelf-kilometres of records, including many tens of thousands of uncatalogued medieval charters, promptly reduced to ashes by Allied bombing.[269] As a result, and not least because so many of these documents had never properly been listed let alone catalogued, any transcripts from the lost Archives de la Manche are today of particular significance. Indeed, in the longer term, it is to be hoped that some attempt may be made to list and inventory such copies, as a step towards reconstructing the vanished archive, in the same style as the heroic labours, made since the 1940s, to reconstitute the contents of other war-damaged archives, most notably those of the city of Naples. Many, but by no means all of the twelfth-century charters copied at St-Lô by Léchaudé d'Anisy were incorporated by Round into his *Calendar*. However, whereas Round deliberately restricted his *Calendar* to documents dating from before 1206, the Léchaudé d'Anisy transcripts continue well into the thirteenth century, preserving texts that survive nowhere else and that no student of Norman history can afford to ignore.[270] For all of these reasons, Léchaudé d'Anisy's three-volume 'Cartulaire de Basse Normandie' deserves to rank today as one of the most important of all the Norman sources housed in England. Nonetheless, Léchaudé d'Anisy was by no means the only copyist to have worked at St-Lô. At Winchester Cathedral, for example, there is a small but extremely important volume of transcripts made from the charters of St-Sauveur-le-Vicomte at St-Lô, preserving in nineteenth-century copies a large part of the archive of St-Sauveur's priory at Ellingham in Hampshire.[271] Likewise,

---

[269] See here the descriptions by J.–C. Brisseau and especially by Y. Nédélec, 'Répertoire des bibliotheques et archives de la Manche', *Revue du Département de la Manche*, iv part 16 (1962), 393–420. For photographs of the old Archives building and reading room, see also the website at *http://archives.manche.fr/historique.asp*.

[270] See, for example, the various charters of Henry de Trubleville, Philip de Aubigny and the Lord Edward, from the archive of Le Mont-St-Michel, in TNA PRO 31/8/140B part 2 pp.321ff. For a recent survey of the few medieval items still at St-Lô having survived the destruction of 1944, see *Documents du XVe siècle des Archives de la Manche. Catalogue de l'exposition organisée par les archives départementales du 1er au 5 décembre 1998 et du 4 janvier au 2 avril 1999*, ed. J.–P. Hervieu and others (St-Lô 1998). More recently and more miraculously still, the archivist at St-Lô, Monsieur Gilles Désiré dit Gosset, has recovered nearly 100 glass plates, made before 1910, preserving photographic images of 20 or more of the lost original charters of Henry II from the archives destroyed in 1944, as well as what are today unique images from the lost cartulary of Savigny and a handful of other sources of the twelfth century and later. These are now stored as St-Lô AD Manche series F (Fonds Dolbet), with a small selection, including images from the Savigny cartulary, also preserved in early photographic prints, at Caen AD Calvados F5690.

[271] Winchester Cathedral Library, Unlisted ms. in 48 folios. From the address on the endpapers (fo.48v), made for Monsieur l'Abbé de Veil in 1898, and sent to him at 41 Rue d'Alsace, Paris. Later forwarded to the Rev. J.S. Trevor Garrick, vicar of Ellingham. The transcripts are taken both from original charters and from the lost cartulary of St-Sauveur-le-Vicomte (listed by Stein no.3561), of which an eighteenth-century copy survives as Bnf ms. Latin 17137. Another series of transcripts from the charters of St-Sauveur, by dom. Louis Guilloreau,

at Salisbury Cathedral, a manuscript once owned by Sir Thomas Phillipps and originally copied for Thomas Stapleton by Léchaudé d'Anisy, includes transcripts of charters for the English priory of Loders, a daughter-house of Montebourg, whose originals were also destroyed in the great bonfire of 1944.[272]

Apart from transcripts of lost charters, English archives beyond Kew can boast significant collections of charters relevant to the history of ducal Normandy, preserved either as originals or in medieval cartulary copies. Such documents fall into two basic groups. To begin with there are the charters and cartulary copies that have always been housed in England but which touch in some way upon landholding or privileges in Normandy. Here, it is worth drawing attention to those English monasteries, such as Southwick, Bradenstoke and Bruton, which before 1204 received gifts of land in Normandy, still recorded in considerable detail in their medieval cartularies.[273] Other English churches, most notably the cathedral church of Canterbury, acquired lands or privileges in France even after 1204, still documented amidst their medieval archives. I have attempted elsewhere to tell the story of these English monasteries and their French possessions, and in the process to supply a census of relevant manuscripts.[274] Below, in a separate chapter, I have endeavoured to bring together and to edit all of the principal charter evidences for the monks of Canterbury and their exemptions and privileges in northern France, previously unpublished.[275] A quittance from toll and customs, similar in many ways to those offered by French lords to the monks of Canterbury, issued by Walter of Coutances, archbishop of Rouen, is preserved for the Augustinian canons of Waltham Abbey in Essex, and there are probably other such charters surviving in English cartularies, as yet unrecognized.[276] The second chief category of

---

at one time at Quarr Abbey (cited by S.F. Hockey, introduction to *The Beaulieu Cartulary*, Southampton Records Series xvii (1974), p.xlvi), remains untraced.

[272] Salisbury Cathedral Library ms.188 (formerly Phillipps ms.10557). For the earlier history of this manuscript, see above, p.62n. For the Loders cartulary, destroyed in 1944, see Stein no. 2211; *Cartulaire de Loders*, ed. L. Guilloreau (Evreux 1908); G.R.C. Davis, *Medieval Cartularies of Great Britain. A Short Catalogue* (London 1958), 67 no.595. For other, episcopal charters, copied from the Archives at St-Lô in 1840, relating to the Somerset church of Martock and its grant to the monks of Mont-St-Michel, see BL mss. Additional Charters 19063–8.

[273] See, for example, *The Cartularies of Southwick Priory*, ed. K.A. Hanna, 2 vols., Hampshire Record Series ix–x (1988–9), ii, 19–21 nos 55, 58, pp.112–115 nos 324–30; *The Cartulary of Bradenstoke Priory*, ed. V.C.M. London, Wiltshire Record Society xxxv (1979), nos 503, 565, 643–4.

[274] N. Vincent, 'The English Monasteries and their French Possessions', *Cathedrals, Communities and Conflict in the Anglo-Norman World*, ed. P. Dalton, C. Insley and L. Wilkinson (Woodbridge 2011), 221-39.

[275] Below, pp.98-108.

[276] *The Early Charters of Waltham Abbey, 1062–1230*, ed. R. Ransford (Woodbridge 1989), p.44 no.81, and see letters of the barons of Dover to the archbp of Rouen and his bailiffs at Dieppe, below appendix no.44. For letters of Walter archbp of Rouen, issued in his capacity as viceregent to King Richard I in the 1190s, see BL ms. Additional Charter 33650, whence *English Episcopal Acta VIII: Winchester 1070–1204*, ed. M.J. Franklin (Oxford 1993), 178–9 no.232.

Norman evidences preserved in England but outside The National Archives, results from precisely that archival chaos to which I have already referred in dealing with Léchaudé d'Anisy and with such shady characters as the Abbé de la Rue. From at least the late eighteenth century onwards, English libraries have regularly been enriched with charters and other manuscripts removed, legally or otherwise, from collections in France. Here, amongst the more important of such sources, I would draw particular attention to the collecting activities of Sir Thomas Phillipps and Thomas Stapleton. From the Phillipps collection, dispersed at auction in the twentieth century, many of the more significant French charters and cartularies were repurchased by the Bibliothèque nationale in Paris. Others, however, entered English libraries or continue to feature in subsequent sale catalogues.[277] Although the majority of documents 'abstracted' from French public collections and sent into exile in England come from the modern départements of Calvados

---

[277] For Phillipps' collecting activities in France in the 1820s, see A.N.L. Munby, *Phillipps Studies*, 5 vols (Cambridge 1951–60), iii, 19–41, abstracted in Munby, *Portrait of an Obsession. The Life of Sir Thomas Phillipps* (London 1967), 15–28, with an interesting letter from Le Prévost to de Gerville, 24 December 1828, not noted by Munby, reporting on a recent visit from Phillipps and upon Phillipps' over-riding concern to acquire Norman cartularies: Evreux, Archives départementales 5F33. The majority of the French cartularies collected by Phillipps were subsequently purchased by the Bnf. For lists see, H. Omont, 'Cartalogue des manuscrits de la bibliothèque de Sir Thomas Phillipps récemment acquis pour la Bibliothèque nationale', *BEC*, lxiv (1903), 490–553; H. Omont, *Catalogue des manuscrits latins et français de la collection Phillipps acquis en 1908 pour la Bibliothèque nationale* (Paris 1909). Others of Phillipps' French and Norman charters have since entered the John Rylands Library at Manchester: *Handlist of Charters, Deeds and Similar Documents in the Possession of the John Rylands Library*, vol.1, ed. R. Fawtier (Manchester 1925), 43–95, including at p.59 three early charters for Mont-St-Michel. For an analysis of various of the items from the collection of St-Etienne at Caen, acquired by Phillipps from the Abbé de la Rue and now in the Bnf mss. nouv.acq. françaises 20218–20, see Sauvage, *Le Fonds de l'abbaye de Saint-Etienne*, p.x note 5, pp.50–4. Originals or very early copies of charters of dukes Richard II and William II of Normandy for Marmoutier (Fauroux, *Recueil*, nos 23, 141), were once Phillipps mss. 34699, 34701), the former sold at Sotheby's (*Bibliotheca Phillippica, n.s. part 3* (26 June 1967) lot no.732, £520 to H.P. Kraus of New York, offered for sale in Kraus' 1969 catalogue). The duke William charter is now in the library of the Fondation Martin Bodmer near Geneva, reference CB169. As recently as 1973, several hundred mostly fourteenth and fifteenth-century documents relating to the financial administration of Normandy, were auctioned at Sotheby's from the residue of the Phillipps collection: *Bibliotheca Phillippica: Catalogue of French, Spanish and Greek Manuscripts and English Charters* (Sotheby's Sale Catalogue, 25–26 June 1973), esp. lots 1949, 2020–4. My attempts to trace the subsequent fate of this collection have proved unsuccessful. Lot no.2020 was sold to Quaritch for £700. Like the other lots, which were either bought in or sold to dealers for much lesser amounts, the collection was thereafter most likely dispersed to the four corners of the earth, via individual private sales. For other, mostly fifteenth-century Norman materials now in the BL, acquired from the Baron Joursanvault from 1831 onwards and from other collections but ultimately deriving from the dispersal of the archives of the French royal Chambre des Comptes, burned in 1737, see Mlle Guitard, 'Documents normands conservés à Londres', *Bulletin de la Société d'Emulation de la Seine-Inférieure* (1933), 65–158 (and separately as a pamphlet, of which a copy is amongst the BL printed books collection); M. Nortier, 'Le Sort des archives dispersées de la Chambre des Comptes de Paris', *BEC*, cxxiii (1965), 460–537, esp. pp.516–19, and cf. the catalogues of Jourasanvault deeds in BL mss. Additional 11539–40. As early as January 1877, an unnamed English collector was already disposing at auction in London of considerable numbers of medieval deeds acquired from France: 'Vent de documents français à Londres', *BEC*, xxxviii (1877), 479–83.

and Manche, whose custody in the early nineteenth century was far from
ideally conducted,[278] all told, no part of Normandy can claim to have escaped
the ravages of nineteenth-century 'collecting'. From the archives of the
abbey of Foucarmont, for example, which in theory entered French public
custody via the fledgling but well-regulated archives départementales at
Rouen, the British Library today possesses a highly significant collection
of archiepiscopal and papal charters, including a bull of Alexander III and
confirmations issued in the names of archbishops Rotrou and Walter of
Rouen, acquired as late as 1869 from a Paris bookseller.[279]

Thomas Stapleton's collecting activities, though less frantic than those
of Phillipps, were clearly on a significant scale, and included at least
one full-blown cartulary, for the Breton monastery of Quimperlé, now
housed in the British Library, as well as a substantial number, approaching
200, of early Norman monastic charters.[280] The exact provenance of these
documents remains obscure. However, there now seems little doubt that

---

[278] See, for example, the significant collections for the monasteries of Montivilliers, Le Valasse,
La Lucerne, Le Mont-Saint-Michel, the Maison Dieu at St-Lô and the bpric of Coutances,
part of a miscellaneous collection of French documents entered in the BL's acquisitions
register as if purchased from William Simpson junior of Mitcham, but endorsed as if
purchased from the London booksellers Boone's, 13 June 1857: BL Additional Charters
13343–13596, esp. nos 13348–57, 13414–29, 13432, 13435–6, 13441, 13445, 13535, 13537.
For further examples, see Vincent, 'A Collection of Early Norman Charters', p.26n. For the
dispersal of documents from the Breton Chambre des Comptes, after 1789, including some
remarkable tales of survival, see M. Jones, '"Membra disjecta" of the Breton "Chambre des
Comptes" in the Late Middle Ages: Treasures Revisited and Rediscovered', *War, Government
and Power in Late Medieval France*, ed. C. Allmand (Liverpool 2000), 209–20.

[279] BL mss. Additional Charters 17839–59, part of a larger collection (Additional Charters
17838–17942), purchased from the Paris bookseller Bachelin de Florenne, 10 April 1869,
including a charter of Ymer abbot of Bec 1299 (Additional Charter 17881) and various
fourteenth-century Norman charters (Ibid. 17905, 17907, 17910, 17915–17, 17927). The
collection includes all of the known papal originals for Foucarmont, which were clearly
'liberated' at some point from the abbey's archive now in the Archives départementales
at Rouen. For the papal charters now in London, see *Papsturkunden in England*, ed. W.
Holtzmann, Abhandlungen der Gesellschaft der Wissenschaften zu Göttingen, Philologisch-
Historische Klasse, neue Folge 25 (1930–1), 3. Folge 14–15 (1935–6) and 33 (1952), i,
174 no.23 (and cf. p.173 no.13, also listing BL Additional Charter 54148, Alexander III for
Rouen); *Papsturkunden in Frankreich. Neue Folge 2. Band: Normandie*, ed. J. Ramackers,
Abhandlungen der Gesellschaft der Wissenschaften zu Göttingen Philologisch-Historische
Klasse 3 Folge 21 (Göttingen 1937), 289–90 no.193 (J–L 13452), and J. Sayers, *Original
Papal Documents in England and Wales From the Accession of Pope Innocent III to the
Death of Pope Benedict XI (1198–1304)* (Oxford 1999), nos 35–6, 190–2, 249, 252, 254–61,
893. What seems to have been a further stray from this collection, a judgement of 1197
by Theobald bp of Amiens in favour of the monks of Foucarmont, entered the archives
départementales at Rouen, by purchase, as recently as 2006: Rouen AD Seine-Maritime
J1157.

[280] The Quimperlé cartulary is now BL ms. Egerton 2802 (listed by Stein no.3125), purchased
by the British Museum 14 December 1895 for 120 guineas, having passed from the Le
Guillou family to Stapleton and from Stapleton to his nephew, Henry 9th Baron Beaumont.
My attempts to list the original charters collected in Normandy by Stapleton suggest a total
approaching 200 individual items.

they were mostly acquired in the summer of 1836, when an otherwise poorly documented visit to Normandy by Gage and Stapleton was followed by enquiries from Stapleton to Achille Deville over the fate of the charters of the priory of St-Gabriel in the archives at Rouen, St-Gabriel being one of the institutions whose early evidences had now come into Stapleton's own hands.[281] Stapleton's charter collection was acquired, apparently for £30, from the Abbé de la Rue, as we can establish from the fact that it was as an 'original charter belonging to Thomas Stapleton Esq from the collection of the Abbé de la Rue' that one of these documents was copied into Gage's correspondence books. In December 1836, we find Stapleton informing Gage that 'the governor' (i.e. Stapleton's father) 'has made me a present of the £30 the Norman charters cost me'.[282] Further traces of Stapleton and Gage's collecting activities have recently come to light amongst Gage's papers in Cambridge, which themselves include at least four medieval Norman charters. Of these, one, dated 14 April 1429, was issued in the name of John d'Alençon as vicomte de Beaumont: a document likely to have caught the eye of Thomas Stapleton, given his Beaumont connection.[283] Two others of the Norman charters now in Cambridge can be traced back to the archives of the sous-préfecture at Mortain where, in 1835, Léchaudé d'Anisy had unearthed a massive collection of original deeds relating principally to the Abbaye-Blanche at Mortain and to the monks of Savigny.[284] Neither of the deeds now in Cambridge features in Léchaudé's inventory of the Mortain originals, apparently compiled in 1839, leading us to suppose either that Stapleton and Gage pocketed the charters, now at Cambridge, whilst Léchaudé's back was turned or, more probably, that at some time after 1835 but before his inventory of 1839, most likely during Gage and Stapleton's tour of Normandy in 1836, Léchaudé himself was giving away or selling various of the Mortain

---

[281] Cambridge University Library ms. Hengrave Hall 21/8/160, Deville to Gage, 29 September 1836.

[282] Ibid. 21/8/74, 179. The transcripts in Gage's correspondence are of a charter of Robert earl of Gloucester for Fécamp (printed from the original in Stapleton's possession, sold in 1920 and since untraced, by R.B. Patterson, *Earldom of Gloucester Charters* (Oxford 1973), 75–8 no.70) and of Richard fitz Thurstan to the priory of St-Gabriel (today Hull History Centre, University Archives ms. Hull DDCA/37/46F).

[283] Cambridge University Library ms. Hengrave Hall 117 (provisional numbering: Norman deeds), granting safe conduct for four months to John Rousseau and Julien Bouvet, and for another deed of the same John d'Alençon, from the Savigny archive, see AN L968 no.304 (relating to Château-Gontier, Mayenne, 24 July 1451). Besides the Beaumont charter, and the charters for the Abbaye-Blanche and Savigny considered below, the fourth document in the Hengrave Hall collection is of Stephen abbot of St-Martin at Sées, appointing a proctor for his English lands, 29 March 1429.

[284] For the earlier of these, see below appendix no.68. The second, endorsed 'Carte de Gatemo Abrncensi' (s.xiii), seal missing and the document itself badly rubbed, takes the form of an acknowledgement by Robert de ... of arrangements made with the abbot of Savigny over the molture owed by the men residing on the land at Gathemo (Manche, cant. Sourdeval) which Robert's ancestors had purchased from the nuns of the Abbaye-Blanche at Mortain, January 1242/3. The grantor was perhaps Robert de Presles (*Praeriis*), heir of Hasculf de Presles, himself married to a daughter of the previous lord of Gathemo (cf. below appendix no.68n.), who in 1236 sold the vicomté of Avranches to Louis IX, who had denied Robert's right to inherit it from his father: *CN*, no.429.

charters as souvenirs.[285] As this suggests, Stapleton and Gage were not above seeking out stolen goods, a fact confirmed by Stapleton's purchase of the 200 Norman charters from de la Rue in circumstances where we know, on Stapleton's own testimony, that he was aware from the outset that de la Rue had come by his collections nefariously and through abuse of public office.[286] As a result, the 200 Norman charters purchased by Stapleton and thereafter preserved at Carlton Towers remained a subject of controversy. The arguments here can be traced in detail from the correspondence of Léopold Delisle.[287]

Delisle had been aware of Stapleton's collecting activities since at least the 1850s, perhaps through their mutual acquaintance, Auguste Le Prévost.[288] In 1881, he had sponsored the efforts of Léon Maître, archivist of Nantes, who at last gained access to the Stapleton archive at Carlton Towers and who, with the permission of the then Lord Beaumont, had made copies not only of the Quimperlé cartulary, but of 190 of the early Norman charters that Stapleton had carried off to England.[289] In 1890, Delisle attempted to enter into further correspondence with Lord Beaumont, enlisting the help of various aristocratic intermediaries, both French and English, in the hope that the Quimperlé cartulary might be repatriated to the Bibliothèque nationale.[290] Obtaining no reply, in May 1895 he wrote again, this time to the French ambassador in London, asking that the ambassador help secure the return not only of the Quimperlé cartulary but of Stapleton's Norman charters.[291] In response, the following month, Delisle received a letter from Violet Lady Beaumont, written from the eminently respectable 49 Eaton Place, informing him that Lord Beaumont had died three years earlier, but offering to sell the manuscripts should a reasonable price be offered.[292] Delisle offered 2000 Francs (£80) for the cartulary, and 2500 Francs (£100)

---

[285] For the circumstances of the discovery, see Léchaudé's memorandum in Bnf ms. Latin 10078 fos. A–C, with a list of the 1569 items for Savigny, dated in pencil '1839' at pp.1–140, and of the 402 items for the Abbaye-Blanche at pp.141–65. Various copies, dated 1835, were made by Léchaudé from originals then in the sous-préfecture at Mortain in his 'Cartulaire de Basse-Normandie', TNA PRO 31/8/140B part 1, for example at p.91 no.4.

[286] For Stapleton's awareness of this point, from the time of his first meeting with de la Rue in 1833, see above p.54.

[287] Delisle's letters on the 'affaire Stapleton', together with various later memoranda, are preserved in Bnf ms. nouv.acq.français 23910 fos.117r–133r.

[288] Memoranda in Ibid. fos.131r–132r.

[289] Maître's copies are now Bnf mss. nouv.acq.latines 1427 (Cartulaire de Quimperlé) and 1428 (Norman charters), and see the published note by Léopold Delisle in *BEC*, xlii (1881), 250–3. Some, but by no means all of the charters transcribed in nouv.acq. latines 1428 are briefly listed by Delisle in his *Catalogue des manuscrits du fonds de la Trémoïlle* (Paris 1889), 19–24.

[290] Bnf ms. nouv.acq.français 23910 fos.118r–120r, draft letters of Delisle to Lord Beaumont, January 1890, noting introductions effected in 1881 by the Marquis de la Ferronnays and more recently by Lady Herbert.

[291] Ibid. fos.121r–123r, draft of Delisle to Monsieur de Courcel, 8 May 1895, referring to Thomas Stapleton as the 'très savant antiquaire anglais'.

[292] Ibid. fos.124r–125v, Lady Beaumont to Delisle, in French, describing these manuscripts as a personal bequest from her husband to herself and assuring him of the 'état parfait' of the Quimperlé cartulary, 10 June 1895.

for the charters.[293] But the offer did not impress. Instead, Lady Beaumont now declared that, on her solicitor's advice, she was proceeding to the sale of the Quimperlé cartulary at Christie and Manson's auction house, the British Museum having already offered a higher price. As for the charters, she declared that she had never set eyes on them and doubted whether they were still to be found at Carlton.[294] The Quimperlé cartulary was duly sold to the British Museum in December 1895 for 120 guineas (£126).[295] Lady Beaumont's power to negotiate here was, to say the least, questionable, since Thomas Stapleton's collections had surely passed out of her control at the death of her husband, the 9th Lord Beaumont, in 1892, into the ownership of the 10th Lord Beaumont, still living in May 1895. Moreover, there is an interesting postscript to this story, that sheds much light on Delisle and not a little on Lady Beaumont. Clearly irked by Lady Beaumont's response, not least because he was then in the midst of a far more serious battle with the British authorities over his attempts, eventually successful, to secure the repatriation of the many hundreds of manuscripts stolen from public libraries in France by the notorious scoundrel, Libri, and since sold to Lord Ashburnham, Delisle sought the advice of the splendidly named Monsieur le comte du Pontavice de Heussey, 'Chef d'Escadron d'Artillerie', then serving as French military attaché in London. From the count, he received an alarming account of Lady Beaumont, preserved amongst Delisle's papers, that deserves to be quoted at length:

> 'Violet Beaumont (est) fille d'une couturière de Paris et d'un riche juif du nom de Isaacson. Elle s'est fait épouser par Lord Beaumont, dont les dettes avaient eté payées par le dit Isaacson. Lord Beaumont, disabusé peu de temps après le marriage, a voulu divorcer; mais le beau père avait pris des précautions, et Lord Beaumont, menacé de la ruine et du déshonneur, s'est contenté de s'eloigner de sa femme. Violet Beaumont est une intrigante tout à fait décriée'.[296]

The economy of expression here, no less than the inaccuracies of reportage, bear witness to Delisle's fury, and the fury of Delisle, like that of so many librarians, is not to be underestimated. The comte, meanwhile, was writing less than a year after a rather more notorious outburst of French military anti-semitism had consigned Captain Alfred Dreyfus to life imprisonment on Devil's Island.

---

[293] Ibid. fo.126r, draft letter from Delisle to Lady Beaumont, headed 'du 15 au 20 Juin 1895', the uncertain date perhaps reflecting the need to consult over prices. The letter refers in passing to Delisle's possession of a 'précieuse correspondance' with Thomas Stapleton, presumably the letters that had passed between Le Prévost and Stapleton (above p.63 n.222), since untraced.

[294] Ibid. fos.127r–128v, Lady Beaumont to Delisle, 28 June 1895.

[295] Information from Julian Harrison.

[296] Ibid. fo.130r, note by Delisle reporting receipt of a letter of 26 October 1895. The calling card of Monsieur le comte du Pontavice de Heussey is preserved in Ibid. fo.129r.

Delisle's attempts to repatriate the Stapleton charters having failed, the majority were dispersed in October 1920 at sale from the Carlton Towers library. At this sale, held at Sotheby's, a single one of the 180 or more charters, in this instance with sign manuals of King William I, fetched £500, supplying some justification for Lady Beaumont's reluctance to accept the £100 offered by Delisle in 1895 for the entire collection.[297] From the sale itself, more than 120 of the charters were purchased by Quaritch acting on behalf of the John Rylands Library in Manchester. Others, purchased privately, have since entered the British Library as a result of resale or gift. The items acquired by the Rylands are well catalogued in print, those in the British Library less so.[298] Meanwhile, several lots, including up to thirty charters for the abbeys of St-Etienne and La Trinité at Caen, sold in 1920 to a variety of buyers, particularly to Maggs, remain untraced.[299] Yet another small cache of Norman charters, including very early royal charters for St-Etienne Caen, went unsold in 1920 and was only removed from Carlton Towers in the 1970s. Today these are to be found in the somewhat unlikely custody of the library of the University of Hull, cited thence and in the more significant cases since published by David Bates.[300] Others of Thomas Stapleton's charters, including an original diploma of Henry I for St-Etienne Caen recently tracked down to the collections of the Morgan Library in New York, continue to surface, sometimes in the most surprising of places.[301]

---

[297] See here BL Additional Charter 75503, with sign manuals of King William I, sold in the Beaumont sale at Sotheby's on 22 October 1920 as lot 185 for £500, resold by Maggs Bros. in 1931 for £2500, and eventually acquired by the BL in 1961: *The British Library Catalogue of Additions to the Manuscripts 1956–1965: Part 1 Descriptions* (London 2000), pp.612–14, with a distinctly garbled version of these events in H.P. Kraus, *A Rare Book Saga* (London 1978), 137–8, and the Sotheby's sale catalogue 22 October 1920, in the BL marked up with purchasers and prices, realizing just under £1000 for the 44 lots of Beaumont charters (BL printed books S.C. Sotheby's, Sale of 22 October 1920 ('The Property of the Baroness Beaumont ... A Valuable Collection of Norman Charters') lots 184–224).

[298] *Handlist of Charters*, ed. Fawtier, 1–19; BL mss. Additional Charters 66980, 67574–93, 75503, mostly catalogued in *British Museum Catalogue of Additions to the Manuscripts 1926–1930* (London 1959), 250–2, listing the items acquired in 1930 from R.A. Coates, in some cases having first passed through the hands of W.A. Lindsay, lots 188, 190–1, 193, 214 and part of lot 194 in the sale of 1920. For the 1920 sale itself, see *Catalogue of Important Medieval Manuscripts ... The Property of the Baroness Beaumont, Carlton Towers, Yorks.*, (Sotheby's, London 22 October 1920), esp. lots 184–228.

[299] From the sale of 1920, a single charter from lot 188, 3 from lot 194, the 12 documents in lots 197–8, the 14 in lots 204 and 206, the 6 in lot 211, one item from lot 218, and 5 items from lots 221 and 224, remain untraced. The majority of these were bought at the sale by Maggs Bros., who retain no record of their subsequent resale. I am indebted to Robert Harding of Maggs for his assistance here. I am currently preparing a full list of the missing items as part of a more detailed study of the collection.

[300] Hull History Centre, University Archives DDCA/37/46a–j, with a full edition of some of the more important items by D. Bates, 'Four Recently Rediscovered Norman Charters', *Annales de Normandie*, xlv (1995), 35–48. A copy of a thirteenth-century survey of the diocese of Coutances, apparently transcribed in 1816, is still amongst the materials now at Hull: DDCA3/7/1.

[301] New York, Pierpont Morgan Library MA 1217, in 1920 bought by Ralph C. Runyon at the Carlton Towers sales whence purchased for the Morgan at the Shattuck sale in 1947, with facsimile and commentary by E.G. Carlson, 'A Charter for St-Etienne, Caen: A Document and Its Implications', *Gesta*, xv (1976) (*Essays in Honor of Sumner McKnight Crosby*), 11–14, and cf. above p.75 n.267 for another of the Stapleton charters likewise 'stranded' in New York.

3. THE EVIDENCES

I hope thus far to have demonstrated that students of ducal Normandy ignore the manuscript resources of England very much at their peril. The proof of this is best demonstrated by a selection of the available evidences. What follows here, save in my edition of the principal surviving French and Norman evidences from Canterbury Cathedral, brought together towards the end of this edition, represents a selection rather than a comprehensive edition: a selection that is deliberately eclectic and that is intended to illustrate the importance of English archives for Anglo-Norman relations in the decades either side of King John's loss of Normandy in 1204. Let us begin here with the evidences of The National Archives and in particular with the so-called Norman Rolls, revived in the fifteenth century as a result of Henry V's conquests after Agincourt. I have edited below an important grant by King Henry I to the monastery of La Trinité at Rouen, which has previously escaped the editors of King Henry's charters.[302] From the same rolls, I have also transcribed below two Norman charters of King John, for the monks of Beaubec and the men of Falaise, issued during the third and fourth years of John's reign – years of vital significance for the duchy of Normandy, but for which the chancery Charter rolls of John's own reign are now missing. The first of these charters, given at Montfort on 26 October 1201, which also survives as an original in the archives of Beaubec at Rouen, merely rehearses the terms of a confirmation issued by King Henry II. It is nonetheless of significance in demonstrating that within a few years of his conquest of Ireland, Henry II had confirmed lands in Ireland, in County Meath, upon the Norman abbey of Beaubec.[303] The second charter of King John printed below, for the men of Falaise, given at Argentan on 11 August 1202, is known otherwise only from a late copy in the municipal archives of Falaise, and is indicative of John's attempts to buy the support of the Norman towns amidst the blandishments extended to the duchy by Philip Augustus, on the eve of the Capetian conquest of the duchy.[304] Complementing these royal documents, a further pair of charters of King John is published below from the thirteenth-century Cartae Antiquae Rolls, the first, undated but assignable to the period before May 1203, involving an exchange of land at Maldon in Essex between the lepers of Le Bois-Halbout and the Norman bishop of London, William de Ste-Mère-Eglise, the second, of 15 September 1208, relating to the confiscated estate of Robert fitz Erneis, a significant Norman baron, who himself had held a moiety of the manor of Maldon before his defection to the Capetian cause, c.1204.[305] A mid thirteenth-century roll of charters, copied for

---

[302] Below appendix no.1.
[303] Below appendix no.2.
[304] Below appendix no.3.
[305] Below appendix nos 4–5.

their significance for the administration of the King's forests in England, supplies a further charter of King John, issued at Rouen on 31 March 1203, conferring assarts within the forest at Weedon Beck in Northamptonshire upon the monks of Bec. The survival of this charter, both in this and other copies, and as an original now at Eton College, allows us to compare the truncated witness list supplied for the copies with the much longer list of witnesses appended to the original.[306]

Returning thence to the fifteenth-century Norman chancery rolls, I have selected a small handful of the private Norman charters which occur in the Henry V enrolments. Amongst fifty or so such inspected charters, a considerable number survive, either in the original or in further copies, in Norman archives. Of those that do not, a charter of Peter de Préaux not only represents a unique survival of evidences relating to the Augustinian Abbey of Beaulieu near Préaux, but complements and adds further details to a charter of King John enrolled on the chancery Charter Roll.[307] Charters of Reginald de Pavilly for the lepers of Rouen, of Robert de Courtenay for the monks of La Noë, and of Nicholas de Montaigne for the monks of Bonport, illustrate the secular patronage of Norman religious institutions either side of the Capetian conquest of 1204, and complement the evidences surviving in Norman archives.[308] The grant of Nicholas de Montaigne includes an important snapshot of the Norman Exchequer, once again at work in Rouen in 1208 only a few years after the collapse of Plantagenet administration.[309] Taken together, these documents are intended to draw the attention of Anglo-Norman historians to the other, more extensive enrolments of early Norman evidences still to be recovered from the Norman chancery rolls. Concluding this section of early evidences taken from enrolments, I have transcribed below a charter of the dean and chapter of Mortain, *c.*1260, relating to their estates in Wiltshire, taken from the Wiltshire Forest Eyre Roll of 1263: a rare survival from the evidences of a Norman institution, the collegiate church of St Evroult and St Guillaume Firmat at Mortain, which have otherwise vanished almost entirely, and a useful reminder of the way in which Norman charters can turn up haphazardly, even amongst the least likely of English enrolments.[310]

Turning from the enrolments to The National Archives' vast collection of original deeds, and in particular to those deeds relating to Norman religious houses or alien priories with lands in England, I have transcribed below a charter of Robert archbishop of Rouen, issued in 1209 or 1210, concerning an annual rent that the archdeacon of Eu was accustomed to receive from the monks of Lewes, and demonstrating that Lewes, like other English houses, had property of its own in Normandy, in this instance a priory or cell at Etoutteville-sur-Mer whose existence has previously gone

---

[306] Below appendix no.6.
[307] Below appendix no.7.
[308] Below appendix nos 8–10.
[309] Below appendix no.10.
[310] Below appendix no.11.

unnoticed by English historians.[311] For a period, Lewes enjoyed jurisdiction both over the priory at Etoutteville-sur-Mer and over the Cluniac priory at Mortemer-sur-Eaulne.[312] From a similar series of miscellaneous deeds, another charter, of February 1258, demonstrates that even fifty years after the Plantagenet loss of Normandy, the monks of Fécamp were entering into new confraternity arrangements with the abbot and monks of Pershore in Worcestershire.[313]

The materials in these Ancient Deeds series are so extensive, and relate so frequently to the alien priories, that no attempt here can be made to supply even a skeleton outline of their riches. By contrast, from the archives of the Duchy of Lancaster, it is possible to aim at a more or less complete edition of Norman evidences. From amongst those that have already been published, I have drawn attention above to exchanges of lands in the Roumare fee in both England and Normandy, published by Stenton and Cazel.[314] These charters can now be supplemented by three further deeds, of the late 1160s or 1170s, by which Roger de Tilleul and Robert le Chalceis (or 'de Caux') abandoned their lands within the Lincolnshire honour of Bolingbroke in return for a confirmation of an extensive estate in the Roumare fee at Roumare, Barentin, Bouteilles and elsewhere.[315] Other Norman evidences in the Duchy of Lancaster series have previously gone entirely unnoticed. These include an inquest returned to King John by abbot Samson of St-Etienne Caen and his three fellow officers who we know, from the Norman charter roll and elsewhere, headed the Exchequer at Caen between 1200 and 1204. The inquest, into the lands held by William de Mandeville at Beuzeval near Bayeux, is interesting in its own right, and all the more so for being returned by the same Peter de Lions who is recorded in the Norman charter roll as clerk at the Exchequer, written in a hand that is remarkably similar, indeed quite possibly identical to that which wrote the surviving roll of Norman charters for the year 2 John.[316]

On the face of things, the next four Duchy of Lancaster deeds printed below have no direct bearing upon Norman history, save that they were issued by an Anglo-Norman family, the Pirous (Pirou, Manche, cant. Lessay), in respect to their estate at Chedzoy in Somerset. However, if we probe a little deeper, the story that these charters tell may well be Norman in focus. William de Pirou, lord of Pirou in Manche, appears to have held part of his estate from the honour of Mortain, losing possession of Chedzoy in the early 1190s almost certainly as a result of support for the rebellion of John count of Mortain, the king's brother. In 1194, after King Richard's return,

---

[311] Below appendix no.12.
[312] See here the list of dependencies assigned to Lewes in BL ms. Stowe 935 (Monks Horton cartulary) fo.56r (183r): 'Prioratus de Estotauilla in Rotomagensi dioc(esi) taxatur, Prioratus de Mortuo Mari in dict(a) dioc(esi) taxatur', and cf. Cottineau, i, 1082, ii, 1991, and the visitations of Eudes Rigaud archbp of Rouen, cited below no.12 note.
[313] Below appendix no.13, with a counterpart from the Fécamp archives, below no.14.
[314] Above p.22.
[315] Below appendix nos 15–17.
[316] Below appendix no.18.

William was restored to possession of Chedzoy, apparently holding it in one form or another from the Mortain estate until 1199, after which it passed to William Brewer, one of King John's closest henchmen.[317] Brewer's title to Chedzoy was nonetheless disputed by the manor's immediate overlords, the Montagu family, who pursued their claim through to the time of Brewer's death in the late 1220s.[318] Our series of charters here begins with letters of William de Pirou in which he informs an unnamed king, possibly Richard but more likely King John or Henry III, that he is sending Richard de Pirou, his son, to seek possession of Chedzoy.[319] The remaining three charters detail the process by which Richard de Pirou transferred the estate to William Brewer in return for an annual rent of 100 shillings.[320] The principal charter here makes plain that the rent was to be reduced according to the amount that Brewer might spend in any year discharging his obligations to the manor's overlord, presumably William de Montagu.[321] However, had only this charter survived we would have no idea that Richard de Pirou further disclaimed his right to the rent until such a time as he could obtain full seisin of Chedzoy from the king and his council – a significant indication of the extent to which the survival of a series of

---

[317] *PR 6 Richard I*, 19, 189; *PR 7 Richard I*, 39, 230, 234; *PR 8 Richard I*, 215; *Rot. Ob.*, 8. William or a namesake served subsequently as keeper of Bristol, one of Count John's principal assets: *PR 8 Richard I*, 109–10; *PR 9 Richard I*, 128. For reference to his debts in Normandy after 1195, see *MRSN*, i, 198, 229, ii, 297, 523, 536. For what appears to be the earliest reference to William Brewer's tenancy at Chedzoy, before 1216, see *RLC*, i, 252b, and cf. *VCH Somerset*, vi, 246. In 1200, William de Pirou fined to take possession of the Tracy lands near Vire in Normandy, remaining in possession until after the conquest of Normandy by Philip Augustus, apparently until at least 1213: *Rot. Norm.*, 38; *Registres*, 268; *Jugements*, 32–3 no.125, 166–7 no.729. A William de Pirou, son of Alexander de Pirou, tenant of Richard de Montagu, occurs in Somerset 1174 X 1180, apparently as successor to an earlier lord of Chedzoy named Alured de Pirou fl. before 1166, Richard de Montagu himself having married a woman named Alice de Pirou: *Two Cartularies of the Benedictine Abbeys of Muchelney and Athelney*, ed. E.H. Bates, Somerset Record Society xiv (1899), 135 no.33; *A Cartulary of Buckland Priory*, ed. F.W. Weaver, Somerset Record Society xxv (1909), 104–5 no.179; *Two Cartularies of the Augustinian Priory of Bruton and the Cluniac Priory of Montacute*, ed. T.S. Holmes, Somerset Record Society viii (1894), 25 no.105. For references to charters of William and Richard de Pirou in favour of the monks of Aunay and Blanchelande, formerly St-Lô, Archives départementales de la Manche H33, H102 and H326, see F.–N. Dubosc, *Inventaire sommaire (des archives départementales de la Manche) série H*, vol.1 part 1 (St-Lô 1875), 5, 15, 52. For a Ralph de Pirou and William de Pirou his son, temp. Richard bp of Coutances (1150–1178), see Paris, BN ms. Latin 17137 (St-Sauveur cartulary) fos.180r–v, 182r–v nos 235–6, 239. William de Pirou 'the elder', together with his wife Prebreia/Ebrea de Tracy, was still living in 1216, but seems to have been succeeded before 1217 when various grants were confirmed by William de Pirou 'the younger': P. Le Cacheux, *Essai historique sur l'Hôtel-Dieu de Coutances, l'Hôpital-Général et les Augustines Hospitalières*, 2 vols (Paris 1895–9), ii ('Cartulaire de l'Hotel-Dieu'), 9–10 nos 10–11, 16–17 no.20, concerning mills and forest rights at Montpinchon (Manche, cant. Cerisy-la-Salle) and La Vendele (Manche, cant. St-Malo-de-la-Lande), for which references I am indebted to Daniel Power.

[318] *CRR*, viii, 29, x, 125, xi, nos 2, 1147, xii, nos 826, 1155, 1435, 1640, 2227; *RLC*, ii, 160; *VCH Somerset*, vi, 246.

[319] Below appendix no.19.

[320] Below appendix nos 20–2. In the 1190s, the manor appears to have been valued at £10 per annum (*PR 7 Richard I*, 39), so that the rent required from Brewer represented roughly half of the manor's true value.

[321] Below appendix no.20.

charters can often disclose details that would be entirely distorted were only a single charter to survive.[322] Throughout, the reference by William de Pirou to sending Richard his son to the king, and Richard de Pirou's own undertaking both to send properly accredited representatives to collect rent at Chedzoy and to obtain a full confirmation of his charter from William, his father, suggest that the Pirous themselves resided at some distance both from the king and from Somerset.[323] What we have here, I would suggest, are letters and charters issued by Normans, in the aftermath of 1204, who though unable to obtain King John's confirmation of their English lands, nonetheless determined to ensure a promise of future advantage, first by investing their claim in a member of the family, Richard de Pirou, who might hope to claim lands in England despite the allegiance of his father in Normandy, and then, when this failed, by transferring the land to the king's henchman William Brewer, on the understanding that Brewer would pay rent if and when the Pirou family could regain seisin in England. The attempt itself failed. It nonetheless suggests that even after 1204 there were Normans who, although most anxious to retain their Norman lands and hence forced to recognise the authority of Philip Augustus, were by no means convinced either that the breach between England and Normandy would prove permanent or that they must abandon all claims to their English estates. As has been argued elsewhere, had John or Henry III shown greater sensitivity to the plight of those Norman lords caught up in the Capetian conquest, and had John not insisted, immediately after 1204, that all men make a clear choice between keeping their lands in England or in Normandy, then the chances of a Plantagenet reconquest might have been considerably improved.[324]

The other charters printed below from the Duchy of Lancaster series concern relations with Normandy in the decades after 1204, and once again, as with the main series of Ancient Deeds in The National Archives, come from an archive rich in charters of the alien priories. We have seen already that a charter of King John, preserved in the fifteenth-century Norman Rolls, is crucial in proving that the abbey of Beaubec received its lands in Ireland as early as the 1180s, perhaps immediately after Henry II's seizure of Ireland in 1172–3.[325] Two of the Duchy of Lancaster deeds concern this same Irish daughter-house of Beaubec alias 'Beybeg', south of Drogheda, to which, at some time after his exile from Ireland during the reign of King John, Walter de Lacy confirmed an estate at 'Killekeran' (perhaps Castlekeeran, Templekeeran or Kilcarn, all in County Meath) together with the church

---

[322] Below appendix no.22.
[323] Below appendix nos 19, 21.
[324] In general, see Powicke, *Loss*, passim, and most recently D.J. Power, 'The French Interests of the Marshal Earls of Striguil and Pembroke, 1189–1234', *ANS*, xxv (2003), 199–225.
[325] Below appendix no.2.

of St Patrick at Trim.[326] Walter's charters are interesting, in part because they show a secular lord endowing a vicarage (a function more usually left to bishops), in part because they distinguish between the English inhabitants of Ireland and the 'Bethani', the native Irish treated here as a subject people of lower legal status. De Lacy's patronage of Beaubec was known to William Dugdale and rehearsed in the *Monasticon*, but only from a subsequent confirmation charter of King Henry III.[327] The Duchy deeds here can be supplemented by a related charter, now preserved in the British Library, recording further grants by Walter de Lacy to the monks of Beaubec in Ireland.[328] The other Duchy charters printed below, confirming a settlement between Simon de Montfort and the proctor appointed by the monks of Bec for their lands in England, represent two of at least three, another surviving in the archives départementales at Rouen, in which that most improbable of francophile English patriots, Simon de Montfort, is to be found negotiating with the religious corporations of Normandy.[329]

We have seen that the Ancient Correspondence series of The National Archives (SC 1) contains numerous letters with a Norman focus. Below, I have printed a letter of 1234 from the archbishop of Rouen, sent in the midst of the upheavals at court occasioned by the king's dismissal of the ministry of Peter des Roches, requesting the assistance of Edmund archbishop of Canterbury in protecting Rouen's estate at Bentworth in Hampshire, menaced by the king's bailiffs of Odiham.[330] A further such Norman petition, from the dean and chapter of the collegiate church at Sauqueville, *c.* June 1286, has to be set in the context of a pair of charters, one in the archives at Rouen, the other in the British Library, setting out the terms of Jordan de Sauqueville's augmentation of the college's rents

---

[326] Below appendix nos 23–4, and cf. M. Potterton, *Medieval Trim: History and Archaeology* (Dublin 2005), 270, for access to which book I am indebted to Marie Therese Flanagan. For the manor of Beaubec near Drogheda, see also *Inquisitions and Extents of Medieval Ireland*, ed. P. Dryburgh and B. Smith, List and Index Society cccxx (2007), 135–6 no.250.

[327] *Monasticon*, vi, 1129, ultimately from *Cal. Chart. R. 1226–57*, 215.

[328] Below appendix no.25. This charter (BL ms. Additional Charter 19803) is one of more than two thousand acquired on 12 July 1873 from G.R. Attenborough. The source of these documents, previously overlooked, was almost certainly the private collection of the Elizabethan antiquary, Sir Christopher Hatton, reported by both Tanner and Dugdale to have possessed large numbers of charters from Sulby/Welford Abbey (in which the Attenborough collection in the BL is particularly rich) and who certainly owned what are now BL mss. Additional Charters 20419, 20544, 20554, printed as from Hatton's collections by Dugdale in *Monasticon*, iv, 285, v, 410, vi, 520, and for Hatton's private collections, see also *Hatton's Seals*, p.xxvii. In 1874, a year after Attenborough's bequest, a large collection of Hatton's correspondence entered the library as BL mss. Additional 29548–85. By no means all of Hatton's charters (which are to be distinguished from those belonging to his fellow antiquaries, temporarily gathered together for the making of Hatton's 'Book of Seals') were acquired with the Attenborough bequest. Some had already strayed as long ago as the seventeenth century. See, for example, BL ms. Cotton Charter XI.13, printed as from the Hatton library, in *Monasticon*, iii, 578.

[329] Below appendix nos 26–7, and see Rouen, Archives départementales Seine-Maritime G1114, noted from a modern photocopy by J.R. Maddicott, *Simon de Montfort* (Cambridge 1994), 198–9 n.30.

[330] Below appendix no.28.

in 1201–2, granting the canons the manor of Helmingham in Suffolk: an important reminder this, of the fact that Anglo-Norman landowners were still making cross-Channel grants of land on the very eve of the Capetian conquest.[331] Jordan de Sauqueville, indeed, was one of those rare Anglo-Norman landowners who, after 1204 and as a satellite of the Marshal earls of Pembroke, was able to retain his property on both sides of the Channel.[332] The subsequent fortunes of his college at Sauqueville, deprived of its revenues from Suffolk and as a result fallen upon evil times, serves as a reminder of the extent to which the religious of Normandy, particularly those heavily dependent upon English revenues, were thrown into financial crisis as a result of the events of 1204.[333]

Turning now from The National Archives to evidences preserved in other English archives, it was not only religious corporations but a large number of secular Anglo-Norman lords who had at one time possessed Norman land. On rare occasions we find charters to secular beneficiaries, still preserved, not only in such archives as those of the Duchy of Lancaster, now in public custody, but in private, family collections in England, in which Norman estates or Norman dignitaries appear. Some of these charters have entered the British Library or the various English local record offices in which such collections are deposited. Others remain in private custody.[334] Since the archivists who catalogued or listed such collections were rarely on the look out for Norman evidences or familiar with the means by which Norman place-names could be identified, it is not surprising that various Norman charters have been misidentified in the past as if they referred to English locations. Amongst the vast muniment collections of Lord Middleton, for example, now deposited in the archives of Nottingham University, there lurk at least two Norman charters, the most important being a grant by Henry de Montfort, lord of Beaudesert in Warwickshire *c.*1185, to Hugh de Montfort his brother, granting all his lands in 'Pychauilla', 'Gouteuilla' and 'Cleuilla' in return for an annual

---

[331] Below appendix nos 29–34.

[332] Power, 'French Interests of the Marshal Earls of Striguil and Pembroke', 219–20; N. Vincent, 'More Tales of the Conquest', *Normandy and its Neighbours 900–1250: Essays for David Bates*, ed. D. Crouch and K. Thompson (Turnhout 2011), 276–87, 300–1.

[333] D.J.A. Matthew, *The Norman Monasteries and their English Possessions* (Oxford 1962), 65–84; A.J. Davis, *The Holy Bureaucrat: Eudes Rigaud and Religious Reform in Thirteenth-Century Normandy* (Ithaca 2006), 94–6.

[334] See the examples from Eaton Hall and Belvoir Castle, cited below p.91 n.338, and see a final concord made in the king's court at Caen in 1204, concerning the English and Norman estates of Ralph de Argosis and Alured de Solenneio, once amongst the muniments of Sir E.O. Every at Egginton, Derbyshire, whence calendared by I.H. Jeayes, *Descriptive Catalogue of Derbyshire Charters in Public and Private Libraries and Muniment Rooms* (London 1906), 220 no.1753, not now to be found amongst the Every charters deposited at Matlock, Derbyshire Record Office, or at Derby, Local Studies Library, as drawn to my attention by Daniel Power. A grant of land in 'Rochude' and Caen by Henry fitz Herbert to William de Aubenes, once amongst the muniments of Reginald Cholmondeley of Condover Hall, Shropshire (*HMC 5th Report* (London 1876), appendix p.534b), was sold at auction in 1887 and is since untraced. For the donor, Henry fitz Herbert (fl.*c.*1170), subsequently a monk of St-Etienne Caen, see L. Jean-Marie, *Caen aux XIe et XIIe siécles: espace urbain, pouvoirs et société* (Condé-sur-Noireau 2000), 261, 270.

quit rent of a pair of spurs.[335] The nineteenth-century cataloguer of this deed sought to identify 'Pychauilla' as Pickwell in Leicestershire. In reality it is Picauville (Manche, cant. Ste-Mère-Eglise), in which commune are to be found hamlets named Gueutteville and Clainville, supplying significant evidence for the Norman landholding of the Montforts of Beaudesert, in this instance lying well beyond the supposed homeland of the family in the Risle valley, in a manor of the Cotentin perhaps acquired by one or other of the Montforts through marriage. By what means this document came into the Middleton collection remains obscure, but it is preserved there in company with at least one other Norman charter, printed below, by which Oliver de Vrigny quitclaimed land in Normandy to John du Hommet, member of a distinguished Norman family.[336] Other such Norman charters, in no small number, still await discovery amongst English family collections. Below, as a further example of the genre, from the muniments today belonging to the Wingfield-Digby family or dispersed from the Wingfield-Digby collection to the British Library, I have reassembled a pair of charters of Arnulf bishop of Lisieux, recording a division of the estate of an English archdeacon of Lisieux, Robert of Arden, for whose date and circumstances I would refer readers to the splendid edition of Mowbray charters by Diana Greenway.[337]

Despite various of the examples cited thus far, even by 1200, and even in royal confirmations, it is unusual to find charters which refer to a mixture of English and Norman estates.[338] The chancery of Henry II already demonstrated a tendency to issue distinct charters of confirmation to Norman houses, listing English lands separately from those held in Normandy itself. In part this must reflect the differences in land law between the duchy and the kingdom, in part the practical difficulties for a Norman landowner in transporting charters and documents across the Channel to defend title in England. In the case of the abbey of Bec, for example, it seems that as early as the 1150s, the monks obtained distinct charters of confirmation for their Norman and their English estates, the Norman charters to be kept at Bec itself, the English charters at one or other of their dependent priories in England.[339] Several examples could be cited from later in the thirteenth

---

[335] Below appendix no.35.

[336] Below appendix no.36.

[337] Below appendix nos 37–8. For the background, see the charters of the Mowbray family printed from later transcripts in *Charters of the Honour of Mowbray 1107–1191*, ed. D.E. Greenway (Oxford 1972), 212–18 nos 330–8, of which two survive as originals, together with other related but as yet unprinted Mowbray charters, at Birmingham, Central Reference Library ms. Wingfield-Digby muniments A1/1–5.

[338] For exceptions, see charters of Henry II relating to the English and Norman estates of Hugh de Mortimer (*Reading Abbey Cartularies*, ed. B.R. Kemp, 2 vols., Camden Society 4th series xxxi, xxxiii (1986–7), ii, 232–3 no.1068, with an original surviving amongst the muniments of the Duke of Westminster at Eaton Hall, Cheshire), and for Henry du Neubourg (*Manuscripts of His Grace the Duke of Rutland preserved at Belvoir Castle*, vol. iv, HMC (London 1905), 22, from an original at Belvoir Castle, Duke of Rutland ms. Royal Charters 425.

[339] For charters of Henry II apparently produced to meet the particular requirements of the monks of Bec for their English priories, as opposed to a charter of confirmation solely for the monks' Norman estates, see *Acta Henry II*, nos 179–80, 184. For distinct charters of Henry

century, in which French churchmen sent transcripts rather than original documents to England, claiming that the perils of the sea crossing were too great to risk the dispatch of the originals.[340] Such fears were by no means unjustified, as demonstrated in the case of the canons of Notre-Dame de Voeu at Cherbourg, who in the 1260s sent to England a charter of Henry II, confirming both their estate at Hough-on-the-Hill in Lincolnshire and their rights in the Norman forest of Brix (Manche, cant. Valognes), only to have the charter disappear amidst the turmoil of the baronial rebellion.[341] The rarity of charters mentioning lands in both England and Normandy must also reflect the tendency, remarked by David Crouch and fully displayed in the three Bolingbroke charters printed below, for Anglo-Norman families, long before the debacle of 1204, to divide into distinct English and Norman branches. Many such families, even as early as the 1150s or 60s, had a very clear idea of the particular side of the Channel on which their principal interests lay and hence, after 1204, were left in little doubt as to whether to side with John or Philip Augustus. This phenomenon, as Professor Crouch remarks, served as an important long-term factor in the collapse of Plantagenet lordship in France.[342] With only the king himself and a few of the greater noble families possessing substantial estates both in England and in France, not only were the ties that bound the old Anglo-Norman realm together slowly loosened, but, after 1204, the king's desire for reconquest met with a less than enthusiastic response from the majority of his English barons and knights.

These same tendencies can be observed in a pair of charters of 1201, issued on the eve of the Capetian conquest, by which Robert count of Meulan sought to endow his granddaughter Mary and her husband, Peter de Préaux, with his entire estate in France, Normandy and England in return for a cash payment of 10,000 marks. Previously known only from a nineteenth-century printing, one of these charters today survives amongst the muniments of the Trevelyan family, deposited in the Somerset Record Office at Taunton. The other is known only from seventeenth-century copies.[343] When this arrangement failed, in part through the defection of Peter de Préaux and of count Robert's own son to the French, on 1 May 1204, Robert attempted a second settlement in favour of his daughter, Mabel, married to William de Vernon earl of Devon, this time known only

---

II confirming the English and Norman possessions of the monks of Cormeilles, see Ibid., nos 691–2.

[340] See, for example, Exeter, Devon Record Office ms. 312M/TY57, letters of William de Beaumont, bp of Angers in favour of Totnes priory, apologising for failing to dispatch the original charters here abstracted 'cum periculosum esset … dictas cartas sigillatas propter alicuius rei infortunium ad partes vestras transmisse'. As early as 1201, see a charter of King John for Fontevraud, sent to England in the form of a vidimus by William des Roches, 'quoniam necesse erat monialibus Fontebraldi ut cartam siue autenticum huius transcripti pro negotiis suis in Angliam mitterent', cited by Delisle, *Recueil*, i (Introduction), 181n.

[341] *CPR 1266–72*, 206–7.

[342] D. Crouch, 'Normans and Anglo-Normans: A Divided Aristocracy?', *England and Normandy in the Middle Ages*, ed. D. Bates and A. Curry (London 1994), 51–67.

[343] Below, appendix nos 39–40, and cf *Hatton's Seals*, 135–6 no.191n.

from an early-modern transcript out of a lost Norman cartulary, to which Thomas Stapleton was the first modern historian to draw attention.[344] On a similar note, two further charters, the first a division of English and Norman lands by the head of the Courcy family today known only from copies made in the seventeenth century by Elias Ashmole, the second the record of a settlement made at the Norman Exchequer but nonetheless referring to lands in Cambridgeshire, demonstrate that, although rare, such mixed, Anglo-Norman settlements are by no means unknown.[345] A third charter, issued by Richard de Barentin, son of Henry II's butler, Alexander de Barentin, reveals an interesting disposition of estates, again on the eve of the conquest of 1204, with Richard disposing of the majority of his Norman patrimony whilst seeking to retain rents from it, payable in England.[346] Letters from the barons of Dover to the archbishop of Rouen, apparently sent after 1197 but before King John's loss of Normandy, reveal the efforts made by the monks of St Augustine's Canterbury to obtain exemption from toll at Dieppe, apparently by claiming to be fellow citizens of the men of Dover, themselves quit from such tolls.[347] Selecting two from the fairly considerable number of charters surviving in English archives relating to the Norman possessions of English monks, Aldulf de Brachy's foundation charter for a Sempringhamite house, intended to be established on his ancestral estate at Brachy in Upper Normandy, is one of the more remarkable examples, from the 1170s or 80s, of attempts made to integrate English monks into Norman society. The attempt was a total failure, so that the churches and lands here assigned to the Brachy house were, by the early 1180s, either recovered by Aldulf and his heirs or, in the case of the English lands, redistributed amongst other Sempringhamite foundations in England.[348] On a slightly more successful note, and following the transfer of the church of Ecrammeville to the monks of St James' Bristol by William earl of Gloucester before 1179, letters of King John to the bishop of Bayeux, sent in March 1202 and preserved only in a Tewkesbury cartulary, record actions over the advowson of the church of Ecrammeville, apparently involving an attempt by the Norman baron, William Infans, to subvert procedures in the Norman courts by bringing an action of 'ultima presentatione' without royal writ and before justices who had not been appointed by the king.[349] As an illustration of the 'slow death' of Anglo-Norman England, and of the tenacity with which not only Norman religious institutions, but Anglo-Norman families in England continued to maintain their cross-Channel connections after 1204, I conclude this particular section of my sample with two transcripts, from the evidences of the Bussy family today divided between the Northamptonshire Record Office and the

---

[344] Noticed by Stapleton in *MRSN*, ii, p.cci from its printing by G.–A. de la Roque, *L'Histoire généalogique de la maison de Harcourt*, 4 vols (Paris 1662), iv, 91, whence *CP*, iv, 315–16n.; *Charters of the Redvers Family and the Earldom of Devon 1090–1217*, ed. R. Bearman, Devon and Cornwall Record Society n.s. xxxvii (1994), 201–2 no.37, and cf. 202–3 no.38.

[345] Below appendix nos 41–2.

[346] Below appendix no.43.

[347] Below appendix no.44.

[348] Below appendix no.45.

[349] Below appendix no.46.

British Library, demonstrating that, as late as 1232, the Lincolnshire knight, Lambert de Bussy, was seeking a place for himself and his parents amongst the benefactors commemorated in the martyrology of the canons of Notre-Dame-de-Voeu near Cherbourg. From a similar date, or slightly earlier, a charter of the abbot of Valmont, today preserved at Eton College, reveals Norman monks not only extending spiritual benefits but dispatching relics of the saints to encourage devotion to an English daughter house.[350]

All of these documents survive because they were kept with the archives of particular English families or estates. As a result, without ever having passed through the Public Records, they were either deposited in English local record offices in the twentieth century, or were sold, ultimately to the British Library, that great mopper-up of historical evidences. On a similar note, the next portion of our collection, a series of more than a dozen deeds, today in the British Library, ranging in date from the mid-twelfth century to the 1290s and for the most part relating to the English estates of the nunnery of La Chaise-Dieu, a dependency of Fontevraud, survived the Middle Ages in English custody, as a result of the arrangements made by the nuns of La Chaise-Dieu, after 1243, by which their English revenues were at first farmed to their fellow Fontevraudists at Nuneaton in return for an annual pension, in 1291 being definitively sold to Nuneaton Priory.[351] It was as part of the muniments of Nuneaton Priory that these charters, together with an isolated charter of the Norman abbey of Cormeilles, were passed down to the post-Reformation landowners who came into possession of the priory site, and thereafter, as recently as 1912, into the custody of the British Library.[352] The collection of charters for La Chaise-Dieu is all the more valuable for the fact that the muniments of the house itself, in Normandy, failed in most cases to survive the French Revolution, so that today only a tiny handful of the charters preserved in the British Library have left any trace amongst the priory's surviving inventories, now in the archives départementales at Evreux.[353]

By contrast to such collections of deeds which have for centuries been in English custody, as I have already indicated, some of the richest of the collections of Norman evidences today in England result not from medieval estate management or the survival of family archives in English collections, but from the collecting activities of eighteenth and nineteenth-century antiquaries, who brought to England either copies or originals of documents in many cases no longer to be found amongst the Norman archives in which they were originally housed. We have seen here the important role played by Léchaudé d'Anisy as a collector and copier of

---

[350] Below appendix nos 47–9.

[351] Below appendix nos 50–62, esp. nos 60, 62 for the arrangements with Nuneaton.

[352] For the Cormeilles charter, see below appendix no.63. All of these charters were acquired by the BL in 1902 together with the muniments of the Aston family of Aston Hall in Birmingham, now BL Additional Charters 47380–53115.

[353] Cf. below nos 57–9, the only three of these deeds for which evidence survives amongst the fragmentary records now at Evreux.

documents. The richest of Léchaudé's collections of transcripts, his so-called 'Cartulaire de Basse-Normandie', is best experienced in the original, by ordering it up in the search room of The National Archives at Kew. There is a great deal in Léchaudé's 'Cartulaire' that was not abstracted in J.H. Round's *Calendar of Documents Preserved in France*, and which has left little or no trace in the French archives in which Léchaudé himself worked. As a foretaste of some of the riches which Léchaudé's transcripts have yet to disclose, I have printed below a charter of Henry II for the abbey of Longues, copied by Léchaudé from what he considered to be his own collection, most likely from evidences 'abstracted' from the departmental archives at Caen, some of which would have vanished without trace had they not been copied into Léchaudé 's 'Cartulaire'.[354]

Léchaudé, like others of the scholar collectors, was not averse to the removal or purchase of documents that by rights had been deposited in French public collections after the Revolution of 1789. We have seen already that Léchaudé was only one of these collectors. Others who were particularly active included the Abbé de la Rue, J.H. Wiffen, Sir Thomas Phillipps and, in some ways the hero of our story, Thomas Stapleton. Of the evidences preserved by such means, I have begun my selection (and once again, it is very much a selection rather than an attempt at anything more comprehensive) with one of the dozen charters from Lower Normandy that entered the British Library as a result of the collecting activities of J.H. Wiffen in 1832. This particular charter from Wiffen's cache – a grant by Philippa de Rosel to the canons of Ardenne – preserves vital information on the membership of the Exchequer court at Caen in 1176.[355] It can be supplemented by two closely associated charters granted by the same Philippa, both of them still in the Archives de Calvados, though the second of them at one time removed thence to what Léchaudé chose to regard as his own private collection, preserving details of the renewal of the gift of 1176 before the Exchequer at Caen in the first year of the reign of King John, once again with valuable details of the Exchequer officials in attendance.[356] The three versions of our charter for Ardenne are followed by a charter for the nuns of Mortain, now amongst the papers of John Gage Rokewode in the Cambridge University Library, in all probability passed on to Gage by Léchaudé d'Anisy, the first discoverer of the Mortain charters, during one or other of the visits that Gage and Thomas Stapleton paid to Normandy in the 1830s.[357] Simple theft explains the presence in

---

[354] Below appendix no.64.
[355] Below appendix no.65, part of a small collection of charters for the Norman houses of La Trinité at Caen, Montmorel, St-Sauveur-le-Vicomte, Aunay, Fontenay and Mont-St-Michel now BL mss. Additional Charters 15278–89, also including fragments of a cartulary for Montebourg (BL ms. Additional Charter 15288, whence Stein no.2525). All of these charters were acquired by the British Museum, 13 October 1860, by purchase from Mrs Wiffen, ultimately from the antiquary and historian of the Russell family, J.H. Wiffen. See here N. Vincent, 'A Collection of Early Norman Charters in the British Library: The Case of Jeremiah Holmes Wiffen', *Cahiers Léopold Delisle*, liii fasc.1–2 (2004), 21–45.
[356] Below appendix nos 66–7.
[357] Below appendix no.68.

the British Library of two extensive archiepiscopal confirmations of the possessions of the monks of Foucarmont, apparently 'abstracted' from the main series of the abbey's muniments which, from the 1790s onwards, were rightfully deposited in the archives départementales at Rouen. The second of these very long charters, issued by archbishop Walter at Rouen in April 1204, supplies a poignant reminder of the way in which former Anglo-Norman courtiers, in this case King Henry II's former seal-keeper, Walter of Coutances, found themselves in 1204 witnesses to a permanent collapse of the old Anglo-Norman realm.[358]

Turning now to Thomas Stapleton's own collection of Norman charters, I have already charted the means by which Stapleton's extensive collection of nearly 200 charters was dispersed from Carlton Towers after 1920, the bulk of them coming to rest in the John Rylands Library at Manchester. Most of these Rylands charters are well calendared in the published catalogue.[359] I have nonetheless printed below two of the Stapleton deeds now in Manchester, one as an example of a charter issued by the prominent Norman baron Robert de Marmion, concerning estates in both England and Normandy, the other for its references to the capture of Arthur of Brittany in 1202, to claims to hold land in Caen by grant of Henry II, and most significantly to the 'royal rolls' in which settlements made before the Norman Exchequer were already being recorded.[360] These are followed by three of the twenty or so Stapleton charters now in the British Library, two of them chosen because of their references to the Norman Exchequer at Caen, both before and after 1204.[361] Finally, and as a reminder that by no means all of the Stapleton charters sold at the Carlton Towers sale of 1920 have since entered public collections, I have concluded this selection with a Stapleton charter, today known only from the copy made of it in the nineteenth century by Léon Maître, which once again emphasises the degree to which inquests and returns to the crown were a standard part of administration in Normandy before 1204, in this instance with letters to King John from the abbot of St-André-en-Gouffern relating to the patronage of churches belonging to the nuns of La Trinité at Caen.[362] Of the 76 charters presented here, only thirteen have previously appeared in print.[363]

---

[358] Below appendix nos 69–70, and cf. above p.79.
[359] Above p.83.
[360] Below appendix nos 71–2.
[361] Below appendix nos 73–5.
[362] Below appendix no.76.
[363] Below appendix nos 2–4, 6, 26, 35, 39, 46, 55, 57, 64–5, 71.

4. THE FRENCH CHARTERS OF CANTERBURY CATHEDRAL

Having dealt with these miscellaneous Norman evidences surviving in English collections, it remains to assess the richest group of French charters to have survived in any English archive from the Middle Ages through to the present day. Although long in the public domain, this collection of documents, from Canterbury Cathedral, has not received the attention that is its due. To date, only a small number of the Canterbury charters have been published. Here, whilst I do not claim to have edited all of the French or Norman charters surviving in the Canterbury Cathedral Archives, I have attempted a more comprehensive survey than is possible for the miscellaneous Norman evidences scattered across other English archives.

Ever since the sixth century and the arrival of St Augustine in England, the church of Canterbury had enjoyed close contacts with northern France.[364] Canterbury's geographical proximity to the straits of Dover, combined with the regular traffic between its religious communities and the papacy in Rome, ensured that the cathedral, and its archbishops and monks, early established links with the religious of northern France, in particular with the Benedictine abbey of St-Bertin at St-Omer.[365] The evidences presented below commence in the 1090s, within thirty years of the Norman conquest of England, with grants of immunity from toll and custom from the counts of Boulogne and Flanders, renewed at regular intervals throughout the

---

[364] For highlights amongst a very extensive literature, see the chapters by Stéphane Lebecq and Ian Wood in *St Augustine and the Conversion of England*, ed. R. Gameson (Stroud 1999), 50–82; W. Levison, *England and the Continent in the Eighth Century* (Oxford 1946); V. Ortenberg, *The English Church and the Continent in the Tenth and Eleventh Centuries* (Oxford 1992). For assistance in the writing of this section, I am indebted to David Crouch, Elisabeth Lalou, Jean-François Nieus, Daniel Power and Cressida Williams.

[365] By the 980s, at the latest, the archbps of Canterbury were accustomed to stay at St-Bertin's whilst journeying to and from Rome to receive their pallium: N. Brooks, *The Early History of the Church of Canterbury* (Leicester 1984), 279; Ortenberg, *English Church*, 26. For a miracle at St-Bertin's supposedly inspired by an archbp of Canterbury who had stopped there on his return from the papal curia and who had heard of the chanting of the psalms in the Holy Land beginning with the letters MARIA see BL ms. Additional 15723 fo.85r, also in Bnf ms. Latin 2040 fo.146r, whence Bnf ms. Baluze 69 fo.40bis r–v, briefly listed by A. Poncelet, 'Miraculorum B.V. Mariae … index', *Analecta Bollandiana*, xxi (1902), 329 no.1352. For attempts to supply a date for this story to the time of bp Andrew of Arras (1161–1173), see H.L.D. Ward and J.A. Herbert, *Catalogue of Romances in the Department of Manuscripts the British Museum*, 3 vols (London 1883–1910), ii, 632–3 no.30. However, the bp of Arras mentioned in the story is perhaps better identified as Peter (1184–1203), formerly abbot of Pontigny and later of Cîteaux (cf. *GC*, iii, 328–9). As a result, the story could apply to any of the archbps of Canterbury from Thomas Becket to Hubert Walter. For the exile to St Bertin's and to the household of Richard de Gerberoy, bp of Amiens (1204–1210), of monks of Canterbury forced to flee during the Interdict of King John's reign, see, for example, C.R. Cheney, *Innocent III and England* (Stuttgart 1976), 298n.; BL ms. Arundel 68 fo.28r.

twelfth and thirteenth centuries.[366] These immunities were at first applied
to the port of Wissant. As early as the 1170s, however, they were being
extended to the ports of Boulogne and Nieulay, the latter transformed
by the 1190s into the port of Calais.[367] The precise savings here to the
Canterbury monks are impossible to calculate. However, in the early
fourteenth century we do know that the archbishop of Canterbury was
expected to pay the considerable sum of 40 marks to the officers of the
count of Boulogne for a single crossing to and from the port of Wissant.[368]
After the wandering exile in northern France of both archbishop Anselm
(1097–1100 and 1103–6) and archbishop Becket (from 1164 to 1170), an
enormous boost to Canterbury's traffic with the northern French nobility
was supplied by Becket's martyrdom and subsequent canonization. From
the early 1170s onwards, large numbers of foreign pilgrims flocked to
Becket's shrine.[369] In particular, in August 1179, the king of France, Louis
VII, came to Canterbury on pilgrimage to pray for the recovery from illness
of his son, the future King Philip Augustus.

Amongst the gifts which Louis presented to the Canterbury monks, then
in the process of rebuilding their cathedral church, destroyed by fire in
1174, was a grant of an annual rent of 100 measures of wine, set to be
paid from the vineyards of Poissy, just to the west of Paris, itself the future
birthplace of Louis's grandson, Louis IX of France.[370] In 1190, the wine
was reassigned for payment from the vineyards of Triel-sur-Seine, close
to Poissy.[371] To safeguard the passage of this wine down the Seine into
Normandy, and in other cases to commemorate their own pilgrimages to
Canterbury, various of the lords of the French Vexin (the frontier region
dividing Normandy from the Ile-de-France) made grants of their own
to the Canterbury monks, including exemptions from toll at Mantes,
Maisons-Laffitte, Rosny-sur-Seine and Meulan, and an annual rent at
L'Isle-Adam, perhaps in compensation for tolls taken there.[372] Apart from
the counts of Meulan, whose loyalty had long been commanded by the
kings of England, most of these lords fell within the Capetian rather than
the Plantagenet sphere of influence at a time of critical significance in the
history of the Norman frontier. Their semi-independence of either Capetian
or Plantagenet authority is nonetheless signalled by the refusal, in the case
of the lords of Poissy, Rosny-sur-Seine and Mantes, to grant complete
remission from the tolls and customs owing on Canterbury's wine, and
this despite the total exemption in theory commanded by Louis VII and his

---

[366] Below nos 94–9, 110–11, 115–8.

[367] Below nos 97–8.

[368] *Lit. Cant.*, iii, 387–8 no.51.

[369] For the cult of St Thomas on the continent, see the various essays of Raymonde Foreville,
collected in her *Gouvernement et vie de l'église au Moyen-Age* (London 1979).

[370] Below no.77. St Louis was born at Poissy on 25 April 1214.

[371] Below no.79, and cf. no.80 where Louis IX refers, in 1235, to wine also payable from nearby
Chanteloup-les-Vignes.

[372] Below nos 100–102, 105–6.

successors, confirmed in turn by King Henry II of England and his sons, Richard I and John.[373]

Similar exemptions from toll were granted before 1200 by the lords of St-Valery-sur-Somme, Ponthieu and Guînes, and by Walter of Coutances, archbishop of Rouen, for tolls payable at his manor of Les Andelys on the Seine.[374] All told, our evidences are of very great significance for the final years of Plantagenet rule in Normandy, and supply a keen insight into the relations between England and the lords of the Norman frontier. One frontier family, the Montfort lords of Montfort-l'Aumary and counts of Evreux, although signally absent from the lists of those granting exemption from tolls and taxes to Canterbury, can nonetheless be inferred to have adopted a favourable stance to the Canterbury monks, from the grants recorded below from Amaury III and IV, and Mabel countess of Evreux, of rents from a mill at Marlow in Buckinghamshire, grants that once again suggest particular personal devotion to the cult of St Thomas Becket.[375] Most of Becket's devotees in northern France took the Capetian rather than the Plantagenet side in the ensuing period of war and conquest, that culminated in 1204 with the Capetian seizure of Normandy. As this should remind us, although the links commemorated below suggest close association between Canterbury and the lords of northern France, Becket's cult was politically ambiguous. Through their generosity to Canterbury, the French aristocracy was not necessarily demonstrating an attachment to England so much as approval of a saint, Thomas Becket, whose entire career could be read as a condemnation of the tyranny of the Plantagenet kings.[376]

Even after the loss of Normandy in 1204, the Canterbury monks continued to benefit from French patronage, most notably from a grant of further vineyards at St-Brice-sous-Forêt by Richoldis de Groslay, confirmed in 1212 by charter of the bishop of Paris, Peter of Nemours.[377] Thereafter, at regular intervals throughout the thirteenth century, the kings of France and the counts of Guînes and of Boulogne, whose ports lay closest to the natural point of embarkation for Canterbury's overseas trade, renewed the privileges granted by their ancestors.[378] At Amiens in January 1264, for example, Louis IX confirmed his ancestors' grants of the 100 measures of wine from Poissy and Triel, in the midst of his negotiation of a settlement between Henry III of England and the rebel barons, and on the same occasion that he himself received letters from the Canterbury monks promising him special obit celebrations after his death.[379] As this last grant

---

[373] Below nos 100, 109, and cf. nos 77–8, 91–3.

[374] Below nos 103–4, 107–8, 113.

[375] Below nos 119–20.

[376] The classic article here remains that by J.C. Russell, 'The Canonization of Opposition to the King in Angevin England', *Anniversary Essays in Medieval History by Students of Charles Homer Haskins*, ed. C.H. Taylor (New York 1929), 279–90.

[377] Below no.112.

[378] Below nos 80–2, 110–11, 114–18.

[379] Below no.81n.

should remind us, the reward of many of the northern French benefactors whose charters are printed below was inclusion within the confraternity, the prayers, or the post-obit celebrations of the Canterbury monks. The Canterbury obit lists are far from comprehensive. They fail, for example, to notice the obits or confraternity which our charters clearly show had been granted to such figures as the counts of Ponthieu, Guînes or Boulogne.[380] Besides Louis VII of France, whose obit was also celebrated at the rival Canterbury abbey of St Augustine's, no doubt as a result of a visit during Louis' pilgrimage of 1179, the earliest of the thirteenth-century Canterbury obit lists suggests that the monks of Christ Church also commemorated such major French magnates as Henry 'the liberal', count of Champagne (d.1181), or, amongst ecclesiastical dignitaries, Master Simon, chancellor and canon of Rouen (fl. 1180–c.1208), for whom no charter evidence now survives in the Canterbury Cathedral archives.[381] Nonetheless, a direct link between obit celebrations and grants to the Canterbury monks can be made for at least half a dozen of our charters, granted by the kings of France and England, by Thomas de St-Valery and by Mabel countess of Evreux.[382]

Even before 1170, various of the grants recorded here had almost certainly been made in commemoration of pilgrimages to Canterbury, including the very earliest which records that Eustace and Baldwin of Boulogne, before 1096, placed the charter of their grant on the altar of Christ, presumably the high altar of the cathedral church of Christ Church in Canterbury itself.[383] The writing by English scribes of various of the original charters recording later French awards once again suggests charters granted whilst physically present in Canterbury.[384] With the death and canonization of Becket, the connection between penance, pilgrimage and grants to the Canterbury monks became markedly closer, and this despite the fact, so splendidly exposed by Richard Southern, that in Becket's lifetime, the Canterbury monks were far from being Becket's keenest friends or supporters. The longstanding tensions between archbishop and monks were only resolved by the events of December 1170, as the monks discovered that their late archbishop, in life best regarded as a disastrous nuisance, had in death become their chief advocate both in heaven and on earth.[385] Becket's one-time secretary, Herbert of Bosham, describing Louis VII's pilgrimage in 1179, drew specific attention to the appropriateness of Louis' gift of a

---

[380] Below nos 104, 107, 111, 114, all of which do not merely imply spiritual benefits for the donor but employ the language of confraternity, including references to the Canterbury monks as the donors' 'brothers'.

[381] For Louis' commemoration at St Augustine's, see below no.77n. For the obit of 'Henricus comes Trecas' frater noster' celebrated at Canterbury on 17 March, see BL ms. Cotton Nero C ix fo.7v (whence Fleming, 'Christchurch's Sisters and Brothers', 136), not retained in the s.xv/xvi version of the Cathedral's obit list in BL ms. Arundel 68. For Master Simon, see BL ms. Cotton Nero C ix fo.15v, whence Fleming, 'Christchurch's Sisters and Brothers', 145; Spear, *Personnel*, 225–6.

[382] Below nos 77–8, 81, 90–3, 113, 120.

[383] Below no.94.

[384] Below no.98, and cf. no.110n.

[385] R.W. Southern, *The Monks of Canterbury and the Murder of Archbishop Becket*, William Urry Lecture (Canterbury 1985).

golden chalice and of wine with which to fill it, to commemorate not only the red blood of Becket shed in the Cathedral but the red blood of Christ remade daily in the sacrifice of the mass.[386] In reality, although Louis was reputed to have granted the monks a great red ruby – the semi-mythical 'regal', supposed to have grown under a unicorn's horn, at one time to have belonged to the emperor Charlemagne and later to have served in the coronation ring of the kings of France, still amongst the cathedral's most treasured possessions at the time of the Dissolution in the sixteenth century – the wine assigned from the French vineyards at Triel and Poissy seems to have been exclusively white.[387] Whatever red wine was produced there (and one can only speculate as to its quality), was reserved for the kings of France.[388] Be that as it may, several of the grants recorded below seem to have been prompted either by the uneasy consciences of those, such as the courtiers Bernard de St-Valery, Walter of Coutances, and not least the kings themselves, Henry II and Louis VII, who had played a part in the Becket conflict, during the 1160s, or by a desire to emphasise Becket's sacrifice in the political context of opposition to the Plantagenet kings, as, for example, with the renewal of quittance from toll granted by Matthew count of Boulogne, a leading figure in the great rebellion against Henry II after 1173.[389] Other grants, such as those by John count of Ponthieu or Robert count of Meulan, can be directly linked to miracles of the 1170s, worked at Becket's shrine and recorded in the extraordinarily rich collections of such stories maintained by the Canterbury monks.[390]

Canterbury's French evidences were not ignored in the later Middle Ages. Only a few years before the dissolution of the monasteries, in 1514, an inspeximus of various of the French charters was prepared at Canterbury, no doubt in expectation of a renewal of the cathedral's quittances and rights.[391] After the Dissolution, it was the French evidences with their magnificent seals that fell particular victim to the collecting activities of the antiquary, Sir Edward Dering (1598–1644), who plundered far and wide amongst the cathedral muniments.[392] Nonetheless in scholarly terms, these charters were first rediscovered by precisely that generation of nineteenth-century antiquaries whose role in the writing of Anglo-French history we have already considered, beginning in 1861, when a local Kent clergyman,

---

[386] *MTB*, iii, 538–9, with commentary by N. Vincent, *The Holy Blood: King Henry III and the Westminster Blood* Relic (Cambridge 2001), 45–6. Herbert is alone in suggesting that the wine was offered for festivities on the day of the martyr's birth, presumably on Becket's feast day, 29 December.

[387] For the 'regal', first documented in the Icelandic *Thómas Saga Erkibyskups*, ed. E. Magnússon, 2 vols, RS (London 1875–83), i, 475–81, ii, 213–23, still pointed out to Erasmus in the sixteenth century, see S. Blick, 'Reconstructing the Shrine of St Thomas Becket, Canterbury Cathedral', *Art and Architecture of Late Medieval Pilgrimage in Northern Europe and the British Isles*, ed. S. Blick and R. Tekippe (Leiden 2005), 425–6.

[388] Below nos 80, 83.

[389] Below nos 77, 91, 97, 103, 108, and cf. no.107n. for connections between Becket and Baldwin count of Guînes.

[390] Below nos 104–5.

[391] CCA ms. Chartae Antiquae F149, reciting the texts nos 77–82, 88–9 below.

[392] For Dering, see below pp.107-8.

the Rev. Lambert B. Larking, printed a facsimile and brief commentary on one of the Canterbury charters of Philip Augustus. Ironically, Larking took his transcript, not from the muniments of the cathedral itself, but from the Dering collection at Surrenden. In 1861, the year of its publication, this same charter of Philip Augustus was sold by the Dering family at public auction for £2 10s., to a London book-dealer.[393] It was not for a further fifteen years that the Cathedral's first 'scientific' archivist, Joseph Brigstocke Sheppard (1828–1895), first drew proper attention to the many other surviving charters associated with Canterbury's French wine.[394] Sheppard went on to edit, for the Camden Society and the Rolls Series, a series of volumes dedicated to letters and documents from the fourteenth and fifteenth-century archives of Canterbury Cathedral, and in particular from the great series of priory registers, in which he carried the history of the French wine from the late thirteenth through to the early sixteenth century.[395]

As Sheppard demonstrated, both from the letter evidence and from surviving financial accounts, by the 1270s, the Canterbury monks had abandoned any attempt physically to transport the wine from Triel, Poissy and St-Brice into England. Indeed, it is doubtful whether they had ever made much effort to take physical possession of their wine given the probable inferiority of these vintages (in Sheppard's words 'a liquid so austere and worthless that <in 1876> it can only be obtained outside the barriers').[396] Rather, they employed a local agent at Paris, to sell the wine *in situ* and to ensure the conversion of any profit, minus a commission, into credit payable in England.[397] Sheppard calculated that the 100 measures of wine first granted in 1179 amounted to at least 1600 gallons of wine, suggesting a potential annual profit to the Canterbury monks of as much as £30 or even £50.[398] He also demonstrated that a very large part of the correspondence between the monks and their French agents concerned non-payment of

---

[393] 'Charter of Philip Augustus, King of France, 1180', *Archaeologia Cantiana*, iv (1861), 127–130 and plates, and cf. below no.77 text A².

[394] J.B. Sheppard, 'A Notice of Some MSS. Selected From the Archives of the Dean and Chapter of Canterbury', *Archaeological Journal*, xxxiii (1876), pp.154–63, published in the same year that various of these documents were noticed by Sheppard in his report on the Canterbury muniments in HMC 5th Report (1876), app. 426–62. For Sheppard himself and for his transformation of the study of the archival resources at Canterbury, see N. Ramsay, 'The Cathedral Archives and Library', *A History of Canterbury Cathedral*, ed. P. Collinson and others (Oxford 1995), 396–7.

[395] *Christ Church Letters*, ed. J.B. Sheppard, Camden Society n.s. xix (1877), esp. pp.xxvi–xxix; *Lit. Cant.*, esp. i, pp.lxxvi–lxxxiv, iii, pp.xix–xxiii.

[396] Sheppard, 'Notice of Some MSS.', 163, and see B. Dobson, 'The Monks of Canterbury in the Later Middle Ages, 1220–1540', in *A History of Canterbury Cathedral*, ed. Collinson, 142, for notes on the true source of the wine consumed by the cathedral convent.

[397] *Lit. Cant.*, i, p.lxxx. For various surviving taxation lists of the vineyards at Triel, written in French, with extensive details of tenants and cultivation, from 1280, 1288–9 and 1300, see CCA mss. Chartae Antiquae F104–7, whence briefly noticed in *HMC 5th Report*, appendix p.461.

[398] *Lit. Cant.*, i, pp.lxxxii–iii, and for attempts to calculate profits, mostly from lists of arrears owing, see Ibid., i, 284–7 no.272, 310–11 no.302, 424–7 nos 407–8.

the profits of the wine, and the agents' reluctance to render accounts.[399] As a result, and in consequence of the regular warfare between France and England from 1294 onwards, the average annual profit to Canterbury never amounted to more than £7 or £8.[400] The very earliest of the Canterbury financial accounts, for the profits of the shrine of St Thomas, suggest that the yield from the French wine was always erratic: 72s. in 1214 with a payment of 10d. owing to 'those overseas', presumably the local collectors; £6 6s. 8d. in 1215; 20 marks in 1216, apparently as a double payment 'de duobus annis per manum magistri Willelmi filii Therrici', at a time when the future Louis VIII was in occupation of Canterbury in the midst of civil war; a mere 4 marks in 1219; £7 13s. 4d. 'for our wine in France of one year sold by the chanter'; 117s. 20d. 'per manum Alani thesaurarii' in 1221, whereafter the proceeds seem to have been shifted to another set of accounts.[401] On the outbreak of war between France and England, in 1294, Philip IV of France entirely suspended payment of the wine, relenting, as our letters demonstrate, in 1300, when 200 livres tournois were offered in compensation for the missing years.[402]

Thereafter, Philip's actions were treated as a precedent by the Canterbury monks, who petitioned and obtained renewals of their wine from Charles IV in 1322, seeking similar confirmation from Philip VI in the 1330s and again, in the 1360s, petitioning for arrears calculated on the basis of Philip IV's earlier grant of 200 livres.[403] Even the Hundred Years War did not entirely put paid to the monks' petitions. In 1419, after Agincourt, and again in the 1440s, there were attempts to reactivate the king of France's award, in part brokered by the poet Charles duc of Orléans.[404] In 1478, during a brief thaw in relations, Louis XI was prevailed upon to issue a charter transferring the wine from the vineyards of northern France to those of Bordeaux and Gascony.[405] This southern wine was paid for the

---

[399] *Lit. Cant.*, i, pp.lxxx–ii, and for a series of letters from 1313 to the mid-1320s, for the most part concerning the arrears owed by the priory's local collector, Robert de Longjumeau, see CCA mss. Chartae Antiquae F141/i–viii; F143/i–5; F159–62. For letters in similar terms, from the 1320s onwards, for the most part concerning arrears and delays in account, see *Lit. Cant.*, i, nos 206, 272, 281, 302, 338, 367, 386, 407–8, 431, 439, 447, ii, nos 516–17, 534–5, 734–5.

[400] *Lit. Cant.*, i, p.lxxxi.

[401] CCA ms. MA1 fos. 55r, 57r–v, 63r, 64v, 66r. For Louis VIII's relations with the Canterbury monks during the civil war of 1216–17, see *The Letters and Charters of Cardinal Guala Bicchieri Papal Legate in England 1216–1218*, ed. N. Vincent, Canterbury and York Society lxxxiii (1996), 10–11 no.11.

[402] Below nos 83–7.

[403] Below no.88; *Lit. Cant.*, i, nos 67–71, 161–2, ii, nos 506–8, 924–5.

[404] *Lit. Cant.*, iii, pp.xix–xx, 138 no.996, 189–90 nos 1030–1; R. Foreville, 'Charles d'Orléans et le "vin de Saint Thomas"', *Cahiers d'Histoire et de Folklore*, i (Dol 1955), 22–32, reprinted in Foreville, *Thomas Becket dans la tradition historique et hagiographique* (London 1981), ch.12. The priory's appointment of Thomas Feelde, doctor of divinity and dean of Hereford, and of John Lamgedon, doctor of theology, to act as proctors in the receipt of the French wine and in any ensuing negotiations, 24 March 1419, is now CCA ms. Chartae Antiquae F144.

[405] Below no.89; *Lit. Cant.*, iii, pp.xx–xxi, with an extensive narrative at pp.292–4 no.1085 and cf. 300–1 no.1089; *Christ Church Letters*, ed. Sheppard, 33–5 nos 30–1, 37–8 no.34, this last including a request from Louis XI for a token of St Thomas to wear in his hat.

next four or five years.[406] As late as 1498 petitions were being addressed by the monks to Charles VIII, and in 1514 the monks were still preparing schedules of their French evidences.[407] But the last practical evidence we have for the wine's dispatch comes in the early 1480s.[408] Nonetheless, for more than three centuries, and long after King John's loss of Normandy in 1204, the 'French wine' represented a tangible reminder of Canterbury's links to the French monarchy and of the abiding links between England and northern France.

Besides the charters relating to the French wine, the taxation exemptions and the charters of the counts of Evreux all printed below, the Canterbury archive continues to boast other, diverse French evidences. Some of these I have dealt with elsewhere: the acquisition, shortly after 1170, for example, of houses in and around Lyons in south-eastern France, still being claimed by the Canterbury monks as late as the 1380s; the right to mercantile privileges at La Rochelle, conferred by Louis VIII of France after 1224; the various confraternity arrangements made between Canterbury and religious communities scattered across northern Europe.[409] Regularly, in the twelfth and thirteenth centuries, French clergy appear in the Canterbury archives, testifying in matters of canon law or issuing inspeximuses of earlier evidence. From the 1170s, for example, we have original letters of Giles bishop of Evreux, surviving in triplicate, addressed to Pope Alexander III and forwarding testimony as to events at the Council of Reims in 1131.[410] From the 1220s and beyond, one might point to a series of inspeximuses of the rights of the archbishops and cathedral church of Rouen in England issued by bishop Richard of Evreux and the abbots of Bec, Jumièges, St-Ouen and Ste-Catherine at Rouen.[411] Various charters in the cathedral collection, relating to the English lands of the counts of Perche, have recently been calendared by Kathleen Thompson.[412] The earliest of the Canterbury letter collections, preserved not as registered copies but to start with as files of original documents now mounted in scrapbooks, contain

---

[406] Below no.89n.

[407] For the petitions of the late 1490s, see CCA mss. Chartae Antiquae F114, F114A, F123, F128.

[408] *Lit. Cant.*, iii, pp.xxii–iii; *Christ Church Letters*, ed. Sheppard, pp.xxvi–xxix, 45–6 no.42; Sheppard, 'Notice of Some MSS.', 159–60.

[409] See here Vincent, 'The English Monasteries and their French Possessions', 221–39.

[410] Printed by H. Wharton, *Anglia Sacra,* 2 vols (London 1691) ii, 'praefatio' pp.v–vi, whence (with detailed commentary) P. Le Brasseur, *Histoire civile et ecclesiastique du comté d'Evreux*, 2 vols (Paris 1722), ii, instr. 4–5, whence Migne, *Patrologia Latinae*, cc, cols.1411–12. Wharton printed the original now BL ms. Cotton Charter XXI.9, still bearing bp Giles' seal. Two further originals, seals now missing, survive in CCA mss. Chartae Antiquae A61 and A62, whence Sheppard in *Lit. Cant.*, iii, 365–7.

[411] CCA mss. Chartae Antiquae C1264, R51–55, and for a sealed original charter of William abbot of Bec (1198 X 1211) relating to land in Dorset, see Ibid. P49.

[412] Ibid. F155, R62, T27, only two of these briefly calendared by K. Thompson, 'Matilda, Countess of the Perche (1171–1210): The Expression of Authority in Name, Style and Seal', *Tabularia*, iii (2003), 84 nos 10–11 (online journal at *http://www.unicaen.fr/mrsh/craham/revue/tabularia*). Another charter of Geoffrey count of Perche from the cathedral archive, granting half a virgate and a mill to Adam de la More, was sold as lot 349 in the Dering sale (Puttick and Simpson, 14 July 1865) to a buyer named 'Wood' for 6s.

extensive correspondence with France, including, for example, petitions from William archbishop of Bourges and John aux Bellesmains, former archbishop of Lyons, to archbishop Hubert Walter, on the eve of the Capetian conquest of 1204, requesting intervention with King John on behalf of the Cistercians of La Grâce-Dieu in the Saintonge.[413] The same source preserves letters of William archbishop of Reims *c*.1190, himself commemorated in the Canterbury obits, addressed to Philip count of Flanders, concerning the will of William de Mandeville, late earl of Essex and a bequest of £20 said to have been made to the Canterbury monks: an interesting document this, not least because it concerns the estate of Earl William whose disposition we have already considered from evidences preserved in The National Archives at Kew.[414] A glance beyond the Canterbury archives to those of the kings of France very quickly reveals that the Archives nationales and the Bibliothèque nationale preserve much that is of relevance to the history of Canterbury's French connections: proof, for example, of the confraternity arrangements promised to the kings of France, and certificates of the discharge of penitential pilgrimages vowed by Frenchmen to the shrine of St Thomas Becket.[415] Rather than attempt a comprehensive edition of such evidences here, I have sought below merely to present the most important of the cathedral's twelfth and thirteenth-century charters directly related to Normandy or northern France.

It remains only to explain the present whereabouts of various of the documents published below. Of our forty-five charters, no less than thirty-five still survive as originals, the other ten being preserved in one, or sometimes more than one, of the cathedral's fourteenth-century cartularies.[416] Of our thirty-five originals, no less than eleven survive in duplicate, and

---

[413] CCA ms. Christ Church Letters II nos 2, 3, both relating to the Cistercian abbey of La Grâce-Dieu (Charente-Maritime, cant. Courçon, com. Benon), the first of these, to be dated after the election of William de Donjeon archbp of Bourges (23 November 1200) and before the death of Hubert Walter (d. 13 July 1205), reading 'Reuerendo in Cristo patri H(uberto) Dei gratia Cantuar' archiepiscopo et totius Angl(ie) prim(ati) W(illelmus) diuina permissione Bituricen' ecclesie minister humilis salutem et sincere dilectionis affectum. Cum dilectus noster W. pro abbatia de Gratia Dei Xancton' diocesis que preter guerrarum incomoda a balliuis domini regis Angl(ie) magna dampna sustinuit ad regiam serenitatem accedat, rogamus paternitatem vestram quatinus erga predictam abbatiam que admodum disolata est et afflicta conpassionis affectum habentes, dominum regem si placet pietatis intuitu velitis inducere ut eidem abbatie restitutionem aliquam faciat de amissis cum balliui ipsius multa de rebus monasterii habuerint sicut litor presentium vobis exponere poterit diligenter'. For John aux Bellesmains, still living (in retirement at Cîteaux) in 1200, see *Letters of Cardinal Guala*, ed. Vincent, 33–4 no.43.

[414] Ibid. Christ Church Letters II no.224, whence printed by A.L. Poole in *HMC Various Collections*, i (1901), 233, and see below appendix no.92. For the Canterbury celebration of the obit of William archbp of Reims (1175 – d. 7 September 1202), himself a son of Theobald count of Champagne, see BL ms. Nero C ix fo.11r, whence Fleming, 'Christchurch's Sisters and Brothers', 140.

[415] See here, below no.81n., and for the presentation of letters testimonial (not recited) from the penitentiary of Canterbury in 1282, testifying that John de Welu, knight, had duly discharged a pilgrimage to Canterbury on the octaves of the feast of the Trinity, having earlier received similar letters from King Charles of Sicily relating to a pilgrimage to Rome, see AN X1a/2 (Olim II) fo.60r, whence *Actes du Parlement de Paris*, ed. E. Boutaric, 2 vols (Paris 1863–7), i, 230 no.2408.

[416] Below nos 83–7, 90, 114, 116, 118, 121 are known only from cartulary copies.

one in triplicate.[417] This is an extraordinary rate of survival for an English medieval archive: testimony first of all to the beneficent neglect of these documents after the 1530s and thereafter to the care lavished upon them since their rediscovery in the 1860s. Nonetheless, a significant number of our originals are no longer to be found at Canterbury itself but in the British Library in London. An explanation here is supplied by the collecting activities of Sir Edward Dering of Surrenden, 1st Baronet (1598–1644) and antiquary, whose pillage of the Canterbury archives is well known.[418] No less than 42 Anglo-Saxon charters, most of them from Canterbury sources, passed by uncertain means from the Cathedral to Dering and thence, from Dering's descendants, before December 1766, into the great collection of charters and manuscripts assembled by Thomas Astle (1735–1803), chief clerk of the Tower Record Office from 1782.[419] Astle's Saxon charters, together with Canterbury charters of kings Henry I and II, mostly acquired from a Canterbury source via Dering, ultimately came to the British Museum Library in 1883 as BL Stowe Charters 1–44.[420] Various other charters, including Canterbury documents acquired by Dering and thence by Astle, were copied when in Astle's possession in continuation of the 'Aspilogia' of John Anstis (1708–1754): an attempt to assemble facsimiles of early writing and seals, now BL mss. Stowe 665–6. By means unknown, but distinct from the Dering/Astle charters sold to the Grenville family and thence to the British Museum as Stowe manuscripts, this particular group of Canterbury originals, including nos 105–6, 110 and 111 below, all of them notable for their especially fine heraldic seals, passed from Astle into the collection of Lord Frederick Campbell (1729–1816), second son of the 4th Duke of Argyll, overseer of Scottish records and of the building of the Edinburgh General Register House, whose own impressive collection of charters was presented to the British Museum Library in 1814.[421] Others of the French charters looted by Dering had either already escaped from Canterbury, via Dering, into the collections of Sir Robert Cotton (below no.81, and cf. no.97 version A[2]), in one case certainly before the Cotton fire of 1731, or remained in the possession of the Dering family at Surrenden, only entering the British Museum in the 1860s, as the result of further sales from the Dering collections at Surrenden in 1811, 1861 and 1865 (nos 78, 81–2, 88, 98).[422] Even then, yet others of our charters, in circulation in

---

[417] Below nos 77–8, 81, 89, 100, 103 (triplicate), 104–8, 112, and cf. no.97 which apparently survived in duplicate into relatively recent times.

[418] For Dering, see *ODNB*; C.E. Wright, 'Sir Edward Dering: A Seventeenth-Century Antiquary and His "Saxon" Charters', *The Early Cultures of North-West Europe*, ed. C. Fox and B. Dickins (Cambridge 1950), 379–80, 386; Ramsay, 'The Cathedral Archives and Library', 371–93, and cf. G.R.C. Davis, *Medieval Cartularies of Great Britain* (London 1958), 21 no.168 (leaves from the Canterbury Register/cartulary E, now BL ms. Additional 25109 as a result of Dering's collecting), also noting at nos 168–9 Dering's own transcripts from Canterbury Registers A and E.

[419] For Astle's acquisition of Dering's 'Saxon' charters, apparently before December 1866, see BL ms. Stowe 1085 fo.91v (p.84); Wright, 'Sir Edward Dering', 380–1, 384–5.

[420] Wright, 'Sir Edward Dering', 380–2.

[421] Today BL mss. Lord Frederick Campbell Charters.

[422] For descriptions of some of the Surrenden charters, still in Dering family possession in the 1850s, and for what remains the most detailed account of Sir Edward Dering's collecting

the seventeenth century as sealed originals, remain untraced.[423] A detached impression of the seal of Robert count of Boulogne, sold at the Dering sale in July 1861, might suggest that an original of one or other of the charters of Count Robert not now known to survive (below nos 116, 118), was once in Dering's possession.[424]

Of the forty-five Canterbury charters edited below, only ten have previously been printed in full, often from copies rather than from the surviving originals. Ten have been printed in part or in calendar form, leaving twenty-five of our documents previously unpublished.

---

activities, see L.B. L(arking), 'On the Surrenden Charters', *Archaeologia Cantiana*, i (1858), 50–65. For the more important of his Saxon manuscripts, see Wright, 'Sir Edward Dering', at pp.378–9 noting the purchase of BL mss. Additional Charters 15480–2 (below nos 78, 82, 88) from the sale at Puttick and Co. of 13 July 1861, further sales, also at Puttick and Simpson's, on 4–7 February 1863 (no.98, although apparently resold later that year) and 13–15 July 1865 (below no.89). Another of the charters below (no.81 version A²), seems already to have left Surrenden as the result of an earlier, and much less extensive sale at King and Lochée, of 3 December 1811 (noted by Wright, 'Sir Edward Dering', p.378n.), being recovered at some point and resold in the Dering sale of 15 July 1865. Dering had earlier, in 1623 and 1630 (Wright, p.380ff) given others of his charters to Sir Robert Cotton, which might explain the survival of no.81 below in the Cotton Library. For another early Christ Church charter, by the 1640s in the hands of the antiquary William Le Neve, see *Hatton's Seals*, 198 no.287. One of the more important of the Christ Church charters to have passed from Dering to Cotton was the sealed bilingual writ of Odo bp of Bayeux, 1071 X 1082 (*Hatton's Seals*, 301–2 no.431 and plate viii), now surviving only in mutilated condition as BL ms. Cotton Charter XVI.31. Another original writ of Odo still survives, unsealed, in the Canterbury Archives ms. Chartae Antiquae S246. Dering's dispersal of the archive perhaps explains the survival of numerous Canterbury charters in the Hatton Wood Collection now in the archives of the University of Keele.

[423] Cf. below no.121, of which a drawing was made by Roger Dodsworth in the 1620s or 30s.

[424] See here the BL's marked-up copy of the sale catalogue: *Catalogue of an Extraordinary Collection of Rare and Interesting Books ... from the famous Surrenden Collection of Sir Edward Dering*, Puttick and Simpson (10–13 July 1861) 4th day, lot no.1113, sold to the dealer Boone for £2 14s. It was from this same sale, lot nos 936–8, that three of the French royal charters, once in Dering's possession, passed to the British Museum/British Library, below nos 78, 82, 88.

APPENDIX OF CHARTERS

1. *Notification by King Henry I of his grant to the abbey of La Trinité(-du-Mont) at Rouen of the churches of Neufchâtel-en-Bray (Seine-Maritime), together with tithes from rents, toll, mills and the fair of the vill.*　　　　　　　　　　　　　Rouen [August 1133 X 1135]

B = TNA C 64/15 (Norman Roll 8 Henry V part 3) m.16, in an inspeximus, 20 February 1421. C = Bnf ms. Moreau 631 fo.61r–v, copy from B by Bréquigny, s.xviii. D = St-Pierre-de-Semilly, Marquis de Mathan ms. Lenoir 69 p.439, partial copy after a copy by Bréquigny from B, s.xviii.

To be dated after the consecration of Adelulf as bp of Carlisle (6 August 1133). The inspeximus of 1421 also recites a charter of Henry II confirming the present award (*Acta Henry II*, no.2254, not in Delisle, *Recueil*). For the abbey's churches of St-Jacques and Notre-Dame at Neufchâtel, see *Pouillés Rouen*, 38–9. Amongst the witnesses, note the appearance of Richard de Beaufou (Calvados, cant. Cambremer), archdeacon of Suffolk, nominated bp of Avranches in 1134, consecrated 1135 (Spear, *Personnel*, 4), here apparently distinguished from the datary, another Richard de Beaufou, described as (the king's) chaplain.

H(enricus) rex Anglie archiepiscopo Roth', episcopis, abb(atibus), com(itibus), iustic(iis), vic(ecomitibus), baron(ibus) et omnibus fidelibus suis totius Norm(annie) salutem. Sciatis quod[a] dedi et concessi Deo et ecclesie sancte Trinit(atis) de Monte Roth' et abbati et monach(is) in ea Deo familiantibus in elemosin(am) perpetuam ecclesias meas de Drincurt et totam decimam meam de censu ville et <de> teloneo et molend(inis) et feria et omnibus aliis redditibus meis qui ad me pertinent et cum decimis et beneficiis burgensium in villa et extra et cum omnibus rebus que ad ipsas ecclesias pertinuerint, et volo et precipio quod ecclesia sancte Trinitatis et abbas et monachi ea bene et in pace et libere possideant nunc et in sempiternum tanquam propriam elimosinam meam. T(estibus) Audino episcopo Ebroic' et Adel(wulfo) episcopo Carl' et Roberto de Sigillo et Rogero archid(iacono) et Ric(ardo) de Bellef' archid(iacono) et Rob(erto) de Ver, Rob(erto) de Curci et Roscelino de Brioldic' apud Roth' per Ric(ardum) de Bellafago capell(anum).

[a] quia B, quod *supplied*

2. *Notification by King John of his confirmation of the possessions and liberties of the abbey of Beaubec.* Montfort, 26 October 1201

A= Rouen AD Seine-Maritime 2H464. Endorsed: *Iohannes rex Angl(ie) de confirmatione om(n)i(um) possess(ionum) nostrarum et omnibus libertatibus quas* ... (s.xiii); *carta iiii. reg(um)* (s.xiv); various illegible or post medieval endorsements. Approx. 188 × 89 + 27mm. Sealed *sur double queue*, single slit, tag and seal impression missing. Foot damaged, with some letters missing. B = Ibid., in an original inspeximus by Henry V of England, 10 January 1421. C = TNA C 64/15 (Norman Roll 8 Henry V part 3) m.12, the enrolment of B, 10 January 1421. D = Rouen AD Seine-Maritime G851 (Coutumier de Dieppe) fo.58r–v, copy made in 1396. E = AN ms. JJ46 (Register of Philip IV) fo.38r–v no.38, in an inspeximus by Philip IV of France, June 1311. F = A lost inspeximus by Charles VI of France dated 1400/1401, formerly in the AD at Rouen. G = AN ms. JJ155 (Register of Charles VI) fo.226r no.376, the registered copy of the inspeximus F, s.xv in. G = Dieppe, Bibliothèque Municipale ms.45 fos.102v–103r, copy from D, s.xvii. H = Bnf ms. Moreau 631 fos.10r–11r, copy from C by Bréquigny, s.xviii.

Printed (from F) Gurney, *House of Gurney*, i, 109–10 no.6; (from C) *Monasticon*, vi, 1069; (calendar from E) *Registres du Trésor des Chartes: Tome 1, règne de Philippe le Bel*, ed. R. Fawtier and others (Paris 1958), 250 no.1312.

The inspeximus of 1421 also recites a charter of Henry I given at Clarendon, but with title as Henry II (*Regesta*, ii, no.1270, and by mistake for Henry II, Delisle, *Recueil*, no.314). For a charter of Henry II, 1172 X 1189, similar to the present confirmation, in which the Irish estate at 'Gilleberan' is also confirmed, see *Acta Henry II*, no.167 (Delisle, *Recueil*, no.477). For the identity of 'Killekeran' or 'Gillekeran', perhaps Castlekeeran co. Meath, see *The Irish Pipe Roll of 14 John, 1211–1212*, ed. O. Davies and D.B. Quinn, Ulster Journal of Archaeology iv, supplement (1941), 40–1n; below nos 23–5. For various of the Norman place names, see S. Deck, 'Le temporel de l'abbaye cistercienne de Beaubec', *Annales de Normandie*, xxiv (1974), 131–56, 221–45. The English lands specified here lay at Aston on Carrant (in Ashchurch, Gloucestershire) and Ashton under Hill (Worcestershire), for which see SC 6/1125/15; *VCH Gloucestershire*, viii, 180, 246; *Calendar of Inquisitions Miscellaneous*, i (London 1916), 145 no.440. The textual variants are noted below to provide some indication of the exactitude with which the inspeximus by Henry V was copied from the original award, and in turn of how accurately the original inspeximus is itself copied into the Norman chancery roll.

I(ohannes) Dei gratia rex Angl(ie), dominus Hibern(ie), dux Norm(annie), Aquit(anie) et comes And(egauie) omnibus ad quos presens scriptum peruenerit salutem. Sciatis nos pro salute anime nostre et animarum antecessorum et successorum nostrorum concessisse et confirmasse Deo et ecclesie de Belbec et monach(is) ibidem Deo seruientibus nemus in quo abbatia fundata est cum omni dominico circa idem nemus et de Mesnilboschet, de Spineto, de Balleteria, de Morimont, de Cantecoc, de Torniaco, de Corcell'[a], de Botell'[b], de Boscoputeorum, de Hadencort[c], de Antiz[d], de Mureaumont, de Sancto Oyno, de Haia Gonnor, de Gillekeran', de Eston' et de Ayston' loca, domos, terras, nemora, vineas, prata, pascua, aquas, vias et semitas cum omnibus pertinentiis suis et omnia maneria, tenementa, terras, villas, redditus, redeuancias, decimas, patronatus ecclesiarum, molendina, viuaria, piscarias, gurgites, salinas, pasturagia, pasnagia, usagia et omnes res alias et possessiones quascumque acquisierunt et in futurum iustis modis acquirere poterunt in villis, burgis, portubus, castris, ciuitatibus et in cunctis aliis locis. Quare volumus et firmiter precipimus quod omnia et singula predicta habeant et per quoscumque voluerint bene et in pace possideant in puram et perpetuam elemosinam, liberam penitus et quietam ab omnibus rebus pertinentibus ad regiam magestatem. Damus etiam eis et omnibus hominibus et seruientibus ipsorum presentibus et futuris per terram et per aquam vend<endo, emendo et tran>sportando[e] omnes libertates quas dare possumus. T(estibus) Garin(o) de Glap' sen(escallo) Norm(annie), Hub(erto) de Burgo camerar(io) nostro, Steph<ano de Longocampo apud M>ont(em)fortem[e] vicesima sexta die Oct(obris) anno regni nostri tercio.

[a] Corcellis BC [b] Botellis BC [c] Hadencourt BC [d] Autis BC [e] *letters in bracke*ts ◇ *illegible* A, *supplied from* BC

3. Notification by King John of his grant to the men of Falaise of quittance from passage, pontage, péage and lestage throughout his lands save at London.   Argentan, 11 August 1202

B = TNA C 64/15 (Norman Roll 8 Henry V part 3) m.21, in an inspeximus, 12 January 1421. C = Caen AD Calvados 386 Edt 1, copied into the 'Cartulaire de la ville de Falaise' fo.6r, 1358. D = Ibid. copy from B by Bréquigny, 17 June 1786. E = Ibid., copy from an unidentified source, s.xvii/xviii. F = Ibid., copy from ?D, shown to Augustine Thierry, s.xix. G = Ibid., copy, s.xix. H = Bnf ms. Moreau 673 fos.53v–54r, copy from B by Bréquigny, s.xviii. J = St-Pierre-de-Semilly, Marquis de Mathan ms. Lenoir 69 pp.337–8, copy by Lenoir after a copy by Bréquigny from B, s.xviii. K = Ibid. Lenoir 73 p.614, copy as in J, s.xviii.

Printed (from a lost register of the Chambre des Comptes) G.–A. de la Roque, *Histoire généalogique de la maison de Harcourt*, 4 vols (Paris 1662), iv, 1414–15, whence P.G. Langevin, *Recherches historiques sur Falaise* (Falaise 1814), 165–6n.; (briefly noticed) F. Galeron, *Statistique de l'arrondissement de Falaise*, 3 vols (Falaise 1826–9), i, 56; P. German, *Histoire de Falaise* (Condé-sur-Noireau 1993), 130.

The inspeximus further recites charters of Philip Augustus granting the leper house of Falaise a fair of seven days, May 1204 (*Actes Philippe Auguste*, ii, 370 no.791); Philip Augustus granting quittance to the men of Falaise from passage, pontage etc, given at Falaise, 1204 (*Actes Philippe Auguste*, ii, 368–9 no.790); Louis (IX) addressed to the bailli of Caen, granting the paupers of the Domus Dei at Falaise timber from the forest of Canivet (Calvados), April 1256; John Marshal lord of Argentan, son of Henry Marshal, granting quittance to the men of Falaise from passage, pontage etc at Argentan n.d.; Philip (III) on the rights to grain of the Domus Dei at Falaise, August 1280, these last three apparently unpublished. For letters patent sent to the newly appointed constable of Falaise in February 1203, commanding him to respect the commune established by the men of the town, see *RLP*, 24, 24b, whence Langevin, *Recherches historiques sur Falaise*, 165. Amongst the town charters of Falaise now deposited at Caen (AD Calvados 386 Edt 1–2) the earliest surviving original is a charter of Charles IV of December 1324.

Iohannes Dei gratia rex Anglie, dominus Hibern(ie), dux Normannie, Acquitanie[a], comes And(egauie) archiepiscopis, episcopis, abbatibus, comitibus, baronibus, iusticiar(iis)[b], vic(ecomitibus), prepositis et omnibus balliuis[c] et fidelibus suis salutem. Sciatis nos dedisse et concessisse et hac carta nostra confirmasse burgensibus nostris de Falesia[d] et heredibus suis quietanciam per totam terram nostram excepta ciuitate London' de passagio, pontagio[e], paagio et lestagio et omni alia consuetudine ad nos pertinente de omnibus rebus et mercandisis[f] suis, et prohibemus ne quis eos aut homines eorum contra hanc concessionem nostram in aliquo vexet vel disturbet super decem librarum forisfacturam. T(estibus) W(illelmo) com(ite) Arundell', comite Willelmo Marescallo[g], Rad(ulfo) Tax'[h] sen(escallo) Norm(annie), Rob(erto) de Harecort[j], Gir(ardo) de Forniuall', Petro de Pratell', Gileb(erto) de Aquila, Ric(ardo) de Reueriis. Dat' per manum Hugonis de Well' apud Argenthoem'[k] xi. die Augusti anno regni nostri quarto.

[a] Aquit(anie) C [b] iustic(iis) C [c] bailliois C [d] Fal'ia C [e] C *inserts* et
[f] markandisis C [g] Maresc' C [h] Taxone C [j] Harecourt C [k] Argent' C

4. Notification by King John of his grant to the lepers of Le Bois-Halbout (Calvados, cant. Thury-Harcourt, com. Cesny-Bois-Halbout) and the canons of Notre-Dame du Val (Calvados, cant. Thury-Harcourt, com. St-Omer) of an annual rent of 30 livres in the manor of Ste-Mère-Eglise (Manche) previously held by William (de Ste-Mère-Eglise) bishop of London, in exchange for a moiety of the manor of Maldon (Essex) which the lepers have by gift of Eudo fitz Erneis, granting the land at Maldon to the church of St Paul's London and to Bishop William in return for obit celebrations and prayers for King Henry II and King John.

[September 1202 X May 1203]

B = TNA C 52/26 (Cartae Antiquae Roll BB) no.11, headed *carta episcopi London' de manerio de Measdon'*, rubbed and illegible at the left and right hand sides, s.xiii in.
C = TNA C 52/1 (Cartae Antiquae Roll A) no.9, s.xiii. in.   D = BL ms. Harley 85 fos.18v–19r (325v–326r), copy from B, s.xvii.

Pd (from C) *Cartae Antiquae Rolls 1–10*, ed. L. Landon, PRS n.s. xvii (1939), 3–4 no.9.

For an annual rent of 35 livres 12s. paid to William de Ste-Mère-Eglise, bp of London (1199–1221), for his lifetime and that of his mother, first recorded in the Norman Pipe Roll account for 1184, still being paid in the account for 1203, see *MRSN*, i, 276, ii, 472,

506. The date of the present charter can nonetheless be fixed in the Exchequer years 4 or 5 John on the basis of entries in the English Pipe Roll where an allowance of £10 17d. from Maldon attributed at Michaelmas 1202 to the lepers of Le Bois-Halbout was transferred by Michaelmas 1203 to bp William of London *per breve regis*, the other moiety of the manor being held at this time by Robert fitz Erneis (*PR 4 John*, 258–9; *5 John*, 123, and for Robert fitz Erneis' English lands, see below no.5). In all likelihood, the present charter was originally entered on the Charter Roll 4 John (May 1202–May 1203), now missing. It does not appear on the surviving Charter Roll 5 John, suggesting a further narrowing of the date to the period before May 1203. For the leper hospital at Le Bois–Halbout, placed under the authority of the abbey of Notre-Dame-du-Val, for Eudo fitz Erneis' grants, confirmed *c.*1170 by Robert fitz Erneis his nephew, and for grants made to the lepers before the present charter, by King Richard I in the manor of Ste-Mère-Eglise, 18 March 1190 renewed 5 November 1198, see M. Arnoux, 'Actes de l'abbaye Notre-Dame-du-Val', *Le Pays Bas-Normand: Société d'Art et d'Histoire*, ccxxxvii–viii (2000), 47–53 esp. nos 26a–b, 28; *Book of Fees*, i, 121; Round, *Calendar*, no.1457; Landon, *Itinerary*, 157 no.233. Cf. *English Episcopal Acta 26: London 1189–1228*, ed. D.P. Johnson (Oxford 2003), no.229, where, in 1223, bp Eustace of London assigned an annual payment of 5 marks for the term of his life from his moiety of the manor of Maldon, acquired by bp William, to be spent by the dean and chapter of St Paul's on obit celebrations for kings Henry II and John.

<Iohannes>[a] Dei gratia rex Angl(ie) etc. Sciatis nos dedisse, concessisse et presenti carta confirmasse Deo et sancto Iacobo et leprosis de Bosco Hereboldi et canonicis de Valle ipsos procurantibus pro salute nostra et anima patris nostri et antecessorum nostrorum <triginta libr>atas[b] terre Andeg(auenses) cum pertinentiis suis quas Will(elmus) London' episcopus de nob(is) tenebat in manerio de Sancte Marie Ecclesia assensu et voluntate ipsius episcopi in puram et perpetuam elem(osinam) in escamb(io) medietatis manerii de Mealdon' quam idem leprosi habeb<ant de do>natione Eudonis filii Ernisii. Et h(oc) fecimus ad instantiam et petitionem dictorum leprosorum pro salute nostra et antecessorum nostrorum quia dicta terra de Sancte Marie Ecclesia eis melius sedens fuit et utilior. Dictam autem medietatem manerii de Meal<don' cum pertine>ntiis[b] quam idem leprosi habebant dedimus Deo et ecclesie beati Pauli Lond'[c] et prefato Willelmo Lond'[c] episcopo et successoribus suis in puram et perpetuam elem(osinam) possidendam pro salute nostra et animabus patris nostri et antecessorum nostrorum, et ipse episcopus tant(um) faciet <quod tempore>[b] suo et successorum suorum in cathedrali ecclesia beati Pauli sollempniter[d] celebrabitur anniuersarium patris nostri singulis annis et pro nobis speciales orationes quamdiu vixerimus in ecclesia sua facient, et post decessum nostrum singulis annis anniuersa<rium>[b] nostrum similiter facient celebrari. Quare volumus et firmiter precipimus quod predictus Will(elmus) episcopus Lond'[c] et successores sui et predicti leprosi de Bosco Hereboldi et canonici de Valle ipsos procurantes habeant et teneant in perpetuum omnia predicta <sicut predictum>[b] est bene et in pace, libere et quiete, integre et plenarie et honorifice cum omnibus libertatibus et liberis consuetudinibus ad predictam pertinentibus. His t(estibus): E(ustacio) Elyensi et H(erberto) Saresbir' episcopis.

ᵃ *illegible* B, Henr(icus) D, Iohannes *supplied from* C ᵇ *letters in brackets* <> *illegible* B, *supplied from* C ᶜ London' D ᵈ sollempnitur D

5. *Notification by King John of his grant to Geoffrey fitz Peter, earl of Essex, of the lands of Robert fitz Erneis in England, namely Wells next the Sea, Warham, Massingham (Norfolk), Hatfield Peverel, Debden (Essex) and Hemingby (Lincolnshire), with provision for restitution should Geoffrey or his heirs recover their own lands in Normandy or Robert and his heirs return to the king's allegiance.*
Winchester, 15 September 1208

B = TNA C 52/26 (Cartae Antiquae Roll BB) no.28, s.xiii. C = BL ms. Harley 85 fo.25r–v (332r–v), copy from B, s.xvii.

Not enrolled in the Charter Roll 10 John, which nonetheless records a further grant of land in London to Geoffrey fitz Peter on 11 September 1208 (*Rot. Chart.*, 182, also in *Foedera*, 102). For various of the lands listed here, see *Book of Fees*, i, 169, 284, 388, 615, 619; *CRR*, ii, 24–5, vii, 342; *Red Book*, ii, 610. The present grant is briefly noted from the confirmation to Geoffrey's son (*RLC*, i, 154b), by R. Turner, *Men Raised from the Dust* (Philadelphia 1988), 59. Robert fitz Erneis seems to have been a relatively late defector to the Capetian allegiance, since his allowance of £10 for a moiety of the manor of Maldon (Essex, cf. above no.4n.) was only stopped in the year to Michaelmas 1207 (*PR 8 John*, 227; *9 John*, 90). With the rebellion of Geoffrey fitz Peter's heir, after 1215, there was a real prospect that Robert fitz Erneis might be restored to his English estates. In 1216, at the height of civil war, Robert was still negotiating, via the Templars, for the restoration of these lands (*Rot. Ob.*, 576), and in 1220, following Robert's death, his younger brother William fitz Erneis, restored to various of the family properties in Lincolnshire in 1217, was promised the restoration even of those estates previously granted to Geoffrey fitz Peter and his Mandeville descendants (*RLC*, i, 309b, 321, 442, and cf. *CFR*, i, 283 no.15). The present charter is of significance, not least for clarifying the identity and landholding of the various twelfth-century branches of the Fitz Erneis family, descended from the first Robert fitz Erneis, nephew of Ralph Tesson who had died at the Battle of Hastings and for whose progeny, see L. Musset, 'Actes inédits du XIe siècle: Autour des origines de Saint-Etienne de Fontenay', *Bulletin de la Société des Antiquaires de Normandie*, lvi (1963 for 1961–2), 17–18, 23, 40–1; Fauroux, *Recueil*, 372 no.190; K.S.B. Keats-Rohan, *Domesday Descendants* (Woodbridge 2002), 883. As compensation to Geoffrey fitz Peter for the loss of his own estates in Normandy, including the Mandeville inheritance, it is interesting to compare the present gift with the valuation of £100 that in 1214 Geoffrey's son, Geoffrey de Mandeville, placed upon his family's lost Norman lands: *CRR*, vii, 110–11.

Ioh(anne)s Dei gratia rex Angl(ie) etc. Sciatis nos concessisse et commisisse et hac carta nostra confirmasse Galfr(ido) filio Petri comiti Essex' totam terram quam Robertus filius Ernisii habuit <in>ᵃ Anglia, scilicet Welles et Waraham' et Massingeham' et Hadfeld' Peuerel et Diepedene et Hemingeby cum omnibus pertin(entiis) suis habendam et tenendam sibi et heredibus suis de <nobis et here>dibusᵃ nostris per idem seruicium quod predictus Robertus nob(is) in(de) facere consueuit pro omni seruicio et exactione, ita tamen quod si nos vel heredes nostri reddiderimus predicto Galfr(ido) vel heredibus suis totam terram <cum>ᵇ pertin(entiis) suis que ad eos pertinere solet in Norman(nia) et saisinamᶜ inde eis fecerimus, tunc nob(is) reddent et quietam clamabunt terram quam predictus Rob(ertus) habuit in Angl(ia), et si predictus Rob(ertus) <vel>ᵃ heredes sui aliquo tempore seruicio nostro vel heredum nostrorum adheserint et nos predictam terram eis reddere voluerimus, tunc dabimus predicto Gaufr(ido) vel heredibus suis escambium ad valenciam in locis <com>petentibusᵃ, et cum de escambio illo saisinamᶜ eis fecerimus predictam terram nob(is) reddent quietam. Quare volumus et firmiter precipimus quod predictus Galfr(idus) et heredes sui post eum habeant et teneant predictam terram cum pertinent(iis) sicut predictum est bene et in pace, libere et quiete et integre, plenarie et honorifice sicut predictus Rob(ertus) illam melius et liberius et integrius habuit. Test(ibus) W(illelmo) comite Saresbir', W(illelmo) de Cantilup' tunc senesc(allo) nostro, Sim(one) de Patteshill', Iacob(o) de Poterne, Thom(a) de Samford', Ioh(ann)e Mariscall', Rad(ulfo) Gernun. Dat' per man(um) Hug(onis) de Welles archidiaconi Well(e)ns' apud Winton' xv. die Septembr(is) anno regni nostri decimo.

ᵃ *letters in brackets* <> *illegible* B, *supplied from* C ᵇ cum *supplied, illegible* B, *shown as already illegible* C ᶜ seisinam C

6. *Notification by King John of his grant to the abbot and monks of Le Bec-Hellouin (Eure, cant. Brionne) of forty-eight acres of new assart and two acres of old assart in the manor of Weedon Beck (Northamptonshire) quit of the forest regard with quittance from swanmoot for the abbey's men.* Rouen, 31 March 1203

A = Eton College Records ECR 27/3. Endorsed: *carta reg(is) Ioh(annis) de (feria,* cancelled) *quitantia essart(orum) de Wedon'* (s.xiii); various post medieval endorsements. Approx. 238 × 180 + 38mm. Sealed *sur double queue,* fine seal impression in green wax on green silk cords through 3 holes. B = TNA C 52/10 (Cartae Antiquae Roll K) no.2, s.xiii in. C = TNA C 47/12/6 no.14, copies of charters relating to the forests, headed *cart(a) abbatis de Becco in com(itatu) Norht'*, s.xiii med.

Pd (from B) *The Cartae Antiquae Rolls 1–10*, ed. L. Landon, Pipe Roll Society n.s. xvii (1939), 136 no.285. Confirmed, but not recited, in a charter of Henry III, 13 February 1227: *Cal.Chart.R. 1226–57*, 9 (with an original also at Eton College Archives ECR 27/4).

For the fine of 100 marks offered by the abbot and monks for the present charter, the money apparently being paid via Hugh de Neville as the king's chief forester, see *PR 5 John*, 135; *6 John*, 31, 36. Note that the names of only the first three witnesses are preserved in the copies BC, omitting five further witnesses named in A.

Iohannes Dei gratia rex Angl(ie), ᵃdominus Hybernie, dux Norm(annie), Aquit(anie), comes Andeg(auie) archiepiscopis, episcopis, abbatibus, comit(ibus), baronibus, iustic(iis), vicecom(itibus), prepositis, ministris et omnibus ball(iu)is et fidelibus suis salutemᵃ. Sciatis nos pro amore Dei et pro salute nostra et pro animabus antecessorum et successorum nostrorum concessisse et presenti carta nostra confirmasse abbati et monachis de Becco quadraginta et octo acras de nouo assarto ad perticam nostram et duas acras de veteri assarto in manerio suo de Wedon' liberas et quietas de essarto et rewardo et de visu forestariorum et ab omni consuetudine et exactione que ad forestariam pertinent et quod in numero assartorum non contineantur et quod homines predictorum abbatis et monachorum de predicto manerio de Wedon' liberi et quieti sint de swanemot' in perpetuum. Quare volumus et firmiter precipimus quod predicti abbas et monachi predicta essarta habeant et teneant bene et in pace, libere et quiete, integre, plenarie et honorifice in omnibus locis et rebus et predictos homines suos de Wedon' liberos et quietos de swanemot' in perpetuum sicut predictum est. Test(ibus) R(oberto) com(ite) Leyc', G(alfrido) fil(io) Petri ᵇcom(ite) Essex'ᵇ, Will(elm)o com(ite) Sar', ᵇWill(elm)o de Breosa, Will(elm)o Bryewerr', Roberto fil(io) Walteri, R(ogero) constab(ulario) Cestr', Sahero de Quenciᵇ. Dat' per manum Sym(onis) prepositi Beuerlac' et archidiaconi Wellen' apud Rothomagum xxxi. die Marcii anno regni nostri quarto.

ᵃ⁻ᵃ etc BC   ᵇ⁻ᵇ *not in* BC

7. *Notification by Peter de Préaux of his grant, for the souls of himself, his father and mother and of Simon, Roger, John and Enguerand his brothers, to the canons of Notre-Dame de Beaulieu of an annual rent of 100 livres Angevin at Rouen in the market and fairs, as granted to Peter by King John, the canons having their own servant to receive this rent and paying an annual rent of 20s. to the Hospital of St Mary Magdalene for the soul of Henry the Young King, Peter's former lord. The canons of Beaulieu will celebrate two daily masses for Peter's soul and the souls of the departed, burning two candles each Saturday night in honour of the Blessed Virgin Mary, for Peter and for Roger his brother.* [*c.* June 1200]

B = TNA C 64/12 (Norman Roll 7 Henry V part 2) m.43, in an inspeximus by Henry V, in the castle at Rouen, 18 January 1420. C = Bnf ms. Moreau 630 fos.43r–44v, copy from B by Bréquigny, s.xviii.

Apparently issued on the same occasion as, and sharing various of the witnesses with a charter of King John, 21 June 1200, first granting the 100 livres rent to Peter, this charter of King John being preserved both in the Charter Roll 2 John and in the Norman Roll, where the text is fuller and includes the names of five witnesses (Guerin de Glapion seneschal of Normandy, Robert of Thurnham, Robert fitz Erneis, Richard de Redvers and William de Cantiloupe) omitted from the Charter Roll version: *Rot. Chart.*, 70b–71; TNA C 64/12 m.43. For the Augustinian abbey, later priory of Beaulieu (Seine-Maritime, cant. Darnetal, com. Préaux) founded *c.*1200 by John de Préaux, whose archives are now almost entirely lost, see Cottineau, i, 300. The supposed extracts from a lost cartulary (Stein no.385) in Bnf ms. Duchesne 22 fos.321–326 are in fact from the cartulary of Beaulieu-sur-Dordogne (Corrèze, cf. Stein no.380; Cottineau, i, 296–7), but that a cartulary of Notre-Dame de Beaulieu did indeed once exist is suggested by the extracts in G.–A. de la Roque, *Histoire généalogique de la maison de Harcourt*, 4 vols (Paris 1662), iv, 1966.

Omnibus tam presentibus quam futuris ad quos presens scriptum peruenerit Petrus de Pratell' salutem. Sciatis quod ego pro salute anime mee et patris mei et matris mee et fratrum meorum, videlicet Simonis et Rogeri, Iohannis et Engerranni, et dominorum et antecessorum meorum dedi et concessi in puram et perpetuam elemosinam sancte Marie de Belloloco et canonicis ibidem Deo seruientibus centum libratas redditus Andeg(auenses) apud Rothom', scilicet in estallis fori Roth' et in feria de Pardone et in feria sancte Marie de Prato, quem s(cilicet) redditum Iohannes Dei gratia rex Angl(ie) dedit michi et concessit pro meo seruicio, et si quid de predictis centum libratis redditus annuatim recipiendis in predictis locis eis defuerit, de vicecomitatu Roth' eis perficietur. Sciend(um) est etiam quod predicti canonici debent habere dominicum suum seruientem ad recipiendas illas centum libratas redditus in prefatis locis una cum vicecomite Roth' vel cum eo qui in loco domini regis ibi erit. Item sciend(um) est quod iamdicti canonici reddant singulis annis viginti sol(idos) Andeg(auenses) hospitarie sancte Marie Magdal(ene) de prefato redditu ad festum sancti Michaelis pro salute anime domini mei Henrici minoris regis. Predicti canonici de misericordia Dei confisi et saluti anime mee et animabus antecessorum meorum subuenire desiderantes concesserunt michi quod singulis diebus cum duobus cereis accensis in honore beate Virginis Marie pro salute nostra unam missam solempniter celebrabunt, alteram vero pro defunctis. Preter hoc autem concesserunt michi quod duos cereos, unum pro me, alterum pro Rogero fratre meo, in honore beate Virginis Marie singulis noctibus sabbatorum in supradicta ecclesia ardere constituent, et ut hec donatio rata et inconcussa permaneat, cartam istam sigilli mei munimine roboraui. T(estibus) domino Waltero Rothom' archiepiscopo, Willelmo de Constantiis, Waltero de Sancto Walerico et magistro Garino Angeli Roth' archidia(co)n(is), Willelmo Marescallo com(ite) de Pembroch, Hugon(e) de Gorn', Willelmo de Cahem, Warin(o) de Glapion', Rob(erto) de Torneham, Willelmo et Engerranno de Pratell' fratribus, Gaufr(ido) de Bosco et Iohanne fratribus, Matheo Grosso maiore Roth', Gaufrid(o) de

Valle Richeri, Iord(ano) Iolm', Gaufrido clerico de Caprau(i)lla et multis aliis.

8. *Notification by Reginald de Pavilly (Seine-Maritime) of his grant to St Thomas (of Canterbury) and the lepers of (Le Mont-aux-Malades at) Rouen, for the soul of his wife Alice, previously known as Pagana, of 10 sous from his rents at Pont-Audemer (Eure).*
[1172 X 1190]

B = BN ms. Français 26476 fo.3 no.1, in an original inspeximus by Henry V, issued in the castle at Rouen, 3 January 1420, formerly AN Chambre des Comptes greffe 23659 (whence listed in the factitious listing AN P1913/2 no.23659), dispersed with other such 'greffes' as a result of the burning of the Chambre des Comptes in 1744, also reciting charters of Henry II (*Acta Henry II*, nos 2283–4) and William his brother (Delisle, *Recueil*, i (Introduction), 488). C = TNA C 64/12 (Norman Roll 7 Henry V part 2) m.25, the enrolment of B, 1420. D = Bnf ms. Moreau 630 fos.5v, copy from C by Bréquigny, s.xviii. E = St-Pierre-de-Semilly, Marquis de Mathan ms. Lenoir 3 pp.319–20, copy from B, s.xviii. F = Ibid. Lenoir 69 p.435, partial copy after a copy by from C by Bréquigny, s.xviii. G = Ibid. Lenoir 76 p.54, copy from E, s.xviii. G = AN S4889[b] no.7, copy from C by William Ryley, 14 September 1674.

After the canonization of St Thomas, and the rededication of the priory of Mont-aux-Malades, previously dedicated to St James, whose prior, Nicholas, had acted as a close friend of Becket during the archbp's exile of the 1160s. Related to an original charter written in a late twelfth-century hand, now Rouen AD Seine-Maritime 25HP1, by which Ralph de Wesneval (Esneval, Seine-Maritime, cant. et com. Pavilly) and William his brother granted St Thomas and the infirm and lepers of the 'Monte infirmis' 20s., comprising 10s. from the mill of Ste-Croix and 10s. from the English rents of William, Ralph's brother, to pay for a pittance on the anniversary of their mother, witnessed by Reginald 'de Palliaco frater meus', Walter my brother, William Calceius, Peter de Deneuilla, Robert de Francchesneio and Ralph de Plaseiz, and for the Wesnevals, active in the 1170s or early 80s with lands at Chippenham (Wiltshire), see Round, *Calendar*, no.277, re-edited as *Acta Henry II*, no.2291n.; Chippenham, Wiltshire Record Office 1213/5. For lands at Pavilly and Pont-de-l'Arche, by the 1540s administered on behalf of the lepers of the Lazarite order, see AN S4890[a]. Reginald himself was a courtier, regular witness to charters of Henry II, and joint founder of the Augustinian abbey of Ile-Dieu (Eure, cant. Fleury-sur-Andelle, com. Perruel), to which he granted the vill of Charlton (near Upavon) in Wiltshire in a charter witnessed by Gilbert and Ralph de Wesneval, for which see Evreux AD Eure H353, and the foundation narrative in *Des clercs au service de la réforme: études et documents sur les chanoines réguliers de la province de Rouen*, ed. M. Arnoux (Brepols 2000), 297–306. In England he granted further land at Charlton to the monks of St-Georges-de-Boscherville (BL ms. Lord Frederick Campbell Charter XXIII.6), and the monks of Stanley part of a moor in Chippenham given him by King Henry II, his gift here being made 'pro salute domini mei regis

Henrici et pro anima domini mei et auunculi Roberti de Peissi et pro anima Roberti de Wendeual': Chippenham, Wiltshire Record Office 473/32, with an equestrian seal, legend <SIGIL>LUM .... DE PAVEILLI+, and cf. Ibid. 473/40 pp.10–13; 473/36.

Sciant uniuersi tam presentes quam futuri quod ego Reginaldus de Pauilleio concessi et dedi sancte Thome martiri Cristi et infirmis de Monte super Rothm' in perpetuam elemosinam pro salute anime mee et patris mei et matris mee Aeles que dicta fuit Pagana x. solidos in redditu meo de Ponte Aldemari singulis annis in festo sancti Mich(ael)is habendos. Testibus Rad(ulfo) de Werneuall' et Willelmo fratre suo, Rogero de Pauilleio, Rob(erto) de Croismare, Rad(ulfo) de Pleisseit et multis aliis.

9. *Notification by Robert de Courtenay of his grant to the abbey of Notre-Dame of La Noë of 40 sous Tours in his prévôté of Conches (Eure) for lights in the chapel of the infirmary.*   [1215/16]

B = TNA C 64/12 (Norman Roll 7 Henry V part 2) m.18, in an inspeximus at Rouen, 3 January 1420, at mm.19–18 reciting a further inspeximus of Henry V, 3 January 1420, reciting charters of Henry II and the Empress Matilda to La Noë (*Regesta*, iii, no.607; *Acta Henry II*, nos 1931–2). C = Bnf ms. Moreau 630 fo.9v, copy from B by Bréquigny, s.xviii. D = St-Pierre-de-Semilly, Marquis de Mathan ms. Lenoir 69 p.417, copy by Lenoir after a copy by Bréquigny from B, s.xviii.

For Robert de Courtenay, a direct descendant of Louis VI of France, lord of Montargis south of Paris, granted extensive lordships in Normandy after the Capetian conquest in 1204, including the castles of Conches and Nonancourt, later active in the Capetian invasion of England after 1215, taken prisoner in 1217 in the battle of Sandwich, see N. Vincent, 'Isabella of Angoulême: John's Jezebel', *King John New Interpretations*, ed. S.D. Church (Woodbridge 1999), 175–6, 201–2, and references; H. Stein, 'Chartes inédites relatives à la famille de Courtenay et à l'abbaye des Echarlis', *Annales de la Société Historique et Archéologique du Gatinais*, xxxvi (1922), 141–65; *Actes Philippe Auguste*, ii, no.875; *Layettes*, i, nos 747, 1262. For subsequent confirmations by his descendants of the rights of the monks of La Noë in the lordship of Conches, see *Sceaux de chartes de l'abbaye de la Noë conservées à la Bibliothèque nationale XIIe-XIIIe siècles*, ed. M. Dalas (Paris 1993), 142–3 nos 167–8.

Nouerint uniuersi presentes et futuri quod ego Robertus de Cortenaio dedi Deo et beate Marie de Noa pro salute mea et uxoris mee puerorumque nostrorum quadraginta solidos Turonensium habendos singulis annis in prepositura mea de Conchis ad festum sancti Remigii <in> puram scilicet et perpetuam elemosinam ad luminare capelle infirmorum eiusdem domus. Quod ut firmum sit et stabile, presenti scripto et sigillo meo apposito confirmaui in anno dominice incarnationis m°.cc. quintodecimo.

10. *Notification by Nicholas de Montaigne and Isabella his wife, eldest daughter of Aldulf de Brachy, of their grant to the abbey of Bonport of the hay of Vidame (Seine-Maritime, cant. Darnétal, com. Bois-Guillaume) to hold for an annual rent of 20 livres. Supported by oaths made in the Exchequer of the king of France at Rouen, and granted in the church of Saint-Eloi.* Rouen, 1208

B = TNA C 64/13 (Norman Roll 8 Henry V part 1) m.6, in an inspeximus at Rouen, 26 March 1420. C = Bnf ms. Moreau 631 fos.111v–112v, copy from B by Bréquigny, s.xviii.

The inspeximus B also recites charters of Richard I, 28 February 1198 (Landon, *Itinerary*, no.486; *GC*, xi, instr. 137–8), Louis IX, February 1246/7 (*Cartulaire de l'abbaye royale de Notre-Dame de Bon-Port de l'ordre de Cîteaux au diocèse d'Evreux*, ed. J. Andrieux (Evreux 1862), 159–61 no.156), the present charter, and charters of Robert de Courtenay, December 1211 (*Cartulaire de Bon-Port*, 47 no.45), Jordan du Mesnil-Jourdain, November 1243 (*Cartulaire de Bon-Port*, 128–9 no.129), William abbot of La Trappe, March 1270/1 selling to Bonport a rent of 60s. given by Robert de Courtenay in the prévôté of Conches, and of Giles Malet, 15 July 1383.

Not in the printed *Cartulaire de Bon-Port*, which nonetheless (406 no.372, from an 'aveu' of 15 November 1456), refers to the same land, here described as 'en la viconte de Rouen, en la paroisse du Bos Guillaume, ung fief noble et basse justice, dont le chief est assis en la dite paroisse, en ung hostel nomme la Haie de Widasne, et se revient en rentes en deniers, terres labourables, corvees, grains, oyseux et autres aides de fief coustumieres', and for the place-name, see *Dictionnaire topographique du département de Seine-Maritime*, ed. C. de Beaurepaire and J. Laporte, 2 vols (Paris 1982–4), ii, 1058. For Nicholas (d.*c*.1230), perhaps to be associated either with Montigny (Seine-Maritime, cant. Maromme) or Montagny (cant. Argueil, com. Nolleval), see also *Jugements*, nos 229, 441, 463, 469. For his father-in-law, Aldulf de Brachy, see below no.45.

Nouerint uniuersi presentem paginam inspecturi quod ego Nicholaus de Monteign' et Isabel uxor mea primogenita filia Aldulphi de Bracheio dedimus et concessimus in perpetuam elemosinam Deo et ecclesie Boniportus et monachis ibidem Deo seruientibus haiam de Vicdasne cum pertin(entiis) suis integre, videlicet terram cum bosco et quicquid iuris et hereditatis ibidem habebamus in dominicis, in hominibus et feodis, in redditibus et seruiciis, in escaetis et releuiamentis et incrementis et in omnibus aliis predicte terre pertinentibus tenend(am) et possidend(am) libere, quiete et pacifice per viginti libr(as) cur(ren)tis monete de redditu nobis vel heredibus nostris, nostris annuatim persoluendas ad duos terminos, in festo sancti Remigii decem libr(as) et in Purificatione beate virginis Marie decem libr(as). Hanc predictam donationem ego Nicholaus et Isabel uxor mea in scacario domini regis Francie apud Rothom' coram domino Waltero camerario et Odone Clement' archidiac(ono) Parisien' et fratre Guarino iuramento confirmauimus tenendam et bona fide custodiendam ut elemosinam liberam et quietam per prefatum redditum ab omni exactione, consuetudine, inquietudine, calumpnia vel reclamatione nostri vel heredum nostrorum penitus absolutam, et in ecclesia beati Eligii presente Laurentio sacerdote et parrochianis eiusdem ecclesie super altare solempniter obtulimus ut elemosinam saluo prenominato redditu nostro, quod si monachi ab eodem redditu persoluendo defecerint, nos solummodo pro defectu redditus nostri et non pro alio ad res feodi donec persoluatur redditus recurremus. Quod ut ratum et stabile cunctis in posterum diebus permaneat, presentis carte testimonio et sigilli mei patrocinio duximus roborand(um). Actum apud Rothom' anno dominice incarnationis millesimo ducentesimo octauo, coram subscriptis testibus: Iohanne de Robereto Osberto, Ric(ard)o de Willicario, Reginaldo de Pierreuilla, Willelmo Freschet de Ginnenuill'militibus, Cadulc(o) castellano Galonis, Willelmo Escua'col et multis aliis.

11. *Notification by the dean and chapter of Mortain to their men of Hanging Langford (Wiltshire) of their grant of their manor and land there to Firminus de Gorron (Mayenne), priest, for the term of his life.*

[*c.*1260]

B = TNA E 32/199 (Wiltshire Forest Eyre 1263) m.1, headed *carta Mortun'*, s.xiii med.

Datable only to the approximate period of the Forest eyre roll in which the charter is recorded. Included here, in part because of the extreme rarity of documentary evidences relating to the collegiate church of St-Evroult and St-Guillaume Firmat at Mortain, in part as an indication of the extraordinary range of source materials in The National Archives from which Norman evidences can still be unearthed. Cf. *VCH Wiltshire*, ii, 133n.; *Book of Fees*, ii, 742, where Hanging Langford (in Steeple Langford) is identified with the Langford held by the count of Mortain at the time of Domesday and, in the case of this particular manor, as 100s. of land recorded in 1242 in the possession of the collegiate church of Mortain by gift of King Richard (I).

Decanus et capitulum sanctorum confessor(um) Ebrulfi et Firmati de Moreton' fidelibus suis hominibus de Hangindelangeford' in Wilt' salutem in Domino. Noueritis nos manerium nostrum et terram nostram de Hangedelangeford' cum hominibus nostris ibidem existentibus et omnibus aliis ad dictum[a] manerium spectantibus tradidisse et de co(mmun)i assensu concessisse Firmino de Gorranno presbitero tenend(um) et possidend(um) pro toto tempore vite sue reddend(o) inde nob(is) per singulos annos cum propriis suis sumptibus apud Moreton' quandam summam argenti prout in carta a nob(is) eidem facta F(irmino) super hoc confecta continetur. Quapropter vob(is) mandamus etc.

[a] dictum *after* dcucum *cancelled*

12. *Notification by Robert archbishop of Rouen that Ralph fitz Gerald, archdeacon of Eu, has resigned an annual rent that he used to receive in England from the monks of Lewes, restoring all the evidences that he had over the same to the prior of Etoutteville and brother Reginald, monks of Lewes.*
Valmont, 18 March 1209 or 17 March 1210

A = TNA E 40/15643. No medieval endorsement. Approx. 137 × 86 + 18mm. Sealed *sur double queue*, single slit, tag and seal impression missing. Faded in part, some letters illegible even under ultra-violet light.

The calendar year in use here is not certain, so the charter might date to either 1209 or 1210. For benefactions by the Anglo-Norman Stuteville family to Lewes Priory, see *EYC*, ix, 2, 29, 118–19 no.43n. That Lewes maintained a small priory at Etoutteville-sur-Mer (Seine-Maritime, cant. Yerville) seems not previously to have been noticed by English historians, although cf. Cottineau, i, 1082, and above pp.86–7 for evidence that Lewes also controlled the revenues of the nearby priory of Mortemer-sur-Eaulne (Seine-Maritime, cant. Neufchâtel). For Robert Pullus, archbp of Rouen 1208–1221, see *GC*, xi, 59–60. For Ralph fitz Gerald, canon of Rouen, official of Rouen *c*.1204–6, archdeacon by 1207, see Spear, *Personnel*, 218, 226–7, 254. By the 1250s, the revenues and communal life of both priories had declined to an alarming extent, with the revenues of Etoutteville, where there were only two monks of Lewes in residence, farmed for life to Master Gilbert de Wyauville, *alias* Gilbert de Caux ('Caleto') who allowed the monks only 20s. tours per week, and with those of Mortemer, again housing only two monks of Lewes, farmed for life to Master Odo de St-Denis: *Regestrum visitationum archiepiscopi Rothomagensis*, ed. T. Bonnin (Rouen 1852), 354, 381, 432, 473, 518, 549, 565, 601, 630.

Omnibus Cristi fidelibus ad quos p<resens> scriptum peruenerit Robertus Dei gratia Rothom' archiepiscopus salutem in domino. Nouerit uniuersitas vestra quod dilectus filius noster Rad(ulfus) filius Geroudi, archid(iaconu)s Augi, pro salute anime sue remisit monachis sancti Pancratii de Leawes totum redditum quem ab eis in Anglia solebat percipere annuatim. Munimenta etiam que inde ab eis habuerat in manus prioris de Estuteuill' et fratris Reinaldi, monachorum eiusdem domus, libere resignauit et quieta concessit. Cartam etiam suam super hac resignatione sua fecit monachis predictis ad maiorem eorum securitatem. Nos vero quod in hac parte a predicto archid(iacon)o factum est volentes ad omnium noticiam peruenire, ad eiusdem facti testimonium presenti scripto sigillum nostrum duximus apponendum. Dat' apud Walemont per manum Rad(ulfi) de I.. capellani nostri anno incarnationis dominice m°cc° nono, die mercurii proxima post festum sancti Gregorii.

13. *Notification by Abbot William and the convent of Fécamp of their grant of confraternity to Abbot Eler and the monks of Pershore (Worcestershire).*   25 February 1258

A = TNA E 210/10188. Endorsed: *conuentio Fiscam'* (s.xiii/xiv). Approx. 200 × 100 + 26mm. Sealed *sur double queue*, two tags through two sets of slits, both seal impressions missing. Decorated initial letter *O* of *Omnibus*.

The feast day of St Mathias fell on a Monday in 1259 so that the present charter appears to be dated using a calendar year beginning on 1 January. For Eler, abbot of Pershore 1251–1264, previously a monk of Fécamp, sent to England *c.*1248 to oversee Fécamp's cell at Cogges in Oxfordshire, royal escheator for lands south of the Trent from 1251 and a baron of the Exchequer, see *VCH Worcestershire*, ii, 136; *The Heads of Religious Houses England and Wales II: 1216–1377*, ed. D.M. Smith and V.C.M. London (Cambridge 2001), 56; *CPR 1247–58*, 7, 77, 92, 104. I am indebted to David Carpenter for the information that Eler was almost certainly the principal patron of the *Flores Historiarum*, in its first incarnation a Pershore as much as a St Albans or Westminster chronicle. Fécamp already enjoyed extensive confraternity arrangements with other English monasteries, including St Augustine's Canterbury (cf. BL ms. Cotton Vitellius C xii fo.155r), and Reading Abbey (BL ms. Cotton Vespasian E v (Reading Almoner's cartulary) fo.37r: 'fratribus de Fiscanno debemus officium et missam in conuentu et missas priuatas et L. psalmos et tricenarium').

Omnibus Cristi fidelibus ad quos presentes littere peruenerint Will(el)mus Dei gratia humilis abbas Fiscannen' et eiusdem loci conuentus salutem in domino sempiternam. Nouerit uniuersitas vestra nos concessisse domino Elerio Dei gratia abbati Persoren' et successoribus suis et eiusdem loci conuentui quod, audito obitu dominorum abbatum eiusdem monasterii Persoren', fiet pro eis sollempniter et plenarie in monasterio nostro sicut pro abbatibus <monast>erii Fiscann' fieri debet et solet in missis, orationibus, psalmis, disciplinis et elemosinis, et audito obi<tu mon>achorum dicti Persoren' monasterii, fiet pro eis similiter in monasterio nostro sicut pro <monachis monaster>ii Fiscann', et nomina eorum in martyrologio Fiscannen' scribentur. In cuius rei testimonium presenti scripto sigilla nostra duximus apponenda. Dat' anno gratie m°cc°l° octauo, die lune proxima post festum sancti Mathie apostoli.

14. *Counterpart notification by Eler abbot of Pershore.*
                                             29 August 1258

A = Rouen AD Seine-Maritime 7H51. Endorsed: *societas Persorens'* (s.xiii); various post medieval endorsements including *L.17* (s.xvii/xviii) Approx. 206 × 78 + 28mm. Sealed *sur double queue*, parchment tag through a single slit on left hand side, white (?hemp) cords through 3 holes at centre, small fragment of dark brown wax, image illegible, legend mostly illegible save from central left hand side of obverse ...<?A>NGELUM... Written in a hand identified by Tessa Webber as English rather than French, and, although similar, probably distinct from that of no.2 above.

Note the delay of six months between the two, more or less identical, parts of this agreement. The fact that both parts of the agreement are written in very similar (?English) hands may suggest that the impetus for these arrangements came chiefly from Pershore.

Omnibus Cristi fidelibus ad quos presentes littere peruenerint Eler(ius) Dei gratia Persorens' ecclesie minister humil(is) et eiusdem loci conuentus salutem in domino sempiternam. Nouerit uniuersitas vestra nos concessisse domino Will(elm)o Dei gratia abbati Fiscann' et successoribus suis et eiusdem loci conuentui quod, audito obitu dominorum abbatum eiusdem ecclesie Fiscann', fiet pro eis solempniter et plenar(ie) in ecclesia nostra sicut pro abbatibus ecclesie Persor' fieri debet et solet in missis, orationibus, psalmis, disciplinis et elemosinis, et audito obitu monachorum dicte ecclesie Fiscann', fiet pro eis similiter in ecclesia nostra sicut pro monachis ecclesie Persor', et nomina eorum in martirologio Persor' scribentur. In cuius rei testimonium presenti scripto sigillum nostrum apposuimus. Dat' anno gratie m°cc°l° octauo, die decollationis beati Ioh(ann)is Baptiste.

15. *Notification by Roger de Tilleul that he has restored to William de Roumare all his lands in England in the soke of Bolingbroke at Hareby, Mavis Enderby and Hundleby in return for life possession of 16 livres angevin of rents in Normandy in Roumare (Seine-Maritime, cant. Maromme) and 'Wiunville' (? Yainville or Yville-sur-Seine, both cant. Duclair), including 100 sous in the multure of the mill of Barentin (cant. Pavilly), William further granting Roger and Ralph his nephew the whole of Roger's land in Bouteilles (Seine-Maritime, cant. Offranville, com. Rouxmesnil-Bouteilles) in hereditary fee.*

[1166 X 1198, ?c.1170 X 1180]

A = TNA DL 27/254. No medieval endorsement, but a parchment schedule sewn on to the front of the linen seal bag: *cart(a) Rog(eri) de Tilliol de terra quam quietum clamauit Will(elm)o de Rom' in soca de Bulingbroc* (s.xii). Approx. 246 × 154 + 14mm. Sealed *sur double queue*, round equestrian seal in pinkish-red wax on tag through 3 slits, legend: SIGILL' ROGERI DE ....IL+. The top of the parchment continues to show the downstrokes of the writing that preceded the writing of the present charter, and the parchment itself exhibits a large hole across which the letters of the name of Roger's nephew (*Butelles et Radul...fo nepoti meo*) have been carefully arranged.

For Hugh abbot of Revesby, witness to the present charter, who occurs after 1166 and before 1208, see *The Heads of Religious Houses England and Wales I: 940–1216*, ed. D. Knowles, C.N.L. Brooke and V.C.M. London, 2nd ed. (Cambridge 2001), 140. Cf. Stenton, *Danelaw Charters*, 377–8 no.520; Cazel, 'Roumare Charters', 86 no.3. For

Roger de Tilleul fl.1172–3, see *Monasticon*, v, 455. Before the death of William III de Roumare in 1198, probably earlier rather than later during this period.

Rog(erus) de Tillol omnibus hominibus suis et amicis Francis et Anglis presentibus et futuris salutem. Notum vobis facio me reddidisse et quietam clamasse domino meo Will(elm)o de Rom' totam terram meam Anglie quam habebam in soca de Bulinbroc, scilicet in Harebi et in Endrebi et in Hundelbi solutam et quietam de me et heredibus meis sibi et heredibus suis in perpetuum pro xvi. libratis redditus ad monetam Andegauensium quas michi dominus meus Will(elmus) dedit in Normannia habendas omnibus diebus vite mee, et post dies meos ille xvi. librate redditus ad se et heredes suos redibunt, et me de ill(is) attornauit in Romara et in Wiunuilla, scilicet in sua sicca moulta Romare que pertinet ad molendinum suum de Barentino de c. solidis Andegauensium ita integre sicut illa supradicta moulta fuit in anno antequam michi daret, scilicet illo anno quo Will(elmus) Pinchewerre emit de Roberto Drou, et si quis illam minuere presumpserit de sicut fuit in illo anno per senescaldum suum Normannie et per seruientes suos Romare adretietur michi ut habeam moultam suam sicut supradictum est plenarie, et me attornauit in x. et nouem acris terre quas Gilleb(ertus) le Tonir tenuit in Romara et una acra terre quam egomet Rog(erus) teneo in Romara de lx. et decem solidis Andegauensium, et in Wiunuilla me attornauit in quinque acris prati quod vocatur Latrenteine et iuxta illud pratum quod vocatur Laquerenteine in tribus acris prati et dimidia de vii. libris et x. solidis Andegauensium. Summa est inter totum xvi. libre Andegauensium. Has xvi. libratas redditus dedit michi habendas omnibus diebus vite mee pro tota terra mea Anglie quam habebam in soca de Bulinbroc, scilicet in Harebi et in Endrebi et in Hundelbi quam ei reddidi et quietam clamaui sibi et heredibus suis de me et heredibus meis, ita quod xvi. librate redditus post mortem meam ad se et heredes suos redibunt. Pro hac autem quietatione et concessione quam ego ei feci de terra mea Anglie concessit michi totam terram meam de Butelles et Radulfo nepoti meo post dies meos tenendam de se in capite et de heredibus suis michi et heredibus meis. His testibus: Hug(one) abbate de Reuesbi, Philippo de Kima, Rabodo de Kales, Gill(elmo) de Bolonia, Matheo de Benigword', Ioslano de Autebarge, Rog(ero) capellano, Dauid de Totint', Rad(ulfo) de Imouilla, Rad(ulfo) Cantel, Ric(ardo) fratre eius, Rob(erto) Nigro, Matheo Nigro, Rog(ero) clerico, Waleranno de Grochet, Rob(erto) de Bolon', Gaufrid(o) de Totintona, Hug(one) nepote eius, Reingoto de Stikefort.

16. *Notification by Roger de Tilleul of his grant to William de Roumare, his lord, of all his land in the wapentake of Bolingbroke in return for hereditary possession of his land of Bouteilles (Seine-Maritime, cant. Offranville, com. Rouxmesnil-Bouteilles).*

[1166 X 1198, ?c.1170 X 1180]

A = TNA DL 27/260. Endorsed: *c(arta) Will(elm)i de Rom'* (s.xii); on a parchment schedule sewn to the front of the linen seal bag: *carta Rog(eri) de Till' de terra quam reddidit Will(elm)o Rom' de wapentac de Bulinbroc* (s.xii). Approx. 185 × 56 + 16mm. Sealed *sur double queue* on a parchment tag through 3 slits, seal impression natural wax varnished brown, equestrian but distinct from that of no.15 above, oval: SIGILL'... Date as above no.15.

Rog(erus) de Till' omnibus hominibus suis et amicis Francis et Anglis salutem. Noscant tam presentes quam futuri me dedisse et concessisse domino meo Will(elm)o de Roum' et heredibus suis in feodo et hereditate totam terram meam de wapentac de Bolinbroc quam auus suus pro seruicio meo michi dedit quietam de me et heredibus meis post dies meos sibi et heredibus suis, et pro ista concordia et pro ista conuentione quam ei concessi dedit et concessit dominus meus Will(elmus) de Roum' michi et heredibus meis terram de Boteilles in feodo et hereditate tenendam de eo et heredibus suis. Hiis testibus: Rogero de Beningorde, Matheo eius fratre, Daui de Totintonne, Rab(odo) de Cales, Rog(ero) clerico, Rob(erto) Marmiun.

17. *Notification by Robert le Chalceis of his quitclaim to William de Roumare, his lord, of all his land held from William's fee in England in Alkborough and Toynton St Peter (Lincs.) in exchange for all the land that William held in Le Bourg-Dun (Seine-Maritime), save for the service of the knights who hold from William there, and all the land that William had in La Chapelle-sur-Dun (Seine-Maritime) save for the service of Walter de Canteleu and Richard de Dun, Robert rendering the service of one knight and an annual rent of 20 livres angevin.* [1166 X 1173]

A = TNA DL 27/259. Endorsed: *c(arta) Willelmi de Romar'* (s.xii/xiii); *xxiiii. s.* (s.xiv); various post medieval endorsements. Approx. 232 × 67 + 17mm. Sealed *sur double queue*, parchment tag through a single slit. Seal impression inside linen seal bag, with a description sewn to the front of the bag, apparently in a s.xii hand distinct from that of the text itself: *carta Rob(erti) Le Chalceis de terra quam quietam clamauit Willelmo de Rom'*. Seal, round, light brown wax, approx. 62mm. diameter, a lion passant facing to the right, its front left paw pointing ahead, elaborate tail curling behind, legend +SIGILL' ROBBERTI LE CALCHIS. B = TNA DL42/2 (Great Coucher Book II) fo.237r (251r) no.24, s. xv in.

The present agreement is confirmed in a charter of Henry II: Delisle, *Recueil*, no.429; *Acta Henry II*, no.2291, which can be dated 1166 X 1173, probably September 1167 X August 1171, and where (as a note in *Acta Henry II*) is transcribed a letter from Robert to King Henry II, referring to the present settlement and entrusting his lands to William his nephew for a term of three years pending Robert's return from pilgrimage to Jerusalem, from Rouen AD Seine-Maritime 24HP75. For a grant by Robert to the Templars of land at Toynton St Peter, see Stenton, *Danelaw Charters*, 378–9 no.522.

Rob(ertus) le Chalceis omnibus amicis suis Francis et Anglis salutem. Not(um) sit vob(is) me concessisse et clamasse quietam domino meo Will(elm)o de Roum' totam terram meam quam habui in Angl(ia) de feodo suo in Altebarge et Totintona in excambio tocius dominii sui quod habuit in Duno exceptis seruiciis militum suorum qui tenent de eo in eadem vill(a), et in excambio tocius terre quam habui in Capella excepto seruicio Walteri de Canteleu et Ric(ardi) de Duno, tenend(am) de eo et de heredibus suis in feodo et hereditate per seruicium unius militis ita quod ego et heredes mei annuatim reddemus sibi et heredibus suis in feodi firma xx. li(bras) And(egauensium) pro isto tenemento ad duo terminos, videlicet ad Pasch(a) x. li(bras) et ad festum sancti Remigii x. li(bras). His t(estibus): Adam de Brus, Will(elmo) le Chauceis, Walt(ero) Enguainne, Math(eo) de Beningworde, Rog(ero) de Dodeuill', Rog(ero) de Till'. Val(ete).

18. *Notification addressed to King John by S(amson) abbot of (St-Etienne) Caen, Ralph L'Abbé, Hugh of Chac(ombe) and Peter de Lions, who, in accordance with the king's mandate, have held an inquest on the oath of twenty-three knights and men, finding that the late earl William de Mandeville died holding Beuzeval (Calvados, cant. Dozulé) in demesne, the land passing thereafter to King (Richard) for half a year until Richard de Montigny had seisin of it.*
[May 1199 X May 1204]

A = TNA DL 25/722. Endorsed: *Boseuall'* (s.xiv). Approx. 190 × 79 +13mm. Sealed *sur double queue*, slits for four tags, two inner tags extant, outer tags and all seal impressions missing.

After the accession of King John and before the evacuation of Peter de Lions and the Exchequer archive to England in May 1204. William de Mandeville died 12 December 1189. For Beuzeval and Ifs (*Yz, Isibus*), see C. Hippeau, *Dictionnaire topographique du département du Calvados* (Paris 1883), 27, 150–1. For Samson abbot of St-Etienne 1196–1214, and his fellow judges, see V. Gazeau, *Normannia monastica*, 2 vols (Caen 2007), ii, 55–7; D. Power, 'En Quête de sécurité juridique dans la Normandie angevine: concorde finale et inscription au rouleau', *BEC*, clxviii (2010), 370–1. For Richard de Montigny, 'bailli' of the Pays de Caux in 1195 and in the same year witness to a charter of King Richard I issued in Normandy, having served during the late disturbances as defender of the castle of Bellencombre, and having apparently deputed his son William de Montigny to carry gold coin into Germany to assist with the payment of the king's ransom, see *MRSN*, i, 2, 134, 147, 157, 163–4, 167, 284, ii, 423, 436, 443; Landon, *Itinerary*, 100 no.441.

I(ohanni) Dei gratia illustri regi Angl(ie), domino Hibern(ie), duc(i) Norm(annie), Aquit(anie) et com(iti) Andeg(auie) fideles sui S(amson) abbas Cad' et Rad(ulfus) Labbe et Hug(o) de Chauc' et Petrus de Liuns

salutem et obsequium. Nouerit excellentio vestra quod iuxta formam
mandati vestri inquisiuimus si Will(elmus) com(es) de Mandeuile fuit
saisitus de Boseual' cum pertinentiis anno quo obiit et die qua incepit
egrotare egritudine qua obiit et die qua obiit in dominico suo sic(ut) de
feodo per sacramentum legalium militum et hominum, scilicet istorum,
Rob(erti) de Yz, Rob(erti) de Isibus, Will(elmi) de Burganuile, Rob(erti) de
Turgisuile, Ric(ardi) de Astin, Galfr(idi) Mani'at, Bose Heard, Ioh(annis)
Aliger, Bernard(i) de Campo Dolent, Saffr(idi) Turoude, Anketil de
Veteriuilla, Simon(is) de Trusseauuile, Hug(onis) de Luiet, Rob(erti) de
Valdoire, Thom(e) de Osberuile, Rumt' de Tol'uile, Rob(erti) de Gisros,
Will(elmi) de Angeruile marescall(i), Thom(e) de Gotteranuile, Thom(e)
de Agernt, Galfr(idi) Keisnel, Ric(ardi) fil(ii) Houte, Rob(erti) Corsond,
qui dic(un)t quod Will(elmus) com(es) de Mandeuile fuit saisitus de
Boseual cum pertinentiis suis in dominico suo sic(ut) de feodo anno quo
obiit, et die qua incepit egrotare egritudine qua obiit et die qua obiit et etiam
quod post mortem predicti Will(elmi) com(itis) fuit terra predicta, scilicet
de Boseual, cum pertinentiis in manu domini reg(is) et eius custodia per
spacium dimidii anni donec Ric(ardus) de Muntigni habuit in(de) saisinam,
set nesciunt per q(uem) vel quomodo. Valeat excellentia vestra.

19. *Letters of William de Pirou informing King (?Henry III) that he is sending Richard his eldest son to seek his inheritance at Chedzoy (Somerset).* [1195 X 1226, ?1217 X 1218]

A = TNA DL 25/199. Endorsed: *rem* (s.xiii). Approx. 122 × 27mm. Sealed *sur simple queue*, tongue and wrapping tie, round seal in natural wax, a shield of arms, a label with five points, legend: .....I DE PIROU+.

For William de Pirou's fine of 30 marks to have possession of Chedzoy, paid in full at Michaelmas 1195, the land having been accounted for by the king's local keeper of escheats from Easter until Christmas 1194, see *PR 6 Richard I*, 19; *PR 7 Richard I*, 39, 234. To be dated after William's recovery of Chedzoy in the 1190s, and apparently after the acquisition of the estate by William Brewer (below nos 20–2), probably after King John's loss of Normandy, and certainly before the death of William Brewer, perhaps of the same date as no.20 below. The reference in no.21 below to seisin being awarded by the king and his council might suggest a date during the minority of Henry III. For further indications of the date, see below no.20.

Domino suo regi Anglie balliuis suis et fidelibus Will(elmus) de Pirou
salutem. Ego transmitto ad vos Ricard(um) filium meum primogenit(um)
et heredem meum causa hereditatis mee perquirende michi et sibi penes vos
apud Chedesie que terra de hereditate mea est, gratum et ratum habiturus

quicquid ipse Ric(ardus) erga vos super hoc negotio tam in seruicio quam
in aliis rebus poterit impetrare.

20. *Notificaton by Richard de Pirou that he has granted his land
at Chedzoy to William Brewer and his heirs in fee, rendering 100
shillings each year at Chedzoy to Richard or his representative
bearing Richard's letters patent, any expense incurred by William or
his heirs in discharging the land's obligations to its chief lord being
deducted from the 100 shilling rent.*   [1195 X 1218, 1217 X 1218]

A = TNA DL 25/201. Endorsed: *in re* (s.xii/xiii). Approx. 186 × 118 + 34mm. Sealed
sur double queue, blue and green silk cords through 4 holes, seal impression in green
wax as below no.21.

Witnessed by Enjuger (II) de Bohon, lord of Midhurst in Sussex, who died after 9
December 1217 but before 10 January 1219: *RLC*, i, 383b, 385, 404b, 429. William
Brewer's tenancy at Chedzoy is first referred to in March 1216, apparently as a gift
made earlier by King John: *RLC*, i, 252b. William de Percy, witness to this and the
next two charters, was a ward of William Brewer from *c*.1204 until his coming of age
in 1218, being married to Brewer's daughter: R.V. Turner, *Men Raised from the Dust*
(Philadelphia 1988), 83. Ralph, son of Hasculf de Subligny, was granted custody of
his father's estates in Cornwall and Somerset in 1220, apparently whilst his father was
absent on the Fifth Crusade from which he may never have returned: *RLC*, i, 410b.
William de Pirou 'the younger' appears to have succeeded to the estate of William
de Pirou 'the elder', his father, *c*.1217 (above pp.87–8), which might suggest that the
present arrangements were provoked by this succession.

Sciant tam presentes quam futuri quod ego Ricardus de Pyro dedi et concessi
et hac presenti carta mea confirmaui Will(elm)o Briwer' et heredibus suis
pro homagio et seruicio suo totam terram meam de Chedesie cum omnibus
pertinentiis suis et quicquid iuris habui in predicta terra et eius pertinentiis,
habendam et tenendam predicto Will(elm)o et heredibus suis de me et
heredibus meis libere et quiete, integre et pacifice cum omnibus libertatibus
et liberis consuetudinibus ad eandem terram spectantibus, reddendo inde
michi et heredibus meis ipse et heredes sui centum solidos sterlingorum
singulis annis ad Pasca pro omni seruicio et exactione ad me et heredes
meos pertinentibus, et debet singulis annis ista solutio fieri ad predictum
terminum in manerio de Chedesie michi et heredibus meis vel certo nuncio
qui literas mei vel heredum meorum patentes predicto Will(elm)o et
heredibus suis inde attulerit, et ipse Will(elmu)s et heredes sui aquietabunt
de predictis centum solidis seruicium quod fieri debet de predicta terra
versus capitalem dominum, et ego et heredes mei computabimus predicto
Will(elm)o et heredibus suis in solutione predictorum centum solidorum

totum id quod capitali domino pacabunt pro seruicio predicte terre, et si forte idem Will(elmu)s et heredes sui non soluerint michi et heredibus meis predictos denarios ad predictum terminum, licebit michi et heredibus meis saisiare predictam terram in manus nostras donec idem Will(elmu)s et heredes sui competenter satisfecerint michi et heredibus meis de predictis centum solidis, saluo seruicio quod debetur capitali domino de eadem terra sicud predictum est, et ego Ricardus de Pyro et heredes mei warantizabimus predictam terram cum pertinentiis predicto Will(elmo) et heredibus suis contra omnes mortales, et ut hec mea donatio et concessio rata et stabilis in perpetuum perseueret, presentem cartam sigilli mei appositione roboraui. Hiis testibus: Rob(erto) de Curtenay, Will(elm)o de Percy, Engeugerio de Boun, Hascullo de Sulinn', Rad(ulfo) Gernun, Baldewino de Ver, Rob(erto) de Gouiz, Oseberto Giffard', Rad(ulfo) de Sulinn', Ricardo Suward, Will(elm)o Suward et multis aliis.

21. *Notification by Richard de Pirou that he has sworn to obtain a charter from William de Pirou, his father, confirming the charter that Richard himself has granted William Brewer over the land of* Chedzoy. [1195 X 1226, ?1217 X 1218]

A = TNA DL 25/200. Endorsed: *rem'* (s.xii/xiii); *in re* (s.xii/xiii). Approx. 130 × 48mm. Sealed *sur simple queue*, tongue and wrapping tie, seal impression on tongue, natural wax, a shield charged with a label of five points, legend: SIGILL'M RICARDI DE PIROIO+

With similar witnesses to, and therefore probably issued on the same occasion as no.20 above.

Omnibus ad quos presens script(um) peruenerit Ricardus de Pyro salutem. Nouerit uniuersitas vestra quod ego tactis sacrosanctis iuraui quod faciam habere Will(elm)o Briwer' cartam Will(elm)i de Pyro patris mei de terra de Chedesie talem qualem idem Will(elmu)s habet de me de predicta terra et in eadem verba, et in huius rei testimonium has litteras meas patentes ei inde feci. Hiis testibus: Rob(erto) de Curten', Will(elm)o de Percy, Rad(ulfo) Gernun, Rob(erto) de Gouiz, Hascullo de Sulinn', Oseberto Giffard', Baldewino de Ver et multis aliis.

22. *Notification by Richard de Pirou that he will not demand the 100 shilling rent referred to in his charter to William Brewer over the land of Chedzoy (above no.18), until he has full seisin of the land from the king and his council.*   [1195 X 1226,?1217 X 1218]

A = TNA DL 25/202. Endorsed: *rem* (s.xii/xiii); *in re* (s.xii/xiii). Approx. 143 × 55mm. Sealed *sur simple queue*, tongue and wrapping tie, seal impression natural wax and hand as in above no.21.

With similar witnesses to, and therefore probably on the same occasion as nos 20–1 above.

Omnibus ad quos presens scriptum peruenerit Ric(ardus) de Pyro salutem. Nouerit universitas vestra quod ego et heredes mei non exigemus nec exigi faciemus de Will(elm)o Briwer' vel heredibus suis illos centum solidos quos michi annuatim soluere tenetur per cartam quam habeo predicto Will(elm)o de centum solidis michi annuatim soluendis pro terra mea de Chedesie quam eidem Will(elm)o et heredibus suis dedi et concessi pro homagio et seruicio suo, donec plenariam saisinam habuero de predicta terra cum omnibus pertinentiis suis per dominum regem et eius consilium, et in huius rei testimonium huic scripto sigillum meum apposui. Hiis testibus: Rob(erto) de Curten', Will(elm)o de Percy, Rob(erto) de Guuiz, Baldewino de Ver, Will(elm)o de Pratellis, Rad(ulfo) Gernun, Oseberto Giffard' et multis aliis.

23. *Notification by Walter de Lacy of his grant to the monks of Beaubec (Seine-Maritime, cant. Forges, com. Beaubec-la-Rosière) of the church of St Patrick at Trim (Ireland, Co. Meath) to pay for the monks' sandals, establishing a vicar's portion in the church.*
[1215 X 1241, ?1235]

A = TNA DL 27/296. Sealed *sur double queue*, parchment tag through a single slit. Endorsed: *W. de Lacy de aduocatione ecclesie de Trim* (s.xiv); *xxvii.a comitum* (s.xiv). Approx. 160 × 88 + 28mm. Sealed *sur double queue*. Fine seal impression in natural wax varnished reddish brown, equestrian, SIGILLUM WALTERI DE LACI+, counterseal, a shield of arms, a fesse, legend: SIGILLUM WALTERI DE LACI+, the seal being described in *Catalogue of Seals in the Public Record Office, Personal Seals II*, ed. R.H. Ellis (London 1981), 64 nos P1642–3, and for Walter's arms, 'or, a fess gules', see *Aspilogia II: Rolls of Arms Henry III*, ed. T.D. Tremlett, A. Wagner and others (London 1967), 67.

To be dated after the restoration of Meath to Walter de Lacy following his disgrace in 1210, and before his death, probably of the same date as no.24 below. For the Irish priory of Beaubec in Co. Meath, near Drogheda, see A. Gwynn and R.N. Hadcock, *Medieval Religious Houses Ireland* (London 1970), 128; *Monasticon*, vi, 1129, and for

Jocelin prior of the Irish house of Beaubec, active in Stephen of Lexington's visitation of the Cistercian houses of Ireland 1228–9, see 'Registrum epistolarum Stephani de Lexinton abbatis de Stanlegia et de Savigniaco', ed. B. Griesser, *Analecta Sacri Ordinis Cisterciensis*, ii (1946) 46 no.37, 59–60 nos 55, 57, whence *Stephen of Lexington's Letters from Ireland 1228–1229*, trans. B.W. O'Dwyer (Kalamazoo 1982), 66 no.27, 96 no.45, 98 no.47. For the term 'Betani', referring to the native Irish peasantry, see J.A. Watt, *The Church and the Two Nations in Medieval Ireland* (Cambridge 1970), 125 and references there cited. According to M. Potterton (*Medieval Trim: History and Archaeology* (Dublin 2005), 270), the church of Trim is to be identified with that granted by John count of Mortain to form a prebend in St Patrick's church, Dublin, apparently for a set period of twenty years from 1193, thereafter renewed in 1213, at a time that the Lacy lands were in royal custody. This suggests that Walter de Lacy's grant to Beaubec was never properly implemented, since the church remained one of the more valuable prebends of St Patrick's from the 1250s onwards. An original charter of Geoffrey de Geneville, husband of Walter de Lacy's grand-daughter and joint heiress Matilda or Maud, 13 May 1259, confirms various lands, but not the churches, to the monks of Beaubec: BL ms. Harley Charter 50.G.38. The castle at Trim is further referred to in a charter of Walter de Lacy in favour of Petronilla his daughter and Ralph (V) de Tosny her husband (d.1239), witnessed by John de Lacy as earl of Lincoln (d.1240) and Richard vicomte de Beaumont-sur-Sarthe (from *c*.1237 to 1242–3), hence datable 1237 X 1239: Taunton, Somerset Record Office ms. DD/SAS H/348 (Hungerford cartulary) fo.59r, whence the calendar in *The Hungerford Cartulary: A Calendar of the Hobhouse Cartulary of the Hungerford Family*, ed. J.L. Kirby, Wiltshire Record Society lx (2007), 12–13 no.999. Amongst the witnesses to the present grant, Potterton notes that Nicholas de 'Ebroicis' (?Evreux) was, by 1234, serving as Walter de Lacy's seneschal for Meath. Note also the way in which an Irish landlord here endows a vicarage, usurping what in England would be regarded as a distinctly episcopal function.

Uniuersis Cristi fidelibus ad quos presens scriptum peruenerit Walterus de Lascy salutem. Ad vestre uniuersitatis noticiam volo peruenire me diuini amoris intuitu et pro salute anime mee, sponse mee, patris mei, matris mee, antecessorum et successorum meorum dedisse et concessisse et hac carta mea confirmasse Deo et ecclesie beati Laurentii de Bellobecco et monachis ibidem Deo seruientibus quantum ad patronum pertinet ecclesiam beati Patricii de Trum cum omnibus pertinentiis suis, habendam et tenendam in liberam, puram et perpetuam elemosinam ad ipsorum monachorum et familiarium suorum calciaturam, salua vicaria perpetua in eadem ecclesia assignata ad quam ego et heredes mei personam idoneam presentabimus et assignabimus. Vicarius autem habebit alteragia eiusdem ecclesie beati Patricii et capelle sancti Thome cum minutis decimis et sepulturis mortuorum. Habebit etiam idem vicarius duodecim marcas assignatas in decimis Betasiorum meorum de Leuure que si in tantum non suffecerint, dicti monachi perficient, et si quid in dictis superfuerit decimis prefatis remaneat monachis. Idem etiam vicarius omnia honera ecclesie pertinentia sustinebit. Ut hec igitur mea donatio et concessio rata et inconcussa permaneat, eam presenti scripto sigilli mei munimine roborato confirmaui. Hiis testibus: Nichol(ao) de Ebroic', Iohanne capellano, Alexandro clerico, Simone capellano, Willelmo de Cenomann', Ric(ardo) de Windesor, Adam de Notingeham' clerico et multis aliis.

24. *Notification by Walter de Lacy of his grant to the monks of Beaubec of the vill of 'Killekeran' (Ireland, ?Castlekeeran, Co. Meath) as he held it before he was deprived of it by King John, further granting a burgage in the 'vill of the mariners' (?Mornington, Co. Meath) with a boat free from toll and custom, and free entry and exit to his lands with freedom from toll on the purchase and sale of the monks' merchandise.*   [1215 X 1235, ?1235]

A = TNA DL 25/532. Endorsed: *carta ann(u)i redditus vi. marc(arum) de Gillikren'* (s.xiv); *dupli(catur)* (s.xiv); *xxii.a comitum* (s.xiv). Approx. 173 × 120 + 26mm. Sealed as no.23 above.

To be dated after the restoration of Meath to Walter de Lacy following the seizure of the Lacy estates by King John in 1210 (A.J. Otway-Ruthven, *A History of Medieval Ireland* (2nd ed., London 1980), 79–86, 91–2), and before the confirmation of the present award by King Henry III, issued on 2 December 1235: *Cal. Chart. R. 1226–57*, 215, and cf. letters of Edward III, 4 May 1348 (summarizing the terms of the present grant and recounting the later history of the abbey, transferred by the monks of Beaubec in Normandy to the keeping of the Cisterican monks of Furness): *Calendar of Close Rolls 1346–9* (London 1905), 459, whence Oxford, Bodleian Library ms. Dodsworth 71 fo.82r, and for the negotiations to alienate Beaubec's Irish estate to Furness, in train since 1322, see also *Inquisitions and Extents of Medieval Ireland*, ed. P. Dryburgh and B. Smith, List and Index Society cccxx (2007), 135–6 no.250; *CPR 1330–4*, 383. Probably issued shortly before the king's confirmation. For the identity of Killekeran, see above no.2n. For Nicholas de Ebroicis, one of the witnesses, as seneschal of Meath by 1234, see above no.23n. Note Walter's specific reference to his deprivation 'per voluntatem regis'.

Omnibus tam presentibus quam futuris Walterus de Lascy salutem in domino. Ad uniuersitatis vestre noticiam volo peruenire me dedisse et hac presenti carta mea confirmasse D(e)o et ecclesie beate Marie sanctique Laurentii de Bello Becco et monachis ibidem D(e)o seruientibus totum dominicum carucarum mearum in villa Gillekeran cum omnibus pertinentiis et libertatibus suis sicut melius, plenius et liberius illud tenui antequam inde dissaisitus essem per voluntatem domini Ioh(ann)is regis Angl(ie). Dedi etiam predicte ecclesie et eiusdem loci conuentui pro salute anime mee et Marger(ie) uxoris mee et omnium antecessorum et successorum meorum totam terram quam Betani et Anglici tenuerunt in villa Gillekeran tenend(am) et habend(am) libere et quiete cum omnibus pertinentiis suis in bosco et plano, in pratis et pascuis, in aquis et molendinis, in omnibus libertatibus et liberis consuetudinibus ad eandem terram pertinentibus, pro qua terra et libertate possidenda sepedicti monachi reddent michi et heredibus meis annuatim quatuor libras esterlingorum, scilicet medietatem ad Annunciationem beate Marie et aliam medietatem ad festum sancti Mich(aelis) pro omni seruicio seculari et exactione et demandis. Preterea dedi et concessi predicte ecclesie et conuentui unum burgagium in villa

Marineri cum libertate habendi unum batellum ad usus proprios sine teloneo et consuetudine et demanda. Concessi etiam predictis monachis liberum introitum et exitum in terra mea et libere emendi et vendendi omnes mercandisas quas ad usus proprios emere voluerint vel vendere sine teloneo, et quia volo quod hec elemosina et concessio mea et donatio predicte ecclesie et monachis ibidem Deo seruientibus imperpetuum remaneat sine contradictione sicut aliqua elemosina melius et plenius et liberius iuris religiosis dari potest, eam presenti scripto et sigilli mei inpressione confirmaui. Hiis testibus: Marger(ia) de Lascy, Will(elmo) de Manns', Rob(erto) Saluage, Will(elmo) Dylun, Nich(olao) de Ebr', Ricardo de Windesour', Will(elm)o clerico, Waltero Ioye, Ad(a) Dachet', Will(elm)o Haket' et multis aliis.

25. Notification by Walter de Lacy of his grant to the monks of Beaubec of the advowson of the church of St Patrick at Trim (Ireland, Co. Meath) to pay for the monks' sandals and 'pottages', saving the right of himself and his heirs to confer a vicarage within the church. [1227 X 1237, ?1235]

A = BL Additional Charter 19803. Endorsed: *carta Galt(eri) de Laci de ecclesia de Trim'* (s.xiii in); *cum xxvii. comitum* (s.xiii). Approx. 145 × 72 + 15mm. Sealed *sur double queue*, parchment tag through a single slit. Seal impression, round, dark brown wax, a shield showing a fess, legend: SIGILLUM WALTERI DE LACI+ Part of a much larger collection of English charters acquired by the British Library from G.R. Attenborough, 12 July 1873, themselves ultimately from the collections of Sir Christopher Hatton of Kirby Hall (above p.89 n.328).

Reproduced in facsimile M. Potterton, *Medieval Trim: History and Archaeology* (Dublin 2005), 288.

For Richard abbot of Stratford Langthorne (1218–1233 X 1237), see Smith, *Heads*, 313–14. After his disgrace in 1210, Hugh de Lacy was not restored as earl of Ulster until April 1227: *CP*, xii part 2, 168–71. Closely related to, and perhaps issued only shortly after Walter's other charter relating to the church, above no.24. Preserved together with a grant by Walter Talbot, confirming the gift by Geoffrey his uncle and Hugh his brother and Richard his father of land at Feltwell (Norfolk) to the monks of Beaubec (BL Additional Charter 19804, and for the Talbot estate at Feltwell and the Talbots as benefactors of Beaubec, see also Ibid. Harley Charters 111.G.50, 112.D.57–9). Note the reference to the monks' 'pottages' ('pulmentorum') or feedings.

Sciant presentes et futuri quod ego Walterus de Lascy dedi, concessi et presenti carta mea confirmaui pro salute anime mee et omnium antecessorum et successorum meorum Deo et ecclesie beate Marie

Belli Beccy et monach(is) ibidem Deo seruientibus aduocationem ecclesie sancti Patricii de Trum cum omnibus pertinen(tiis) suis salua tamen mi(chi) et heredibus meis vicaria eiusdem ecclesie in perpetuum conferenda et pretaxata, habendam et tenendam ipsis monachis de me et heredibus meis in liberam, puram et perpetuam elemosinam ad aumentum emendationis calciamentorum et pulmentorum eorum in perpetuum, et ego Walterus et heredes mei warantizabimus predictis monachis aduocationem predicte ecclesie cum omnibus pertin(entiis) suis contra omnes gentes in perpet(uum), et ut hec mea donatio et concessio et carte mee confirmatio rata sit et stabilis in perpet(uum) perseueret, sigilli mei appositione eam roboraui. Hiis testibus: Ric(ardo) abbate de Straford', Hugon(e) de Lascy com(ite) de Uluester', Willelmo de Lascy, Simone de Clifford', Waltero le Petit', Iohanne de Cranford', Ric(ardo) de Stangeland', Nich(olao) de Criketon.

26. *Convention made between Simon de Montfort, earl of Leicester, and Brother William de Gineuil', proctor in England of the abbot and convent of Bec, by which Earl Simon grants the monks of Bec the service, rent, land, a burgage and rights in Hungerford in exchange and recompense for pasture and commons for his beasts within the wood of Baltelay (in Hungerford, Berkshire).*   8 September 1246

A = TNA DL 36/1/152. Endorsed: *conventiones facte super parco de Hungerford'* (s.xiii/ xiv); *xxvi s.* (s.xiv/xv). Indented cyrograph. Approx. 207 × 195 + 20mm. Sealed *sur double queue*, slits for 2 tags, tags and seal impressions missing. B = TNA DL 42/2 (Great Coucher Book II) fo.72r–v (50r–v) no.26, entered by mistake amongst deeds for Leicestershire, s.xiv. C = Windsor, St George's Chapel Muniments ms. XI.G.28, copy, s.xv.

Pd (calendar from C) *The Manuscripts of St George's Chapel, Windsor Castle*, ed. J.N. Dalton (Windsor 1957), 46.

For Baltelay *alias* Batele in Hungerford, see *The Place-Names of Berkshire Part 2*, ed. M. Gelling, English Place-Name Society 1 (1974), 307, and for further exchanges of land there in the late 1240s involving Simon de Montfort in negotiations with Geoffrey Posard of Hungerford and William de Erpeham, see TNA DL 25/2296–7, whence DL 42/2 fo.176r–v (159r–v). The endorsements to the present award suggest that these transactions may have been related to the creation of a park at Hungerford, Simon having been granted licence by King Henry III to enclose his wood of 'Bauteleg' within Savernake forest by a charter of 3 May 1246: *Cal. Chart.R. 1226–57*, 293. For Simon's jurisdiction at Hungerford, where by 1248 he was attempting to exclude the king's bailiffs from entering to make distraints, see *The Roll and Writ File of the Berkshire Eyre of 1248*, ed. M.T. Clanchy, Selden Society xc (1973), 309 no.756. For Bec's lands in Wiltshire, see also letters of abbot H. of Bec 1234, in TNA DL 42/2 fo.205r–v (188r–v).

CONVENTIO CIROGRAPHATA

Anno regni reg(is) Henr(ici) filii reg(is) Ioh(ann)is tricesimo ad festum Nativitatis beate Marie virginis facta est hec conventio inter dominum Simonem de Monteforti comitem Leicestr' ex una parte et fratrem Willelmum de Ginevill' procuratorem abbatis et conventus de Becco tunc temporis in Anglia generalem ex altera. Videlicet quod dictus Simon dedit, concessit et confirmavit Deo et ecclesie beate Marie de Becco et monachis ibidem eis servientibus in escambium et recompensationem pasture et commune omnium mobilium suorum infra boscum suum de Baltelay secundum quod vetus fossatum et antique bunde eiusdem bosci se habent et proportant totum servicium et redditum de tenemento Iordani de Mareis cum omnibus pertinent(iis) suis et omnimodis exitibus et escaetis que inde aliquo casu dicto S(imoni) vel heredibus suis possent accidere, et unam cotsetlandam terre cum marisco cum omnibus pertinent(iis) suis quam Iohannes Ginegone tenuit in villa de Hungerford', excepta una acra que iacet apud Hanechull' inter terram Ade de Helme et Iordani de Mareis. Preterea unam acram terre que fuit Regin(aldi) Hareng que vocatur Bergacra extra cimiterium de Hungerford'. Ad hec concessit et dedit eis unum dimidium burgagium cum omnibus pertinent(iis) suis quod Rogerus Pogge tenuit in villa de Hungerford' et redditum quatuor denariorum que de terra quam Petrus le Sagiehere tenuit annuatim capere consuevit. Dedit insuper eis et concessit pro se et heredibus suis quod ipsi et eorum homines ac tenentes liberi sint et quieti tam in agris et villis quam extra et in omnibus aliis locis de omni servicio seculari, actione, querelis et demandis et omnimodis sectis curiarum suarum et hundredorum tam de tenemento prati quod vocatur Widemerch' quam de omnibus aliis terris, tenementis et possessionibus suis unde dicto S(imoni) vel heredibus suis aliquod seruicium seculare vel secta posset pertinere, ita quod dictus Simon nec heredes sui vel balliui aliquid ab eis in vite occasione alicuius servicii secularis de terris vel tenementis eorum exigere capere possint vel extorquere. Dicti vero monachi vel eorum successores nich(il) occasione herbagii pasture et commune infra antiquas bundas bosci de Baltelay prenominati exigere in perpetuum vel clamare poterunt vel debebunt. Quare memoratus S(imon) com(es) de Leicestr' voluit et concessit pro se et heredibus suis quod dicti monach(i) et eorum succ(essores) habeant et teneant omnia prenominata et omnes possessiones suas cum omnibus pertinen(tiis) suis et libertatibus tam in rebus spiritualibus quam secularibus in potestate sua in parochia de Hungerford' constitutis in puram et perpetuam elemosinam libere, quiete, honorifice, bene et in pace de omnibus serviciis secularibus, querelis et exactionibus sicut predictum est ita libere sicut dictus Simon aliquid liberius potuit conferre. Dictus vero S(imon) et heredes sui prefatis monach(is) et succ(essoribus) suis omnia suprascripta cum omnibus pertinent(iis) et libertatibus suis contra omnes gentes in perpetuum warantizabunt, et ut ista conventio stabil(is) et inconcussa utrinque permaneat, presenti scripto in modum cirographi confecto partes sigilla sua alternatim apposuerunt. Hiis testibus: dominis Roberto de Erpenham, Willelmo de Brettinuores, Iohanne de Columbar', Alano filio Warini, Hug(one) de Standen' militibus, Ricardo de Hauering',

Nicholao de Ingepenne, Galfr(ido) Ponchehart, Waltero de Ferchedon', Adam Bat et aliis.

27. *Notification by Abbot R(obert) and the convent of Bec of their confirmation of a settlement made between Simon de Montfort, earl of Leicester, and Brother William de Gineuill', their proctor in England, over the pasture of Baltelay in the parish of Hungerford (Berkshire).*

24 July 1247

A = TNA DL 27/101. Endorsed: *de parco de Hungerford* (s.xiii); *iiii.s* (s.xiv). Approx. 195 × 38 + 8mm. Sealed *sur double queue* on parchment tags through 3 slits, two seal impressions in brown wax, on the left the double-sided seal ?of an abbot, more or less entirely defaced, on the right the conventual seal of Bec, round, the Virgin and child seated, legend SI.................CI+, counterseal round, a monk's head, legend SIGILLUM ....ECCI+ B = TNA DL 42/2 (Great Coucher Book II) fo.176v (159v), s.xv in.

For Robert I de Clairbec, abbot of Bec, elected 22 July 1247, blessed by the bp of Evreux at Rouen during a vacancy in the archbpric, 8 September 1247, died 1265, see *GC*, xi, 232. The present charter was thus made only two days after Robert's election as abbot, and before his blessing at Rouen, in confirmation of no.26 above.

Omnibus presentes litteras inspecturis vel audituris R(obertus) divina permissione abbas de Becco Herluini totusque eiusdem loci conventus salutem in domino. Noverit universitas vestra quod nos habemus ratam et gratam compositionem factam inter nobilem virum dominum Symonem de Monteforti comitem Leicestr' ex una parte et dilectum nostrum in Cristo filium fratrem Willelmum de Ginevill' procuratorem nostrum in Anglia generalem ex altera super pastura de Baltelay in parrochia de Hungerford', et ad ipsius compositionis confirmationem presentibus lit(t)eris sigilla nostra duximus apponenda. Dat' anno domini m°cc°xl° septimo, die mercurii proxima post festum sancte Marie Magdalene.

28. *Letters of Maurice archbishop of Rouen to Edmund archbishop of Canterbury, following complaints from the men of the manor of Bentworth (Hampshire) that the king's bailiffs of Odiham have infringed their liberties and privileges conferred by earlier kings of England. Maurice requests Edmund's intervention with the king.*

20 July 1234

A = TNA SC 1/11 no.89. Endorsed: *domino Cantuar' archiepiscopo* (s.xiii, ?contemporary address). Approx. 144 × 88mm. Foot cut away, originally sealed ?*sur simple queue*.

Sent shortly after the fall of Peter des Roches, King Henry III's previous chief minister, at a time when archbp Edmund was in a position of authority at court. For the history of Rouen's property at Bentworth and elsewhere in England, see Maddicott, *Simon de Montfort*, 198–9; J. Peltzer, 'The Slow Death of the Angevin Empire', *Historical Research*, lxxxi (2008), 563ff, esp. p.566.

Reuerendo in Cristo patri ac domino Ead(mundo) Dei gratia Cantuar' archiepiscopo Maur(icius) diuina permissione Rothomag' ecclesie minister indignus salutem et sinceram in domino cartitatem. Intimatum est nobis ex parte hominum manerii nostri de Bintewurdhe quod balliui domini regis Anglie de Odiham contra libertates et priuilegia ab antecessoribus suis Rothomagen' ecclesie et ipsis hominibus concessa eosdem homines vexant multipliciter et molestan<t>, ab ipsis hominibus exactiones indebitas extorquendo. Verum cum de vobis dicatur et sic esse credamus quod vos saluti anime dicti regis salubriter prouidentes, eidem consulitis quod Dei ecclesiam et eius ministros diligat et eosdem in libertate et iure suo conseruet, et idem rex tanquam deuotus ecclesie filius salubribus paternitatis vestre consiliis et monitis libenter obtemperet, paternitatem vestram attentius duximus exorandam quatinus memoratum regem efficaciter inducatis ut balliuos suos conpellat desistere a predictorum hominum molestatione indebita, et eos in suis immo potius Rothomagen' ecclesie libertatibus tueatur. Valete in domino paternitas vestra. Dat' in festo sancte Margarite <anno domini m°> cc° tricesimo quarto.

29. Notification by Jordan de Sauqueville of his grant to the collegiate church at Sauqueville (Seine-Maritime, cant. Offranville) of the manor of Helmingham (Suffolk), 10 livres in the vill of L'Epinay (?Seine-Maritime, cant. et com. Dieppe), the churches of either Fawley (Buckinghamshire) or Marlesford (Suffolk) at the next vacancy, and rents at Epreville (?Seine-Maritime, cant. St-Valery, com. Veules-les-Roses) and Les Hameaux (Seine-Maritime, cant. Tôtes, com. Gonneville-sur-Scie) to augment the collegiate establishment from two to six canons, for whose regular life rules are here established relating to discipline, residence and liturgy.

[c.1200 X 1202]

A = Rouen AD Seine-Maritime J294. An original, or possibly a contemporary copy. Mounted, dorse inaccessible. Approx. 200 × 425mm. No indication of sealing, perhaps foot cut away. Badly damp damaged, especially along folds and at left hand side, many letters missing or crumbling. Letters in brackets <> below supplied, for the most part from the confirmation, no.30 below. Recovered with no.30 in the 1880s from the collections of a local notary, cf. Stein no.3625, where this and no.30 below are falsely described as a cartulary roll.

Of the same date as the archiepiscopal confirmation, no.30, whose date is discussed below. For Jordan, d.<u>c</u>. 1234, lord of Sauqueville in Normandy and of Fawley in Buckinghamshire, and for his rights in Helmingham passed down to his wife, Clementia, apparently as daughter and coheiress of William de Chesney of Norfolk, see W. Farrer, *Honors and Knights' Fees*, 3 vols (London 1923–5), i, 210–13, iii, 317–18; *CRR*, xi, no.254; D. Power, 'The French Interests of the Marshal Earls of Striguil and Pembroke, 1189–1234', *ANS*, xxv (2003), 219–20; N. Vincent, 'More Tales of the Conquest', *Normandy and its Neighbours 900–1250: Essays for David Bates*, ed. D. Crouch and K. Thompson (Turnhout 2011), 276–87, 300–1. The present charter shares at least one witness in common with no.31 below, and perhaps two if the reconstruction of the witness name 'Elias de Tillol' be allowed. For the form 'Faneleia' or 'Fanle' to denote Fawley, and for the descent of the advowson there together with the lordship of the manor, neither of them, in the event transferred to the college at Sauqueville, see *VCH Buckinghamshire*, iii, 42; *Book of Fees*, i, 464, 467. For further charters or bequests by the grantor relating to his lands in Normandy, see Rouen AD Seine-Maritime 24HP45; 24HP75/1; 16H14 (Cartulary of St-Wandrille) fo.90v; *Monasticon*, vi, 1091.

<Omnibus Cristi> fidelibus ad quos presens scriptum peruenerit Iord(anus) de Sauqueuill' salutem in domino. Nouerit uniuersitas vestra <ego Iordanus de Sauqueuill' pro amore Dei et pro salute anime mee> et uxoris mee Clement(ie) et antecessorum et heredum meorum dedisse et concessisse et presenti carta mea <confirma>ss<e Deo et ecclesie beate Marie de S>auqueuill' totam terram meam de Helmingeham cum omnibus pertinentiis suis et omnibus obuenti<onibus et f>ructibus que ad <u>s<us> suos spectare solent, que terra valet ad minus per annum cent(um) sol(idos) sterlingorum. Hoc siquidem concessi per concessi<onem et donationem domini> Walt(eri) Dei gratia Rothom' archiepiscopi et uxoris mee Clement(ie) que heres est eiusdem terre de Helmingeh', ita quod de terra illa <quatu>or fiant prebende in ecclesia de Sauqueuill', quilibet de cent(um) sol(idis) Andeg(auensibus) preter illas duas prebendas que ab antiquo ab antecessoribus me<is in> ecclesia illa ordinate sunt. Preterea decano illius ecclesie qui unus erit ex illis sex canonicis canonice electus dedi et concessi decem li(bras) And(egauenses) <in villa de Spin>eto <de> redditu <meo> assiso annuatim nomine personatus d<onec> ecclesia de Faneleia vel ecclesia de Merlesford' vaca<uerit nis>i inter<im de alio ecclesiastico beneficio poter>o prouidere ad valenciam decem librarum. Cantori qui similiter unus erit ex illis sex dedi et concessi quinquaginta sol(idos) <Andegauenses in redditu meo de Sauqueuill' annu>atim nomine personatus. Thesaurario qui similiter unus erit ex illis sex dedi et concessi <unam> marcam <argenti in redditu meo assiso de> Es<peruilla annuati>m <nomine> personatus <et> ad luminare ecclesie <qui>nquaginta sol<idos>. Similiter de <r>edd<itu> ....<thesaurarii>. Preterea a<d com>m<un>iam ec<clesie> dedi et concessi predicte ecclesie et canonicis in perpetuum t.........de H<ameau> ....tonum ducentas et sexaginta <min>as ordei, et statui quod de illa com<munia habeat qui>li<bet c>anoni<cus in> die <d>uos panes et un(um) <galone>m <c>eru<isie> et <si> predictum do<nationem> ad hoc non possit sufficere, ego d<e meo proprio qui>cquid defecerit perficiam. D<uo canonici> presb<iteri> qui ab antiquo <fuerunt et> sunt in ecclesia predicta habebunt <domo>s et redditus quos habent <et> successores eorum in perpetuum, qui semper <sac>erdotes erunt, et tenetur quil<ibet eorum> habere clericum suum sufficientem ad deseruiendum ecclesie. Aliis vero quatuor canonicis dedi et concessi ad e<dificia s>ua construenda et qui<cquid habeo> in domini<o> in magno gardino de <S>auqueuill' iuxta ecclesiam. Omnes isti canonici tenen<tur> face<re res>id<entiam>, et qui residentiam n<on fecerit tantum> modo percipiet per annum quinque sol(idos) Andeg(auenses), et residuum de beneficio suo percipient illi qui resident<iam fec>erint et tenentur habere hab<itum> ca<n>onical alioquin hora canonica non intrabunt ecclesiam. Tenentur etiam canonici ad matutinas <sur>gere, et qui non interfuerit matutinis non habebit ea die communia sed illi qui interfuerint <totam> communiam habebunt. Decanus cum assensu meo <et heredum> meorum et <c>anonicorum canonice electus archiepiscopo per me et heredes meos et per canon<icos> presentabitur et <in>stituendus qui ei et successoribus su<is cano>n<icam> obedientiam et reuerentiam pr<est>a<bit> et eandem securitatem q<uam> decanus Rothom' ecclesie <facit meo et meis heredi>bus et ecclesie <de Sau>queuill' facere tenetur <sa>luo ordine suo et salua obedienti<a> <debita> arch<iepiscopo>. Ego vero et <heredes mei> prebend<am cum> vacau<er>it <infra> xx. dies, si in prouincia Rothom' fuerimus, persone idonee conferemus <et illam per>son<am> decano de Sauqueuill' presentabimus instituend<am. Canonic>i autem honeste et ordinate <obserue>bunt usu<m et ordi>n Rothom' ecclesie in omnibus, et intrabunt in capitul<um> et legent ib<idem o>bit<us statuto>s et cetera que ad capitulum pertinent. Ad......... ego et heredes <mei> sta<tui>mus quod u>nus canonicorum sacerdos si voluerit et nos vol<uerimus s>uccurret nob(is) et co<nsul>et ubicum<que> simus et quamdiu apud nos er<it poterit habere> unum sacerdotem idoneum ad des<eruiendum. Aliud sacerdos> autem poterunt aliquem ponere in locum suum. O<mnia hec> predicta in personati<s> et <in> communis ...p......... <ecclesias>tico <be>neficio ad valentiam .... cuiuslibet .... preter ......de............. Hec autem omnia que prescripta sunt ecclesie de Sa<uque>uill' data et statut<a> guarant<izabo> .... et fite....im et a........... in perpet<uum contra omnes> homines. Q<uod> ut rata et constanter in perpetuum permaneant .... sigilli<s nost>ris munim<us> et c<on>fi<rmamus>. Hiis testibus: R<i>c<ardo> decano <Rothom'> ecclesie, Rogero <cantore>, ...rio, ma<gistro> Ioh<anne> de <Vil>liers, Will(elm)o de Brue<r'> et Ric(ardo) Hairun canonicis Rothom', Ro<berto de Sancto Nicolao, G>ill<eberto> de W<alemunt>, Ric(ardo) Briton(e), Bart<holomeo de .... de S......, magistro Ioh(anne) de Sa.................. illar', Will(elm)o Marcei, Alano Marce...............<Wi>ll(elmo) de ...., Hel(ia) de <Ti>ll<ol'>, ...o. Will(elm)o Clare, Rad(ulfo) de ....el', Will(elmo) de ....H..f.... et multis <aliis>

30. *Confirmation by Walter archbishop of Rouen of no.29, adding quittance from synodal exactions, limited freedom from excommunication by archdeacons or deans, and granting licence for a school.* Rouen, 17 January [1200 X 1202]

A = Rouen AD Seine-Maritime J294. Mounted, dorse inaccessible. Approx. 275 × 280 + 45mm. Foot flattened out. Originally sealed *sur double queue*, 4 holes for cords, cords and seal impression missing, B = Ibid. G8685, paper copy by the notaries of the Châtelet at Paris, apparently from A, 13 May 1762. Passages marked below as ..... shown as illegible in the copy by use of straight lines ____

Letters in brackets [] now illegible in A, supplied from B. Letters in brackets <> illegible in either A or B, supplied, for the most part from no.29 above.

The secondary authorities, apparently working from a copy of this charter, suggest a date of 17 January 1201 (i.e. 1201/2): M.–T. Duplessis, *Description géographique et historique de la haute Normandie*, 2 vols (Paris 1740), i, 167; *Registre des fiefs et arrière-fiefs du bailliage de Caux en 1503*, ed. A. Beaucousin, Société de l'Histoire de Normandie (Rouen 1891), 80, referring to possessions at Sauqueville, Gonneville and Les Hameaux. However, the final initial of the date 'c°', still visible in A, might nonetheless suggest a date of 1200 ('ducentissimo'). For various of the witnesses, including Richard dean (1200–1207), Roger de Foucarmont chanter, and probably Amicus du Neubourg treasurer of Rouen, see Spear, *Personnel*, 204, 220, 222–3, 248, 256, 265–6.

Omnibus Cristi fidelibus ad quos presens scriptum peruenerit Walterus Dei gratia Rothom(agensis) archiepiscopus salutem in domino. Adeo nostris temporibus [seua m]alignandi cupiditas inualuit ut vix bene gesta debita possint firmitate gaudere. Ad rep(ri)mendam igitur malignantium temeritatem et ut ea que pie et iuste ecclesiis [seu] ecclesiasticis viris conferuntur debita gaudeant firmitate, ne obliuione vel inuidentium siue etiam ambitiosorum malignitate aliquatenus valeant deperire, ad uniuersitatis vestre volumus notitiam peruenire dilectum filium nostrum Iordane[a] de Sauqueuill'[b] pro amore Dei et pro salute anime sue et uxoris sue Clementie et[c] antecessorum et heredum suorum dedisse et concessisse et carta sua confirmasse Deo et ecclesie beate Marie de Sauqueuill'[b] totam terram suam de Helmingehan cum omnibus pertinentiis [suis et omnibus obuentionibus] et [fructibus qu]e ad usus suos spectare solent, ita quod de predicta terra quatuor [fiant] prebende in ecclesia de Sauqueuill'[b] preter illas duas prebendas q[ue ab antiquo ab antecessoribus suis] in e[cclesia illa] ordinate sunt. Preterea decano [illius ecclesie qui unus erit ex i]ll[is sex] canonicis canonice electus dedit et concessit decem [libras] Andeg(auenses) in villa de Spineto de redditu suo assiso annuatim nomine personatus <donec ecclesia de Fan>eleia vel ecclesia de Merlefordia[d] vacauerit nisi [interim de a]llio [ecclesiast]ico beneficio poterit prouidere ad [vale]ntiam decem librarum. Cantori qui <unus erit ex illis sex> dedit et concessit quinquaginta sol(idos) Andeg(auenses) in redd[itu suo] de Sauqueuilla[b] annuatim nomine personatus. Thesaurario qui similiter <unus erit ex illis sex dedit unam> marcam de redditu suo assiso de Esperuill'[e] annuatim nomine personatus

et ad luminare ecclesie quinquaginta solidos sim<iliter de redditu>
.... thesaurarii. Preterea ad communiam
ecclesie dedit et concessit predicte ecclesie et canonicis in perpetuum
..............de Hameau....quod ....<ducentas> et sexaginta minas
ordei, et statuit quod de illa communia habeat quilibet canonicus in die duos
panes et unum galonem ceruisie, et [si] predictum <donationem> [ad] hoc
non possit sufficere, ipse de suo quicquid defuerit perficiet. [Duo] canonici
presbiteri qui ab antiquo fuerunt et sunt in ecclesia predicta habebunt [do]mos
[et redditus] quos habent et successores eorum similiter in perpetuum, qui
semper sacerdotes [erunt et] tenetur quilibet eorum habere clericum suum
sufficientem ad deseruiendum ecclesie. Aliis vero quatuor canonicis dedit et
concessit ad edificia sua construenda quicquid habuit in d(omi)nio in magno
gardino de Sauqueuill'[b] iuxta ecclesiam. Omnes isti canonici tenentur
f[acere reside]ntiam, et qui residentiam non fecerit tantum modo percipiet
per annum quinque sol(idos) Andeg(auenses) et residuum de beneficio suo
percipient illi qui residentes fuerint, et tenentur canonici habere habitum
ca[non]ical[em alioquin hora canonica non intrabunt] ecclesiam. Tenentur
etiam canonici ad matutinas surgere, et qui non interfuerit matutinis non
habebit ea die commun(i)am s[ed] illi qui interfuerint <totam> commun(i)am
habebunt. Decanus cum assensu Iord(ani) et heredum suorum et canonicorum
canonice electus nob(is) et successoribus nostris [per] ipsum Iord(anum)
et heredes suos et per canonicos presentabitur instituendus, qui nob(is) et
successoribus nostris canonicam obedientiam et reuerentiam prestabit et
eandem securitatem quam decanus Rothom(agensis) nob(is) et ecclesie
Rothom(agensi) facit prefato Iord(ano) et heredibus suis et ecclesie de
Sauqueuill'[b] faciet, saluo ordine suo et salua obedientia nob(is) debita. Ipse
vero Iord(anus) et heredes sui prebendam cum vacauerit infra viginti dies,
si in prouinicia Rothom(agensi) fuerint, persone idonee conferent et illam
personam dec(ano) de Sauqueuill'[b] presentabunt instituendam. Canonici
autem honeste et ordinate usum et ordinem Rothom(agensis) ecclesie in
omnibus obseruabunt et intrabunt[f] [in capitulum quot]idie et legent ibidem
obitus stat[utos] et cetera que ad capitulum pertinent. Ipse vero I(ordanus)
et heredes sui statuerunt quod unus canonicorum sacerdos, si voluerit et
eis placuerit, [succurr]at eis et consulat ubicumque sint et quamdiu[g] apud
eos fuerit poterit <habere> [in] locum suum unum sacerdotem idoneum ad
deseruiendum prebende sue, nec aliquis alius canonicus poterit aliquem
ponere in locum suum. Hec autem omnia [que prescrip]ta [sunt] ecclesie
de Sauqueuill'[b] data warantizabit[h] ipse Iord(anus) et heredes sui [prefate]
ecclesie canonicis in perpetuum contra omnes homines. Nos autem hec
omnia que prescripta sunt rata habentes et firma, presenti scripto et s[igilli]
<nostri munimine confirmamus>. Concessimus etiam eis in perpetuum
quod quieti sint ab omni tallia et sinodalibus consuetudinibus et omnibus
exactionibus que ad nos seu ad archidiaconos [et] decanos spectant, statuentes
quod [nullus] archid(iaconu)s vel decanus po[ssit sententia]m suspensionis,
excommunicationis aut interdicti [in] ecclesiam illam seu in canonicos nisi
de sp[eciali] mandato nostro aut capital(is) offic(ialis) nostri promulgare.
Concessimus etiam .... [quod libere] et sine contradictione habeant
scolas in ecclesia vel in villa de S[auqueuilla]. Testibus: domino Ri(cardo)
decano, Rogero cantore, ...rario, magistro Ioh(anne) de Vi[llers],
Will(elm)o[j] de Bruer'[k] et Ric(ardo) Hayrun[l] canonicis Rothom(agensibus),

Rob(erto) de Sancto N[icolao], Gilleb(erto)[m] de Walemunt et <multis aliis>.
Actum a<nno incarnationis Domini millesimo> .... c° apud Rothom(agum)
xvi. kal(endas)[n] Febr(uarii).

[a] Iordanum B [b] Sauqueuilla B [c] et not in B [d] Melefordia B [e] Esperuilla B [f] introibunt
B [g] quandiu B [h] garantisabit B [j] Willermo B [k] Bruyere B [l] Hayrum B [m] Gilberto B
[n] calendas B

31. *Notification by Jordan de Sauqueville, with the assent of Clementia his wife and Jordan his son, of his confirmation to Richard of Bocking of a grant made by the dean and chapter of Sauqueville (Seine-Maritime, cant. Offranville) of a perpetual farm of the land of Helmingham (Suffolk) in return for an annual rent of 100s. [c.1202]*

A = BL Additional Charter 9810. No medieval endorsement. Approx. 135 × 70 +
21mm. Sealed *sur double queue* on pink, blue and white cords through two holes, seal
impression round, brown wax, equestrian image facing to the right (approx. 30mm.
diameter), legend defaced, counterseal an oval intaglio, illegible, legend: SECRE[T'
SAUNGVILL'], here supplying letters now illegible from the description given by
W.G. Birch, *Catalogue of Seals in the Department of Manuscripts in the British
Museum*, 6 vols (London 1887–1900), ii, 351 no.6417.

Of the same date as nos 29–30. At his death, Jordan left a son and heir, Bartholomew
de Sauqueville, perhaps the witness to the present charter, suggesting that his elder son,
mentioned below, had predeceased him. Despite the new endowment from Helmingham,
and no doubt as a result of disruptions brought about in the aftermath of the Capetian
conquest of Normandy, by the 1250s the college at Sauqueville was reported to be
in a perilous state of both moral and financial collapse, its prebendaries more often
resident in the local tavern than in the church: *Regestrum visitationum archiepiscopi
Rothomagensis*, ed. T. Bonnin (Rouen 1852), 116, 145, 209, 285, 409, 652.

Sciant tam presentes quam futuri quod ego Iord(anus) de Sauq'will'
concessu uxoris mee Clem(en)c(ie) et Iord(ani) heredis mei confirmo et
concedo Ric(ardo) de Bocking' donationem G. decani ecclesie beate Marie
de Sauq'will' totiusque capituli eiusdem, ita quod predictus Ric(ardus)
et heredes sui tenebunt terram de Helmingeh' cum omnibus pertinentiis
ad firmam perpetuam de predicto capitulo ecclesie predicte de Sauq'uill'
per c. sol(idos) stelling(os) per annum reddend(os) sicuti carta quam ipse
habet de predicto capitulo testatur. Testibus hiis: Helya de Tillol, Willelmo
Clar', Iohanne Hosbermesnil, Rog(ero) de Viuar', Iord(ano) de Fanel',
Ric(ardo) fil(io) Roberti, Barth(o)lom(eo) de Sauq'uill' cum multis aliis
hoc videntibus et scientibus.

32. *Mandate from King Edward (I) to Edmund earl of Cornwall, to do justice in respect to the enclosed petition from the dean and chapter of Notre-Dame de Sauqueville (below no.33).*

Paris, 13 June 1286

A = TNA SC 1/20 no.124A. Endorsed: *Habent ad mandatum regis a cur(ia) quicquid curia facere poterit* (s.xiii ex). Approx. 220 × 54mm. Sealed *sur simple queue*, step for tongue or wrapping tie at lower left hand corner and similarly at lower right hand corner, sew holes at left hand side for attachment to the petition no.33 below.

Despite the forwarding of the petition (below no.33), there is no record in the chancery Charter, Patent or Close Rolls, of the king's administration taking action in response to the dean and chapter's request.

Edwardus Dei gratia rex Angl(ie) dominus Hibern(ie) et dux Aquitann(ie) dilecto consanguineo suo Edmundo comiti Cornub' salutem. Requisiuit nos magnificus princeps rex Franc(ie) ut decano et capitulo ecclesie beate Marie de Sauqueuill' super quibusdam redditibus, arreragiis et debitis que eis debentur ut dicunt in Angl(ia) subueniri per ministros nostros seu iusticiarios curaremus, et quia sumus et esse debemus iusticie debitores, ponderantes etiam requisitionem regis Franc(ie) supradictam vobis mandamus quatinus, inspecta peticione decani et capituli predictorum presentibus interclusa, communicatoque consiliariorum nostrorum assistenċium vobis consilio, memoratis .. decano et capitulo vel attornato ipsorum per viam qua poteritis breuiorem sine lite de plano fieri faciatis celeris iusticie complementum. T(este) me ipso Paris', terciodecimo die Iun(ii), anno regni nostri quartodecimo.

33. *Petition from the dean and chapter of Notre-Dame de Sauqueville, placed under the patronage of the king of France, asking that the king of England write to his bailiffs or justices to ensure the payment to the dean and chapter of all rights, rents or arrears arising from grants made in England by Jordan de Sauqueville or Matilda his wife or their heirs.* [*c*.June 1286]

A = TNA SC 1/20 no.124. No medieval endorsement. Approx. 174 × 44mm. Sealed *sur simple queue*, step for tongue at bottom left hand corner.

For the response to this petition, by which Edmund earl of Cornwall forwarded it and the king's letters to W(illiam) de Hamilton, requesting investigation and execution, see TNA SC 1/25 no.78. The reference to Jordan de Sauqueville and Matilda his wife rules out an identification with the Jordan and Clementia of nos 27A–28, and could refer either to Jordan's grandfather or grandson (fl.1240), for whom see Vincent, 'More Tales of the Conqueror' (above no.30 note).

Regie maiestati Anglie supplicant .. decanus et capitulum ecclesie beate Marie de Sauqueuill' Rothomagen' dyoc(esis) cuius ecclesie dominus rex Francie patronus existit quatinus dominus rex Anglie bailliuis seu iusticiariis suis scribere ac eis precipere dignetur ut cum ipsi decanus et capitulum sint pauperes nec habeant unde iura seu redditus et arreragia eiusdem ecclesie repetere seu defendere cum iudiciorum strepitu valeant in partibus Anglicanis, dicti bailliui aut iusticiarii Anglie redditus, arreragia et debita que debentur eisdem decano et capitulo coniunctim vel diuisim nomine suo vel ecclesie supradicte a Iordano de Sauq(ue)uill' milite, Matildi eius uxore et eorum heredibus ac quibusdam aliis coniunctim vel diuisim in Anglia sine litis et more dispendio faciant et percipiant liberari sicut in litteris et conuentionibus predictorum Iordani et Matildis continetur.

34. *Notification by Ralph of Dean of his grant to Jordan de Sackville and his wife Ela, Ralph's daughter, of a hide of land at Waldrington with the church of the same vill, and a virgate of land at Chalvington (Sussex) together with the land of 'Geyle' in Normandy with a promise to assist Jordan to acquire the whole of Ralph's inheritance and right in Normandy, without offering Jordan monetary assistance.*
[*c.*1170]

B = BL ms. Additional 14291 fo.66r (p.125), a copy by John Anstis (1669–1744) from an original charter belonging to the Earl of Dorset, no longer in the Sackville family archives at Knole House or in the Kent Record Office at Maidstone, noting a large seal 'with the arms of Den fritee or et vert circumscribed +SIGILLUM RADULPHI DE DEN'.

Noted as part of the appallingly confused genealogy of the Sackville dukes of Dorset in *Collins' Peerage of England*, ed. E. Brydges, 9 vols (London 1812), ii, 92–3, apparently from a fuller version of the lost charter 'ex charta Rad(ulfi) de Dene in stemmate' (perhaps from a heraldic visitation), referring to Ralph's gifts as noted above but adding 'the land which Robert Franceis held at Sutton's fee, the manor of Saperton, and a yard land in Chalventune, with the mansion thereto belonging'.

The present charter, as noted by N. Vincent, 'More Tales of the Conquest', *Normandy and its Neighbours 900–1250: Essays for David Bates*, ed. D. Crouch and K. Thompson (Turnhout 2011), 277 n.14, refers to Jordan de Sauqueville (d.*c.*1175), a namesake and cousin distinct from the Jordan of Fawley, Helmingham and Sauqueville who granted above nos 29.31. The Jordan of the present charter was son of Robert de Sauqueville who had served as steward to King Stephen during Stephen's time as count of Mortain, and brother of Stephen de Sauqueville who in 1180 was serving as the king's bailli for the vicomté of Cérences. This Jordan, of Mount Bures and West Bergholt (Essex), married Ela daughter of Ralph of Dean (d.1187, himself the son of Robert of Dean, *alias* Robert 'pincerna', butler to the count of Mortain fl.1147). The date of the present charter can be supplied only approximately, from the fact that in 1185 Ela was said to have been a widow for the past ten years. Ela herself was still living in 1205: TNA E 40/4221. For supporting evidence here, in part drawn to my attention by Daniel Power, see H.M. Colvin, *The White Canons in England* (Oxford 1951), 109–11; L.F. Salzman, 'Some Domesday Tenants II: The Family of Dene', *Sussex Archaeological Collections*, lviii (1906), 171–3, 177, 189; *Rotuli de Dominabus*, ed. J.H. Round, PRS xxxv (1913), 70n.; *MRSN*, i, 14–15; E. King, 'Stephen of Blois, Count of Mortain and Boulogne', *EHR*, cxv (2000), 287. 'Geyle' is perhaps one or other of the estates named La Geôle or Le Gal, Seine-Maritime, as listed in the *Dictionnaire topographique de du département de Seine-Maritime*, ed. C. de Beaurepaire and J. Laporte, 2 vols (Paris 1982–4), i, 422–3, 430.

Radulphus de Dene omnibus hominibus suis et amicis Francis et Anglis salutem et dilectionem. Sciatis me dedisse et concessisse Iordano de Saucauill et Hele uxori sue filie mee hidam de Waldene cum ecclesia eiusdem ville etc et unam virgatam terre in Chaluentune etc et in Normannia terram meam de Geyle et omnem hereditatem et rectum meum Normannie illi perquirere adiuuabo ad posse meum cum labori absque pecuniam dare. Hii sunt testes: Reginaldus de Warenne etc Helias de Saccauill etc.

35. Notification by Henry de Montfort of his grant to Hugh de Montfort, his brother, of his lands in Picauville, Gueutteville and Clainville (Manche, cant. Ste-Mère-Eglise, com. Picauville).

[1178 X 1199]

A = Nottingham University Archives Mi D 3317. Endorsed: *Hug(onis) de Mont 'fort' confirmat(io) sine dato* (s.xv); various post medieval endorsements. Approx. 289 × 98 + 22mm. Sealed *sur double queue*, parchment tag through single slit to the left of the centre of the plica, seal impression cut away.

Printed *HMC Middleton*, 35–6 (as if relating to Pickwell Leics.).

For the Montfort family of Beaudesert (Warwickshire), ultimately perhaps from Montfort-sur-Risle (Eure), and for Henry de Montfort, lord of Beaudesert *c*.1183–*c*.1199, son of Thurstan de Montfort (d.*c*.1170) by his marriage to Juliana daughter of Geoffrey Murdac, and younger brother of Robert de Montfort, see *CP*, ix, 120–2; *CRR*, v, 311; *Mowbray Charters*, ed. Greenway, p.xxxiv, 240–1 no.372, 264 no.25. Henry's inheritance in England may have come to him some years before the generally accepted date of 1183. His elder brother, Robert de Montfort, was the victim of a series of punitive fines, in part for forest offences, in the year to Michaelmas 1176, which seem to have led to temporary seizure of various of Robert's lands, including Uppingham in Rutland (*PR 22 Henry II*, 109, 129, 176, 186; *PR 23 Henry II*, 32–4. 74, 104). By Michaelmas 1178, whether or not Robert was still living, his debts were assumed by Henry his brother, who thereafter emerges as the principal representative of the family in England, without any further evidence that Robert was still alive (*PR 24 Henry II*, 81; *PR 25 Henry II*, 113; *26 Henry II*, 74; *27 Henry II*, 74; *28 Henry II*, 93, and cf. the sheriffs' account for the manor of Wellesbourne, Warwicks., described as an escheat from Robert de Montfort and first recorded in the king's hands for the year ending at Michaelmas 1179, *PR 26 Henry II*, 105; *27 Henry II*, 79). In these circumstances, it is tempting, although wrong, to assume an identity between Robert de Montfort of Beaudesert and the great Norman landowner Robert de Montfort(-sur-Risle), rebel during the civil war of 1173–4, who died in 1178 and who was succeeded, in Normandy, by a son named Hugh (V), by his marriage to Clemence, a sister of Ralph de Fougères, with Hugh having brothers named Ralph, William and Henry and a sister named Aelina, a nun at Mortain: 'Torigny', 279; AN L979 no.72. Robert de Montfort of Beaudesert, by contrast, is described as son of Thurstan de Montfort, a Warwickshire and Rutland landowner, in the last years of King Stephen, and left a widow named Alice de Harcourt: N. Vincent, *The Lucys of Charlecote: The Invention of a Warwickshire Family 1170–1302*, Dugdale Society Occasional Papers xlii (2002), 32–5 nos 3, 5; Oxford, Bodleian Library ms. Dugdale 21 fo.148r. The genealogy of the Norman Montfort family is extremely complicated and has still not achieved certainty. Amongst the parties and witnesses to the present charter, Hugh de Montfort occurs as witness to a charter of Henry his brother (Oxford, Bodleian Library ms. Dugdale 17 p.5). There were two Warwickshire knights named Aytrop Hastang, Aytrop (I) who was active from 1120 until 1158, and Aytrop (II), his son, who died in 1204: R. Dace, 'The Hastang Family and their Lands, 1086–1204', *Warwickshire History*, xii (2004/5), 221–38. Peter 'the clerk', identified as writer of the present charter, is perhaps the same man as Peter de Montfort who occurs as writer of another of Henry de Montfort's charters, with similar witness list: BL ms. Harley 506 fo.122r (p.244). The senior branch of the Montfort family, although inconvenienced in Normandy after 1204, did not entirely lose possession of their estates, still controlling land there in the 1250s: AN L979 no.57. Nonetheless, Picauville was given by Philip Augustus, after 1204, to Matthew de Marly, a junior member of the Montmorency family: *RHF*, xxiii, 525l, 611c; *Pouillés Rouen*, 299. Since the Montforts of Beaudesert held in England of the Neubourg earls of Warwick, it is possible that Picauville came to them from the Neubourgs, who certainly possessed land in the Cotentin (*RHF*, xxiii, 610–11). Alternatively, it may have been the Montforts' original Norman patrimony, before they achieved far greater possessions in the 1080s with the creation of the earldom of Warwick for their cousin, Henry de Beaumont.

Henr(icus) de Monte Forti omnibus hominibus suis et amicis Francis et Anglicis, clericis et laicis tam futuris quam presentibus salutem. Ad uniuersorum noticiam referatur me dedisse et concessisse et hac mea presenti carta confirmasse Hugoni de Monte Forti fratri meo et heredibus suis totas terras meas de Pychauilla et de Gouteuilla et de Cleuilla cum omnibus eisdem terris pertinenciis et libertatibus, ad tenendum hereditarie de me et de heredibus meis, reddendo annuatim m(ich)i et heredibus meis duo calcaria deaurata pro omnibus seruiciis m(ich)i et heredibus meis pertinentibus. Quare volo et firmiter precipio quatinus predictus Hugo et heredes eius post illum habeant et teneant totas prenominatas terras de me et de heredibus meis libere et quiete et honorifice cum omnibus libertatibus et liberis consuetudinibus in bosco, in plano, in foro et extra, in pratis, in pascuis, in piscariis, in stangnis, in molendinis, in aquis, in viis, in semitis, in exitibus et in omnibus aliis locis prefatis terris pertinentibus per prefatum seruicium. His testibus: Aytrop Hasteng, Willelmo et Waltero de Monte Forti, Ric(ardo) capellano, Willelmo de Hulehale, Roberto filio Nic(olai), Clare de Beldesert, Willelmo de Rameham, Iohanne Brusle, Rand(ulfo) et Reimbaldo fratre suo, Gileberto de Brahal, Adam fil(io) Lamberti, Roberto fil(io) Henr(ici), Aytrop de Boilest', Petro clerico qui hanc cartam scripsit et aliis multis. Valete.

36. *Notification by Oliver de Vrigny (Orne, cant. Mortrée) of his quitclaim to John du Hommet of his land in Airel (Manche, cant. St-Clair-sur-l'Elle) held of John's fee, undertaking that, should he or his heirs contravene the terms of this grant, John and his heirs are to have Oliver's land of Ecrammeville (Calvados, cant. Trévières).*
[1192 X 1223, ?1204 X 1216]

A[1] = Nottingham University Archives, Middleton Collection Mi D 4825. Endorsed: *Hum'* (s.xiii); *vacat* (s.xiii); various post medieval endorsements. Approx. 162 × 62 + 25mm. Sealed *sur double queue*, parchment tag through 3 slits, seal impression round, green wax, an eagle or phoenix looking back to the right over its shoulders, legend SIGILL'..........INGNE+ A[2] = Ibid. Mi D 4826. Endorsed: *Oliuer de Veney vacat* (s.xiii); various post medieval endorsements. Approx. 162 × 64 + 45mm. Sealed *sur double queue*, parchment tag through 3 slits, seal impression missing. Written in the same hand as A[1].

The following information is for the most part supplied by Daniel Power. John du Hommet (d.*c*.1223) was the elder son of Jordan du Hommet (d.1192), himself the third and youngest son of Richard du Hommet (d.1179), constable of Normandy under King Henry II. John's allegiance after 1204 was in doubt, although he eventually settled in England (cf. Powicke, *Loss*, 336), where he was taken prisoner as a rebel against the king after 1215 (*RLC*, i, 249, 289b; *Patent Rolls 1216–25*, 6). After his death, *c*.1223 (*RLC*, i, 552; *CFR 1216–24*, 359 no.156, and cf. *CRR*, x, 199), his English lands passed to his daughter Lucy and her husband, Richard de Gray of Codnor, and were subsumed into the Gray estate (whose archives themselves, in large part, have come to reside amongst the Middleton papers now at Nottingham). His lands included Humberstone (Leics. acquired by Jordan du Hommet by marriage with Hawise de Crevecoeur), and Sheringham (Norfolk, given by Henry II to Richard du Hommet, Jordan's father). The fate of his lands at Cléville (Calvados, cant. Troarn) and around Lisieux is complicated and was marked by attempts made by Lucy, his daughter, to reobtain possession, as late as 1260. Oliver de Vrigny was perhaps the heir of Wigan de Vrigny, in 1200 recorded in the wardship of Guérin de Glapion and thereafter apparently dragged into rebellion in Guérin's wake, losing his lands in England as a result (*Rot. Chart.*, 59b; *Rot. Lib.*, 66; D. Power, 'Guérin de Glapion, Seneschal of Normandy (1200–1): Service and Ambition under the Plantagenet and Capetian Kings', *Records, Administration and Aristocratic Society in the Anglo-Norman Realm*, ed. N. Vincent (Woodbridge 2009), 164, 173, nn.52, 110). Airel was a Hommet manor in which several of the cadet branches of the family possessed an interest. Amongst the witnesses, Enguerrand de Fornet had strong links to the Hommet family. Perhaps to be dated shortly after King John's loss of Normandy, at a time when John du Hommet's allegiance was not as yet certain.

Sciant presentes et futuri quod ego Oliuerus de Verigni[a] quietam clamaui in perpetuum de me et de heredibus meis Ioh(ann)i de Humet et heredibus suis totam terram cum pertinenc(iis) quam habui in Arel de feodo prefati Ioh(ann)is excepto masagio quod emi de Galfrido filio Mabilie, et si ego Oliuerus vel heredes mei aliqua occasione huic carte contraire voluerimus, concedo quod prefatus Iohannes et heredes sui totam terram meam de Escremeuvile absque contradictione habeant. Pro hac vero quieta clamacione dedit m(ich)i prefatus Ioh(anne)s unum equum et unam robam. Ut autem hec quieta clamacio rata sit et stabilis, illam sacramento et sigillo meo roboraui. Hiis testibus: Ingeramo de Furnet, Willelmo de Beggeuill'[b], Iordano de Hotot, Willelmo de Tolewast, Alano de Euintona[c], Rob(erto) Barre, Willelmo filio Walkelini et aliis pluribus.

[a] Vereigni A[2] [b] Begeuill' A[2] [c] Euinton' A[2]

37. Notification by Bishop Arnulf, Dean Fulk and the (cathedral) chapter of Lisieux, informing R(oger) de Mowbray and Nigel his son that Robert of Arden, archdeacon of Lisieux, has in their presence granted his whole land of Hampton in Arden with the advowson of the church there to Peter and Roger his brothers, to hold from R(oger) and Nigel for the same service by which Robert previously held it, with remainder to whichever of the brothers lives longest.

[1148 X 1161, ?1154 X 1161]

A[1] = BL Additional Charter 21175. Endorsed: *carta Luxouiensis episcopi et decani eiusdem* (s.xii ex.). Approx. 125 × 108 + 16mm. Sealed *sur double queue*, 2 sets of single slits, right hand side tag and seal missing, left hand tag with fragment of seal impression in brownish wax, a bishop with both arms raised in blessing, legend: AR... Part of a much larger collection of English charters acquired by the British Library from G.R. Attenborough, 12 July 1873, ultimately from the collections of Christopher Hatton, cf. above p.89 n.328. A² = BL ms. Cotton Charter XI.35. Endorsed: *Luxsuriencis episcopi* (s.xii/xiii); various post medieval endorsements. Approx. 121 × 86 + 12mm. Sealed *sur double queue*, single slit, tag and seal impression missing. Listed in the pre-fire catalogue of Cotton charters as Cotton Charter Augustus A.28.

Briefly noted from A¹ in *Mowbray Charters*, ed. Greenway, 218 no.336n.

For Fulk dean of Lisieux from before 1142, died or resigned before 1161, and for Robert of Arden serving as archdeacon *c.*1148–after 1171, possibly as late as 1191, see C.P. Schriber, *The Dilemma of Arnulf of Lisieux* (Bloomington 1990), 58, corrected by Spear, *Personnel*, 172, 175 Hence after the return of Arnulf of Lisieux from the Second Crusade, in which Roger de Mowbray had also taken part (*Mowbray Charters*, ed. Greenway, p.xxvi), perhaps at the time of Arnulf's first contacts in England with the Empress Matilda and the future King Henry II (*The Letters of Arnulf of Lisieux*, ed. F. Barlow, Camden Society 3rd series lxi (1939), pp.xxv–viii). However, the address of the present letter to both Roger de Mowbray and Nigel his son (born only *c.*1142, cf. *Mowbray Charters*, ed. Greenway, p.xxix) might suggest a charter issued later rather than earlier within the period 1148–62, almost certainly after the accession of Henry II and the consequent easing in relations between England and Normandy. If dated to the period shortly after the Second Crusade, an interesting indication of Roger de Mowbray's rapprochement with the Angevin party in the period 1149–53 (*Mowbray Charters*, ed. Greenway, pp.xxvi–vii).

Arnulfus[a] Dei gratia Lex' episcopus et Fulco Lex' decanus et totum capitulum eiusdem ecclesie dilectis amicis suis R(ogero)[b] de Molbraio et Nigello filio suo [c]et omnibus fidelibus ad quos presentes littere peruenerint[c] salutem. Sciatis quod Rob(ertus) de Ard' Lex' archid(iaconus) in vita sua et libera potestate nobis presentibus et multis aliis clericis et laicis dedit Petro et Rogero fratribus suis totam terram suam de Hantona[d] cum aduocatione ecclesie que in eadem terra est et boscum et omnia que tenebat de vob(is) apud Hanton'[d] ad tenendum de vob(is) sicut ipse tenuit per seruicium quod vobis faciebat, ita tam(en) quod ambo simul possideant[e] predictam terram in vita sua et ille qui diutius vixerit totum tenementum possideat. Valete.

[a]Arn(ulfus) A² [b] Rogero A² [c-c] *not in* A² [d] Hant' A [e] possideant A, teneant A

38. Notification by Bishop Arnulf and the (cathedral) chapter of Lisieux that Robert of Arden, their archdeacon, has granted the land of Hampton in Arden and the advowson of the church there to Peter and Roger his brothers with remainder to whichever of them lives longest.   [1148 X 1161, ?1154 X 1161]

A = Birmingham Central Reference Library, Wingfield-Digby A1/6. Endorsed: *v.*

(s.xiv). Approx. 108 × 59 + 18mm. Sealed *sur double queue*, 2 sets of single slits, left hand side tag survives without seal impression, right hand tag with central portion of seal impression in natural wax, a seated figure of ? St Peter, legend lost.

Date apparently as above no.37. Robert of Arden was succeeded as rector of Hampton in Arden by his brother Peter before 1179: *Mowbray Charters*, ed. Greenway, 129 no. 179n., citing BL ms. Harley 3650 (Kenilworth Cartulary) fos.22v–23r.

Arn(ulfus) Dei gratia Lex' episcopus et uniuersum capitulum eiusdem ecclesie omnibus in Cristo fidelibus salutem et D(e)i bened(i)c(tionem). Nouerit uniuersitas vestra Rob(ertum) de Ard' archidiaconum nostrum concessisse et donasse fratribus suis, Petro videlicet et Rogero, terram suam de Hantona in Ard' et aduocationem ecclesie eiusdem ville, ita videlicet ut uter illorum diutius viueret totum iure hereditario possideret. Ne igitur taliter facta concessio in dubium decetero reuocetur, ipsam sigillorum nostrorum munimine duximus roborandam. Valete.

39. Notification by Robert (II) count of Meulan of his mortgage and gift to Peter de Préaux and to Mary, daughter of William earl of the Isle (of Wight, i.e. William de Vernon) and of Mabira, Count Robert's own daughter, of his lands in France, Normandy and England, one third of it as a marriage portion, the other two parts in return for a payment of 10,000 marks, with reversion to Robert and his heirs should Peter and Mary die without issue.

March 1201 X March 1202

A = Taunton, Somerset Record Office ms. DD/WO Box 10 Bundle 3. No medieval endorsements. Approx. 248 × 113 + 22mm. Sealed *sur double queue* on green silk through 2 holes and a slit, central portion of a single sided seal impression in natural wax, varnished brown, the horse's head from an equestrian seal.

Printed (by 'W.C.T.', i.e. Walter Calverley Trevelyan, of Wallington, Northumberland, from the original, then in the possession of his kinsman Sir John Trevelyan, Bart., of Nettlecombe in Somerset) *Collectanea Topographica et Genealogica*, ii (1835), 390 no.43; (calendar from A) R. Bearman, 'Charters of the Redvers Family and the Earldom of Devon, 1090–1217: An Addendum', *Report and Transactions of the Devonshire Association*, cxlii (2010), 96 no.13.

For the witness Geoffrey, abbot of St-Ouen at Rouen (after 1193–1208), see *GC*, xi, 146; V. Gazeau, *Normannia Monastica*, 2 vols (Caen 2007), ii, 260–1. The second witness was prior of the Augustinian house of Beaulieu, founded in the vill of Préaux (Seine-Maritime, cant. Darnetal) *c*.1200 by another of the witnesses, John de Préaux, for which see above no.7. The story underlying the present charter and no.40 below is a complicated one. It is nonetheless of central importance to our understanding of the descent of two of the greatest estates in the Anglo-Norman world. It also has much to tell us of the collateral damage inflicted upon the Anglo-Norman aristocracy as a result of King John's defeat by Philip Augustus. In 1200, arrangements were made by King John for the two daughters and chief heirs of William de Vernon, earl of Devon, born to his wife Mabira *alias* Mabel, daughter of Robert count of Meulan, to be married to the courtiers Peter de Préaux and Hubert de Burgh. Keen to purchase the support of Peter de Préaux, a key player in Anglo-Norman affairs, in January 1200, the king offered Peter the islands of Jersey, Guernsey and Alderney, £60 of land at Alton (Hampshire) and 100 livres of rents in Rouen (themselves destined for the Préaux family foundation of Beaulieu, cf. above no.7n.), for the service of three knights' fees and pending Peter's betrothal to Mary, eldest daughter of Earl William, and Peter and Mary's inheritance of Earl William's estate. As yet, no formal betrothal had taken place between Peter and Mary, but the 100 livres of rents in Normandy were promised by the king to Peter and his heirs whether or not such a betrothal was concluded, with the king insisting that the Channel Islands and the £60 of land in England were to be considered a gift to Peter and his heirs should the king die before any final arrangements could be made for Peter's marriage: *Rot. Chart.*, 33b, with a fuller version in TNA C 64/12 (Norman Roll 7 Henry V) m.43. By April 1200, Hubert de Burgh had entered into formal arrangements to marry Earl William's younger daughter, Joan. According to the written settlement here, Joan's elder sister, Mary, was to bring her husband (unidentified, but undoubtedly Peter de Préaux) the chief claim to the Vernon/Redvers earldom of Devon together with the castle of Plympton. The younger daughter, Joan, was to bring Hubert de Burgh Christchurch and the Isle of Wight. Since there was still a possibility that Earl William and his wife Mabira might produce a male heir, Hubert was promised £60 of land and 10 knights' fees from Earl William's estate, even should the arrangements over Christchurch and the Isle of Wight come to nothing. In all probability, similar guarantees were extended to Peter de Préaux, who for the previous few months had been identified as the potential husband for Earl William's elder daughter: *Rot.Chart.*, 52b–53. These arrangements over the earldom of Devon were made as distinct transactions, but clearly in expectation of the present division of the even more extensive honour of Meulan, from which the two daughters of William de Vernon and Mabira could hope for some portion as heiresses of their grandfather, Count Robert (II) of Meulan. Robert's division of his estate was no less complicated than the carving up of the earldom of Devon, and was overshadowed by Anglo-French hostilities in which his own sons and grandson were closely involved. Robert, who had succeeded to his county as long ago as 1166 and who was thus already an old man, had at least three sons: Waleran, the eldest, Peter and Henry. Waleran died at some time between 1195 and 1203 (*MRSN*, ii, pp.cxcix–cc; below no.106n.), leaving a son, Ralph, and at least one surviving brother, Peter, a clerk in orders (*MRSN*, ii, pp.cxcvii–viii note). Apparently disregarding the claims of these, his own male heirs, and hoping to secure the descent of the honour of Meulan intact, whatever might happen in the disputes between King John and Philip Augustus, by the present charter Count Robert in effect declared Peter de Préaux, the betrothed of his granddaughter, Mary, heir to all his lands in France, Normandy and England. There were, nonetheless, significant caveats. Robert conferred a third of his estate as a marriage portion upon Peter and Mary, entailed to their joint issue. The entail is specified in the present charter, unlike the details of the land assigned which are reserved to a separate charter, below no.40, in which this third of the estate is defined as Count Robert's lands at Vatteville, Brotonne and Pont-Audemer (Eure). The remaining two thirds of the estate were governed by the present charter, but in complicated fashion. These portions were mortgaged to Peter and Mary in return for 10,000 marks, according to the present charter already paid to Count Robert. Since it was presumably Peter de Préaux who advanced this money, it was agreed that should Mary die before him, Peter was to retain a life interest in the two thirds of Count Robert's estate. Should Peter die before Mary, by contrast, the two thirds were immediately to revert to Count Robert and his heirs. However, if Peter and Mary produced issue, the two thirds, like the remaining third, were to be entailed upon such issue in perpetuity. All of this suggests an attempt to guarantee the descent of Count Robert's vast estate through a single line of inheritance, setting aside his own son and grandson, but instead allowing descent to his eldest granddaughter and her husband, Peter de Préaux. In the process, Count Robert himself was bought out with a payment of 10,000 marks. Two events transpired to frustrate these arrangements. Firstly, perhaps very soon after April 1200, Earl William of Devon and his wife, Mabira the daughter of Count Robert, produced a son, Baldwin de Redvers, whose claims now trumped those of his older sisters and their prospective husbands, Hubert de Burgh and Peter de Préaux. As a result, and amidst the collapse of King John's lordship in Normandy, both marriage partners seem to have repudiated their brides. Instead of marrying Hubert de Burgh, Earl William's daughter Joan was married (before 1211) to William Brewer. Peter de Préaux, due to marry the elder daughter, Mary, remained loyal to King John but as a result found himself serving as the king's commander of Rouen when the city was forced to surrender to Philip Augustus, in August 1204. He thereafter seems to have sought refuge in England. There is no evidence that his marriage to Mary was ever solemnized, and Mary herself was by 1211 promised in marriage to Robert de Courtenay of Okehampton, whose heirs succeeded to the earldom of Devon in the 1330s, following the extinction of the main Redvers line: *Charters of the Redvers Family and the Earldom of Devon 1090–1217*, ed. R. Bearman, Devon and Cornwall Record Society n.s. xxxvii (1994), 15–16, 172–3 nos 30–1; Powicke, *Loss*, 261–2, 350; *MRSN*, ii, p.ccxxxi; *Pipe Roll 13 John*, 61. Secondly, and with Count Robert's own loyalty undecided between the French and English camps, in May 1203 his eldest surviving son, Peter de Meulan, betrayed the great family fortress of Beaumont-le-Roger to the French, leading in effect to the forfeiture of the family lands in both England and Normandy. Peter died shortly afterwards, at some time between April and October 1203. In May 1203, Count Robert had been obliged to enter into arrangements whereby King John offered him 5000 marks for the succession to the Meulan lands in Normandy, the king taking Pont-Audemer in the meantime and carving off another significant portion of the count's estate, Elbeuf-sur-Seine (Seine-Maritime), as a peace offering to another Norman baron, Richard de Harcourt: *MRSN*, pp.cc–cci; Powicke, *Loss*, 161, 344–5; *Rot. Chart.*, 104b–5; Power, *Norman Frontier*, 209, 285. Count Robert responded to the French victories in Normandy with an attempt, on 1 May 1204, shortly before the fall of Rouen, to declare his daughter, Mabira countess of Devon, heiress to all his lands in England, Normandy and France: *Charters of the Redvers Family*, ed. Bearman, 201–3 nos 37–8. This, however, was ignored by both the French and English kings. Instead, Robert's Norman and French estates were redistributed to King Philip's supporters, with King Philip himself retaining Meulan for the French crown. Count Robert lived on until his death, *c*.1207, apparently as a pensioner of the English crown, his widow thereafter supported from dower in Cornwall and elsewhere, inherited from her father, Reginald earl of Cornwall (d. 1175), but unable to prove her title to her husband's principal English manor at Sturminster in Dorset, which passed instead to William

Marshal. The Marshal claimed to possess Sturminster by a charter of Count Robert issued long before the recent turmoils. Even so, and whatever the precise terms of Count Robert's gift, its acquisition was one of the collateral consequences of King John's loss of Normandy: Ibid., 202–3 no.38n.; *CP*, vii, 739–40 appendix I; *Hatton's Seals*, 135–6 no.191n.; *CRR*, iii, 124; D. Crouch, *William Marshal: Knighthood, War and Chivalry, 1147–1219* (2nd ed., London 2002), 95. I am indebted to Robert Bearman and David Crouch for their assistance with these notes.

Notum sit tam presentibus quam futuris quod ego Robertus comes Melleti inuadiaui Petro de Pratell' et Marie filie Willelmi comitis de Insula et filie Mabirie filie mee duas partes tocius terre mee et tocius terre que ad me pertinere debet quicumque illam teneat vel possideat ubicumque fuerit tam in Francia quam in Normannia et in Anglia pro decies mille marcis argenti quas michi propter negotium meum accomodauerunt. Cuius terre terciam partem ego dedi et carta mea confirmaui predicto Petro in maritagium cum predicta Maria nepte mea habendas et possidendas ipsis et eorum heredibus ab ipsis procedentibus, et si predicti Petrus et Maria obierint absque herede ab illis progenito, ille duas partes reuertentur ad me et ad meos heredes quiete, et si predicta Maria obierit priusque predictus Petrus, predictus Petrus illas duas partes tenebit quamdiu vixerit. Si autem predictus Petrus obierit antequam prefata Maria, ille due partes reuertentur ad me et ad meos heredes statim post decessum sepedicti Petri quiete. Si autem sepedicti Petrus et Maria heredem vel heredes ab illis progenitos habuerint, ille due partes tocius terre mee remanebunt ipsis et eorum heredibus post eos in perpetuum. Et ut hoc ratum et stabile futuris temporibus perseueret, presentem cartam sigilli mei appositione confirmaui. Actum est hoc anno incarnationis domini m.cc.i. Hiis testibus: Galfrido abbate sancti Audoeni, Galfrido priore Belli Loci, Iohanne, Willelmo, Engerammo de Pratell' fratribus, Galfr(ido) de Bosco, Roberto filio Land(ulf)i, Willelmo de Chaumont, Osberto de Bosco, Roberto Grandi, Willelmo de Putot et multis aliis.

40. *Notification by Robert (II) count of Meulan of his gift to Peter de Préaux in marriage with Mary, the daughter of William earl of the Isle (of Wight, i.e. William de Vernon), and of Mabiria, Count Robert's own daughter, of a third portion of his lands in France, Normandy and England, namely Vatteville, Brotonne and Pont-Audemer (Eure), with descent to Peter, Mary and their issue in perpetuity, and with the right to Robert to recover these lands should they represent more than a third of his estate.*

March 1201 X March 1202

B = London, College of Arms ms. Vincent 59 p.84, copy from a lost original, amongst a miscellaneous heraldic collection once belonging to Augustine Vincent (d.1626), the present transcript perhaps not in Vincent's own hand, s.xvii. Vincent's source is listed Ibid. p.208 as 'A deed of Robert erle of Millent with a seale annexed', so presumably from a lost sealed original.   C = Oxford, Bodleian Library ms. Dodsworth 90 fo.114r, partial copy marked Vincent, perhaps from B, s.xvii.   D = Stafford, Staffordshire Record Office D1744/73, copied from an unknown source, perhaps ultimately from C, s.xvii.   E = Rouen AD Seine-Maritime 7H1 (Inventory of the charters of Fécamp), briefly listed as a French abstract, as drawn to my attention by David Crouch, s.xvi.

For the circumstances, see the note to above no.39.

Notum <sit>[a] omnibus tam presentibus quam futur(is) quod ego Robertus comes Melenti[b] dedi [c]et concessi et hac presenti carta mea confirmaui[c] Petro de Pratellis[d] in maritagium[e] cum Maria filia Will(el)mi comitis de Insula et filia Marb(i)rie filie mee tertiam partem totius terre mee [f]et totius terre[f] [c]que ad me pertinere debet[c] tam in Francia quam [c]in[c] Norman(n)ia et [c]in[c] Anglia ubicumque fuerit et quicumque illam teneat[g] [h]vel possideat[h], et super illam tertiam partem assignaui predicto Petro totam terram meam de Wateuilla[j] et [c]de[c] Bretona[k] cum omnibus pertinentiis suis tam in bosco [l]quam in[l] plano, et Pontem Audomari cum omnibus pertinent(iis) suis tam in feodis militum quam in aliis rebus, habendas et possidendas[m] ipsis et heredibus suis de me et heredibus meis iure hereditar(io) in liberum maritagium integre, [n]plenarie et honorifice, libere et quiete, bene et in pace, ita quod si Watteuilla et Breton cum pertinentiis et Pont(em) Audomari cum pertinentiis magis valuerunt quam tertia pars terre mee, ego recuperabo super predictas Petrum et Mariam.   Si autem minus valuerunt, ego vel mei heredes perficiemus[p] predictis Petro et Marie valentiam tertie partis totius terre mee.   Et ut hec mea donatio et concessio rata et stabilis futuris temporibus perseueret, present(em) chart(am) sigill(i) mei appositione muniui[q] et roboraui[n]. Actum est hoc anno incarnat(i)onis dominice[r] m°cci°s. Hiis testibus: Ioh(ann)e de Pratellis, Will(elm)o de Pratellis[d], Engeramo de Pratellis[d], Galfrido de Bosco, Stephano de Longocampo, Gautero de Brionia, Will(elm)o de Chaumont[t], Rob(er)to filio Landri, Rob(er)to Pontell, Roberto Grandi, Osberto de Bosco et multis aliis.

[a] sit *not in* B, *supplied from* CD   [b] Melle.... C, Mellenti D   [c-c] *not in* D   [d] Pratell' C
[e] maritagio D   [f-f] *not in* BD, *supplied from* C   [g] tenet B *over* tenuit *erased*, teneat *supplied from* CD   [h-h] *not in* CD   [j] Watteuilla CD   [k] Brotona C, D *ends here* Actum est hoc anno incarnationis domini 1201 Test(ibus) Ioh(anne) de Pratellis Willelmo de Pratellis   [l-l] et C
[m] possidendas B, tenendas D   [n-n] *not in* D   [p] proficituius B, perficiemus *supplied*   [q] maniui B, muniui *supplied*   [r] domini C   [s] 1201 B, moccio C   [t] C *ends here* etc

41. *Notification by Robert (IV) de Courcy of the peace and final concord made with Roger de Escures, by which Robert granted Roger and his heirs the vill of Farlington (Hampshire) as Roger son of Walter, uncle of the said Roger, and William son of Walter, Roger's father, held it from Robert de Courcy, Robert's uncle, and from William de Courcy, Robert's father; also granting Roger whatever right Robert has in the church of Farlington, and the fees of Geoffrey Polain and Thomas la Gatte, saving the rights of Geoffrey and Thomas, and whatever Robert has in the same vill. In Robert's vill of Courcy (Calvados, cant. Morteaux-Coulibeuf), Robert grants Roger the tenement of Richard de Castello saving Richard's right and that of the lord of the fee of Cropuz (unidentified, ?Calvados, com. Courcy) that remained to Robert in demesne as the result of a fine made between Robert and Robert de Cropuz. Roger and his heirs are to hold these lands in England and Normandy from Robert and his heirs in perpetuity for the service of half a knight's fee. In return Roger has released to Robert all the lands which Roger claimed against him.* 1202/3

B = BL ms. Lansdowne 203 fos.42v–43r, copy by Elias Ashmole, apparently from a lost original, s.xvii. C = Oxford, Bodleian Library ms. Dugdale 18 fos.43v–44r, copy by Dugdale from an unidentified source, s.xvii.

For the Courcy family, early divided into English and Norman branches, and for the Robert de Courcy of the present award, holder of the Norman honour with only minor lands in England, who defected to the French in John's reign though perhaps not until 1204, see Powicke, *Loss*, 337; D. Power, 'Angevin Normandy', *A Companion to the Anglo-Norman World*, ed. C. Harper-Bill and E. van Houts (Woodbridge 2003), 75–6; *RLC*, i, 9b; *Cartularies of Southwick Priory*, ed. Hanna, ii, 141 no.393; S. Flanders, *De Courcy: Anglo-Normans in Ireland, England and France in the Eleventh and Twelfth Centuries* (Dublin 2008), esp. p.96 for Farlington, with a family tree at p.181. For disputes over the advowson of Farlington between Robert de Courcy and Roger de Escures *alias* Scures in the summer of 1200, during which Roger claimed to possess the advowson by grant to Roger his uncle and William his father, the sons of Walter, by Robert de Courcy (d.1157) steward to King Henry II, as confirmed by charter of Henry II, see *CRR*, i, 200–1, 239. Robert (III) de Courcy the steward (d.1157) was the father of the Norman landowner William de Courcy (not to be confused with William de Courcy of Stogursey in Somerset who also adopted the title of steward) and grandfather of the Robert (IV) de Courcy active in 1200: *Acta Henry II*, no.2448; Flanders, *De Courcy*, p.181. Whatever the rights of Roger de Scures, immediately after the hearings between Scures and Courcy in the summer of 1200, Robert de Courcy sued Roger de Merlay for the advowson of Farlington (*CRR*, i, 244, 438), and it was subsequently Roger de Merlay (d.c.1250) who held the manor from Matthew fitz Herbert and from Matthew's son Herbert fitz Matthew, and who granted the advowson of the church there to Southwick Priory: *English Episcopal Acta IX: Winchester 1205–1238*, ed. N. Vincent (Oxford 1994), nos 64–5. Amongst the witnesses to the present grant, Theobald Pantolf appears in 1200 as steward of Roger de Scures, subsequently acting as attorney for Robert de Courcy, suggesting that the suit between Scures and Courcy may have been a fictitious one, intended to set the scene for the subsequent ligitation against Roger de Merlay: *CRR*, i, 200–1, 244. The charter itself appears to have been granted in place of any more formal final concord issued by the king's court, since there seems to be no foot of fine relating to these transactions amongst the relevant files of Hampshire feet of fines (TNA CP 25/1/203/1 et seq).

Omnibus hominibus presentibus et futuris ad quos presens scriptum peruenerit Rob(ertus) de Corci salutem. Notum sit omnibus vobis quod pax et finalis concordia talis facta est inter me et Rogerum de Escuris, quod ego Rob(ertus) de Corc(i) concessi et confirmaui predicto Rogero de Escur'[a] et heredibus suis villam de Felling'tone cum pertinentiis sicut Rog(erus) filius Walteri auunculus predicti Rog(eri) et Willelmus[b] filius Walt(eri) pater prefati Rog(eri) de Escur'[c] prius tenuerunt eandem de Rob(erto) de Corc(i) auunculo meo et de Willelmo de Corc(i) patre meo. Preterea ego Rob(ertus) de Corc(i) dedi et concessi predicto Rog(ero) de Escur'[c] pro pace et finali concordia quicquid habebam in ecclesia de Felling'ton'[d] et feodum Gaufr(idi) Polani[e] et feodum Thome la Gatte[f], saluo iure predictorum scilicet Gaufr(idi) et Thome, et quicquid in predicta villa habebam cum omnibus libertatibus et consuetudinibus integre ad predictam villam de Felling'ton'[g] pertinentibus. Donaui etiam et concessi predicto Rog(ero) et heredibus suis in villa mea de Corc(i) masuram Ric(ardi) de Castello saluo iure predicti Ric(ardi) et illam terram de feodo de Cropuz que mi(c)hi remansit in dominio pro finali concordia facta inter me et Rob(ertum) de Cropuz. Hec autem omnia tenementa tam in Anglia quam in Norm(annia) dedi et concessi predicto Rog(ero) de Escur'[a] et heredibus suis tenenda de me et heredibus meis integre et plenarie, libere et honorifice cum suis libertatibus et consuetudinibus per seruicium dimidii feodi militis, tali modo quod predictus Rog(erus) omnia tenementa que aduersus me clamabat ab eo et heredibus suis mi(c)hi et heredibus meis quieta reliquit, et ut hec ratum et stabile nec aliqua fraude possit dequassari, hac carta presenti et sigilli mei testimonio confirmaui. Hoc autem factum est anno domini m.cc. secundo, Iohanne rege Angl(ie) regnante. Test(ibus) hiis: Willelmo de Corc(i) fratre meo, Ric(ardo) de Corc(i), Teob(aldo) Pantof, Iord(ano) de Maigni, Willelmo Bozon, Willemo de Valle Logiarum, Fulc(one) de Maigni, Willelmo de Cad', Willelmo de Mascel et aliis pluribus.

[a] Escuris C   [b] Willielmus C   [c] Escures C   [d] Fellingetone C   [e] Polain C   [f] Gaite C
[g] Felling'tone C

42. *Notification by Matthew de Alençon of his lease to Walter of Ely, for 150 marks, of the land which William de Longchamp, bishop of Ely, granted Matthew for service and homage at Stretham and Wilberton (Cambridgeshire), to hold for twelve years from 29 September 1199, with restoration to Matthew and his heirs at the end of this term or thereafter if the money is repaid, and with provision for the compensation of Walter for any improvements or repairs.*
The King's Court at Vaudreuil [*c*.29 September 1199]

A = BL Harley Charter 45.C.9. No medieval endorsement. Approx. 173 × 200 + 24mm., spade shaped parchment. Sealed *sur double queue*, 3 holes for cords, cords and seal impression missing.

Briefly noticed *English Episcopal Acta 31: Ely 1109–1197*, ed. N. Karn (Oxford 2006), 238, appendix 3 no.19.

Highly significant as evidence that English landholding was occasionally regulated by the king's courts meeting in Normandy. The king himself was at Vaudreuil in mid July, mid August and mid October 1199, but on 29 September 1199 was at Le Mans (*RLP*, itinerary of King John). For Matthew de Alençon as chamberlain of Bp William Longchamps, recorded in the company of Walter of Ely, the bp's steward *c*.1191, see *English Episcopal Acta 31*, ed. Karn, pp.cxxii, 182 no.140. Walter of Ely occurs as a knight in the tournament at Lagny-sur-Marne *c*.1179 in the company of William Marshal, and later as a witness to charters of King John: *History of William Marshal*, ed. A.G. Holden and D. Crouch, trans. S. Gregory, 3 vols, Anglo-Norman Text Society Occasional Publications Series iv–vi (2002–7), i, 236 lines 4625–30, iii, 90, noting the longstanding close association between Walter of Ely and Robert de Wanchy, witness to the present charter. Amongst the other witnesses, both William de l'Etang (*Stagno*) and Hugh de Corny (Eure, cant. Les Andelys) occur in the *History of William Marshal* (ii, 6 lines 10137–40, 46, lines 10937–8, iii, 128, 135) as knights of Richard I.

Sciant omnes tam presentes quam futuri quod ego Math(eu)s de Alencon inuadiaui Galtero de Ely totam terram meam quam Will(elmu)s de Longo Campo Elyensis episcopus mi(chi) dedit pro seruitio meo et homagio apud Estreham et apud Wilbretone pro centum et quinquaginta marc(is) argenti sibi tenendam et heredibus suis de me et heredibus meis a proximo festo sancti Michaelis post mortem domini regis Ricardi usque in duodecim annis, tali conditione quod si ad predictum terminum predicto Galtero predictam peccuniam reddido, predicta terra mi(chi) quieta remanebit vel heredibus meis. Sin autem totam terram illam tenebit de anno in annum donec totum debitum ei persoluatur vel heredibus suis. Hanc vero predictam terram debet tenere predictus Galt(erus) libere et quiete et absolute in terris, in pratis, in mol(end)inis, in piscariis, in aquis, in alnetis, in viis, in semitis, in hominibus, in redditibus et in omnibus aliis exitibus illius terre sicut karta mea quam de illa terra habui testatur, saluo dominico seruitio quod debetur domino Elyensi episcopo, et si predictus Galt(erus) in predicta terra aliquid edificii vel costamenti posuerit, per visum legalium hominum ad disuadiationem illius terre illi computabitur et reddetur. Hanc conuentionem tenendam predicto Galtero et heredibus suis affidaui tenere de me et heredibus meis et ut hoc ratum et inconcussum permaneat, sigilli mei munimine presentem kartam confirmaui. Hoc autem factum fuit in curia domini regis apud Vallem Rodolii, coram Willelmo filio Radulfi tunc senescallo Normannie et coram aliis iusticiis domini regis. Hiis testibus: Roberto de Vanci, Willelmo de Stagno, magistro Rocelino, Petro Picot, Petro de Estoques, Galtero filio Godefr(idi), Nic(olao) de Witone, Iohanne de Brai, Hug(one) de Corni, Willelmo de Lanceles, Willelmo de Ely, Y(u)one filio Milonis et pluribus aliis.

43. *Notification by Richard, son of Alexander de Barentin, of his grant to Walter de La Rivière of the whole of his land in Barentin and Pissy-Pôville (Seine-Maritime, cant. Pavilly) with his mill at Barentin, retaining the multure of the men of Croix-Mare and Mont-de-L'If (cant. Pavilly) of the fee of Nicholas de Londe. Walter and his heirs are to pay an annual rent of 40s. to Richard and his heirs at Yeoveney (in Staines, Middlesex).* [1193 X 1212, ?1193 X 1197]

A = BL Additional Charter 20236. Prepared as a polled cyrograph, with the word CYROGRAPHUM written down the right hand side of the document. Endorsed: *Iueneye* (s.xiv). Approx. 185 × 130 + 23mm. Sealed *sur double queue*, green silk cords through two holes, seal impression, round, dark green wax, equestrian figure with shield and sword facing to the right, legend: + SIGI<LLUM WAL>TERI DE LARIVERE. Part of a much larger collection of English charters acquired by the British Library from G.R. Attenborough, 12 July 1873, in many cases ultimately from the collections of the great antiquary, Sir Christopher Hatton of Kirby Hall, Northamptonshire (above p.89 n.328).

Witnessed by William Longuespée as the king's brother, and hence after the accession of Richard I and before the death of King John. Alexander de Barentin, who occurs as butler of King Henry II in the 1170s and 80s, acquired an extensive English estate, including property in London by gift of Richard of Ilchester, bp of Winchester, with reversion to Alexander's sons Richard and Thomas, described as Bp Richard's nephews, presumably as a result of a marriage between Alexander and a kinswoman, perhaps a sister of Bp Richard: *Acta Henry II*, nos 100–103. Alexander was dead by Michaelmas 1192, when Herbert Poer, archdeacon of Canterbury, himself son of Richard of Ilchester, fined for custody of Alexander's heirs and their land: *PR 3–4 Richard I*, 305, and cf. *PR 5 Richard I*, 20, 182, where, in the following year, custody of the heir passed to the royal clerk William de Ste-Mère-Eglise. Richard was of age by 1203, lying ill at his estate at Yeoveney in 1204, may have joined the king on the Irish campaign of 1210, but was dead by 1212, when his younger brother Thomas fined for possession of his lands: *CRR*, iii, 11, 111, iv, 6, 93; *Rot. Lib.*, 190, 200, 217; *RLC*, i, 120b; *Rot. Chart.*, 159; *Book of Fees*, i, 71; *PR 14 John*, 85. Walter de Riparia, *alias* de la Rivière, was a familiar of William Longuespée, which explains Longuespée's appearance as witness to the present charter: cf. *Cartulary of Bradenstoke*, nos 278, 646, 649. The failure, nonetheless, to credit Longuespée with title as earl of Salisbury suggests a date before William's marriage to the earldom's heiress, *c*.1196–7.

Sciant omnes presentes et futuri quod ego Ricardus de Barentino filius Alexandri de Barentino concessi et tradidi et presenti carta confirmaui Waltero de Riparia totam terram meam de Barentino et de Pissi et molendinum meum de Barentino cum omnibus pertinentiis ad easdem terras et ad molendinum prefatum pertinentibus, ita tamen quod ego in manu mea retinui moutam hominum de Croismare et de Montdelif qui sunt de feodo Nicholai de Londa, qui sine contradictione et impedimento molere debent ad molendinum predictum. Concessi autem predicto Waltero hec omnia predicta sibi et suis heredibus pro seruicio et homagio suo de me et heredibus meis iure hereditario tenenda, reddendo in(de) m(ich)i et meis heredibus singulis annis pro omnibus seruiciis et consuetudinibus m(ich)i et meis heredibus pertinentibus quadraginta sol(idos) sterlingorum apud Iueneiam in Anglia duobus terminis anni, scilicet viginti sol(idos) ad festum sancti Michael(is) et viginti sol(idos) ad Pascha, et predicta feoda adquietabit singulis annis de dimidio modio auene ipse Walterus et sui heredes post ipsum, et ut hec mea concessio futuris temporibus rata et inconcussa permaneat, eam presenti scripto et sigilli mei munimine confirmaui. T(estibus) Willelmo Longeespee fratre domini reg(is), Henrico de Mara, Lamberto le Tieis, Willelmo Talebot, Ricardo de Wrauuill', Ricardo Commin, Willelmo Pantof, Roberto de Tilluel, Radulfo fratre suo, Roberto de Barentino, Roberto de Pissi, Geru(asio) Angl(ico), Nicholao de Deppa, Willelmo Norman et aliis.

44. *Notification from the barons of Dover to the archbishop of Rouen and his bailiffs at Dieppe that the abbot and convent of St Augustine's and their household are fellow burgesses of the men of Dover and therefore should be quit of toll and customs throughout the lands of the king of England on either side of the sea.* [1197 X 1204]

B = BL ms. Cotton Julius D ii (Cartulary of St Augustine's Canterbury) fo.89v (82v) no.179, s.xiii med. C = BL ms. Stowe 924 fos.214v–215r, copy from B by Sir Edward Dering, s.xvii.

After the transactions of October 1197 by which Dieppe passed to the archbps of Rouen in exchange for the manor of Les Andelys (Landon, *Itinerary*, 123 no.482), and apparently before King John's loss of Normandy.

Viro venerabili in Cristo Dei gratia Rotomagen' archiepiscopo et balliuis suis de Diepe et ceteris burgensibus eiusdem barones Douor' salutem et tam debitum quam deuotum in omnibus obsequium. Sanctitati vestre duximus nunciandum dominum abbatem sancti Augustini Cant' et totum eiusdem loci conuentum una cum illis qui eorum mensam sequuntur esse comburgenses nostros et per omnia ea qua et nos frui libertate debent ergo esse liberi de theloneo per uniuersam terram domini reg(is) Angl(ie) tam in partibus nostris quam vestris et de omnibus consuetudinibus de quibus et nos liberi debemus existere. Valeat sanctitas vestra in domino.

45. *Notification by Aldulf de Brachy of his foundation of a priory at Brachy (Seine-Maritime, cant. Bacqueville) placed under the authority of Gilbert of Sempringham, here granted land at Rainfreville, Le Mesnil in the territory of Royville (cant. Bacqueville), the churches of Brachy, Saint-Ouen-sur-Brachy (com. Brachy), Greuville (cant. Bacqueville), Bornambusc and Manneville-la-Goupil (cant. Goderville), and in England the church of South Croxton (Leicestershire) and a tithe of rents in Eaton Bray (Bedfordshire).* [c.1165 X 1184]

B = BL ms. Cotton Claudius D xi (Malton cartulary) fo.217r (213r), s.xiii ex.

Briefly noticed J. Nichols, *The History and Antiquities of the County of Leicestershire*, 4 vols (London 1795–1811), iii part 1, 231.

For Aldulf, see B. Golding, *Gilbert of Sempringham and the Gilbertine Order c.1130–c.1300* (Oxford 1995), 256–7, at p.258, dating the present charter after c.1170 and Aldulf's acquisition of the Martel estates (though at p.257 n.282 suggesting that Osbert Martel died or forfeited and that Aldulf succeeded to his English lands perhaps as early as 1165–6), and before 1184, by which time the land specified below at South Croxton was certainly in the hands of Malton Priory. For further examples of Aldulf's religious patronage in England and Normandy, see *Acta Henry II*, nos 260, 798, 1344, 1658, 1660, and for his lands in South Croxton, see *HMC Rutland*, iv, 8 no.28. Of the Norman churches listed here, a valuation of the 1330s assesses them at a total of 174 livres, of which Manneville-la-Goupil (60 livres) and Brachy (50 livres) were much the more valuable. By the same date, both Greuville and Bornambusc were in the hands of the Augustinian abbey of L'Ile-Dieu (Eure, cant. Fleury-sur-Andelle, com. Perruel), to which Aldulf was already making grants by 1188, including land at Greuville: *Acta Henry II*, no.1344; *Pouillés Rouen*, 20–1, 30–1.

Omnibus sancte matris ecclesie filiis Aldulf(us) de Braci filius Gwerne, nepos Osberti Martel salutem. Sciatis uniuersi quod ego Aldulfus assensu heredis mei Gwerne et fratris sui Aldulfi fil(ii) mei dedi et p(resenti) c(arta) m(ea) confir(maui) Deo et sancte M(ari)e et can(onicis) de ordine et capitulo de Sempinham totum d(omi)nium meum quod habui in cultura mea que est inter villam de Ranfruiuile et Le Maygnyl in territ(orio) de Rouile, exceptis x. acris quas dedi ecclesie Sancti Wandregisili et duabus acris Gyleberti de Bouule et vii. acris et vii. acris Osberti de Royuile que sunt de eadem cultura, ut ipsi can(onici) predicti faciant in prefato d(omi)nio meo mansionem suam et prioratum constituant unius conuentus de can(onicis) sui ordinis secundum quod terra illa et el(emos)i(n)e que date fuerint illis can(onicis) sustinere rationabiliter poterunt. Ad sustentationem autem predictorum can(onicorum) dedi etiam et confirmaui ecclesiam de Bracy et ecclesiam de Sancto Audoeno et ecclesiam sancte M(ari)e de Greuuilla et ecclesiam de Burnebusc et ecclesiam de Magneuile cum omnibus el(emos)inis tam in decimis quam in terris et omnibus aliis rebus que ad easdem ecclesias pertinent. Dedi etiam omnem decimam omnium reddituum meorum in Normania tam in denar(iis) quam in blado et in mol(e)ndinis et furnis et altilibus et gallinis et aucis et pauibus et ouis. De d(om)inniis autem carrucar(um) mearum aliam decimam non dedi nisi decimam garbarum debitam ecclesie. Preterea dedi eis in Anglia ecclesiam de Crokestune cum omnibus pertin(entiis) s(ui)s et decimam reddituum meorum de Eituna. Hec omnia dedi eis et confirm(aui) in perpetuam possessionem et puram el(emos)inam soluta et quieta ab omni exactione et seculari seruicio. Preter h(ec) dedi eis totam medietatem feudi mei de Criokestun tam in terra quam extra villam in terris et pratis et pascuis et toftis et croftis et viis et semitis et bosco et plano et in omnibus aliis rebus et libertatibus que m(ich)i et heredibus m(eis) adiacebant in perpetuam possessionem et puram el(emos)inam solutam et quietam ab omni exactione et seculari seruic(io) quantum ad me et ad heredes meos attinet, saluo tamen seruicio reg(is) et dominorum meorum quod ipsi per manum meam vel heredum meorum facient. Excipitur t(ame)n una bou(ata) terre quam canon(ici) de Crokestune iuxta Bealum habent in campo de Crokestun' de ista medietate feudi et terra Rad(u)l(f)i Puintel quam tenet de eod(em) feodo de qua ipse Rad(u)lfus et heredes sui facient forinse(cum) seruicium quantum pertinet ad terram suam, scilicet octauam partem de milite. Sciendum autem quod prefata medietas de isto feudo est illa quam Rog(erus) de Mustun tenuit. Hec omnia dedi predictis can(onicis) pro anima patris et matris mee etc. Et ego et heredes mei warantizabimus et manutenebimus hec omnia predictis can(onicis) in perpetuum, et sciend(um) est quod ego adduxi de Anglia ad hanc mansionem et prioratum primum priorem et quod accepi a Gyleberto primo magistro ordinis de Sempinham quod nullus poterit prior(em) constitui in hoc prioratu in diebus meis vel in diebus heredis mei proximi post me nisi per electionem conuentus de isto prioratu et per assensum meum vel heredis proximi post me. Post dies autem nostros constituatur prior siue de illis de prefato prioratu si ibi fuerit quis ad h(oc) ydoneus, siue de ceteris de ordine de Semplingh' secundum quod institutiones eiusdem ordinis exigunt, etiam absque assensu ceterorum aduocatorum. Sed et priores de h(oc) prioratu debent recurere ad magnum cap(itu)l(u)m de Semplingh' singulis vel s(e)c(un)dis annis secundum quod iddem capitulum sibi disposuerit. Teste etc.

46. *Notification by King John to H(enry) bishop of Bayeux, informing him that it has been determined in the king's court that a settlement 'de ultima presentatione' over the church of Écrammeville (Calvados, cant. Trévières), disputed between the abbot of Tewkesbury and William Infans, was held without the king's order or warrant of the seneschal, before justices who were not the king's and who had no right to take the case, and in contradiction of earlier charters. The king orders the bishop to restore the church to the abbot, removing the incumbent whom the bishop placed there after the earlier settlement at the presentation of William Infans.*

Montfort-sur-Risle, 13 March [1202]

B = BL ms. Cotton Cleopatra A vii (Tewkesbury cartulary) fo.92r (88r, 90r), s.xiii.

Pd (from B) *Monasticon*, ii, 79 no.79.

For the king's presence at Montfort on 13 March 1202, see *RLP*, 7; *Rot. Lib.*, 27–8. The present letters are otherwise unrecorded, although they might conceivably have been enrolled on the lost Norman chancery Contrabrevia Roll for the year 3 John. The same source (BL ms. Cotton Cleopatra A vii fos.90r–92r) recites the original grant of the church of Écrammeville to the church of St James Bristol (1164 X 1183, cf. Patterson, *Earldom of Gloucester Charters*, no.38), and its confirmation by King Henry II (1172 X 1179, cf. *Acta Henry II*, no.323), Henry bp of Bayeux (after 1165) and Rotrou archbp of Rouen (1164 X 1183, cf. *Monasticon*, ii, 78 no.79).

I(ohannes) Dei gratia etc venerabili in Cristo patri H(enrico) eadem gratia Baioc' episcopo salutem. Sciatis iudicatum esse in curia nostra quod stare non debet recognitio illa que facta fuit inter abbatem Theok' et Willelmum Infantem de ultima presentatione ecclesie de Escromouill' quia recognitio illa capta fuit sine precepto nostro et warento senescalli vestri[a] coram aliis quam iust(iciis) nostris, et coram talibus coram quibus capi non debuit et contra cartam predicti abbatis quam habet de Willelmo quondam com(ite) Glouc' qui ecclesiam illam dedit ecclesie sancti Iacobi Bristll' que est cella de Theok' et contra confirmationem H(enrici) reg(is) patris nostri et confirmationem Rotrodi quondam Rotomag' archiepiscopi et etiam contra confirmationem vestram, et ideo vobis mandamus quatinus eidem abbati faciatis habere sine dilatione talem seisinam de predicta ecclesia qualem inde habuit antequam predicta recognitio inter ipsum et Willelmum Infantem processisset, ammouentes omnino personam illam quam in ea posuistis post illam recognitionem ad presentationem ipsius Willelmi Infantis. Teste <me> ipso apud Munford xiii. die Marcii.

[a] *sic, ?recte* nostri

47. *Notification by Lambert de Bussy, knight, of his grant to the abbey of Notre-Dame-de-Voeu near Cherbourg (Manche) of a piece of land lying between the river Witham and his own estate.* [1226 X 1233]

B = Northampton, Northamptonshire Record Office ms. Brudenell-Bruce D.v.10, single sheet copy s.xiv/xv.

For Lambert de Bussy, who in 1209 offered a £20 relief for the lands of Hugh de Bussy his father, consisting of at least two knight's fees held of the bps of Lincoln at Hougham (Lincs.), a rebel knight in the service of William of Lancaster, captured by King John at the siege of Rochester in 1215 and thereafter forced to pay a ransom of at least £40 to Peter de Maulay, see *PR 11 John*, 75; *PR 12 John*, 25; *PR 17 John*, 58; *PR 5 Henry III*, 95; *Memoranda Roll 10 John*, PRS new series xxxi (1955), 144; *RLC*, i, 289, 481b; *Patent Rolls 1216–25*, 11–12; *Book of Fees*, i, 186; *The Registrum Antiquissimum of the Cathedral Church of Lincoln*, ed. C.W. Foster and K. Major, 12 vols, Lincoln Record Society xxvii–ix, xxxii, xxxiv, xli–ii, xlvi, li, lxii, lxvii–viii (1931–73), vii, 96 no.2060n., ix, 51 no.2442. Lambert de Bussy probably attended at Rochester as a knight of Gilbert son of Robert fitz Reinfrey, by whom he had been granted land at Lambrigg in Westmorland: *Facsimiles of Early Charters from Northamptonshire Collections*, ed. F.M. Stenton, Northamptonshire Record Society iv (1930), 138-40 no.53. A Lincolnshire knight of assize in 1223, Lambert was still alive in the year to December 1234 when he exercised the patronage of the church of Thistleton (Rutland) in favour of John de Bussy, perhaps a kinsman, but had been succeeded by 1241 by his son Hugh, later recorded in possession of land at Hougham (Lincs.) and Wigsley (Notts.): *CRR*, xi, no.631; *The Acta of Hugh of Wells Bishop of Lincoln 1209–1235*, ed. D.M. Smith, Lincoln Record Society lxxxviii (2000), 210 no.438; *Close Rolls 1237–42*, 352; *Close Rolls 1247–51*, 18, 191–2; *Cal.Chart.R. 1226–57*, 471. The origins of the Bussy family remain unknown, although possibilities include both Boucey (Manche, cant. Pontorson) and Le Boussey (Manche, cant. Barenton, com. St-Georges-du-Rouelley). Lambert's attachment could possibly have been more to the cell of Cherbourg at Hough-on-the-Hill (Lincs.) than to the mother house in Normandy, although a Norman connection seems much more probable. Although the location of the grant is not specified, it almost certainly refers to Lambert's estate at Hougham (Lincs.), skirted by the river Witham, lying within only a few miles of Notre-Dame-de-Voeu's daughter house at Hough-on-the-Hill (Lincs.), the present charter being preserved together with a transcript of other charters relating to Hougham church (Northampton, Northamptonshire Record Office, ms. Brudenell-Bruce D.x.27). The date is presumably before that of no.48 below but after the promotion of the witness named as Master W(illiam) de Insula, who was presented by Lambert to the church of Hougham in the 17th year of Bishop Hugh of Lincoln, i.e. December 1225–6, and who is probably the same man, described as chaplain, presented in the year June 1238–9 by the canons of Cherbourg as vicar of the church of Hough-on-the-Hill: *Rotuli Hugonis de Welles Episcopi Lincolniensis A.D. MCCIX-MCCXXXV*, ed. W.P.W. Phillimore and F.N. Davis, 3 vols., Canterbury and York Society i, iii, iv (London 1907–9), iii, 148; *Rotuli Roberti Grosseteste*, ed. F.N.Davis, Canterbury and York Society x (London 1910–13), 34.

Sciant presentes et futuri quod ego Lambertus de Bussh' miles dedi et concessi et hac presenti carta mea confirmaui Deo et abathie sancte Marie de Voto iuxta Cesarisburgum et canonicis ibidem Deo seruientibus in puram et liberam et perpetuam elemosinam quandam particulam terre que iacet inter Wythom' et culturam meam cuius longitudo continet xxviii. percatas, et latitudo in capite versus orientem continet tres percatas et dimediam[a], et medium contenet[b] quatuor percatas et decem pedes, et in capite versus occidentem contenet vii. percatas et sex pedes, et perc(at)a est decem et octo pedum scicut[a] per(cet)i diuidentes se extendunt ab oriente versus occidentem, et hanc don<ationem> et concessionem feci eis pro anima patris mei [c]et matris mee[c] et pro anima mea et uxoris mee et Hugonis filii mei et o<mnium> antecessorum et successorum meorum et omnium fidelium defunctorum Dei, et ego Lambertus et heredes mei warantisabimus predictam particulam terre predictis canonicis contra omnes homines imperpetuum. Hiis testibus: domino T. de Multon', Alano fratre suo, Hugone de Calkurtorp', magistro W(illelmo) de Insula tunc persona, Roberto scriptore et multis aliis etc.

[a] sic B [b] contenes B, contenet *supplied* [c-c] *interlined*

48. *Notification by Abbot William and the convent of Notre-Dame-de-Voeu near Cherbourg (Manche) of their reception, at the petition of Lambert de Bussy, knight, of the souls of his father and mother, himself and his sons and ancestors into annual commemoration within their house, deputing the recital of requiems to the house's canons established at Hough-on-the-Hill (Lincolnshire), with the names of Lambert's father and mother being recorded in the abbey's martyrology.* 1232/3

B = BL ms. Harley 1756 (Sir John Bussy's Book of Fees) fo.47v, s.xv/xvi. C = BL ms. Harley 1436 (Lincolnshire pedigrees with evidences) fo.123v, copied from an unspecified source fo.56, perhaps ultimately from B, s.xvii/xviii.

For Abbot William (fl.1230), see *GC*, xi, 942.

Universis Cristi fidelibus ad quos presens scriptum peruenerit Willelmus dictus[a] abbas sancte Marie de Voto iuxta Cesarisburgum[b] et eiusdem loci conuentus humilis salutem in domino. Ad universitatis vestre volumus[c] notitiam peruenire nos ad iustam peticionem domini Lamberti de Bussy militis recepisse animas patris et matris sue et suam animam et filii sui et antecessorum suorum specialiter in anuali[d] quod sit assidue in conventu nostro [e]<et> in omnibus aliis bonis que fiunt et fient decetero in domo nostra, ut eorum sint participes et divine retribucionis premium sicut et nos communiter expectantes. Volumus etiam et concedimus quod canonici nostri apud manerium de Hogg processione temporis commorantes in qualibet septimana[f] in qua debent cantare requiem semel celebrent pro animabus antecessorum iamdicti Lamberti si sint tales qui possint et debeant celebrari[e], et preterea quod nomina patris et matris sue[g] in nostro matirologio conscribantur[h] et eorum anniversorium semel in anno solemniter[j] celebretur[k]. Quod ut ratum permaneat et stabilis, presenti scripto patrocinio et sigillorum nostrorum apposissione duximus roborandi, anno domini m°.cc°.xxx°.ii°., huismodi scripto penes nos reservato.

[a] Deus C [b] Cesarnbugn C [c] nostre voluimus C [d] annali C [e-e] *not in* C [f] septimana septimana B [g] sue B, dicti Lamberti C [h] conscribatur C [j] solempnit C [k] C *ends here* celebrat etc anno domini 1232

49. Notification by Nicholas abbot of Valmont of his dispatch of relics from Valmont to the dependent hermitage of St Leonard (Stratfield Saye, Hampshire) for the support of the monks of Valmont serving there and to attract visitors, granting annual commemoration and three weekly masses to all benefactors, listing the relics themselves, which include relics of Christ, the Virgin Mary, the Holy Innocents, St Thomas the apostle, St Andrew, St Leonard, St Mary Magdalene, St Gregory and St Katherine. [1211 X 1228]

A = Eton College Records ECR 18/24. Endorsed: *orac(i)ones de Wylmnt* (s.xiii); *Q.* (?s.xvi). Approx. 262 × 154 + 20mm. Sealed *sur double queue*, 2 sets each of 3 slits, parchment tags, both seal impressions missing. B = BL ms. Additional 24319 fo.45r, copy from A, 1724.

There were two abbots of Valmont named Nicholas (*GC*, xi, col.279). The script of the present letters suggests the early thirteenth-century Nicholas I (*c*.1211 X *c*.1228) rather than Nicholas II (1290–1301). For Valmont's cell at Stratfield Saye in Hampshire, the result of patronage extended by the Stuteville family, confirmed to the mother house in a charter of Henry II before 1184, see Delisle, *Recueil*, no.636; *Acta Henry II*, no.2720. The present letters are of interest for the continued contacts between Valmont and its English daughter house, for what they disclose of the relics held by the mother house and for their evidence of the rise of perpetual prayers for the dead. The very careless copying (as noticed in the textual notes below) suggests that, as with other such appeals, this may be the sole survivor from what was originally a mass-produced sheaf of such documents intended for distribution to the faithful. For comparisons here, see the mass-produced offer of indulgences described by R.N. Swanson, 'Fund-Raising for a Medieval Monastery: Indulgences and Great Bricett Priory', *Proceedings of the Suffolk Institute of Archaeology and History*, xl (2001), 1–7.

Omnibus sancte matris ecclesie fidelibus ad quos presentes littere peruenerint Nich(olaus) abbas sancte Marie de Walemont et eiusdem loci conuentus salutem in domino et precum assiduitatem. Gloria sanctorum est quotiens reliquie et patrocinia eorum ad laudem et gloriam domini nostri Ihesu Cristi et eorum venerandam memoriam exaltanda per diuersas terrarum prouincias deferuntur. Inde est quod ad noticiam omnium volumus peruenire nos communi assensu de reliquiis sanctorum quorum corpora et reliquie in nostra continentur ecclesia ad heremum Sancti Leonardi super Lodanum ad loci promotionem et fratrum nostrorum qui ibidem Deo ᵃseruiunt sustentationemᵃ et ut ibi aduenientium et loci benefactorum orationes efficiatius exaudiantur aduenientium partes quasdam transmisisse. Concedimus autem omnibus sanctarum reliquiarum veneratoribus et Dei loci benefactoribus et fraternitatem suscipientibus omnia communia bona domus nostre in missis, in vigiliis, in disciplinis, in ieiuniis, in orationibus et elemosinis et omnibus aliis bonis. Preterea concedimus omnibus loci benefactoribus unum annuale in perpetuum faciendum in domo nostra et per unamquamque ebdomadam tres missas in perpetuum celebrandas, primam de sancto spiritu, alteram de sancta Maria ut pro ipsis filium suum deprecetur, terciam pro defunctis ut anime omnium fidelium defunctorum per misericordiam Dei requiescant in pace amen. Et quoniam os quodᵇ mentitur occidit animam[1], ne aliquis de sancti reliquiis mentiri audeat, nomina earum in hoc scripto commendauimus, de ligno Domini, de pane cene, de mensa Domini, de petra montis Caluarie, de innocentibus, de vestimento beate Marie quo induebatur quando peperit Cristum, de sancto Thoma apostolo, ᶜde + sancti Andree apostoliᶜ, de sancto Leonardo, de capillis sancte Marie Madalene, de sancto Gregorio, de capill(is) sancte Katerine et alie reliquie de pluribus sanctis.

[1] Wisdom 1:11

ᵃ⁻ᵃ seruiunt(ur) sustemtationem A, seruiunt sustentationem *supplied* ᵇ qil' A, quod *supplied* ᶜ⁻ᶜ *sic* A *for* cruce sancti Andree, *with the cross sign interlined.*

50. *Notification by Amicia countess of Leicester of her grant to Notre-Dame de Chaise-Dieu, with the assent of Earl Robert, her husband, of 26 shillings from the gold which she receives from the soke of Wimborne (Dorset).*   [1153 X 1168]

A = BL ms. Additional Charter 47381. Endorsed: *hec est carta Amicie comitisse Leencestrie* (s.xii); *Attisboro* (s.xiv); various post medieval endorsements. Approx. 185 × 65 + 14mm. Sealed *sur double queue*, parchment tag through a single slit, seal impression, vessica shaped, applied sideways, in natural wax varnished green, a female figure standing with a bird on her right hand and long flowing sleeves reaching almost to her feet, legend: ....SE LERECEST......

For the countess Amice, married to Robert earl of Leicester (d. 5 April 1168), herself entering the convent of Nuneaton after the death of her husband, dying 31 August, year uncertain, see *CP*, vii, 529–30. For her possible role in the foundation of the dependency of Fontevraud at Nuneaton, originally established by Earl Robert *c*.1153 at Kintbury in Berkshire, see B.M. Kerr, *Religious Life for Women c.1100–c.1350: Fontevraud in England* (Oxford 1999), 69–70. As pointed out to me by David Crouch, almost certainly to be dated after 1153 and the restoration of Robert of Leicester to his interests in Normandy. For the circumstances of the Leicester patronage of La Chaise-Dieu, see below no.51n.

Notum sit omnibus sancte D(e)i ecclesie filiis quia ego Amicia comitissa Leigr' beneplacito D(e)i et assensu domini mei Roberti comitis Leigr' dono et concedo Deo et beate Marie de Casa Dei et dominabus ibi Deo seruientibus xxxvi. sol(idos) quos habebam in socha Winburne in unciis meis auri, hoc autem dono ut Deus sanitati et incolumitati domini mei et mee et puerorum nostrorum sit prouisor, et etiam pro salute propinquorum et omnium amicorum nostrorum et etiam pro animabus patrum et matrum nostrorum et omnium antecessorum nostrorum. Quare volo et precor ut predicte famule Dei hanc prefatam elemosinam bene et in pace et honorifice et quiete teneant. T(estibus) Ern(aldo) de Bosco, Roberto de Craf, Reg(inaldo) de Bordigni, Gileberto de Vernet, Ric(ardo) Mallore, Ada de Ros, Rog(ero) de Cranford, Ric(ardo) de Teuerai, Willelmo de Bordigni, Sim(one) de Labelueisinera.

51. *Notification by R(obert) earl of Leicester, addressed to Arnold du Bois and all his barons and men, that the land which the nuns of Chaise-Dieu held in his fee in 'Olueia' has been exchanged for six virgates and meadow in Nuneaton and Attleborough (in Nuneaton, Warwickshire).* [1153 X 1159]

A = BL ms. Additional Charter 47382. Endorsed: *de terra quam comes Leencestrie eschambiauit aput Etoniam et Eschebergam* (s.xii); *12* (s.xiv); various post medieval endorsements. Approx. 182 × 98mm. Sealed *sur simple queue*, tongue and step for wrapping tie, seal impression in patterned silk seal bag, natural wax varnished reddish brown, round, equestrian, legend illegible.

Briefly noticed D. Crouch, *The Beaumont Twins* (Cambridge 1986), 204 (where 'Olueia' is assumed to lie in the Norman honour of Breteuil); *VCH Warwickshire*, iv, 167 (where it is identified with Olney in Buckinghamshire, despite the absence of any evidence for such a connection in the Olney entry of *VCH Buckinghamshire*, iv, 433). One possibility would be Olney in Coventry (J.E.B. Gover and others, *The Place-Names of Warwickshire*, English Place-Name Society xiii (Cambridge 1936), 167), but this seems always to have been an estate belonging to the earls of Chester, with no Leicester connections (P.R. Coss, *Lordship, Knighthood and Locality: A Study in English Society c.1180–c.1280* (Cambridge 1991), 38–9). David Crouch suggests Les Aulnaies (Orne, cant. L'Aigle, com. St-Martin-d'Ecublei), not far from La Chaise-Dieu and adjacent to Earl Robert's bourg of Rugles (Eure), with a place-name within this hamlet at La Chaise-Château. He further suggests that Earl Robert's decision to found a nunnery, eventually settled at Nuneaton, may have been taken at the same time that he founded Leicester Abbey for Augustinian canons (*c.*1139), perhaps with La Chaise-Dieu as the intended mother house, plans which would have collapsed following Robert's loss of his Norman estates *c.*1140. After the restoration of his Norman lands in 1153, Earl Robert not only granted the nuns of La Chaise-Dieu the present land in England but usages in the forest of Breteuil (*Mémoires et notes de M. Auguste le Prévost pour servir à l'histoire du département de l'Eure*, ed. L. Delisle and L. Passy, 3 vols (Evreux 1862–9), i, 482 from *CN*, 2 no.6). Set against this, the land at Attleborough and Nuneaton, already in the possession of the nuns of La Chaise-Dieu, was specifically excluded from Earl Robert's foundation charter for Nuneaton Priory, itself expedited 1153 X 1159, suggesting that patronage of La Chaise-Dieu was intended to supplement the patronage granted to Fontevraud at Nuneaton, not to channel or supercede it: Round, *Calendar*, 376 no.1062; Crouch, *Beaumont Twins*, 203–4.

R(obertus) comes Legrec' Ern(aldo) de Bosco et omnibus baronibus et hominibus suis Franc(is) et Angl(is) salutem. Sciatis quia terram illam quam sanctimoniales de Casa Dei habebant in elemosina de feudo meo in Olueia escambiam in Etona et in Atreberga de dominio meo tenendam de me in elemosina perpetue, scilicet vi. virgatas terre cum prato. Quare volo et firmiter precipio quatinus predicte sanctimoniales prefatam terram bene et libere et quiete et honorifice teneant. T(estibus) Ern(aldo) de Bosco, Ric(ardo) de Teurai, Rogero de Cranefort, Reginaldo de Bordigni, Gaufrido Abbate.

52. Notification by the countess Margaret (of Warwick) of her grant to the nuns of Chaise-Dieu of 25 shillings worth of land in Basildon (Berkshire) as confirmed by Robert du Neubourg.

[1139 X 1159, ?1153 X 1159]

B = BL ms. Additional Charter 47383. Endorsed: *335* (s.xviii). No indication of sealing. Hand of late s.xiv. Headed: *Transcript' cartarum que sunt apud Casam Dei. Inquiratur de istis cart(is) et aliis pro terra de Bastenden' et mittantur ad domum de Eton' quia impl(aci)tantur de dicta terra etc in curia reg(is)*.

During the episcopate of Rotrou bp of Evreux (Spear, *Personnel*, 134–5) and before the death of Robert du Neubourg (d.1159), probably of the 1150s. For Margaret (d. after 1156), daughter of Rotrou I count of Perche, married to Henry de Beaumont, earl of Warwick (*c.*1088–d.1119), herself mother of Roger second earl of Warwick (d.1153) and of Robert (d.1159), Rotrou (bp of Evreux, later archbp Rouen, d.1183) and Henry du Neubourg, see

CP, xii part 2, 360–1n.; Power, *Norman Frontier*, 511. For her widowhood and lands, see D. Crouch, 'Oddities in the Early History of the Marcher Lordship of Gower, 1107–1166', *Bulletin of the Board of Celtic Studies*, xxxi (1984), 133–41. She was still living in 1156, when, in the chapter of St-Etienne near Le Neubourg, she made grants to the Templars from her Gower estates: G.T. Clark, *Cartae et alia munimenta quae ad dominium de Glamorgancia pertinent*, new ed. by G.L. Clark, 6 vols (Cardiff 1910), iii, 963–4 no.837. For her confirmation of the church and tithes as Basildon to the monks of Lire as granted by William fitz Osbern her ancestor, see *The Cartulary of Carisbrooke Priory*, ed. S.F. Hockey, Isle of Wight Records Series ii (1981), 30–1 nos 31–2; *Monasticon*, vi, 1093 no.7. For the fee of La Chaise-Dieu at Basildon, recorded in 1220, see *Book of Fees*, i, 296. The witnesses below cause some small difficulties, because of the limited name-stock of the Norman Neubourg family. But plainly, the Robert who granted the act is the Robert who was seneschal of Normandy and died in 1159, elder brother of Bishop Rotrou, the first witness. The Henry de Neubourg who follows Rotrou must be Robert's son of that name, for he had a brother Robert du Neubourg, who was successively dean of Evreux before 1163 and moved to Rouen in 1176 (Spear, *Personnel*, 137–8, 202–3). This clerical Robert had a block grant of all the churches in his father's lordship of Le Neubourg, before 1159: BN ms. Latin 9212 (Copy of the lost Bourg-Achard cartulary) fo.4r (reference courtesy of David Crouch).

Notum sit omnibus quod comitissa Margareta dedit terram monachabus de Casa Dei apud Bastendene de qua habent annuatim viginti quinque solid(os) sterlingorum et hoc concessit Robertus de Nouo Burgo ipso teste Rotrod(o) Ebroycensi episcopo, Henr(ico) de Nouo Burgo, Roberto fratre suo, Gilberto capell(an)o et pluribus aliis.

53. *Notification by Henry du Neubourg of his confirmation to the nuns of Notre-Dame de Chaise-Dieu of the land of Basildon (Berkshire) granted by his ancestors, quit of all secular customs.*
[1160 X 1193]

B = BL ms. Additional Charter 47420, in an inspeximus by the official of the court of Evreux, 11 October 1276. C = BL ms. Additional Charter 47383, copy as in 52 above, s.xiv.

For a grant by Henry du Neubourg and Robert his son to Richard de Vernon of a moiety of Basildon and Ashampstead (Berkshire) in exchange for Radepont (Eure, cant. Fleury-sur-Andelle), and for a confirmation by the same of the churches and a tithe of his demesne at Basildon and Ashampstead as granted to the monks of Lire by his grandmother, the countess Margaret, see *HMC Rutland*, iv, 21; *Monasticon*, vi, 1093 nos 6–7. In these circumstances, the present charter is much more likely to have been granted by Henry du Neubourg, son of Robert (d.1159), witness to no.52 above, rather than by Henry I du Neubourg, who took his family's lands in Gower but who, in the present context, would have been more likely to refer to the grant of Basildon as one made by his mother rather than by his ancestors. A grant of rents at Pont-Audemer made by Henry the younger to the abbey of Bec at Le Neubourg in 1193 appears to have been a deathbed disposition: BN ms. Latin 13905 (Jouvelin's copies for Bec) p.55 (reference courtesy David Crouch). For the family, see Crouch, 'Oddities' (as above no.52 note); Power, *Norman Frontier*, 511.

Henr(icus) dominus Noui Burgi omnibus qui presentes litteras viderint tam presentibus quam futur(is) salutem. Noueritis me concessisse et confirmasse Deo et beate Mar(ie) et conuentui monialium Case Dei pro salute anime mee et antecessorum meorum terram de Bastendene quam antecessores mei eisdem monialibus in perpetuam elemosinam donauerunt, et volo ut terra illa et homines in ea habitantes sint quieti a scutagio et talliata et ab omnibus consuetudinibus secularibus que ad me vel heredes meos pertinent. Quod ut ratum sit et firmum presentem cartam meam sigilli mei munimine roboraui[a].

[a] C *ends here* etc

54. Notification by Earl R(obert) son of Robert earl of Leicester of his confirmation to the nuns of Chaise-Dieu of six virgates of land in Nuneaton and Attleborough granted by his father in exchange for land which the nuns previously held from Earl Robert's fee in 'Olueia'.   [1168 X 1190]

A = BL ms. Additional Charter 47385. Endorsed: *de Atleberg, carta R. com(itis) Leyc' facta priorisse de Casa Dei* (s.xiii/xiv); *Non inrotulat(a) sed t(ame)n mensio sit* (s.xiv/xv); various post medieval endorsements. Approx. 150 × 58 + 23mm. Sealed *sur double queue*, parchment tag through 3 slits, double-sided seal impression in natural wax, equestrian, legend illegible, counterseal illegible.

For the witness named William de Breteuil (d.*c*.1189), elder brother of earl Robert (1190–1204), placing the present charter in the lifetime of their father earl Robert (1168–1190), see *GC*, vii, 533n. For 'Olueia', perhaps in Normandy rather than England, see above no.51n.

R(obertus) comes filius Rob(erti) com(itis) Legr' omnibus hominibus suis salutem. Sciatis me concessisse et hac presenti carta mea confirmasse sanctimonialibus de Casa Dei in perpetuam elemosinam vi. virgatas terre cum prato quas pater meus de dominio suo in Etona et in Atleberga eis escambiauit pro terra quam antea tenebant de feudo suo in Olueia. Quare volo et firmiter precipio quatinus predicte sanctimoniales prefatam terram bene et libere et quiete et honorifice teneant. Testibus his: Willelmo Britolii filio com(itis) et Rob(erto) fratre eius, Ernaldo de Bosco filio Ernaldi, Hug(one) de Halneto, Willelmo de Camp', Gilleb(erto) de Plesseit, Nichalao Nicholao (sic) de Glotis, Hanschitillo Mall' et multis aliis.

55. *Notification by Earl David, brother of the king of Scots, of his grant to the nuns of La Chaise-Dieu of an annual rent of a mark payable from the proceeds of his mill at Fotheringay (Northamptonshire).*
[1190 X 1208]

A = BL ms. Additional Charter 47386. Endorsed: *Frodrige d(e) i. marc' redd(itus) concess' priorisse de Casa Dei* (s.xiii/xiv); *Non irrotulatur q(uia) domus de Eton' nich(il) ind(e) h(abe)t ut intellegit(ur)* (s.xiv/xv); various post medieval endorsements. Approx. 144 × 82 + 35mm. Sealed *sur double queue*, tag through 3 slits, central portion of round equestrian seal in natural wax, legend illegible.

Pd K.J. Stringer, *Earl David of Huntingdon 1152–1219* (Edinburgh 1985), 239–40 no.36.

Dated by Stringer August 1190 × 1194, or perhaps 1190 × 1208, after Earl David's marriage and before the death of Reginald of Oakley. As noted by Stringer, *the pro anima* clause for Thomas Bigod, perhaps a younger son of Earl Roger Bigod (d.1221), suggests a connection between the Scottish royal house and the senior Bigod line, a generation before Isabel, daughter of William the Lion, was married to Earl Roger Bigod (d.1270).

Omnibus sancte matris ecclesie filiis presentibus et futuris comes Dauid frater regis Scotie salutem. Sciatis me dedisse et concessisse et hac carta mea confirmasse Deo et ecclesie sancte Marie de Casa Dei et monialibus ibidem Deo seruientibus in puram et liberam et perpetuam elemosinam tenendam de me et heredibus meis unam marcam argenti ad festum sancti Michael(is) annuatim recipiendam de exitu molendini mei de Frodrigee pro anima patris mei et pro anima matris mee et pro salute anime mee et anime comitisse Matil(dis) sponse mee et pro anima regis Dauid aui mei et pro anima Malcolmi regis fratris mei et pro anima Thome Bigot et pro animabus antecessorum meorum et successorum. T(estibus) W. de Warennia, Rog(ero) conestab(u)l(ario) Cestrie, Eustacio de Vesci, Rob(erto) de Mortuo Mari, Henr(ico) filio meo, Simo(ne) de Sancto Licio, Ric(ardo) de Lindesia, Rob(erto) de Basingham, Will(elmo) de Essebi, Will(elmo) de Foleuill', Regin(aldo) de Acle, Will(elmo) Daco, Rob(erto) de Lah'neill' cum multis aliis.

56. Notification by Peter de la Rivière of a grant made by Rose de Helion his wife to the church of La Chaise-Dieu of a moiety of the vill of Sturmer (Essex), confirmed by Peter and by Daniel, Rose's son.
[1190 X 1204]

A = BL ms. Additional Charter 47387. Endorsed: *E(odem) mod(o) vill' de Estrumele ......ss' domui de Casa Dei* (s.xiii/xiv); *non irrotulatur quia domus de Eton' nichil inde habuit ut estim(aui)* (s.xiv/xv); various post medieval endorsements. Approx. 180 × 56 + 24mm. Sealed *sur double queue*, pink cords through 3 slits, seal impression in green wax, round, a shield of arms, arms and legend defaced.

Rose de Helion, daughter of Robert de Helion (ultimately of Breton descent, from Helléan, Morbihan) was married first to Ailward, chamberlain of Henry the Young King. Ailward, eventually succeeded by their son John, was dead by 1191, whereafter Rose made or confirmed a number of awards in the manor of Sturmer (Essex), clearly as part of her dower: *Acta Henry II*, no.34n.; *The Cartulary of the Knights of St John of Jerusalem in England Secunda Camera Essex*, ed. M. Gervers (Oxford 1982), 191–3 nos 322–4; *Stoke by Clare Cartulary*, ed. C. Harper-Bill and R. Mortimer, 3 vols, Suffolk Records Society Suffolk Charters iv–vi (1982–3), ii, 193–4 nos 260– 1, 203 no.281; *Rot. Lib.*, 59; *Book of Fees*, i, 233. Peter de la Rivière, a Norman landowner and a member of the garrison of Verneuil in 1194 whose local knowledge is specifically referred to in the *Histoire de Guillaume le Maréchal*, was charged scutage on a single fee in Essex in 1201, payment not pursued after 1204 presumably because of his defection to the French: Power, *Norman Frontier*, 76–7; *PR 3 John*, 72; *5 John*, 129. In June 1203, he was promised possession of a marriage portion worth 80 marks in England, his wife being identified as Rose de Helion later that year: *Rot. Lib.*, 40–1, 59. In these circumstances, the present charter can be dated after the death of Rose's first husband, and before Peter's defection to the French. Daniel, Rose's son, is otherwise unrecorded. There is no evidence that the grant of a moiety of Sturmer to the nuns of La Chaise-Dieu was ever allowed to take effect, although Rose de Helion undoubtedly made grants in the manor to other communities of nuns, at Chicksands and Shouldham: *Stoke by Clare Cartulary*, ii, 193–4 nos 260–1.

Petrus de Riueria omnibus tam presentibus quam futuris ad quos presens carta peruenerit salutem in domino. Nouerit uniuersitas vestra quod Roes <d>e Helyon uxor mea assensu meo et voluntate dedit Deo et ecclesie sancte Marie de Casa Dei et monialibus ibidem Deo seruientibus in liberam et quietam et perpetuam elemosinam pro salute anime sue et antecessorum suorum medietatem ville de Estrumele que est de patrimonio suo in terris et pratis et redditibus et generaliter in omnibus extra magistrum herbergagium et insuper brociam que est extra herbergagium ad faciendam granchiam suam et ut hec donatio firma esset et stabil(is) carta sua et sigillo suo confirmauit sui compos et in sua ligia potestate me presente et volente presente etiam Daniele filio suo et concedente qui et ipse inde habebit per manum predicte ecclesie xxiiii. sol(idos) stellinorum quamdiu vixerit. Ego vero P(etrus) de Riueria predicte R. sponsus hanc eius donationem ratam habens et approbans concessi et presenti carta et sigilli mei a(u)ctoritate confirmaui perpetuo duraturam. Test(ibus) Gilleb(erto) de Aquila, Rich(ardo) Gastinel, Galt(ero) de Castello, Auberto Iumell', Girard(o) de Roseria, Randol filio Guihummar, Willelmo Calcio et pluribus aliis.

57. *Notification by King John of his grant to the nuns of Chaise-Dieu (Eure) of an annual rent of 20 livres angevin from the prévôté of Verneuil.* Verneuil, 25 November 1201

B = Additional Charter 11352, copy under the seal of obligations of the vicomté of Verneuil, 2 March 1379/80. Endorsed: de *xxx. lib. de Vernniel* (s.xiv/xv); *pro Chezidieu* (s.xiv/xv); *puchased Moore's sale 28 .... 1856*; various post medieval endorsements. Sealed *sur simple queue*, tongue, seal impression missing. Notarial signiture: *nSpoincel.* C = TNA C 64/3 (Norman Charter Roll 2 John) m.2, s.xiii in. D = Evreux AD Eure H1437 p.77, copy from a lost cartulary of Chaise-Dieu (Stein no.1786) no.187, s.xviii. E = St-Pierre-de-Semilly, Marquis de Mathan ms. Lenoir 69 p.654, copy after a copy by Bréquigny from C, s.xviii.

Pd (from C) *Rot.Norm.*, 17; (fragment only, from an unidentified source, probably from D) *Mémoires et notes de M. Auguste le Prévost pour servir à l'histoire du département de l'Eure*, ed. L. Delisle and L. Passy, 3 vols (Evreux 1862–9), i, 482.

For La Chaise-Dieu-du-Theil (so-called to distinguish it from the Benedictine abbey of La Chaise-Dieu, in the diocese of Clermont, dép. Haute-Loire), founded as a dependency of Fontevraud on the river Iton (Eure, cant. Rugles) by Richer de L'Aigle *c.*1132, see Cottineau, i, 669. The surviving archives of the house are now housed in Evreux AD Eure (H1419–39), with fragments, from the fourteenth century onwards, in the archives of the mother house at Fontevraud (Angers AD Maine-et-Loire 128H1–5). Of those at Evreux, the most important comprise a s.xviii paper register of 43 folios including copies of earlier charters (H1437, cf. Stein no.1786), and another similar in 16 folios (H1438). Note that the 'Norman Roll' copy (C) lacks much that is preserved in the copies B and D. The anathema clause (phrased slightly differently in each of the three principal copies) is also worthy of note.

Iohannes[a] Dei gratia rex Angl(ie) [b]dominus[c] Hybern(ie) dux Norm(annie) et Aquit(anie) et comes And(egauie)[d] archiepiscopis, episcopis, abbatibus, comitibus, baron(ibus), [e]iustic(iis), senescall(is), vic(ecomitibus) et omnibus balliuis[e] et fidelibus suis salutem[b]. Sciatis nos dedisse, concessisse et presenti carta confirmasse Deo et ecclesie sancte[f] Marie de Casa Dei et monialibus ibidem Deo seruientibus in puram et perpetuam elemosinam[g] viginti[h] libras Andegauen(ses) singulis annis percipiendas de prepositura Vernolii ad duos terminos, scilicet medietatem ad Pascha et aliam medietatem in festo sancti Michaelis. Quare volumus et firmiter precipimus quod predicte monial(es) elemosinam[g] illam singulis annis percipiant de nobis et successoribus nostris ad illos duos terminos in perpetuum, [j]integre et libere[j] sine omni contradictione et inpedimento[k], et si quis eis inde molestiam fecerit[l] vel grauamen, Dei et nostram incurrat maledictionem auctoritate[m] qua rex inimic(os)[n] maledicere potest. [p]Hiis testibus: Willelmo Ymeliren'[q] episcopo, R(oberto) comite Leircestr'[r], Gilleberto de Aquila[s], Roberto de Harecort[t], A(imerico) vicecom(ite) Hoarcen'[v], Hugone de Menill'[w], Henr(ico)[x] de Gray, Garin(o) de Glapion[y], Bricio camerario[p]. Dat'[z] per manum Simonis archidiaconi [aa]Wellensis[bb] apud Vernol'[aa] xxv. die Nouembr(is) anno regni nostri tercio.

[a] Ioannes D [b-b] etc C [c] duc D [d] Andegauensis D [e-e] iusticiariis, seneschallis, vicegerentibus et omnibus bailliuis D [f] sancte BD, beate C [g] eleemosinam D [h] vigenti D [j-j] libere et integre C [k] impedimento D [l] faceret D [m] authoritate D [n] inunctus C, indignatus D [p-p] *not in* C [q] Hymelicensis D [r] Rotrodo comite Leirtrestenei D [s] Gileberto de Aquilo D [t] Harecorto D [v] Andrea vicecomite Toarcensi D [w] Neuilla D [x] Hinrico D [y] Clapion D [z] Datum D [aa-aa] de Verellensi apud Vernolium D [bb] Wellen' C

58. Notification by Gilbert de L'Aigle of his grant, made with the assent of Elizabeth his wife and Gilbert his eldest son to the nuns of Notre-Dame de Chaise-Dieu, of an annual rent of 45 shillings from the rent of his manor of Willingdon (Sussex), intended to pay for the nuns' shoes. 1215/16

A = BL ms. Additional Charter 47388. Endorsed: *carta Gilberti de Aquila* (s.xiii med) *de xlv. s(olidis) redd(itus) in Guillenden' concess(is) priorisse de Casa Dei* (s.xiii/xiv); *Guillenden'* (s.xiii/xiv); *non inrotulatur quousque stare poterit sed domus de Eton' aliquid inde habere adhuc necnon* (s.xiv/xv); various post medieval endorsements. Approx. 227 × 105 + 19mm. Sealed *sur double queue*, parchment tag through a single slit, round seal in white wax, an eagle with outstretched wings, legend illegible, smaller oval counterseal, ?a classical cameo of a man or boy, legend illegible. B = Evreux AD Eure H1418 p.8 no.19, notice only, after December 1673, claiming that the letter 'O' was endorsed on the charter, citing the original as 'Cotte 15 Iere liasse des anciennes chartes' and noting its appearance in 'premier inventaire page 43 .... 2eme inventaire p.3 no.15'.

Cf. Evreux AD H1419, for a s.xviii copy, taken from a lost parchment register, of a charter by which Gilbert de L'Aigle and Elizabeth his wife and Gilbert their son and Richer, Gilbert the elder's brother, confirmed the nuns of La Chaise-Dieu in all grants *in Nouam Landam* made by Gilbert's grandfather and father, both named Richer, 10 June 1209. For Gilbert's lands in England, seized following his defection to the Capetian cause in 1203, but held in custody from 1207 by William earl Warenne, brother of Gilbert's wife Elizabeth alias Isabella, recovered by Gilbert himself during his time in England in 1215/16, thereafter held in conjunction with his Norman estate, as one of the few cases of continuing Anglo-Norman lordship through to his death in 1231, with Gilbert choosing to be buried at the new Augustinian priory he had established in the 1220s at Michelham (in Arlington, Sussex), see K. Thompson, 'The Lords of Laigle: Ambition and Insecurity on the Borders of Normandy', *ANS*, xviii (1996), 193–

5, at p.193 n.85 noting the present grant and suggesting that a grant by Gilbert to the Premonstratensian priory of Otham (in Hailsham, Sussex) (TNA E 210/3640) dates from much the same time.

Sciant omnes tam presentes quam futuri ad quos presens carta peruenerit quod ego Gislebertus dominus Aquile assensu et voluntate Elisabet uxoris mee et Gisleberti primogeniti mei et aliorum amicorum meorum dedi ecclesie beate Marie de Casa Dei et sanctimonialibus ibidem Deo seruientibus in liberam et perpetuam et quietam helemosinam pro salute anime mee et Elisabet uxoris mee et omnium antecessorum meorum quadraginta et quinque solidos stellinorum in meo redditu mei manerii de Guillendone et volui et firmiter precepi quod quicumque balliuus meus erit de predicto manerio sine dilatione et absque contradictione reddat benigne nuntio sanctimonialium predictos quadraginta quinque solidos per singulos annos in perpetuum ad festum beati Petri ad vincula intrante Augusto. Iterum volui et precepi ut dominus quod si predictus nuntius sanctimonialium apud Guillendone moram fecerit pro defectu et dilatione predicti balliui, a die transacto termini ad sumptus et grauamen ipsius balliui moretur donec ab illo predictum redditum libere recipiat et quiete. Stabiliui autem hos predictos quadraginta quinque solidos stellinorum ad calciamenta predictarum sanctimonialium, et ut hoc ratum et inconcussum permaneat presentem cartam sigilli mei testimonio confirmaui pluribus testibus. Actum anno ab incarnatione domini m°cc°x°v°.

59. Notification by William de Minières (?Les Minières, Eure, cant. Damville, or Les Minières, Eure, cant. Conches, com. Beaubray) that whereas he earlier granted an annual rent of 10 livres from the prévôté of Verneuil to two of his daughters, nuns of La Chaise-Dieu, specifying that the convent of Chaise-Dieu was to hold half of this rent in perpetuity and the other half only for the lifetime of his daughters, he now grants the entire rent of 10 livres in perpetuity.

February 1241/2

B = BL ms. Additional Charter 11353, as above no.57, copy under the seal of obligations of the vicomté of Verneuil, 2 March 1379/80. C = Evreux AD Eure H1437 p.77, copy from a lost cartulary (Stein no.1786) no.187, s.xviii.

Uniuersi(s) presentes litteras inspecturis Guillermus[a] de Mineriis miles salutem. Nouerit uniuersitas vestra quod cum dedissem duabus filiabus meis monialibus apud Casam Dei decem libr(as) annui redditus in prepositura Vernol'[b] percipiendas, quarum decem libr(arum) redditus concesseram medietatem conuentui[c] dicte domus in perpetuum tenendam et possidendam post decession(em) earum et alteram medietatem ad vitam earum, ego volo et concedo quod conuentus dicte domus post decessum filiarum habeat et possideat totas decem libr(as) predictas annui redditus in perpetuum sine reclamatione mei vel heredum meorum, quas decem libr(as) annui redditus predicto[d] conuentui ego et heredes mei in perpetuum tenemur garantizare vel alibi in hereditate nostra valore ad valorem excambire[e]. In cuiusdic(t)i[f] confirmationem et testimonium sigillum meum presentibus litteris apponere[g] dignum duxi. Actum anno domini m.cc.xl. primo, mense Febriar(ii)[h].

[a] Guillelmus C [b] Vernolii C [c] conuintui C [d] predictas dicto C [e] escambire C [f] cuius rei C [g] apponere *not in* B, *supplied from* C [h] Februario C

60. *Notification by Audelina prioress and William prior of La Chaise-Dieu of their grant to Ida prioress and Robert prior of Nuneaton of their manor of Attleborough and all their possessions at Basildon at a perpetual annual farm of 12 marks.*   La Chaise-Dieu, July 1243

A = BL ms. Additional Charter 47998. Bipartite polled cyrograph, with two diagonal indentations at the top. Endorsed: *Atlebergh' et Bastendene terra dimiss(a) priorisse de Eton' ad perpetuam firmam per priorissam de Casa Dei* (s.xiii/xiv); *ex(tr)a* (s.xiii/xiv); *Attleberge* (s.xv/xvi); *Amannoy* (s.xv/xvi); various illegible or post medieval endorsements, including *365* (s.xviii/xix). Approx. 220 × 112 + 15mm. Sealed *sur double queue*, two parchment tags each through three sets of slits, both seal impressions missing. B = Ibid. 47999, copy of an inspeximus of A by Abbess Aalidis and the convent of Fontevraud, January 1243/4, s.xiii med.

CYROGRAPHUM

Notum sit omnibus tam presentibus quam futuris quod hec est conuentio facta inter Adelinam priorissam et Willelmum priorem et conuentum de Casa Dei et Idam priorissam et Robertum priorem et conuentum de Eton', videliced[a] quod dicti Adelina priorissa et Will(elmu)s prior et conuentus de Casa Dei tradiderunt et concesserunt dictis Ide priorisse et Roberto priori et priorissis et prioribus qui pro tempore erunt in domo Eton' et conuentui manerium suum de Atleberge cum pertinentiis ad perpetuam firmam cum omnibus etiam que habent apud Bastenden' pro duodecim marcis bonorum et legalium sterlingorum singulis annis soluendis apud Casam Dei infra Pentecost', quas dictas duodecim marcas dicti priorissa, prior et conuentus Eton' qui pro tempore fuerint facient deportare apud Casam Dei suis sumptibus et suo periculo infra Pentecost', et si contigerit quod dicti priorissa, prior et conuentus Eton' qui pro tempore fuerint in dicta solutione dictarum duodecim marcarum in dicto termino cessauerint, licebit priorisse vel priori qui pro tempore fuerint apud Casam Dei vel eorum mandato statim possessionem dicti manerii sui de Atleberge et de

Bastenden' cum omnibus pertinentiis integre, pacifice, sine contradictione aliqua et reclamatione dictorum priorisse, prioris et conuentus Eton' qui pro tempore erunt et omnium aliorum hominum quorumcumque, et omnia mobilia et immobilia que ibidem fuerint inuenta pacifice possidere sine contradictione aliqua et reclamatione, nisi dicta solutio per guerram vel per mortem nuncii deferentis pecuniam dictam vel aliam iustam et rationabilem causam seu excusabilem fuerit impedita. Ut autem hec conuentio fidelitatis robur optineat in perpetuum, huic scripto in modum cyrographi confecto apponita sunt signa utriusque partis, videliced[a] scripto quod remanebit penes conuentus de Casa Dei sigilla priorisse et prioris Eton' et scripto quod remanebit penes conuentum Eton' sigilla priorisse et prioris de Casa Dei. Actum anno gratie m°.cc°.x°liii°. apud Casam Dei mense Iulii.

[a] *sic* A

61. *Notification by Margaret prioress of Chaise-Dieu of her receipt of 12 marks for the Pentecost term of her rent owing from the prioress and prior of Nuneaton, paid by Henry, servant of Grove Priory (Bedfordshire).*   2 November 1286

A = BL ms. Additional Charter 47389. Various post medieval endorsements. Approx. 185 × 102mm. Sealed *sur simple queue*, fragment of small oval seal in green wax on tongue, an eagle with wings folded, legend illegible.

For the rent itself, see above no.60.

A touz ceus qui verront et orront cestes presentes lettres suer Marguerite priouresse de Chese De salut en nostre segniour. Sachent tuyt que nos auon et comfesson a avoir receu par la mein' Henri sergant an priour de la Graue on non don de la priouresse et dou priour de Estonne et pour icelz douze mars de estellins pour le terme de Penthecouste derrennement passe es quex los diz priours et priouressez sont tenuz a nos chascun an de certainne caus de quex douze mars desus diz nos nos tenon pleniement pour paiez, en quel tesmoing de ces presentes lettres audiz priour et priouresse donames ces presentes lettres seellees de nostre seel. Ce fut fet en len de grace mil et deus cc. et quatre vinz et sis, on jour dou semadi enpre la feste de Touz Seinz.

62. *Notification by Stephania, prioress, and Ralph, prior of La Chaise Dieu, of their receipt of 300 marks via Nicholas de Fengerons, their proctor, with the assent of M(argaret) abbess of Fontevraud, paid by the prior and convent of Nuneaton via their clerk, Thomas of Ludbrook, as the sale price in place of the annual fee farm of 12 marks previously paid for lands and tenements in Attleborough and Basildon, which 300 marks were previously deposited with the prioress of Belhomer (Eure-et-Loir) until the prioress and prior of La Chaise-Dieu could find equivalent rents to substitute for those previously received from England.*

La Chaise-Dieu, 28 October 1291

A = BL ms. Additional Charter 48002. Endorsed: *Acquiet' priorisse Cas(a) Dei de solutione den(ariorum)* ...... *renunc'* (s.xiv); *carta de Attylborogh et Bastenden'* (s.xv); *ii.* (?s.xvi); various post medieval endorsements including *410* (s.xviii/xix). Approx. 210 × 74mm. Sealed *sur simple queue*, two tongues, upper tongue carrying an oval seal impression in natural, brownish wax, an eagle or bird with head craned backwards over its right wing, legend +STHEOPHAN' PRIOROSSE DE CASA DEI, lower tongue carrying a round seal impression in red wax, two mitred figures, one with right hand carrying crook, the other with head inclined to the right, legend +FRA... RAD......

Cf. the confirmation of this sale by Margaret abbess of Fontevraud, December 1291: BL ms. Additional Charter 48003, referring to the 300 marks desposited by Brother William de Verny, late proctor of Grovebury Priory, previously responsible for the payment of the 12 mark annual farm, *apud Bellum Mare prioratum nobis subditum ... sub clauibus*, now transformed into an outright sale *ut per hoc posset precludi via maris et regionum periculis*. For the Fontevraudist priory of Belhomer (Eure-et-Loir, cant. La Loupe, com. Belhomer-Guéhouville), see Cottineau, i, 326–7.

Tenore presentium pateat uniuersis nos sororem Stephanam priorissam de Casa Dei et fratrem Radulfum loci eiusdem priorem recepisse per Nicholaum de Fengerons presbiterem mandatum nostrum seu attornatum assensu domine nostre domine M. Dei gratia Font' Ebr' abbatisse interueniente a relig(iosis) mulieribus priorissa et conuentu de Nunne Eton' in Anglia per manus Thom(e) de Lodbrok' earumdem dominarum clericum tricent(um) marcas steling(orum) pro duodecim marcis annui redditus quas ab eisdem percipere solebamus annuatim pro terris et tenementis in Attleberge et Bastenden' cum suis pertin(entiis) que prius ad perpetuam feodi firmam pro predictis duodecim marcis annuis de nob(is) tenuerunt per nos predictis priorisse et conuentui venditis et remissis, qui quidem denar(ii) antedicti iuxta assensum domine nostre abbatisse antedicte necnon et assensum nostrum resterant in deposito apud Bellum Mare sub custodia domine priorisse loci eiusdem quousque redditus aliquos ad valentiam dictorum denar(iorum) ad comperand(um) inuenire poterimus. In cuius rei testimonium has litteras nostras sigill(is) nostris consignatas predictis priorisse et conuentui fieri fecimus patentes. Dat' apud Casam Dei, in festo apostolorum Symonis et Iude, anno Domini m°.cc. nonagesimo primo.

63. *Notification by Abbot Harduin and the convent of Cormeilles of their grant to Roger son of Robert, earl of Leicester, of the first church in their gift to fall vacant.* [1174 X 1189]

A = BL ms. Additional Charter 47392. Various post medieval endorsements. Approx. 130 × 41 + 16mm. Sealed *sur double queue*, parchment tag through 3 slits, seal impression missing.

For Harduin, formerly prior of St-Hymer, abbot of Cormeilles (1174– d. 18 December, before 1200), see *GC*, xi, 847. For Roger (d.1202), son of Robert III earl of Leicester (d.1190), chancellor of William King of Scotland (1187), elected bp of St Andrews in 1189, and finally consecrated in 1198, see *CP*, vii, 533n.; *Fasti Ecclesiae Scoticanae medii aevi ad annum 1638*, ed. D.E.R. Watt and A.L. Murray (revised edn, Edinburgh 2003), 379. If Roger obtained his see at the earliest possible canonical age of 30, then he was born in 1159, which might fit the evidence of his having two elder brothers subsequent to his parents' marriage *c.*1153. Cormeilles was an abbey in the advocacy of his father, Earl Robert, and had most likely been solicited for benefices with which to endow Roger. I am indebted to David Crouch for various of the details here.

Harduinus Dei gratia abbas Cormel' totusque couentus eiusdem loci uniuersis sancte matris ecclesie filiis salutem in domino. Ad communem omnium volumus noticiam peruenire nos karitatis intuitu concessisse Rogerio filio Roberti comitis Leg(re)cestrie ecclesiam que prius in nostra donatione vaccauerit saluo iure antiquo ecclesie Cormel'. Ut igitur hec nostra concessio stabil(is) et rata futuris temporibus habeatur, eam presenti scripto sigilli nostri attestatione munito roboramus.

64. *Notification by King Henry II of his confirmation to the abbey of Longues (Calvados, cant. Ryes) of the land at Pouppeville (Manche, cant. Ste-Mère-Église, com. Ste-Marie-du-Mont) granted by Ra(ndu)lph Druel.*
Bur-le-Roi [October 1174 X 1182, ? October 1174 X May 1175]

B = TNA PRO 31/8/140B part 2 pp.89–90 no.2, copy by Léchaudé d'Anisy from amongst his own collection ('de ma collection'), 1836.

Printed (calendar from B) Eyton, *Court, Household and Itinerary of Henry II*, 221, 235 (February 1178, and again June X September 1180); Round, *Calendar*, no.1449; *Acta Henry II*, no.1655.

Supposedly after the consecration of Richard of Ilchester as bp of Winchester, and before the promotion of Walter of Coutances as bp of Lincoln in May 1183, and hence before the king's departure from Normandy for the south in 1182. Probably before the promotion of William fitz Ralph as seneschal of Normandy, and hence before the king's return to England in May 1175. The similarity of the present text to another charter of Henry II also dated at Bur-le-Roi (Delisle, *Recueil*, ii, no.691, from an original still at Caen AD Calvados H6296) must at least raise a suspicion that, in making his final copy for the English Record Commissioners, Léchaudé d'Anisy conflated two distinct documents: a charter relating to Pouppeville (as in Delisle, *Recueil*, no.691), and another carrying the present witness list.

Henricus Dei gratia rex Anglorum, dux Normannie et Aquit(anorum) et comes Andegau(orum) archiepiscopis, episcopis, abbatibus, comitibus, baronibus, iusticiariis, vicecomitibus et omnibus ministris et fidelibus suis Normannie salutem. Sciatis me concessisse et presenti carta confirmasse abbatie de Longis et monachis ibidem Deo seruientibus terram de Pupeuilla quam Radulfus Druel dedit in perpetuam elemosinam. Quare volo et firmiter precipio quod predicti canonici habeant et teneant terram illam cum omnibus pertinentiis suis bene et in pace, libere et quiete, integre et honorifice cum omnibus libertatibus et liberis consuetudinibus suis. T(estibus) Richardo episcopo Wintoniensi, Henrico episcopo Baiocen', mag(is)tro Waltero Constan', Gaufrido de Lucy, Hamo pincerna, Willelmo filio Radulfi apud Burum.

65. Notification by Philippa, daughter of Hugh de Rosel, of her grant to the (Premonstratensian) abbey of Ardenne (Calvados, cant. Caen, com. St-Germain-de-la-Blanche-Herbe) by placing a book on the Lady altar, of ten acres of her demesne land at Gruchy (Calvados, cant. Creully, com. Rosel) lying in four fields. In return the canons have received her and her ancestors in their prayers and benefits and those of their order, granting her burial at Ardennes after her death, acquitting her of 30 livres angevin that she owed to the king, and giving her a further 100 sous angevin. The present grant has been made in public in the king's hall at the castle of Caen, before the king's justices sitting at the Exchequer.

Caen, 1176/7

A = BL ms. Additional Charter 15278. Endorsed: *ii.a Philippe de Rosello* (s.xii/xiii); *Groucie iiii. carta* (s.xiv); various post medieval endorsements. Approx. 338 × 70mm. Sealed *sur simple queue*, two slits in middle of the foot, parchment tag through the upper slit, seal impression, oval in dark green wax, a ?female bust in profile facing to the left, legend: SIGILLUM PHIL..E DE ROSELLO+.

Printed (with English translation 'from the original deed at Caen', and drawing of the seal) J.H. Wiffen, *Historical Memoirs of the House of Russell*, 2 vols (London 1833), i, 77–8, 82, 530 no.15; (calendar from A, then untraced) Round, *Calendar*, 182–3 no.517;

(brief notice from A) Haskins, *Institutions*, 174 n.104; (part only from A) Vincent, 'A Collection of Early Norman Charters', *Cahiers Léopold Delisle*, liii fasc.1–2 (2004), 31–2 no.1.

The diplomatic of the act is surprisingly archaic for a charter of the late 1170s, including the reference to the offering of the book (presumably the present charter), and an elaborately worded 'corroboratio'. Possibly the earliest surviving reference to Richard of Ilchester's period of government in Normandy, although not listed amongst the earliest records of the Norman assizes cited by Haskins, *Institutions*, 334. For Philippa and her grant, see also *The Charters of the Anglo-Norman Earls of Chester c.1071–1237*, ed. G. Barraclough, Record Society of Lancashire and Cheshire cxxvi (1988), 319–21 nos 319–20 (with an original now Caen AD Calvados H322); D. Power, 'Les Dernières années du régime angevin en Normandie', *Plantagenêts et Capétiens: confrontations et héritages*, ed. M. Aurell and N.–Y. Tonnerre (Turnhout 2006), 171, 181 nos 1, 4, 183 nos 33, 38, below nos 66–7.

Notum sit omnibus tam presentibus quam futuris quod ego Philippa filia Hugonis de Rosello dedi D(e)o et ecclesie sancte Marie de Ardena et canonicis ibidem Deo seruientibus offerendo per unum librum super altare beate Marie circumstante conuentu ecclesie et aliis pluribus pro salute anime mee et animarum patris et matris mee et antecessorum meorum in perpetuam elemosinam solutam et quietam ab omni exactione x. acras terre de proprio dominio meo ad Groceium in iiii. campis, campum qui vocatur Pratum et campum Wigo et campum Fullonis et ex alia parte vie dimidiam acram. Pro hac autem elemosina canonici receperunt me et antecessores meos in orationibus et beneficiis suis et ordinis sui et ad mortem meam liberam sepulturam concesserunt m(ich)i quam apud illos elegi. Preterea de rebus ecclesie sue adquietauerunt me ad scacarium regis de xxx. lib(ris) And(egauensium) quas debebam regi et m(ich)imetipsi iam dederant c. sol(idos) And(egauensium). Eapropter quod in multiplici hominum genere multiplex viget genus fallatie, ne hoc obliuione deleretur et ne aliquis super hoc aliquam iniuriam predictis canonicis agere possit, sed firmum et illibatum futuris temporibus conseruetur, presenti carta sigilli mei impressione munita eis confirmare curaui. Actum est autem hoc publice in aula regis in castello Cadomi coram iudicibus regis ad scacarium sedentibus, anno ab incarnatione domini mclxxvi. Super hoc autem testes sunt dominus Ric(ardus) Wint' episcopus qui tunc temporis erat capital(is) iusticia, Gisleb(ertus) Pipart', Ric(ardus) Giphart, Simon de Tornebu, Gaufridus Monacus, Rannulfus de Grantual, Simon de Scuris, Rob(ertus) Belet, Will(elmus) de Caliz, Rog(erus) de Scuris, Willermus Tanetin et alii plures.

66. *Notification by Philippa, daughter of Hugh de Rosel, of her confirmation of no.65 (recited in slightly different terms from no.65 above, with different witnesses and notice that the payment in 1176 included 30 livres to acquit Philippa's debts at the Exchequer and a further 12 livres in money, rather than the 10 livres of no.65), made in the full pleas of the king, at the king's Exchequer, in the first year of King John, in return for a further 4 livres and 15 sous angevines.* [Caen] in the Exchequer, May 1199 X May 1200

A = Caen AD Calvados H322. Endorsed: *Philipe de Rosello de terra de Groceio* (s.xiii); *Groucie iii. carta* (s.xiii/xiv); *Groucy* (s.xvi/xvii). Approx. 188 × 132 + 26mm. Sealed *sur double queue*, single slit, parchment tag and seal impression missing. Written in the same hand as no.67 below. B = Bnf ms. Latin 10063 fo.107r no.4, copy from A by Léchaudé d'Anisy, s.xix. C = Caen AD Calvados AD F4068 Liasse 1 nos 32–33, copy by Léchaudé d'Anisy from A, cited as 'Archives de Calvados', s.xix.

Pd (calendar from BC) Léchaudé, *Extrait*, i, 2 no.3.

The lists of witnesses supplied here, both in augmentation of the witnesses listed in no.65 and for the confirmation of 1199/1200, are particularly valuable. The additions to the witness list of no.65 are entirely plausible. Master Hugh de Gaiet may possibly be identifiable as Master Hugh of Gayhurst, elsewhere recorded as a leading figure in the household of Richard of Ilchester as bp of Winchester: *English Episcopal Acta VIII: Winchester 1070–1204*, ed. M.J. Franklin (Oxford 1993), p.lviii. For a charter issued by Philippa in 1202, granting land at Rosel (Calvados, cant. Creully) to the nuns of La Trinité at Caen, see *Charters and Custumals of the Abbey of Holy Trinity Caen: Part 2 The French Estates*, ed. J. Walmsley (Oxford 1994), 39–40 no.6.

Notum sit omnibus tam presentibus quam futuris quod ego Philipa filia Hug(onis) de Rosello carens marito et omni matrimonio tempore Henr(ici) reg(is) Angl(ie) dedi Deo et ecclesie sancte Marie de Ardena et canonicis ibidem Deo seruientibus pro salute anime mee et antecessorum meorum in puram et perpetuam elemosinam apud Groceium x. acras terre et dimidiam in his vi. campis, in campo qui vocatur Pratum, et in campo qui est inter campos Odonis filii Hosmundi sub vico, et in campo qui est iuxta viam de Carun, scilicet in capite predicti campi, et in campo Wigo et in campo Fullonis et ex alia parte vie dimid(iam) acram de proprio dominico meo sine redditu et seruicio et omnimoda exactione, et apud illam ecclesiam sepulturam elegi, et Garinus tunc temporis illius abbas ecclesie et canonici de rebus suis et amicorum suorum dederunt michi xl. libras et ii. Andeg(auenses), scilicet de xxx. lib(ris) adquietauerunt me ad scacarium domini reg(is) et xii. libr(as) alibi ad voluntatem meam persoluerunt. Quod totum carta mea confirmaui. Actum fuit hoc apud Cad' publice in castello reg(is), anno ab incarnatione Domini m°.c°.lxx°.vi°., coram his iudicibus tunc ad scacarium sedentibus: Ric(ardo) Winton' episcopo tunc capitali iusticia, Rog(ero) de Arre, magistro Hug(one) de Gaiet, Ric(ardo) capellano de Falesia, Sym(one) de Tornebu, Gaufr(ido) Monacho, Gillebert(o) Pypart, Ric(ardo) Gifart et aliis pluribus. Postea autem, primo anno Ioh(ann)is reg(is) Angl(ie) com essem vidua et carens omni matrimonio, in plenis placitis domini reg(is) et ad scaccarium eius eamdem donationem meam prefatam coram omnibus ibi presentibus recognoui et concessi et ad opus predicte ecclesie de Ardena presenti carta mea in puram et perpetuam elemosinam com terra quam Rob(ertus) le Franceis de feodo meo eidem dederat ecclesie fideliter confirmaui, et Rob(ertus) tunc temporis abbas Ardene et conuentus de bonis ecclesie sue iterum dederunt michi iiii. lib(ras) et xv. sol(idos) Andeg(auenses) et concesserunt unam acram illius terre ad luminare ecclesie sue. Hiis presentibus: Sansone tunc abbate Cad', Rad(ulfo) dicto Abbate tunc capitali iusticia, magistro Henr(ico) clerico domini regis, magistro Rad(ulfo) de Luxou', magistro Gaufr(ido) de Curtonia, Hug(one) Destas, Rad(ulfo) Maleherbe, Ric(ardo) filio Henr(ici), Rog(ero) de Gouiz, Henr(ico) de Caliz et aliis pluribus.

67. *Notification by Philippa de Rosel as in no.66 above, but here with yet further details and witnesses.*
[Caen at the Exchequer], May 1199 X May 1200

A = Caen AD Calvados AD H322. Endorsed: *carta Philipe de Rosel de terra de Groceio* (s.xiii); *Philippe de Rosel* (s.xiii); *Groucie ii. carta* (s.xiii/xiv); *Groucy* (s.xvi/xvii). Approx. 176 × 210 + 30mm. Sealed *sur double queue*, parchment tag through a single slit, seal impression missing, B = Ibid. F4068 Liasse 1 nos 32bis–33, copy by Léchaudé d'Anisy from A cited as 'tiré de ma collection', s.xix.

Date as above no.66.

Notum sit omnibus tam presentibus quam futuris quod ego Philipa filia Hug(onis) de Rosello carens marito et libera ab omni matrimonio tempore Henr(ici) regis Angl(ie) dedi Deo et ecclesie sancte Marie de Ardena et canonicis ibidem Deo seruientibus x. acras et dimidiam terre offerendo eas com matre mea Aeliz per unum librum super altare beate Marie, circonstante conuentu ecclesie et laicis multis, scilicet Gaufr(ido) de Cambernol et Rad(ulfo) de Taun et Serlone de Buron, Willelmo filio Auberee, Rad(ulfo) Ruffo, Rob(erto) de Secheuill' et aliis pluribus pro salute anime mee et antecessorum meorum in perpetuam elemosinam libere et quiete ab omni redditu et seruicio et omnimoda exactione de proprio dominico meo ad Groceium in sex campis, in campo qui vocatur Pratum, et in campo qui est inter campos Odonis filii Hosmundi sub vico, et in campo qui est iuxta viam de Carun, scilicet in capite predicti campi, et in campo Wigo, et in campo Fullonis, et ex alia parte vie dimidiam acram. Pro hac autem elemosina canonici receperunt me et antecessores meos in orationibus suis et ad mortem meam liberam sepulturam concesserunt m(ich)i quam apud illos preelegi. Preterea de rebus ecclesie sue et amicorum suorum dederunt michi xl. et ii. libras Andeg(auenses), scilicet de xxx. libris adquietauerunt me ad scacarium domini reg(is) et duodecim libras alibi ad voluntatem meam persoluerunt, et ne ego vel aliquis alius huic elemosine et donationi mee contraire vel eam in aliquo perturbare presumat, set firma et inconcussa in perpetuum perseueret, presentis scripti munimine et sigilli mei appositione eam confirmare et corroborare curaui. Actum est hoc publice in aula domini reg(is) in castello Cadom' coram iudicibus domini reg(is) ad scacarium sedentibus anno ab incarnatione Domini m°.c°.lxx°.vi°. Super hoc autem testes sunt isti: dominus s(cilicet) Ric(ardus) Winton' episcopus qui tunc temporis erat capitalis iusticia, Rog(erus) de Arre, mag(ister) Hug(o) de Gaiet, Ric(ardus) capellanus de Falesia et de laicis Sym(on) de Turnebu, Gaufr(idus) Monachus, Gillebert(us) Pipart, Ric(ardus) Giffart, Ran(ulfus) de Grantual, Willelmus de Caliz, Sym(on) de Escuris et alii plures. Anno iterum Ioh(ann)is reg(is) Angl(ie) primo, super prefata terra inter Rob(ertum) abbatem et conuentum Ardene ex una parte et me prefatam Philipam ex altera in curia domini reg(is) mota est discordia coram Sansone abbate Cad' et Rad(ulfo) dicto Abbate tunc capitali iusticia et magistro Henr(ico) clerico domini reg(is) in plenis placitis, et ad scacarium domini reg(is) in hunc modum est terminata. Ego siquid prefata Philipa sicut supradictum est carens marito, totam prescriptam terram in puram et perpetuam elemosinam sepedictis abbati et canonicis dedi ab omni reclamatione mea et heredum meorum et ab omnimoda exactione liberrima, et Rob(ertus) tunc abbas Ardene iiii. lib(ras) et xv. solid(os) Andeg(auenses) pro hac recognitione et donatione et concordia ad scacarium domini reg(is) apud Cad' in aula reg(is) michi donauit. Ad petitionem vero meam prefatus abbas concessit unam acram predicte terre ad luminare ecclesie sue. Quod totum com terra quam Rob(ertus) le Franceis dedit abbatie Ardene de feodo suo ego sepedicta Philipa presenti carta mea confirmaui. Hiis presentibus: magistro Rad(ulfo) de Luxou', Gaufr(ido) de Curtunna, Ioh(ann)e Ruffo clericis et de laicis Hug(one) Destas, Rad(ulfo) Maleherbe, Willelmo de Serenz, Geruasio de Locell', Walt(ero) de Annell', Henr(ico) de Caliz, Dinam[a] de Carun et aliis pluribus.

[a] *sic* A

68. Notification by Richard Silvain, with the assent of Richard his son, of his grant to the nuns of the Abbaye-Blanche at Mortain of his lordship of Plain-Landes (Manche, cant. Sourdeval, com. Gathemo) within specified bounds.   [1150 X 1180]

A = Cambridge University Library ms. Hengrave Hall 117 (provisional numbering: Norman deeds). Endorsed: *Ricardus Siluanus* (s.xii/xiii); *de Guatemo. Abrinc'* (s.xii/ xiii). Approx. 133 × 53 + 20mm. Sealed *sur double queue*, white leather tag through a single slit, seal impression, natural wax varnished reddish brown, round, a lion passant gardant facing to the right, legend mostly illegible SIGILL.... RI......, counterseal round, a lamb with a cross and a star behind (the Agnus Dei), legend S' RICARDI SILVANI.

Cf. the abbé Desroches, *Annales civiles, militaires et généalogiques du pays d'Avranches ou de la toute Basse-Normandie* (Caen 1856), 192, calendaring what appears to be the present charter, but from a lost cartulary copy: 'Nous voyons dans le Cartulaire de l'Abbaye-Blanche que Richard Silvain, ou Servain, du consentement de Richard Servain, son fils, donna pour le salut de son âme, de ses prédécesseurs et de ses héritiers, aux moniales de Mortain, son domaine de Plain-Laudes (*sic*), comme il était divisé et comme les fossés l'indiquaient jusqu'au chemin qui vient de Artay, comme on va au château de Vire, et jusqu'au domaine du comte', noticing a further charter of the same, with the consent of his son Richard, granting the monks of Savigny two measures of corn from his mills at St-Pair, made in the presence of John 'curé' of Bellefontaine and Guy de Serlant, with another charter to Savigny given by the same Richard, with similar witnesses, granting land at Martigny.

The date of the charter can be established only approximately. The Silvanus or Silvain family were lords of St-Pois (Manche, arr. Avranches, between Mortain and Vire). The first Richard Silvain was killed during Stephen's reign (*Orderic*, vi, 490–2). Another, benefactor of Montmorel and of the Abbaye-Blanche, was prominent at the Norman Exchequer and in assizes under kings Richard and John, being one of the knights of Mortain who later, *c*.1211, did homage to Philip Augustus. This man had a daughter, Margaret, married to Hasculf de Presles, and was succeeded by a son named Adam: AN L967 no.128; L979 nos 69, 108. For an attempted reconstruction of the family, see J. Pouëssel, 'Les structures militaires du comté de Mortain (XIe et XIIe siécles)', *Revue de l'Avranchin*, lviii no.307 (1981), 115–17, where, on the basis of the present charter (from the notice of it by Desroches) and another, to Savigny, the author suggests that the Richard of the present charter succeeded the Richard d. *c*.1137, being father to the Richard of the Norman Exchequer still active in 1211. Alternatively, the successor to the Richard of Stephen's reign and the Richard active in 1211 may have been one and the same man, eventually succeeded by a (younger) son named Adam, since another charter of Richard's to the Abbaye-Blanche, like this one witnessed by Guy and William de Basoches and by Jordan Cormall', claims the assent of Adam his son: Bnf ms. nouv. acq. françaises 21823 fo.299r–v no.155, and for further grants by Richard Silvanus to the nuns of Mortain and the Augustinian canons of Montmorel, cf. fos.298r, 300r–302r nos 140, 142, 144, 156; Bnf ms. Latin 10078 p.144 nos 22–3; AN L972 no.679, L979 no.108; *Cartulaires de la Manche: Abbaye de Montmorel*, ed. M. Dubosc (St-Lô 1878), no.169.

Quoniam temporalia transitoria sunt et caduca et subito labuntur a memoria, idcirco ego Ricardus Siluanus assensu Ricardi Siluani filii mei presentium etati et eorum posteritati notum fieri volui me pro salute anime mee et antecessorum meorum et heredum meorum in perpetuam elemosinam dedisse D(e)o et beate Marie de Moret' et sanctimonialibus ibidem Deo seruientibus et presenti carta confirmasse meum dominic(um) de Plano Landeto sicut fuit diuisum coram me extra tenementum hominum Renaldi Visus Lupi et hominum Willelmi Martini de Spina superiori Lande Ermouim sicut fossatum demonstrat usque ad caminum per quod venitur de Ateis sicut itur ad castell(um) Vire usque ad dominicum comitis, et ut hoc ratum maneat et immobile, sigilli mei munimine roboraui. T(estibus) Guidone de Basoc', Willelmo de Basoc' militibus, Roberto Siluano, Petro de Cormeliis, Petro de Bellofonte clericis, Willelmo Maubeec', Iordano Cormail burgensibus et aliis pluribus.

69. *Notification by Rotrou, archbishop of Rouen, of his confirmation to Foucarmont Abbey of possessions and privileges.* [1165 X 1183]

A = BL Additional Charter 17839. Endorsed: *Rotro Dei gratia Roth' arch(iescopus)* (s.xii); *OO LXIIII* (s.xii/xiii); various post medieval endorsements in French and English including the archival note *premier tiroir 5e liasse 1e(re) lettre de l'arch(vesque) de Rouen* (s.xviii). Approx. 558 × 700 + 40mm. Sealed *sur double queue*, two holes for cords, cords and seal impression missing. 67 lines of a very fine bookhand. Pen decoration to the initial capital *R*.

To be dated to the archiepiscopate of Rotrou (Spear, *Personnel*, 199). Note the address to the abbot and convent, rather than a general address as might be expected, carried through with remarks later in the charter referring to 'your church'. The first two thirds of the present charter recite the lands and possessions of the abbey in almost exactly the same order as a confirmation charter of King Henry II, to be dated 1156 X May 1162: *Acta Henry II*, no.1071 (Delisle, *Recueil*, no.176). The whole appears to be an earlier recension of the confirmation by Rotrou, dated 1178, recited in the Foucarment cartulary: Rouen, Bibliothèque Municipale ms. 1224 fos. 20r-22r.

Rotro Dei gratia Roth' arch(iepiscopus) dilectis filiis suis abbati et conuentui beate Marie sanctique Ioh(ann)is de Fulcardimonte tam presentibus quam futuris in perpetuum. Exigit officii nostri sollicitudo immo et caritas nos compellit iustis filiorum nostrorum annuere precibus <et> eorum precipue quos amplior comendat religio. Unde q(uonia)m in qualibet diocesi elemosine et beneficia ecclesiis et monasteriis collata in possidendo plus obtinent securitatis cum pontificis manu donata et eius confirmata fuerint priuilegio, domum vestram et omnia ad eam pertinentia ab insidiis malignantium munire volentes, uniuersa sub protectione nostra et ecclesie Rothomag' tuenda et conseruanda suscipimus, auctoritate Dei et nostra prohibentes ne quis vos super eis violenter aut iniuste perturbare presumat. Elemosinas autem vestras et beneficia nequis inscienter usurpare presumat pagina annotauimus presenti, scil(icet) ex dono Henrici com(itis) Augi et Ioh(ann)is comitis filii eius Barilsartum, Engueriliisartum, Nouam Landam, per totam forestam Augi pasnagium, herbagium, ignem, edificium, decimam annone et denariorum in ministerio de Fulcardimonte, molendinum de Escenla cum pratis adiacentibus, in molendino castelli vii. modios frumenti, tres modios auene ad horreum apud VII. Molas, medietatem pratorum suorum, maeriam Augi, omnes culturas suas de Fulcardimonte cum corueiis carrucarum pro suprapositis vii.modiis frumenti et tribus auene, decimam vicecomitatus eiusdem ville, totam Beeleiam inter eandem villam et forestam ad extirpandum, maeriam de Blangeio totam, procuratorem quoque ipsius sic(ut) et maerie de Augo ab

omni consuetudine liberum, sartum iuxta Nouam Landam ad excolendum
ad extirpandum quoque quicquid nemoris est a Noualanda usque ad agros
foris positos, in foresta Augi v. acras ad grangiam de Barilsarto
transferendam, ad grangiam quoque de Garinprato in eadem foresta
construendam v. acras, terciam partem molendini de Maisneels, fratribus
quoque ecclesie et famulis et quibuslibet mercennariis suis per totam
terram suam in omnibus vendendis et emendis quietantiam et de omnibus
que in curte abbatie vel in grangiis venduntur quieti sint vendentes et
ementes, Criolii hospitem unum, Septemmol' alterum ab omni consuetudine
utrumque liberum, omnes messes eorum et mercedes triturantium a
molatura et alia consuetudine quietas, quod si inter fratrum famulos vel
mercennarios aliqua contigerit querimonia vel clamor auditus fuerit per se
seu per alios quos voluerint terminetur. Curtes etiam et mansiones ad
grangias in foresta ubicumque necessarium fuerit construendas, ad
Campanesiamuillam in foresta loc(um) ad grangiam construendam et
quicquid nemoris est circa ipsam a via que ad eam venitur de Fulcardimonte
usque ad angulum Sancti Martini ultra ipsam grangiam quousque terra
fratrum protenditur et usque ad fundum vall(is) subtus eandem grangiam
iacentis et totam terram cultam que per diuisionem ei remansit apud
eandem villam inter forestam et terram quam de vauassoribus habebant, eo
t(ame)n tenore quod ei tales redditus in(de) soluent quales antea
vauassoribus reddebant. Preterea etiam pro ortis quos ei dederunt apud
Fulcarm' de cultura iuxta opidum dedit eis in elemosinam liberam apud
Campenesiamuillam terram fossato claudendam directe an(te) portam
grangie et iuxta Maram Roilleice et inter duos campos Petricurie et sic(ut)
fossata que precep(it) facere claudunt terras eorum iuxta forestam suam
ubique, decimam omnium que in Anglia Ioh(anne)s comes Augi acquisierit.
Hec omnia quieta et ab omni consuetudine libera et in perpetuam
elemosinam a fratribus possidenda. Porro ad Campenesiamuillam duas
carrucatas terre prorsus quietas, unam ex dono Roberti de Fanencort,
alteram ex dono Roberti de Restoual et Oelardi filii sui assensu Roberti de
Fanencort, ex dono Radulfi Rastel et Beatricis uxoris eius totum feodum
suum proprium de Campanesiauilla etiam doarium uxoris Engerranni de
Scoteigniis ad campartum solum, terram etiam vauassorum ad firmam vel
campartum in presentia sua suscipiendam omni alia consuetudine et
exactione remota. Cum vero doarium ad ipsos redierit quod in campo de
Beroumont a fratribus marlatum non fuerit ipsorum erit quicquid vero a
monachis marlatum fuerit, monachos ad solum campartum remanebit.
Quod si vauassores a seruitio defecerint nich(il) a fratribus exigi poterit
preter firmam vel campartum vauassoribus debitum, terras etiam cultas et
a cultoribus desertas ad campartum solum concesserunt quoadusque
cultores earum redeant vel pro eis alii succedant. Cum vero tempus
affu<e>rit quo campartum reddi debebit predicte ecclesie fratres Radulfum
vel eius famulum in Campanesiauilla semel submonebunt et in eius
presentia si venerit campartum dabunt. Qui si inuentus non fuerit vel
inuentus venire distulerit, ipsi fratres per se campartum dabunt. Hoc totum
concessit Guido de Auesnis et Berhesia uxor eius preter terram Eustachii
Harenc qui t(ame)n preter predictam pactionem x. acras terre Eustachii
Harenc grangie fratrum viciniores commutauerunt pro aliis x. in dominico

fratrum. Ex dono Engerranni et Will(elm)i de Gislemariuilla assensu matris eorum totam terram ad Campenesiamuillam ab angulo Fanencort usque ad metas iuxta campum Eu(er)ardi affixas ad campartum solum. Ex dono Roberti de Restoual et Oelardi filii sui totam terram suam incultam apud eandem villam et in terra a rusticis marlata campartum solum et preter h(ec) ortum unum. Hec omnia ab omni consuetudine libera preter firmam xii. minarum frumenti et totidem auene. Quod si rusticani vel manentes vel inde recedentes terram suam incultam reliquerint, liceat monachis eam colere ad predictam firmam. Si vero rusticani terram suam marlatam monachis vendere voluerint, possunt monachi emere nich(il) in(de) d(omi)nis tribuentes. Ex dono Heleboldi de Fanencort v. acras terre apud Campanesiamuillam in angulo sancti Martini pro v. minis bladi, medietate frumenti et medietate auene, ad mensuram grangie que olim fuit de Fulcardimonte. Item ex dono Engerranni filii Gihel ibidem ii. acras pro duabus minis lege qua supra. Ex dono Walteri Peurel et Pagani filii sui culturam de prato et illam de Busco Reinardi et campum supra viam de Predosauilla et duas acras in pomerium (e)cclesie[a], hec omnia quieta et assensu Gisleberti Caletot donata. Item ex eorumdem dono iii. acras in Campo Terrici et quod habent ad Busc(um) Noberti et sartum fratris Gisleberti et supra acram unam nemoris et iii. iuxta campum Willelmi filii Seburgis et campum ante domum infirmorum et alterum supra istum a Willelmo filio Seburgis olim excultum, tercium quoque iuxta domum infirmorum et quicquid habent pratorum inter abbatiam et Fanencort. Omnia quoque auenna sua supra abbatiam et quicquid habent nemoris inter montem et Campum Terrici et ii. acras iuxta culturam monachorum. Hec omnia quieta preter annuum censum v. solidorum, et a Richolde et Cecilia sororibus concessa. Ex dono Bernardi molendinarii et fratrum eius et Alberee matris eorum concedentibus Cecilia et Recholde cum filiis suis quicquid habent ad Maisnil Ranulchon quietum, et iii. acras terre nemorose liberas. Ex feodo Willelmi filii Nicholai et Gisleberti Caletot et Walteri Peuerel et Richoldis et Cecilie sororum et Alberee et Bernardi filii eius omnia prata inter abbatiam et Fanencort. Ex dono Angerii Longi concedentibus Radulfo Rastel cum uxore sua et Guidone de Auesnis cum sua et Lamberto Girardi filio vi. acras ex una parte abbatie et iiii. ex altera quietas. Ex dono Gisleberti filii Solicie et Ricardi filii eius concedente Thoma de Sancto Leodegario campum unum ad Nemus Noberti et alterum iuxta culturam ecclesie, tercium in monte super abbatiam, quarrariam quoque cum subiacente auenna, omnia hec quieta. Ex dono Hugonis Machonis et Radulfi filii eius predicto Thoma concedente iii. acras terre supra abbatiam quietas. Ex dono eiusdem Thome Nemus Noberti pro xx. solid(is) Prouiniens(ibus). Ex dono Rogeri de Salceio i. acram terre foris Osberni Maisnilii et totam eius terram in Monte Hastreie utrumque liberam. Ex dono Osberni de Pilo Ceruino et Widonis filii eius quicquid habent inter marleriam suam et abbatiam et ipsam marleriam et par(tem) nemoris ultra eam, preter h(ec) i. acram terre, omnia quieta. Ex dono Rainaldi et Rogeri de Septemmol' et Amabil(ie) matris eorum iii. acras liberas. Ex dono Roberti sacerdotis prefato Reinaldo concedente iii. acras quietas. Ex dono Heruei de Sancto Sulpicio et Willelmi filii sui in molendini sui decima viii. minas frumenti et iiii. bustellos et iii. nummos et obolum. Ex dono Galterii de Sancto Aniano Torfrescalis iii. acras terre liberas et totam decimam illius feodi preter terciam partem, post obitum suum totum feodum suum cum decima liberum. Ex dono Roberti Augi ii. salinas apud Briencon quietas. Ex dono Lamberti filii Girardi concedente Radulfo Rastel cum uxore sua iii. acras terre quietas et iiii. ad Nemus Noberti ad campartum solum. Ex dono Radulfi filii Tustini campum unum supra abbatiam quietum. Ex dono Ioh(ann)is comitis Augi totam Beeleiam inter Fulcardimontem et Nemus Gaufridi ad extirpandum. Ex dono Guidonis de Bouencort et Cecilie uxoris eius dimidium territorii Nemoris Ulberti cum decima ab omni consuetudine quietum preter annuum censum lx. sol(idorum) Romesinorum. Residuum quoque eiusdem territorii totum. Ex dono Thome et Rainaldi de Sancto Leodegario sedem ville nemoris Ulberti cum dimidio eiusdem ville territorii et ecclesiam cum tota decima assensu Rogeri de Freeluilla et Rogonis filii eius, omnia quieta preter annuum censum lx. sol(idorum) Prouiniensium. Ex dono Rogeri Baillol iiii. minas frumenti in molendinis de Fanencort de decima, concedente Roberto de Fanencort. Ex dono Roberti de Hastinguis et Isabel uxoris sue et Aueline matris Isabel quicquid habebant et clamabant in territorio Nemoris Ulberti. Ex dono Hug(onis) de Hisleis xii. acras terre in Fraitiz liberas et dimidiam culturam ad campartum solum. Reliquum vero eiusdem culture liberum, ex dono Roberti de Caneceris et uxoris eius assensu Ansoldi et Henrici Biset. Ex dono Ingelranni de Hisleis decimam iiii. acrarum. Ex dono Willelmi de Porcmort et Girardi filii eius terram suam de Fraitiz et x. acras in Plaisencia totid(em) ad Fossatum Regis, omnia quieta concedente Roberto de Alneto. Ex dono Ric(ardi) de Holgueuilla et Rogeri fratris eius, Galteri quoque et Radulfi de Salsosamara xviii. acras quietas, concedente Rogero filio ipsius Walteri. Residuum vero eiusdem feodi usque ad viam Mortumaris totum cum decima. Campum quoque Walteri Franchelin assensu ipsius et filiorum eius ad campartum solum et decimam per totum feodum. Ex dono Hugonis de Bosco ad Fossatum Regis xii. acras quietas. Ex dono Ricardi Calemel x. acras liberas. Ex dono Engelranni de Hisleis xii. acras ad campartum solum que omnia concesserunt Robertus de Alneto et Hugo de Bosco. Ex dono Radulfi de Nouauilla unam acram liberam et quicquid ab illa est usque ad viam Mortuimaris liberum concedentibus Waltero de Barc, Ansoldo Biset et Henrico filio eius. Ex dono Baldrici de Flamens unam acram liberam concedentibus Waltero de Barc et Radulfo de Nouauilla. Hec omnia de feodo et dono Willelmi comitis Albemarle. Ex dono Hugonis de Sancto Germano et Will(el)mi fratris eius quietanciam de moltura in terris suis ad Onesmaisnil concedente Hugone de Mortuomari. Ex dono Willelmi de Onesmaisnil et Agnetis uxoris eius et Roberti filii eorum xvi. acras terre quietas et liberas ab omni seruitio et communem pasturam animalibus eorum in omni terra sua. Ex dono Roberti prepositi viii. acras terre prorsus liberas concedente predicto Vill(el)mo et Agnete uxore eius. Ex dono Willelmi camerarii de Tancaruilla apud Arculas lxxx. sol(idos) annuatim. Ex dono quoque Ricardi filii comitis Gisleberti terram de Garimprato et de Frainello liberam et quietam a molturis et corueiis et omni consuetudine preter seruicium vauassorum a quo si ipsi defecerint a predictis fratribus nich(il) comes extorquere poterit preter firmam vel campartum a monachis vauassoribus debitum. Ex dono Oelardi de Cleies totam terram suam de

Garinpre ad campartum solum. Ex dono vero predecessoris nostri bone memorie Hugonis archiepiscopi duas partes decime de Garinpre quas Oelardus in manu eius refutauit sicut ille ecclesie vestre in perpetuum habendas concessit et nos concedimus. Conuentionem quoque illam que inter vos et ecclesiam de Fesquis super decimatione de Warinpre et Fraisnello in presentia Hugonis archiepiscopi facta est consensu Willelmi sacerdotis ipsius ecclesie confirmamus, videlicet ut pro decimatione illa dimidium modum frumenti et dimidium auene ad mensuram ville singul(is) annis predicte ecclesie sacerdoti reddatis. Ex dono vero Will(el)mi de Fraisnello unam carrucatam terre concedentibus Osberno de Rouerai et Gaufrido de Salceio omnino liberam preter firmam viii. minarum frumenti melioris presem(iti), viii. quoque ordei et totidem auene ad mensuram de Luceio, reliquum quoque feodum ad campartum solum. Si vero prefatus Guill(el)mus a seruitio prenominatorum Oelardi et Gaufridi resilierit, ipsi nich(il) aliud a monachis nisi predictam firmam vel campartum exigent. Ex dono Radulfi de Fesques annuente Oelardo de Cleies totum feodum suum de Garinpre ad campartum solum. Ex dono Roberti de Fraisnello et uxoris sue et Willelmi filii eorum annuente Oelardo de Cleies totum feodum suum de Warinpre et in feodo de Fraisnello xv. acras annuente Will(el)mo fratre suo ad campartum solum. Ex dono Abberici de Fesques quicquid habent de feodo suo in perpetuum ad Garinpre quietum et ab omni exactione liberum preter campartum. H(ec) scil(icet) campum Vall(is) Petri, campum mare, campum orti, campum castellarii, valliculam caue rue. Has autem auennas concessit prorsus quietas, auennam Frogerii, auennam de capite rogi. Insuper vero ii. garbas totius feodi sui Garimprati de decima similiter liberas et omnino quietas annuente Oelardo de Cleies. Ex dono Nicholai de Galteriuilla totum feodum suum de Garinpre pro xii. minis bladi, medietatem frumenti et medietatem auene. Ex dono Alberee filie Adelelmi totum feodum suum de Garinpre ad firmam x. minarum frumenti, totidemque auene ad mensuram de Luceio. Cum vero tempus affuerit quo campartum dari debebit, predicte ecclesie fratres Oelardum vel eius famulum reliquos quoque prenominatos ad eundem modum in villa de Fesques semel submonebunt et in eius presentia si venerit campartum dabunt. Quod si ibi inuentus non fuerit vel inuentus venire distulerit, ipsi fratres per se facient quod in eius ocul(is) securius ideoque libentius facerent. Si vero prenominati vauassores in seruitio dominorum suorum minus quam debent fecerint, ipsi domini a monachis nichil exigent preter firmam vel campartum vauassoribus debitum. Ex dono Gisleberti de Sartis totam terram suam de Garinpre et quicquid iuris habebat in ea cum omnibus pertinentiis suis in pascuis, in viis et semitis et in omnibus aliis locis et aliis rebus ad illam pertinentibus nich(il) sibi in ea retinens preter reditum l. solidorum Rotomagensis monete quem ei predicti monachi annuatim reddituri sunt. Ex dono Reinaldi de Mediana concedente Helia de Keurecort duas partes decime per totum feodum de Fraisneto liberas et omnino quietas preter annuam firmam xii. minarum frumenti cum sextario brasii minaque pisorum ad mensuram de Garinpre que fuit de Luceio. H(ec) vero concessit Osbernus de Roueraio. Guillelmus vero de Fraisnello et filii eius concesserunt monachis quicquid in eadem decima clamabant. Ex dono Rogeri de Scakerlanda et uxoris eius Alberee et Guill|(el)mi filii eiusdem

Alberee terciam partem decime de Fesques in omibus territoriis ad eandem parrochiam pertinentibus nich(il) omnino ibi retinentes preter modum frumenti et sextarium brasii et minam pisorum per annum ad minam horrei de Garinpre que olim fuit[b] de Luceio concedente et testificante presbitero de Fesques Willelmo. Ex dono vero predecessoris nostri Hugonis pie recordationis archiepiscopi ecclesiam de Campanosauilla cum decima eidem ecclesie adiacente. Decimam quoque loci qui dicitur Fraitiz de feodo Willelmi de Salcosamara et decimam lande de Barilessart atque decimam de Noualanda nemorisque quod est inter utrumque. Item ex dono eiusdem ecclesiam de Fesques cum iure patronatus et institutione sacerdotis liberam et quietam saluo iure pontificali et parrochiali. Animalium etiam vestrorum et nutriture vestre decimam ac terrarum vestrarum quas propriis laboribus et sumptibus laborabitis prout dominus papa concedit et nos concedimus et in usus pauperum et hospitum distribuenda specialius denunciamus. Ex dono Engelranni de Hisleis et uxoris eius et filii eorum primogeniti ii. garbas decime terre sue de Campo Belli quas in manus nostra reddiderunt et nos illas coram eis donauimus monachis et abbatie Fulcardimontis in perpetuam elemosinam, et q(uonia)m terra illa erat de dote uxoris Engelranni, excambium dedit ei coram nob(is) pro ea, curtillum i. et mansuram unam in villa de Hisleis et sic ipsa predicta elemosina concessit et dedit. Ex dono Walteri Peuerel ii. garbas decime terre sue. Ex dono Hugonis de Sancto Mauricio et Willelmi fratris eius salinas suas quas tenebant apud Ulterioremportum de comite Augi liberas et omni exactione quietas. Ex dono Richoardi et filiorum eius totam decimam feodi sui de Bosco Ulberti. Ex dono Rahier de Onomasnil duas acras terre prorsus quietas concedente Roberto de Flames. Ex dono Odonis de Oireual et Heldeardis uxoris eius Rogerique filii amborum duas garbas in feodo quod tenent de Helia de Cheurelcurt omnino liberas. Ne quis vero super his prefatum monasterium perturbare aut inquietare presumat, sub anathemate prohibemus et uniuersa que dicta sunt presenti scripto et sigilli nostri munimine confirmamus.

[a] ccll'ie A, (e)cclesie *supplied* [b] fuit *repeated* A, *marked for deletion*

70. *Notification by Walter (of Coutances), archbishop of Rouen, of his confirmation to Foucarmont Abbey of possessions and privileges.* Priory of Le Parc near Rouen, 11 April 1204

A = BL Additional Charter 17841. Endorsed: *Walteri Roth' arch(iepiscopi) de confirmatione cartarum nostrarum* (s.xiii); *CLXVIII* (s.xii/xiii); *episcoporum p.xii* (s.xv); *Walterus* (s.xii/xiii); *1er tiroir 5e liasse 2e lettre de l'arch(vesque) de Rouen* (s.xviii); various other post medieval endorsements. Approx. 258 × 476 + 37mm. 72 lines of a neat business hand. Sealed *sur double queue*, 3 holes for cords, cords and seal impression missing. B = Rouen, Bibliothèque Municipale ms. 1224 (Foucarmont cartulary) fos.16v–18v, with significant variations, s.xiii.

Note that the *arenga* and closing remarks on rapine and pillage might well have been judged suitable to the circumstances of the charter's issue, in April 1204, in the midst of the Capetian invasion of Normandy. For a chronology of the final days of Plantagenet rule, with the investiture of Rouen in May 1204 and its surrender on 24 June, see Powicke, *Loss*, 260–3; T.K. Moore, 'The Loss of Normandy and the Invention of "Terre Normannorum", 1204', *EHR*, cxxv (2010), 1084–6. For Robert I, abbot of Foucarmont, occ.1196 and 1209, see *GC*, xi, 305. For Master Simon, chancellor of Rouen, see Spear, *Personnel*, 225.

Omnibus sancte matris ecclesie filiis ad quos presens scriptum peruenerit Walterus Dei gratia Rothom' archiepiscopus salutem in domino. Ex approbata descendit consuetudine ea que pie ecclesiis vel monasteriis seu ecclesiasticis viris et religiosis intutitu Dei conferuntur, ne obliuione vel inuidentium seu etiam ambiciosorum malignitate depereant litterarum apicibus annotare et auctoritate pontificali communire. Inde est quod ad uniuersitatis vestre noticiam volumus peruenire nos diuine karitatis intuitu ad petitionem et instantiam dilectorum filiorum in Cristo R(oberti) abbatis et conuentus beate Marie de Fulcardimonte cartas continentes donationes et elemosinas eis pie factas diligenter inspexisse et easdem donationes secundum tenorem ipsarum cartarum quas inspeximus ad maiorem securitatem presenti scripto inseruisse in hac forma. Ex dono videlicet Henrici quondam comitis Augi quadraginta sex acras terre iuxta Beeleam ad faciendum anniuersarium suum et ad ceram emendam unde sufficienter fiant candele in die Purificationis et ad vinum emendum ad missas celebrandas per annum, et septem acras ad Buscum Tachel. Item ex dono eiusdem unam carrucatam terre iuxta eandem Beeleam pro anima Roberti fratris sui omnino liberam et quietam. Item pro anima Henrici reg(is) Anglorum iunioris decimam denariorum ministerii sui de Fulcardimonte in foresta et decem acras terre iusta Beeleam liberas et quietas, et quatuor acras pro Roberto filio Nichol(ai) ibidem. Ex dono Ioh(ann)is de Vilers concedente Emmelina uxore sua et Ermengalda filia sua angulum de Potimou per desuper campum Roberti Moret, et de suo dominico alium campum qui est inter campum Odardi medici et eius Valcellum. Item alium campum de uno Iornello in Valle Gouberti omnia libera et quieta. Item ex dono Roberti Moret unum campum assensu eiusdem Ioh(ann)is. Ex dono Luce de Ioncaria masuram unam cum curtillo liberam ab omni exactione et tallia et alia consuetudine preter censum sex denariorum. Ex dono Rogonis de Freeluilla concedente Roberto filio eius apud Ioncariam masuram unam et unam acram terre omnino liberam preter dimidiam minam auene de brenagium reg(is). Ex dono Roberti de Cagni assensu Odardi medici domum unam in foro de Fulcardimonte ad opus monachorum infirmorum omnino liberam. Ex dono eiusdem Odardi apud Hanneis quadraginta acras terre et quinque acras in feodo de Lucue et partem nemoris sui de Cokerello Monte sicut fossatum proportat, et unum hospitem apud Hainues omnino liberum. Ex dono Gilleberti medici decem sol(idos) annui redditus apud Augum ex curtillis quos Rob(ertus) Maillarz tenebat de ipso assensu heredum suorum. Ex dono Gilleberti de Euremeu assensu Gaufridi fratris eius decem sol(idos) annui redditus in molendino apud Euremeu. Ex dono Simonis de Gillem'cort assensu Gaufr(idi) fratris sui et sororum suarum masuram Will(elm)i filii Moberti et sex acras terre et dimidiam eidem masure appendentes omnino liberas et quietas. Ex dono Rogeri fratris eiusdem Simonis masuram unam in eadem villa quam Robertus Pichon tenebat. Item in eadem villa ex dono Gilleberti de Sancto Audoeno masuram unam singulis annis reddentem septem sol(idos). Ex dono Ric(ardi) Destriemont apud Assigneium septem acras quietas et liberas. Ex dono Walteri de Sancto Martino assensu Isabel uxoris sue et Walteri filii sui duos modios bladi ad molendinum suum de Sancto Martino, unum circa festum sancti Thome apostoli et unum ad Pascha, et sciendum quod cuicumque isdem Walterus assignauerit molend(inum) suum primo omnium isdem redditus assignabitur. Ex dono Will(elm)i le Borgue decem sol(idos) annui redditus apud Augum in una masura super ripam aque. Ex dono Gaufridi de Augo decem et octo sol(idos) ex tenemento quod Trosse tenebat. Ex dono prepositi Augi apud Merleuill' vi. sol(idos) et sex capones. Ex dono Walteri de Sancto Aniano culturam viginti acrarum apud Torfreescales assensu Walteri de Grancort et Ingerranni de Auesnes et unam acram apud Puis. Ex dono eiusdem Walteri de Grancort dimidiam molturam eiusdem culture viginti acrarum que eius erat et totam molturam aliarum duarum acrarum secundum quod carta ipsius testatur. Item apud Arculas quatuor libras Andeg(auenses) ex dono Will(elm)i camerarii de Tankaruill'. Ex dono Simonis de Sancto Remigio duodecim acras terre ad Crucem Fornullet omnino liberas et quietas assensu abbatis sancti Wandreg' et conuentus eiusdem loci. Ex dono Matildis comitisse Augi centum sol(idos) Andeg(auenses) singulis annis ad molend(inum) suum de Torchi, quinquaginta sol(idos) ad Pascha et quinquaginta ad festum sancti Remigii. Hunc autem redditum reddet ecclesie quicumque molend(inum) seruauerit. Ex dono Gaufridi de Berengeruill' viginti sol(idos) et unam libram piperis ad Mesnill super Waregnam. Ex dono Helie de Allage et Isabel uxoris eius et Agnetis filie eius totam terram dominici sui de feodo de Erables et de Busco Tachel, illam de Erables ad sextam garbam, illam de Busco Tachel ad garbam, exceptis decem acris quas ecclesia omnino liberas et quietas habebit. Sciendum au(tem) quod si monachi de terra vauassoris eius aliquid adquisierint et seruicium defecerit ei, ad monachos tamen ad campartum recuperabit. Item si monachi de terra rusticorum adquisierint si terra fuerit des Erables de feodo ad pactum eiusdem feodi si de feodo Buschitac Tachet ad pactum eiusdem feodi monachi eam habebunt. Item ex dono Rad(ulfi) Trichiet quinque sol(idos) annui redditus apud Augum ex domo que fuit Ancheri clerici ad festum sancti Remigii reddendos. Ex dono Willelmi Torel triginta acras terre que est inter diuisiones ville de Caable et Nuillemont omnino liberas et quietas. Ex dono Roberti de Restolual quatuor minas bladi ad antiquam minam ad grangiam de Campenesiauilla. Ex dono Gaufr(idi) de Berengeruill' octo sol(idos) Andeg(auenses) apud Fulcardimontem in domo Geroldi Bote. Item ex dono Ric(ardi) de Isleis totum campartum de decem acris terre quas ecclesia de Fulcardimonte tenet de illo ad Isleis assensu uxoris sue et Hug(onis) filii eius. Item ex dono eiusdem Ric(ardi) et antecessorum eius simulque filii ipsius quicquid habebant in dominico suo in sede grangie de Fraitiz. Totam etiam culturam cum uniuersa decima ante ipsam grangiam iuxta viam de Albamarla liberam penitus et quietam ab omni seruicio, consuetudine et exactione preter septem minas bladi annui redditus, tres scilicet minas et dimidiam auene reddendas ad caput Quadragesime et tres et dimidiam frumenti ad rogationes. Totam etiam terram de Bella Fossa de feodo de Flameis preter tres acras quas Rogerus de Gardin' tenet ad garbam perpetuo possidendam. Item ex proprio dono ipsius Ric(ardi) in excambiam pro Valle de Bello decem acras ad Isleis omnino quietas. Item ex dono Rad(ulfi) de Drenuill' campum de Corneual. Item ex concessione eiusdem Rad(ulfi) donationem quam Walterus de Gardin fecit, scilicet terram de Rotunda Spina et campum Gilleberti le Blont. Item terram de Rupticio, tres scilicet illas acras quas Raherius Hescelin, Guibertus et Robertus homines sui antea dederunt. Item ex dono ipsius proprio terram illam quam habebat inter tenementum Ricardi le Blont et terras de Agnemesuill'. Item donationem Guiberti de Haudricort et Ric(ardi) le Blont quam tenebant de ipso in predicto campo Rupticii. Item in Hastleia campum Bernardi de Ronceio. Hec omnia quieta et libera in perpetuum concessit tenenda. Item ex dono Adan[a] Duredent concedente Hug(onis) filio suo et matre sua Herm(en)gart assensu etiam abbatisse de Sancto Paulo et conuentus eiusdem loci viginti quatuor acras terre de qua terra dedit decem acras omnino quietas preter sex nummos singulis annis ad festum sancti Remigii reddendos. Residuum vero eiusdem terre ad campartum solum. Ex dono eiusdem Adan[a] Duredent totam terram suam super Bellam Fossam omnino quietam preter duas minas bladi et duas auene ad Pentecosten reddendas. Ex dono Will(elm)i Thorel de Maisnil D(aui)d decem acras terre illius que est inter viam que ducit Goislenfontaines et nemus de Flamez viciniores grangie de Fraitiz omnino liberas et quietas a camparto et omni alio redditu, seruicio et consuetudine. Residuum vero eiusdem terre ad campartum t(antu)mmodo. Ex dono Eremburgis matris Radulfi Poun[b] decimam totius feodi sui in Plaisentia. Item ex dono predicti Will(elm)i Thorel quinque acras terre, scilicet pratella Boschier omnino libera et quieta preter campartum solum. Concessit etiam nouem acras terre et ex toto dimisit quietas iuxta culturam ad Fossatum Regis quas aduersus prefatos monachos aliq(uan)d(o) clamabat. Ex dono Renaldi de Fisquis unum pratum apud Fesques quod Radulfus pater eius emerat a Math(e)o de Luceio. Ex dono Adan[a] de Warwanna concedente Will(elm)o filio suo assensu etiam Renaldi de Fesques pratum unum apud Fesques quod dicitur Pratum Garnerii. Ex dono Will(elm)i de Busco filii Rad(ulfi) unam acram terre omnino liberam et quietam. Ex dono vero Gilleberti auunculi eiusdem Will(elm)i aliam acram eodem Will(elm)o concedente. Item ex dono Alelmi Rambout quatuor minas bladi annui redditus ad minam de Luceio quas in grangia de Gariniprato recipiebat et quas de feodo iamdicti Will(elm)i iure hereditario tenebat. Ex dono Raineri Loisel tres acras terre ad garbam iuxta buscum Veteris ville et ex dono iamdicti Will(elm)i duas virgatas similiter ad garbas, unam in Valle Auberti et aliam iuxta buscum Veteris ville. Hec omnia quieta et libera a tallia, releuagio, auxilio et omni alia seculari exactione preter quinque sol(idos) Beluac(enses) quos in supradicto redditu prefati Alelmi Rambout iamdictus Will(elmu)s singulis annis recipiebat. Ex dono Reginaldi de Meduana duodecim minas frumenti et duas minas brasii et unam minam pisorum ad antiquam minam de Luceio quas in grangia de Gariniprato pro decima Veteris ville quasi iure patrimonii singulis annis recipiebat, que omnia iamdictus Regin(aldus) in manu dilecti filii Phil(ippi) archid(iacon)i Augi sponte resignauit et ecclesie et monachis de Fulcardimonte in perpetuam elemosinam confirmari postulauit. Ex dono Reginaldi de Fesques omnia camparta sua que habebat in terra que est ante grangiam de Gariniprato et preterea decem et octo denarios Beluacenses annui redditus quos habebat in eadem terra. Item ex dono eiusdem octo acras terre assensu Wiberti de Sancto Sansone, quinque in uno loco et tres in alio, omnino quietas et liberas ab omni consuetudine, seruicio, tallia, auxilio, moltura et omni seculari exactione. Ex dono Guidonis de Peucheruin assensu Ermengarde uxoris sue et Will(elm)i filii eius masuram unam apud Daiencort cum augmento coram eiusdem ville hominibus designato omnino quietam. Item ex dono Walteri de Castello concedente Thoma Rastel domino suo et Bonafilia uxore iamdicti Walteri et Matheo filio suo tres ortos inter culturam monachorum et villam de Foucardimonte omnino quietos preter duos sol(idos) Andeg(auenses) annui redditus ad luminare ecclesie sancte Marie de Foucard(i)monte pro quibus tam(en) duobus sol(idis) isdem Walterus excambiauit monachis alium redditum duorum solidorum in duabus masuris apud Fulcarmont quas Gilleb(ertus) Michael et Rogerus de Furno de ipso tenebant. Item ex dono <Hu>gonis filii Ricardi de Petricuria concedente Nicholaa uxore eius et Simone filio suo quicquid in decima ecclesie sancti Petri de Petricuria ipse et antecessores sui <pos>sederant et hec decima elemosinata fuit assensu et voluntate Phil(ippi) tunc archid(iacon)i Augi et in manu Will(elm)i de Boaffle tunc decani de Folcard'monte. Item ex dono <Willelmi> Marescalli comitis de Pembroc quietantiam trium solidorum et quatuor denariorum quociens prefati monachi ferrum ad proprios usus emerant in villa de Orbec. Item <ex> dono Berte de Freauuill' concedentibus Roberto et Thoma filiis suis quinque sol(idos) Andeg(auenses) annui redditus in vicecomitatu Criolii. Nos igitur videntes mundum adeo deditum esse concupiscentiis et rapinis, quod calumpniantium et inuid<ium> maliciis veritas sepius impugnatur, cupientes paci et indempnitati sepedictorum monachorum de Fulcardimonte intuitu Dei et religionis ipsorum pia sollicitudine prouidere ut liberius et quietius vacent orationi, predictas donationes et elemosinas eis pie factas secundum quod in cartis donatorum plenius continentur eis in puram et perpetuam elemosinam auctoritate nostra confirmamus, easque ad maiorem securitatem presentis scripti annotatione et sigilli nostri appositione communimus, volentes et sub pena excommunicationis districtius inhibentes ne quis contra hanc nostre confirmationis paginam in preiudicium predictorum monachorum aliquid temere attemptare presumat. Quod si facere presumpserit, maledictionem et iram omnipotentis Dei se nouerit incursurum. Dat' per manum magistri Simonis cancellarii Rothom' apud domum Grandimont(is) iuxta Roth', anno incarnationis dominice m°.cc°. quarto, iii°. Idus Aprilis.

---

^a *sic* A ^b *reading uncertain* A, ?Porin *or* Porm

71. *Notification by Robert Marmion of his grant to the monks of Barbery for his own soul and that of Philippa his wife and for the absolution of his journey to Jerusalem, of 500 livres angevins for the building of their church and of all his lands of Checkendon and Littlestoke (in Checkendon, Oxfordshire) saving various services owed to Robert and saving an annual payment of two pounds of wax from the monks to the monks of Thame for the wood of Hained-in-Wood (in Ipsden, Oxfordshire), the present grant being made in exchange for an earlier assignment made by Robert of £10 a year from his manor of Berwick (Sussex) for the monks' vestments, and with the assent of William Marmion the clerk, Robert's son, to whom he had previously given these lands.*   [1200 X 1218, ?c.1217/18]

A = Manchester, John Rylands Library Beaumont Charter 43. Endorsed: *R. Marm'* (s.xiii/xiv); various post medieval endorsements. On the plica *216/5* (s.xx lot number), with attached paper sheet declaring this to be charter no.151. Approx. 140 × 143 + 16mm. Sealed *sur double queue*, single slit, tag and seal impression missing. Burned on the right hand side, with some letters illegible. B = Aylesbury, Buckinghamshire Record Office ms. AR.38/62/1 (Boarstall/Rede family cartulary) no.25, s.xv. C = Bnf ms. nouv.acq. latines 1428 fo.128r no.151, abstract from A (then in the possession of the Stapleton family at Carlton Towers) by Léon Maître, *c.* August 1881.

Pd (from A) *GC*, xi, instr. 87; *MRSN*, ii, p.ci note (without indicating provenance); (from B) *The Boarstall Cartulary*, ed. H.E. Salter, Oxford Historical Society lxxxviii (1930), 14–15 no.25.

To be dated after 1200, when the abbot of Thame secured lands from William and Robert Marmion in Benson including the wood of Hained-in-Wood (in Ipsden, Oxfordshire) in return for an annual rent of 2lbs of wax, and before the death of Robert Marmion. For Robert, of Fontenay-le-Marmion (Calvados, cant. Bourguébus), assumed to be the Robert Marmion son of Robert son of Millicent, who rendered homage for his father's English lands late in the twelfth century, in the presence of at least 63 witnesses, and who crossed to England definitively after 1204, leaving his family's Norman estates in the custody of a son and namesake, Robert 'the elder', dying *c.*1218, whereafter his English lands, including Tamworth (Staffordshire), were allowed to pass to another son of his, named Robert, half-brother of the Robert 'the elder' resident in Normandy since 1204, in return for a fine of £500 to the crown, see N. Vincent, *Peter des Roches* (Cambridge 1996), 162–3, 193–4, 361; *The Thame Cartulary*, ed. H.E. Salter, 2 vols, Oxfordshire Record Society xxv–vi (1947–8), i, 118–19 nos 166–7; *Boarstall Cartulary*, 12–13 nos 20–1; *CFR*, i, 20–1 no.75; Powicke, *Loss,* 339, with a particularly full account, by Thomas Stapleton, of the family and its religious patronage in *MRSN*, ii, pp.xcvi–cvii. In addition to grants to Cistercian Barbery, a family foundation, Robert's father had granted the church of Checkendon to Coventry Cathedral Priory and much of his land there to a cadet branch of the Marmion family headed by Geoffrey Marmion and William Marmion 'the knight'. William Marmion 'the clerk' purchased an estate there from Robert for £100, saving the service of William 'the knight', but seems to have forfeited in 1221, after fleeing to

France. The abbots of Barbery subsequently granted the estate conferred upon them by the present charter, to William 'the knight' and then, following William's death, *c.*1221, to another Geoffrey de Marmion whose heirs, *c.*1246, for 115 marks, purchased release from an annual farm of 12 marks to Barbery, provided that Geoffrey and his heirs continued to render the annual pension of wax to the monks of Thame: *Boarstall Cartulary*, 4–5 nos 1–2, 12–16 nos 20–31; *CFR*, i, 246–7 no.108, 253 no.161; *MRSN*, ii, p.ciii note. The 'journey to Jerusalem' from which Robert hereby sought to purchase absolution was presumably the Fifth Crusade, suggesting that the present charter represents a deathbed attempt to settle spiritual and wordly accounts.

Uniuersis Cristi fidelibus ad quos presens scriptum peruenerit Robertus Marmion salutem in domino. Nouerit uniuersitas vestra quod ego pro salute anime mee et Philippe uxoris mee et omnium antecessorum et successorum meorum et pro absolutione itineris mei Ierosolimitani donaui Deo et beate Marie de Barbereio et monachis ibidem Deo seruientibus ad edificandam et construendam ecclesiam suam quingentas libras Andegauen(ses), et preterea pro eadem absolutione dedi eis in puram et perpetuam elemosinam liberam et quietam ab omni seruicio, auxilio et scutagio et omni s<ecula>ri exactione et ab omnibus ad me vel ad heredes meos pertinentibus penitus absolutam <omnes> terras meas de Chekendane et de Estokes in hominibus et terris, pratis et nemor<ibus> cum omnibus pertinentiis suis, saluo michi et heredibus meis seruicio quod Willelmus M<armyon>[a] miles et Hugo de Migehan debent michi pro tenementis que tenent de me apud Chekend<ane> et Estokes, excepto quod ipsi monachi duas libras cere annuatim persoluent monachis de Thame quas ego pro quadam parte nemoris que vocatur Hainges singulis annis soluere solebam. Hanc autem donationem feci eis in excambium decem librarum esterlingorum annui redditus quas ego illis ad eorum vestimenta singulis annis inuenienda in manerio meo de Berwic assignaueram, et hoc factum est concessione et assensu Willelmi Marm' clerici, filii mei, cui antea easdem terras donaueram, et sciendum quod ego et heredes mei hanc meam donationem prefatis <monachis> garantizare tenemur et defendere. Quod ut ratum et inconcussum teneatur in p<resen>tis scripti testimonio et sigilli mei appositione confirmaui.

[a] *letters in brackets illegible* A, *supplied from* B

72. *Notification by Geoffrey of Repton (Derbyshire) that Walter fitz Aiulf has granted to the (Premonstratensian) abbey of Ardenne (Calvados, cant. Caen, com. St-Germain-la-Blanche-Herbe) an oven and associated property at Caen, in the Rue Ecuyère, which Geoffrey had earlier, in error, claimed to hold by grant of King Henry (II), but which he later restored to the abbey, in the year that the lord Arthur was captured at Mirebeau (Vienne) together with many noblemen, granting all his rights there with the assent of Alice his wife and Gilbert his kinsman and heir, notwithstanding any recognizances or oaths or writings in the royal rolls, with Geoffrey decreeing that his burial should take place at Ardennes.*

Ardennes [*c*.1202]

A = Manchester, John Rylands Library Beaumont Charter 4. Endorsed: *de furno nostro de Cad'* (s.xiii); *Caen denariorum c.xvi.* (s.xiv); *Gaufridi de Rapendonia de furno nostro* (s.xiii); various post medieval endorsements. On the plica, *rue escuyere four ibidem* (s.xix); *69* (pencil, s.xix/xx); *202/6* (pencil s.xx lot number from the 1920 sale). Approx. 192 × 150 + 27mm. Sealed *sur double queue*, pink, blue and white cords through 2 holes, seal impression missing. B = Bnf ms. nouv.acq. latines 1428 fo.69r no.69, abstract from A (then in the possession of the Stapleton family at Carlton Towers) by Léon Maître, *c*. August 1881.

Pd (part only from A) D. Power, 'En Quête de sécurité juridique dans la Normandie angevine: concorde finale et inscription au rouleau', *BEC*, clxviii (2010), 348n., identifying the 'rolls' here as the enrolments of final concords equivalent to that which survives for the second year of King John, above pp.7–9.

Apparently soon after the capture of Arthur at Mirebeau in May 1202. For the Rue Ecuyère, and for Geoffrey of Repton, an important royal official at Caen from at least 1186, *bailli*, farmer of the town fair 1199–1200, mayor of the commune on the eve of the Capetian conquest, with significant properties at Caen and Anisy, his daughter and her descendants remaining prominent urban landowners after 1204, see below no.73; L. Jean-Marie, *Caen aux XIe et XIIe siècles: Espace urbain, pouvoirs et société* (Condé-sur-Noireau 2000), 116, 231, 235, 237, 261, citing another grant of his to Ardenne from Caen AD Calvados H119 (Ardenne cartulary) fo.8r.

Omnibus Cristi fidelibus ad quos presens scriptum peruenerit ego Gaufridus de Rapendonia salutem. Nouerit uniuersitas vestra quod Walterus filius Aiulfi dedit Deo et abbatie sancte Marie de Ardena pro salute anime sue in perpetuam elemosinam apud Cadom' in vico escuereio quendam furnum quem ibi habebat et duas domos in anteriori parte a dextra et a sinistra et quandam plateam in posteriori parte in qua alias duas domos edificaui, eumdem furnum omnes continue tangentes sicut ex multis scriptis auctenticis que inde habet predicta abbatia et ex testimonio multorum bonorum virorum diligenter didicimus, et ego predictus Gauf(ridus) furnum et domos predictas ex dono Henr(ici) illustris regis Anglorum existimans ad me pertinere errore non modico seductus, eumdem furnum et domos iniuste diu detinere presumpsi. Postea autem anno quo captus est dominus Arturus com multis nobilibus viris apud Mirebel a domino Iohanne rege Angl(ie), intuitu pietatis et caritatis et pro salute anime mee furnum et omnes domos prefatas et quicquid fuit ibi de omni tenemento prescripti Walteri totum prenominate abbatie de Ardena reddidi, et sicut iustissimam elemosinam suam concessi, et quicquid in predictis furno et domibus erat mei iuris et reclamationis et heredum meorum de assensu Aeliz uxoris mee et Gilleb(erti) generis mei in puram et perpetuam elemosinam sepenominate abbatie de Ard' spontaneus donaui, non obstantibus recognitionibus vel sacramentis vel scriptis in rotulis regiis vel quibuscumque impedimentis si forte contra abbatiam de Ardena a me vel ab aliis aliqua inde fuerint facta. Hanc autem meam redditionem et recognitionem et ius et reclamationem et donationem super altare beate Marie de Ardena ego et Gillebertus gener meus diligenter obtulimus et pro posse nostro ubique garantizare promisimus, et Rob(ertus) tunc abbas eiusdem loci et conuentus in fraternitatem domus sue et tocius ordinis sui et orationes et beneficia ad peticionem meam pro amore Dei me et uxorem meam et heredes meos receperunt, quia apud eos Cristianam elegi sepulturam, et abbas et conuentus prefati <pro> hac concessione et donatione mea xl. lib(ras) Andeg(auenses) in caritate michi donauerunt. Actum hoc apud Ardenam his presentibus: Rob(erto) tunc abbate de Ardena et conuentu, magistro Rad(ulfo) de Fonte et Iuone fratre suo, magistro Willelmo de Seren'tot, Thoma de Agnell', Rob(erto) de Burum, Thoma de Nouilla clericis, Sansone de Esperun', Rob(erto) de Landa presbiteris, Willelmo de Pyrou, Gilleb(erto) de Vilers militibus, Rad(ulfo) de Sancto Aniano, Ric(ardo) de Curceio laicis et multis aliis.

73. *Notification by Hugh 'the villein' that he has granted Roger his clerk and servant six and a half acres of land at Loucelles (Calvados, cant. Tilly-sur-Seulles) to hold in perpetual fee from the abbey of St-Etienne Caen for an annual rent of one pound of pepper, two chickens and 20 eggs.* Caen, 1187/8

A = BL ms. Additional Charter 67578. Endorsed: *carta Hug(onis) Willain de vi. acris t(erre) apud Locell'* (s.xiii.); *F* (s.xiii/xiv); long s.xviii endorsement with archival reference *cotte 25*. Approx. 156 × 86 + 24mm. Sealed *sur double queue*, pink and white cords through 2 holes, seal impression missing. B = Bnf ms. nouv.acq. latines 1428 fo.18r no.17, copy from A (then in the possession of the Stapleton family at Carlton Towers) by Léon Maître, misdated 1186, *c*. August 1881.

Briefly noted (from B) L. Delisle, *Catalogue des manuscrits du fonds de la Trémoïlle* (Paris 1889), 20 no.17 (misdated); Haskins, *Institutions*, 335 no.15 (also misdated).

For Hugh's grant of 20 acres of land at Loucelles to St-Etienne Caen confirmed before

1185 by King Henry II, see *Acta Henry II*, no.419; Delisle, *Recueil*, no.582; Round, *Calendar*, no.1413, and cf. Léchaudé, *Extrait*, i, 282 no.71.

Notum sit presentibus et futuris quod ego Hug(o) villan(us) dedi et presenti carta confirmaui Rog(ero) clerico seruienti meo vi. acras et dim(idiam) terre mee de Locel' pro seruicio suo tenendas feodaliter sibi et heredibus suis de monasterio et monachis beati Stephani de Cad', soluendo in(de) eis annuatim ad feriam de Prato i. lib(ram) piperis et ad Natalem Domini ii. gall(inas) et in Pascha xx. oua. Est autem terra h(ec) in locis istis, in Perrella i. ac(ram), in Planicie ac(ram) et dim(idiam), super domum Corbelli i. ac(ram), in Nigra Terra i. ac(ram), in via Sancte Crucis ii. ac(ras). Hoc autem factum anno incarnationis dominice m°c°lxxx°vii° apud Cadom'. T(estibus) W(illelmo) fil(io) Rad(ulfi) tunc senesc(allo) Normann(ie), W(illelmo) de Mara, W(illelmo) de Caluiz, Ric(ardo) fil(io) Henr(ici), Gaufr(ido) de Rapend' tunc bailliuis reg(is), Rog(ero) priore Cad', Rob(erto) de Curl', Osb(erto) de Sag', Rob(erto) de Longocampo, W. Rasulano monachis, Ric(ardo) Ospinel, W. Tailleb', Rog(ero) de Cheus, Rad(ulfo) Bigerel, Rob(erto) de Platea et aliis multis.

74. *Notification by Bartholomew de Livet that for 25 livres angevin Luke his butler has purchased from Roger the clerk the land at Loucelles (Calvados) which Hugh 'the peasant', Bartholomew's uncle, granted Roger and which Roger held from Bartholomew until he resigned it into Bartholomew's hand. Luke and his heirs are to hold the land from Roger and his heirs for the same service rendered by Roger. Luke has given Bartholomew 65 sous angevin.*

[1197 X 1214]

A = BL ms. Additional Charter 67579. Endorsed: *carta Barth(olomei) de Liuet de emptione Luce pincerne apud Locell'* (s.xiii; *G* (s.xiii/xiv); long s.xviii endorsement referring to *Loncelles*. Approx. 193 × 105 + 20mm. Sealed *sur double queue*, parchment tag through 3 slits, seal impression missing. B = Bnf ms. nouv.acq. latines 1428 fo.17r no.14, abstract from A (then in the possession of the Stapleton family at Carlton Towers) by Léon Maître, *c.* August 1881.

To be dated to the time of Samson abbot of Caen (above no.18n.). For Bartholomew and Luke, see also Léchaudé, *Extrait*, i, p.13 nos 106, 110, p.276 no.34, p.281 no.67.

Omnibus ad quos presens carta peruenerit Bartholomeus de Liuet salutem. Nouerit uniuersitas vestra quod Lucas pincerna assensu meo et voluntate emit a Rogero clerico pro xxv. libris And(egauensium) terram illam apud Locellas quam Hugo rusticus auunculus meus eidem Rogero pro suo seruicio donauit et quam idem Rog(erus) de me tenebat, ita quod prefatus Rog(erus) terram predictam in manu mea reddidit et forisiurauit, quod decetero nichil in ea reclamabit. Ego autem tunc eandem terram tradidi

et concessi predicto Luce tenendam et habendam sibi et suis heredibus de
me et meis heredibus bene et pacifice, libere et quiete per talem redditum
qualem memoratus Rog(erus) de illa terra m(ich)i faciebat. Pro hac autem
concessione mea eidem firmiter tenenda et garantizanda, dedit m(ich)i idem
Lucas lv. sol(idos) And(egauensium) et inde fecit m(ich)i hominagium,
et ut hoc ratum et inconcussum habeatur in posterum, presenti scripto
et sigillo meo duxi confirmandum. Inde sunt test(es) S(amson) abbas
Cad', Rob(ertus) Rastel et Will(elmu)s de Cormeliis monachi, Rob(ertus)
B(e)n(e)d(i)c(t)i, Henricus le Rebree, Rog(erus) de Cheus, Will(elmus) de
Montelles et alii plures.

75. *Notification by Albereda de Ros that, following a dispute with
Henry fitz Richard over lands and rents and a mill at Caen and
Hérouville (Calvados, cant. Caen) which Albereda claimed Henry
should hold from her at farm rendering 15 livres tournois each year,
and which Henry claimed he held from Albereda for the same rent
but in hereditary right by the terms of a charter of King Henry (II),
Albereda hereby concedes Henry's claim, Henry having paid her 73
livres tournois when he rendered homage to her.*
In the assize at Caen, March 1214/15

A = BL ms. Additional Charter 67582. Endorsed: *Cad'* (s.xv); various post medieval
endorsements. Approx. 200 × 124 + 22mm. Sealed *sur double queue*, parchment tag
through 3 slits, seal impression missing. B = Bnf ms. nouv.acq. latines 1428 fo.22r
no.22, abstract from A (then in the possession of the Stapleton family at Carlton Towers)
by Léon Maître, *c*. August 1881.

Briefly noticed (from B) *RHF*, xxiv, introduction p.134* n.4.

Omnibus ad quos presens scriptum peruenerit Albereda de Ros salutem.
Noueritis quod cum contentio esset inter me ex una parte et Henric(um)
fil(ium) Ric(ardi) ex alia super quibusdam terris et redditibus et molendino
in villa et territorio Cadomi et Herouuille quas dicebam me debere habere
in dominicum meum sicut illas de quibus m(ich)i reddebat per annum
xv. lib(ras) Tur(onensium) ad firmam et ille Henricus e contrario dicebat
quod illas tenebat de me iure hereditario reddendo inde annuatim xv.
lib(ras) Tur(onensium) et unde habebat cartam regis Henr(ici), tandem ita
concordauimus quod predicte terre et redditus et molendinum remanent
sepedicto Henrico possidendas iure hereditario sibi et heredibus suis
de me et heredibus meis reddendo inde annuatim m(ich)i et heredibus
meis xv. lib(ras) Tur(onenses) ad feriam Prati pro omnibus redditibus et
auxiliis m(ich)i pertinentibus sicut continetur in carta regis Henr(ici) quam

sepedictus Henr(icus) inde habet. Actum est hoc in viduitate mea, anno domini m°cc° quartodecimo, mense Martio, in assisa apud Cad' coram Petro de Teill' tunc iusticiario domini regis Franc(ie) et pluribus aliis. Et sepedictus Henr(icus) inde m(ich)i dedit lxxiii. lib(ras) Tur(onenses) quando eius hominagium recepi. Quod ut ratum hab(e)atur, sigilli mei munimine roboraui.

76. *Notification by Robert abbot of St-André-en-Gouffern to King John, that the churches of La Trinité and St-Gervais at Falaise and Notre-Dame at Guibray (Calvados, cant. et com. Falaise) pertain to the presentation and gift of the abbess and convent of La Trinité at Caen, the nuns drawing annual pensions from these churches and having presented the late priest, Erneis, to the church of La Trinité (at Falaise).* [1199 X 1204]

B = Bnf ms. nouv.acq. latines 1428 fo.42r no.40, copy by Léon Maître from the Stapleton charters then at Carlton Towers, noting that the seal was missing, s.xix ex. The original was sold as one of the six charters in Lot 197 of the Sotheby's sale of the Stapleton charters, 22 October 1920, to Maggs for £6 15s., since entirely untraced.

To be dated after the accession of King John but before the loss of Normandy. For Abbot Robert of St-André-en-Gouffern (pre 1190 – d. September 1221), see *GC*, xi, 744. For King John's control over the patronage of Norman churches, see also above no.46. For these particular churches, grouped together for the purposes of taxation, taxed *c.*1335 at the value of 200 (Guibray), 120 (La Trinité) and 50 livres (St-Gervais), with respectively 400, 700 and 500 estimated parishioners, see *Pouillés Rouen*, 203–4, 208, 229–30.

Reuerentissimo domino suo I(ohanni) Dei gratia illustrissimo regi Angl(ie) domino Hibern(ie) duci Norm(annie) Aquit(anie) et comiti Andeg(auie) frater Rob(ertus) dictus abbas et conuentus sancti Andr(ee) de Bosco perpetuam in domino salutem cum omni reuerentia et constanti orationum deuotione. Quoniam vicinarum ecclesiarum patronatus et iura longo usu et certo et frequenti testimonio nobis innotuerunt, magnitudini vestre notum facimus et in veritate, que D(eu)s est, testificamus ecclesias sancte Trinitatis et sancti Geruasii de Fales et sancte Marie de Wiby' ad presentationem et donationem abbatisse et conuentus sancte Trinitatis de Cadomo indubitanter pertinere ut pace de quibus singulis annuas et certas percipiunt pensiones scimus etiam et proculdubio prohibemus Ernesium presbiterum qui nuper decessit per presentationem dictarum abbatisse et monialium fuisse rationabiliter et canonice in ecclesia sancte Trinitatis institutum. Quamobrem supplicamus vobis deuotius et cum ipsis humillime petimus in Domino quatinus sicut decet honorem regium, exclusis malignis suggestionibus, ius ipsarum conseruare curetis illesum. Bene et diu valeatis in Cristo.

THE CANTERBURY CHARTERS

77. Notification by King Louis (VII) of France that, at the instance of St Thomas at whose tomb the king sought the salvation of his soul and bodily healing, he has granted to the monks of Holy Trinity Canterbury 100 measures of wine to be taken during the vintage each year within the lordship of the castle of Poissy (Yvelines), further granting freedom from all passage for this wine and all the other food and drink of the monks. Canterbury, [23/24 August] 1179

A¹ = CCA ms. Chartae Antiquae F90. Endorsed: *carta Ludowici regis de centum modiis vini* (s.xiii/xiv); *i.* (?s.xii/xiii); various post medieval endorsements. Approx. 221 × 209 + 53mm. Sealed *sur double queue*, pink cords through 4 slits, fine seal and counterseal impressions in natural wax varnished reddish brown. A² = Ibid. F91. Written in the same hand as A¹. Endorsed: *carta L. regis Francorum de c. modiis vini* (s.xii/xiii); *carta prima Ludowici regis Francie de centum modiis vini* (s.xiii/xiv); *i.* (s.xiii); various post medieval endorsements. Approx. 208 × 185 + 34mm. Sealed *sur simple queue*, four slits apparently for cords, cords and seal impression missing. B = Ibid. Register E fo.34r, copy from A¹, s.xiv in. C = Ibid. Register A fo.267r (339r), copy from A¹, s.xiv. D = Ibid. F108, copy from ?A², s.xv ex. E = Ibid. F109, copy as in D, s.xv/xvi. F = Ibid. F110, copy as in DE, s.xv/xvi. G = Ibid. F112, copy, s.xv/xvi. H = Ibid. F113, copy, s.xv/xvi. J = Ibid. F149, in an inspeximus by Nicholas Hyllington, official of the archdeaconry of Canterbury, 15 September 1514. K = Ibid. Register L fo.96v (92v), copy from A¹, s.xiv med. L = BL ms. Stowe 924 fo.89r, partial copy from B, made for Sir Edward Dering, 1630.

Printed (from A¹K) *Lit. Cant.*, ii, 480–1 no.926; (facsimile from A¹) *The English Channel: The Link in the History of Kent and the Pas-de-Calais. Archival Texts* (Arras, Conseil Géneral du Pas-du-Calais, and Maidstone, Kent County Council, 2008), 6–7 no.1.

Besides the present grant to Christ Church, Louis' Canterbury pilgrimage of 1179 may explain his inclusion in the obit list of St Augustine's Canterbury: BL ms. Cotton Vitellius C xii fo.141v, *Ob(iit) Lodoueus frater noster rex Francorum, sub* 14 Kalends October (Louis VII died 18 September 1180). For his obit at Christ Church, and for letters of confraternity issued in his favour in the aftermath of the present gift, see BL ms. Cotton Nero C ix (Christ Church obits) fo.12r, whence (misdated) Fleming, 'Christchurch's Sisters and Brothers', 140; BL ms. Cotton Claudius C vi (Christ Church martyrology) fo.197r, whence *English Episcopal Acta II: Canterbury 1162–1190*, ed. C.R. Cheney and B.E.A. Jones (Oxford 1986), 136 no.164; *The Church Historians of England Vol.IV part ii: The History of William of Newburgh, The Chronicles of Robert de Monte*, ed. J. Stevenson (London 1856), 794–5n., noting that Louis made his gift symbolised by his presentation of a golden cup.

In nomine sancte et indiuidue Trinitatis amen. Ludouicus Dei gratia Francorum rex. Pium est ut que ad pias erogantur causas litterarum beneficio ad hoc indeficienti memorie tribuantur, ne Deo seruientium quies perturbetur in posterum et elemosina deuote facta per obliuionem postmod(um) sopita depereat. Nouerint itaque uniuersi presentes pariter ac futuri quod intuitu beatissimi martyris Thome quondam Cantuar' archiepiscopi, ad cuius tumulum pro salute anime et corporis in multa deuotione profecti fuimus impetranda[a], conuentui monachorum sancte Trinitatis ibidem Deo famulantium centum modios vini ad mensuram Parisiensem singul(is) annis tempore vindemiarum in castellaria Pissiaci accipiendos in elemosinam concessimus. Conuentui etiam predicto indulximus quatinus de prescriptis centum modiis vini et de omnibus que ad esum et potum suum pertinere sacramento unius seruientis de mandato alic(uius) monachi de eodem conuentu probari poterit in omnibus passagiis nostris quantum ad nos attinet sunt[b] omnino liberi et immunes. Que omnia ut perpetuam stabilitatem optineant, sigilli nostri auctoritate ac regii nominis karactere subtus annotato presentem cartam precipimus communiri. Actum Cantuar' anno ab incarnatione domini m°.c°.lxx°ix°. astantibus in palatio nostro quorum nomina supposita sunt et signa. Sign(um) Theobaldi comitis[c] dapiferi nostri. Sign(um) Guidonis buticularii. S(ignum) Reginaldi camerarii. S(ignum) Radulphi constabularii. Data per manum [MONOGRAM] secundi Hugonis cancellarii.

[a] inpetranda A[2] [b] sint A[2] [c] comitis Theobaldi A[2]

78. *Notification by King Philip (II) of France of his confirmation of no. 77 above.*   Mantes, [April X September] 1180

A[1] = CCA ms. Chartae Antiquae F92. Endorsed: *carta Philippi regis de centum modiis vini* (s.xiii); *ii.* (s.xiii); various post medieval endorsements. Approx. 268 × 264 + 50mm. Sealed *sur double queue repli redoublé*, pink cords through a single trapezoid shaped hole, fine seal and counterseal impressions in natural wax varnished reddish brown. Written in the same hand as A[2] below. A[2] = BL ms. Additional Charter 15480. Endorsed: *carta Philippi regis Francie de centum modiis vini* (s.xiii ex); *ii.* (s.xiii); various post medieval endorsements including *lot 936* (s.xix, i.e. lot 936 from the Dering sale of 13 July 1861, whose catalogue records the sale of this item to the dealer Boone, for £2 10s.). Approx. 264 × 230 + 46mm. Sealed *sur double queue repli redoublé*, pink cords through a single trapezoid shaped hole, detached seal and counterseal impression in dark green wax. B = CCA Register E fo.34r, copy apparently from A[1], s.xiv in. C = Ibid. Register A fo.267r (339r), copy from A[1], s.xiv. D = Ibid. F108, copy from ?A[1], s.xv ex. E = Ibid. F109, copy as in D, s.xv/xvi. F = Ibid. F110, copy as in DE, s.xv/xvi. G = Ibid. F112, copy, s.xv/xvi. H = Ibid. F149, in an inspeximus by Nicholas Hyllington, official of the archdeaconry of Canterbury, 15 September 1514. J = Ibid. F113, abstract only, s.xv/xvi. K = Bnf ms. Bréquigny 76 fo.34r, copy from A[2], s.xviii. L = Ibid. ms. Moreau 625 fo.53r, copy from A[2], s.xviii. M = CCA ms. Register L fo.96v (92v), s.xiv med.

Cf. below no.80, where the present charter is inspected in full in an inspeximus of 1235.

Printed (calendar from ?K) *Catalogue des Actes de Philippe-Auguste*, ed. L. Delisle (Paris 1856), 1 no.1; (from A², then in the Dering library, with facsimile) (L.B. Larking), 'Charter of Philip Augustus, King of France, 1180', *Archaeologia Cantiana*, iv (1861), 127–30; (from A¹M) *Lit. Cant.*, ii, 481–2 no.927 (from A²KL) *Actes Philippe Auguste*, i, 2–3 no.2, and cf. subsequent notice of A¹ and identification of the scribe in Ibid., v, 255 supplement to no.2, identifying the scribe of both originals as Gasparri scribe 2, cf. F. Gasparri, *L'écriture des actes de Louis VI, Louis VII et Philippe Auguste* (Geneva 1973).

As dated by Delisle and by Delaborde (in *Actes Philippe Auguste*), according to the dates of Reginald the chamberlain. Delaborde also notes the unique nature of the monogram employed in A², subsequently altered in all known originals of Philip Augustus. For a petition from Prior Alan of Canterbury, addressed to Philip apparently very shortly after the death of Louis VII, asking that he confirm the late king's gifts to the monks of Canterbury, see *Alani Prioris Cantuariensis postea abbatis Tewkesberiensis scripta quae extant*, ed. J.A. Giles, Caxton Society (Oxford 1846), 33–4 no.1. For the commemoration of King Philip's obit at Canterbury Cathedral on 13 July each year, see BL ms. Arundel 68 fo.34r. For a suggestion that he was cured of haemorrhoids by the merits of the relics of St Thomas at Dommartin, one of the principal cult centres of St Thomas in northern France, see below no.98n.

In nomine sancte et indiuidue Trinitatis amen. Philippus Dei gratia Francorum rex. Ea que ab antecessoribus nostris et precipue que a patre nostro Ludouico rege Francorum[a] pietatis intuitu sanctis ecclesiis vel aliis locis venerabilibus sunt indulta non est nostri propositi aliquo modo extenuare sed opera misericordie immobili firmitate conseruare. Nouerint igitur uniuersi presentes pariter ac[b] futuri quod intuitu beatissimi martiris Thome quondam Cantuariensis[c] archiepiscopi, ad cuius tumulum pro salute anime et sanitate corporis impetranda pater noster in multa deuotione fuerat profectus, conuentui monachorum sancte Trinitatis ibidem Deo seruientium centum modios vini ad mensuram Parisiensem singulis annis tempore vindemiarum in castellaria Pissiaci accipiendos in elemosinam concessit. Conuentui etiam predicto indulxit quatinus[d] de predictis centum modiis vini et de omnibus que ad esum et potum suum pertinere sacramento unius seruientis de mandato alicuius monachi de eodem conuentu probari poterit in omnibus passagiis suis et nostris quantum ad ipsum attinebat sint omnino liberi et immunes. Quod factum patris nostri ne aliqua possit obliuione deleri vel aliqua malignantium inuidia violari manu nostre confirmationis apposita precipimus immutabiliter custodiri, unde et sigilli nostri auctoritate ac regii nominis karactere inferius annotato presentem cartam voluimus communiri. Actum Madunte anno incarnationis domini m°.c°.lxxx°. regni nostri anno primo, astantibus in palatio nostro quorum nomina supposita sunt et signa. Signum comitis Theobaudi dapiferi nostri. S(ignum) Guidonis buticularii. S(ignum) Reginaudi camerarii. S(ignum) Radulphi constabularii. Data per manum secundi [MONOGRAM] Hugonis cancellarii.

^a Franc(orum) A^{2 b}ac A¹, et A^{2 c} Thome martiris quondam Cantuar' A²
^d quatenus A²

79. *Notification by King Philip (II) of France to the prévôt of Poissy of his grant of 100 measures of wine to the monks of Canterbury in his close and rents at Triel-sur-Seine (Yvelines) or elsewhere from his cellar at Poissy, ordering him to hand over this wine during the vintage from the coming feast of St John the Baptist for the next three years, unless the king returns meanwhile from his pilgrimage (to the Holy Land).* March 1190

A = CCA ms. Chartae Antiquae F94. Endorsed: *carta Philippi regis Francie de c. modiis vini* (s.xiii/xiv); *ut vinum detur monachis Cant' vel eorum nuntiis dum rex fuit in peregrinatione* (s.xiii); *iii.* (s.xiii); various post medieval endorsements, including old reference numbers *V58* and *T94*, both cancelled. Approx. 165 × 61 + 16mm. Sealed *sur double queue*, single slit, tag and seal impression missing. B = Ibid. Register E fo.34r, s.xiv in. C = Ibid. Register A fo.267r (339r), s.xiv. D = Ibid. F112, copy, s.xv/xvi. E = Ibid. F149, in an inspeximus by Nicholas Hyllington, official of the archdeaconry of Canterbury, 15 September 1514, noting a seal on cords.

Briefly listed, but not recited, in the abstracts of French royal charters in CCA mss. F108, F109, F110 and F113 (s.xv/xvi).

Printed (from A) *Actes Philippe Auguste*, v, 14 no.1832, where Nortier questions whether the earlier charter of Philip referred to in the present letters is to be identified as no.78 above (in which there is no mention of Triel), and where it is proposed that the present letters suggest that the rent may have gone unpaid for some time before 1190. During the late 1180s, King Philip had consistently supported the monks of Canterbury in their great dispute with Archbishop Baldwin: *Epistolae Cantuarienses*, ed. W. Stubbs, Rolls Series (London 1865), 10 no.10, 86 nos 104–5, 146 no.169, 155–6 no.177, 222–3 no.241, 305–6 nos 320–1, and cf. 351 no.382. The first of these letters, in which, *c.* December 1186, the monks of Canterbury express their hope to drink from the chalice of their forefathers, might be construed as a veiled reference to the French wine.

Ph(ilippus) Dei gratia Franc(orum) rex preposito Piss' salutem. Noueris quod dilectis nostris monachis Cantuariensis monasterii viris religiosis assignauimus centum modios vini ad mensuram Paris(iensem) sicut in carta nostra continetur in clauso nostro et redditibus nostris apud Triel. Si autem in clauso et redditibus predictis centum modii vini non possent inueniri, residuum habeant monachi in cellario nostro de Pissiaco. Unde tibi precipimus quatinus tempore vindemiarum ab instanti festo sancti Ioh(ann)is Bapt(ist)e in tres annos, nisi interim a peregrinatione nostra redierimus, predictis monachis vel eorum nunciis vinum sic(ut) eis assignauimus sine dilatione et contradictione aliqua tradas. Act' anno incarnati verbi m°.c°.lxxx°. nono, mense Martio.

80. *Notification by King Louis (IX) of France of his confirmation of no.78 above, specifying that the wine is to come from Triel and Chanteloup-les-Vignes (Yvelines, cant. Andrésy), saving to the king the red wine from the close of Triel.* Saint-Germain-en-Laye, 1235

A = CCA ms. Chartae Antiquae F99. Endorsed: *carta Lodowici regis Francie de centum modiis vini in certis locis recipiend(is)* (s.xiii); *iiii.* (s.xiii); various post medieval endorsements. Approx. 280 × 400 + 64mm. Sealed *sur double queue*, fine seal and counterseal impressions in green wax on pink and green cords through 2 holes. B = Ibid. Register E fo.34r–v, s.xiv in. C = Ibid. Register A fo.267r–v (339r–v), s.xiv. D = Ibid. Chartae Antiquae F100, in an inspeximus by Robert, abbot, and Eudo prior of St Augustine's, and Nicholas prior of St Gregory's Canterbury, 24 August 1244. E = Ibid. Chartae Antiquae F101, in an inspeximus by Roger, abbot, and Gervase prior of St Augustine's, and Hugh prior of St Gregory's Canterbury, May 1263. F = Ibid. Register L fos.96v–97r (92v–93r), in an inspeximus by William Thibout, keeper of the prévôté of Paris, 18 July 1300 (and cf. below no.87). G = Ibid. F112, copy, s.xv/xvi. H = Ibid. F149, in an inspeximus by Nicholas Hyllington, official of the archdeaconry of Canterbury, 15 September 1514.

Briefly listed but not recited in the abstracts of French royal charters in CCA mss. F108, F109, F110 and F113 (s.xv/xvi).

Louis succeeded as king following the death of his father in November 1226, so the ninth year of his reign ran to November 1235.

In nomine sancte et indiuidue Trinitatis amen. Lud(ouicus) Dei gratia Franc(orum) rex. Notum facimus quod nos litteras clare memorie regis Ph(ilipp)i k(arissi)mi aui nostri vidimus in hec verba: *(recites no.78 above, apparently after A²)* Nos igitur piis antecessorum nostrorum deuotionibus volentes obsequi donationes et concessiones predictas, volumus et concedimus et ut predictorum centum mod(ium) elemosina firmior in posterum permaneant et stabilior nec ullo tempore sortiri valeat detrimentum eos in locis assignauimus subnotatis, videlicet in censu Trelii decem et nouem mod(ios) et dimid(iam) et tres sextar(ios) ad mensuram Pissiac', residuum in clauso nostro apud Trelium et in vineis Cantus Lupi, saluo nob(is) vino rubeo de clauso nostro de Trel', omnem iusticiam et omnia alia que in dictis locis habebamus nob(is) et nostris heredibus retinentes, et si aliquid de dictis centum mod(iis) vini in locis determinatis deficeret, volumus quod residuum in castellania Pissiac' capiatur. Isti autem centum modii per manum seruientis nostri qui pro tempore fuerit deliberabuntur et tradentur. Volumus autem firmiter et precipimus ut ubicumque fuerimus, seruiens noster qui pro tempore fuerit nuncio credibili dicte ecclesie cum patentibus litteris conuentus vina predicta sine difficultate qualibet et absque mora integre et sine diminutione deliberet atque tradat. Quod ut perpetue stabilitatis robur obtineat, presentem cartam sigilli nostri auctoritate et regii nominis caractare inferius annotato fecimus communiri. Actum apud Sanctum Germanum in Laya, anno incarnationis dominice m⁰.cc⁰. tricesimo quinto, regni vero nostri anno nono, astantibus in palatio nostro quorum nomina supposita sunt et signa. Dapifero nullo. Signum Roberti buticularii. Camerario nullo. S(ignum) Amalrici constabularii. DATA VACANTE [MONOGRAM] CANCELLARIA.

81. *Notification by King Louis (IX) of France of his confirmation of the grants made by Louis VII and Philip Augustus, renewing the monks' quittance from passage money.* Amiens, January 1264

A¹ = BL Cotton Charter xvi.47 (formerly Cotton charter Tiberius 4). Mounted, dorse inaccessible. Approx. 278 × 220mm. Originally sealed *sur double queue*, on cords through 2 holes, foot now fire damaged and cut away. Written in the same hand as A². A² = BL Additional Charter 16355. Endorsed: *carta Ludouici reg(is) Francorum nona de centum modiis vini et omnibus aliis ad usum conuentus pertinentibus* (s.xiii/ xiv); *v.* (s.xiii/xiv); various post medieval endorsements including *Puttick and Co. 15 July 1863 lot 697* (?Madden, s.xix). On the lower part of the face of the plica: *DTP 1811 from the library of Sir Edw(ard) Dering of Surrendon Kent* (s.xix, perhaps the ownership mark of the antiquary the Rev. David Thomas Powell *c*.1773–1848, and presumably referring to the sale of Dering manuscripts from Surrenden at King and Lochée's Rooms, 3 December 1811, cf. Wright, 'Sir Edward Dering', 378n.). Entered in the Puttick and Simpson sale catalogue for 15 July 1865 lot no.677 as 'From the Dering Collection (former sale)', in the 1865 sale bought by Boone for £2 2s. Approx. 284 × 173 + 45mm. Sealed *sur double queue*, pink and green cords through 2 holes, central portion of seal and counterseal impressions in dark green wax. B = CCA ms. Register E fo.34v, s.xiv in. C = Ibid. Register A fos.267v–268r (339v–340r), s.xiv. D = Ibid. F112, copy, s.xv/xvi. E = Ibid. F149, in an inspeximus by Nicholas Hyllington, official of the archdeaconry of Canterbury, 15 September 1514, noting a seal on silk cords. F = AN J655 Angleterre pièces sans dates no.32, copy of the confirmation by Philip IV below no.82, s.xiii ex. G = Northampton, Northamptonshire Record Office ms. Finch-Hatton 170 (Sir Christopher Hatton's Book of Seals), copy in facsimile from A¹, noting the endorsement *carta Ludouici regis Francorum noni de centum modiis vini et omnibus aliis ad usum conuentus pertinentibus* (s.xiii), and with fine drawing of a seal and counterseal impression in green wax on green and red cords, s.xvii. H = BL ms. Additional 22641 fos.32r–33r, copy from G, s.xix.

Briefly listed but not recited in the abstracts of French royal charters in CCA mss. F108, F109, F110 and F113 (s.xv/xvi). Cf. below no.82, where the present charter is recited in an inspeximus of 1286, itself recited in a further inspeximus of 1322, below no.88.

Printed (from G) *Hatton's Seals*, 297–8 no.427; (from F) *Layettes*, iv, 86 no.4906.

Issued at the same time as Louis IX's Mise of Amiens, intended to bring peace between King Henry III and the rebel barons, made in Henry III's presence at Amiens in January 1264. Almost certainly to be associated with the grant of confraternity and the promise of obit celebrations made to Louis IX and his queen and children, issued at Canterbury by J. the subprior and the convent of Christ Church, today surviving as a sealed original in AN J461 Fondations II no.22[15], whence *Layettes*, iv, 51–2 no.4803, there dated 5 January 1263 but more likely, allowing for a year dated by the incarnation, to be assigned to 4 January 1264. This followed an earlier award, of 1232/3, by which the prior and convent had granted Queen Blanche, Louis IX's mother, and her immediate family participation in the prayers and masses of their church in recognition of her devotion to St Thomas and the church of Canterbury, undertaking to celebrate the obit of Louis (VIII), her late husband (who had died on 8 November 1226), with all the solemnities reserved for the obit of an archbp of Canterbury, on 31 October each year, the vigil of the feast of All Saints: AN J461 Fondations II no.9, a sealed original, whence calendared but not printed in *Layettes*, ii, 243 no.2221, and cf. BL ms. Arundel 68 fo.47v for Louis VIII's obit at Canterbury, in the sixteenth century apparently still being celebrated on 8 November each year. Note the specific reference to the making of the present charter in duplicate 'propter casus fortuitos'.

Lud(ouicus) Dei gratia Franc(orum) rex notum facimus uniuersis tam presentibus quam futuris quod cum bone memorie Lud(ouicus) rex Franc(orum) pater inclite recordationis reg(is) Ph(ilippi) karissimi aui nostri olim intuitu beatissimi Thome martiris quondam Cantuarien' archiepiscopi conuentui monachorum in ecclesia ipsius beati Thome martiris Deo seruientium centum modios vini ad mensuram Parisien(sem) singulis annis tempore vindemiarum in castellaria Pissiaci accipiendos in elemosinam concesserit ac eisdem indulserit ut de predictis centum modiis vini et de omnibus que ad esum et potum suum pertinere sacramento unius seruientis de mandato alicuius monachi de eodem conuentu probari poterunt in omnibus passagiis suis quantum ad ipsum attinebat essent omnino liberi et immunes, et postmod(um) idem karissimus auus noster Ph(ilippu)s rex Franc(orum) concessionem huiusmodi confirmauit, et nos etiam post predictum auum nostrum donaciones et concessiones predictas voluerimus et concesserimus prout in litteris nostris super hoc confectis vidimus[a] contineri, nos volentes eidem conuentui ob reuerentiam predicti martiris facere super hiis gratiam ampliorem, concedimus eisdem ut de predictis centum modiis vini et de omnibus que ad usum suum pertinere sacramento unius seruientis de mandato alicuius de eodem conuentu monachi ad hoc ab eodem conuentu deputati probari[b] poterunt, in omnibus passagiis nostris quantum ad nos attinet sint omnino liberi et immunes. Hanc autem cartam propter casus fortuitos fecimus dupplicari. Quod ut ratum et stabile permaneat in futur(um), presentes litteras sigilli nostri fecimus impressione muniri. Actum Ambian' anno domini m°.cc°.sexagesimo tercio, mense Ianuario.

[a] <vi>dimus A[1], *supplied from* A[2] [b] pro<bari> A[1], *supplied from* A[2]

82. *Notification by King Philip (IV) of France of his confirmation of no.81 above.*   Le Château de Lyons–la-Forêt, August 1286

A = BL Additional Charter 15481. Endorsed: *carta Philippi regis Francie de centum modiis vini et omnibus aliis ad usum et esum conuentus pertinentibus* (s.xiv); *vi*. (s.xiii/ xiv); various post medieval endorsements including *lot 937* (s.xix, i.e. lot 937 from the Dering sale of 13 July 1861, whose catalogue records the sale of this item to the dealer Boone, for £3 8s.). Approx. 305 × 230 + 53mm. Fine pen and ink decorations to six capital letters. Sealed *sur double queue*, red and green cords through 2 holes, fine seal and counterseal impressions in dark green wax inside a magnificent silk seal bag in blue and pink stripes with flowers and stars. B = AN J655 Angleterre pièces sans dates no.32, contemporary copy in an English hand preserved together with a petition to King Philip in French from the Canterbury monks, s.xiii ex. C = CCA ms. Register E fos.34v–35r, s.xiv in. D = Ibid. Register A fo.268r (340r), s.xiv. E = Ibid. fo.268r–v (340r–v), s.xiv. F = Ibid. Chartae Antiquae F112, copy, s.xv/xvi. G = Ibid. F149, in an inspeximus by Nicholas Hyllington, official of the archdeaconry of Canterbury, 15 September 1514, noting a seal on silk cords.

Briefly listed but not recited in the abstracts of French royal charters in CCA mss. F108, F109, F110 and F113 (s.xv/xvi).

Printed (only the charter of Louis IX, from B) *Layettes*, iv, 86 no.4906, whence noticed by E. Lalou, *Itinéraire de Philippe IV le Bel (1285–1314)*, 2 vols (Paris 2007), ii, 26.

Ph(ilippus) Dei gratia Francorum rex. Notum facimus uniuersis tam presentibus quam futuris quod nos litteras inclite recordationis Ludouici quondam Francorum regis aui nostri carissimi vidimus in hec verba: (*recites no.81 above*) Nos vero dictorum antecessorum nostrorum pia sequentes vestigia concedimus predicto conuentui immunitatem in omnibus passagiis nostris quantum ad nos attinet de dictis centum modiis vini et de omnibus que ad usum suum pertinere probari poterunt in forma predicta. Quod ut firmum et stabile perseueret, presentibus litteris nostrum fecimus apponi sigillum. Actum in Castro Leonum anno domini m°.cc°. octogesimo sexto, mense Augusto.

83. *Memoranda of the procedures by which the monks of Canterbury obtained their rents from the vineyards of Triel, Chanteloup-les-Vignes (Yvelines, cant. Andrésy) and of the means by which the monks' local proctor could seek redress from the king of France's bailli at Poissy, referring to the red wine of Triel reserved for the king of France (cf. above no.80), to the monks' farming of their vineyards at St-Brice-sous-Forêt (Val-d'Oise, cant. Ecouen) to a local farmer who would render them half his wine as farm, to the proctor's oversight of the pressing of wine to ensure that it be not adulterated, and to the disruptions caused by the period of war from 1294 to 14 July 1300, when the king of France restored the wine and gave 200 livres tournois as damages and arrears, Prior Henry of Eastry then being present with the king in France.* [c.1300]

B = CCA ms. Register A fo.272v (344v), headed *diuersa memoranda et alia munimenta de vinis Francie reperta in registris ecclesie Cantuar'*, s.xiv.

Printed (part only, in English translation) J.B. Sheppard, 'A Notice of Some MSS. Selected From the Archives of the Dean and Chapter of Canterbury', *Archaeological Journal*, xxxiii (1876), 160–1.

Followed by the recital of nos 84–7 below, in the order 86, 84, 87, 85.

Apud Trielium et Cantuslupi sunt quidam tenentes qui tenent vineas suas de rege Francie reddendo inde annuatim conuentui ecclesie Cristi Cant' certum redditum siue censum, videlicet certam mensuram vini singuli secundum quantitatem vinearum suarum tempore vindemiarum secundum mensuram Pesciat', et si aliqui ipsos mensuram vini ipsos contingentem procuratori conuentus tempore videmiarum non soluerint, tunc procurator conuentus nomina ipsorum scire faciet in script(is) balliuo reg(is) Franc(ie) apud Pesciat', et idem balliuus statim iusticiabit omnes qui in arrerag(iis) fuerint per graues districtiones quousque huiusmodi arrerag(ia) procuratori conuentus plenarie persoluerint, et pro transgressione iniuste detentionis emendas ab eis capiet.

Item apud Triel rex habet unum claustrum vinee et continet quatuor arpent', et istam vineam tenet quedam mulier de Pesciaco, reddendo inde annuatim ad opus reg(is) ad celar(ium) reg(is) de Pesciaco medietatem totius vini rubei dicte vine, et alia medietas vini rubei remanebit penes ipsam pro cultura vinee, et de eodem clauso reg(is) reddet dicta mulier procuratori conuentus ecclesie Cristi Cantuar' medietatem totius albi vini eiusdem vinee, et alia medietas vini albi remanebit penes ipsam pro cultura vinee.

Et memorandum quod collectis et receptis vinis predictis, procurator conuentus ecclesie Cristi Cantuar' ibit ad ball(iuu)m de Pesciaco et iurabit quantum recepit de vino tam de redditu Trieli et Cantuslupi quam de predicto clauso reg(is), et quantum defuerit de centum modiis vini, idem balliuus statim liberabit dicto procuratori de celario reg(is) apud Pesciacum.

Apud Sanctum Bricium habet conuentus ecclesie Cristi Cantuar' duas pecias vinee que continent circiter unam arpentam et dimid(iam), quarum una pecia continet in longitudine x. perticatas et in latitudine viii. perticatas, et altera pecia continet in longitudine septemdecim perticatas et in latitudin(e) quinque perticatas, et sunt dicte vinee ex parte australi ville sancti Bricii distantes a villa circiter tres quarentenas, et traditur dicta vinea per procuratores conuentus supradicti Cantuar' singulis annis ad firmam aliquando uni aliquando alteri, reddendo inde annuatim medietatem totius vini inde prouenient(is), et alia medietas remanebit firmario pro cultura vinee et omnimod(is) aliis expens(is) suis.

Et memorandum quod tenentes predicti tam de Trielo et Cantilupi quam clauso reg(is) ac etiam firmarius conuentus apud Sanctum Bricium non debent fullar(e) vina sua nisi per visum procuratoris conuentus, ne forte apponerent aquam vel facerent deterius vinum ad opus conuentus quam ad opus proprium.

Item memorandum quod una arpenta vini quando vinum com(muni)ter se habet respondebit de octo modiis vini, et aliquando de sex, et aliquando de decem.

Et memorandum quod anno domini millesimo cc.^{mo} nonagesimo quarto, orta guerra inter regem Angl(ie) et Franc(ie) pro terra Vascon', rex Franc(ie) cepit in manu sua omnia vina nostra ac etiam omnia bona omnium Anglicorum que habebant in regno Franc(ie).

Postea anno domini millesimo ccc.^{mo}, ii. Idus Iulii, rex Franc(ie) restituit conuentui omnia vina et alia bona sua que prius ceperat in manum suam, et dedit conuentui cc. libras Turonens(es) pro dampnis et arrerag(iis) suis, et super hoc concessit ei litteras suas tenorem qui sequitur continentes, Henr(ico) de Estria, priore ecclesie Cristi Cantuar' tunc in Franc(ia) coram rege presente.

84. *Mandate from King Philip (IV) to his treasurers at Paris to pay 200 livres tournois to the prior and convent of Christ Church for four years' arrears of wine owing from Poissy, Triel and St-Brice-sous-Forêt (Val-d'Oise, cant. Ecouen).* Arrabloy, 13 July 1300

B = CCA ms. Register A fo.273r (345r), s.xiv.

The king's appearance here at Arrabloy (Loiret, cant. Gien) supplies an addition to the king's published itinerary.

Philippus Dei gratia rex Franc(ie) dilectis et fidelibus suis the(saurar)iis nostris Paris' salutem et dilectionem. Mandamus vobis quatinus priori et conuentui ecclesie Cristi Cantuar' vel eorum mandato ducentas libras Turonens(es) pro arrerag(iis) vinorum que apud Pesciacum, Trielum et apud Sanctum Bricium ex concessione predecessorum nostrorum habent et percipere consueuerunt de quatuor annis ultimo preteritis soluatis de nostro, visis presentibus et retentis. Act' apud Arrablenum die mercur(ii) post festum translationis Sancti Benedicti anno domini millesimo ccc.^{mo}

85. *Mandate from King Philip (IV) to his keepers of lands and ports to grant safe conduct to the prior of Christ Church travelling to England with his household, horses, silver vessels and other possessions.* Arrabloy, 13 July 1300

B = CCA ms. Register A fo.273r (345r), s.xiv, headed *et quia inhibitum fuit per totum regnum Anglie et Franc(ie) ne aliquis extra regna predicta duceret vel mitteret aurum vel argentum, vasa vel iocalia, aurea vel argentea sine speciali licentia regum predictorum, dominus rex Franc(ie) concessit priori qui tunc temporis cum ipso rege erat in Franc(ia) pro negotiis predictis litteras suas patentes de saluo conductu in forma sequenti.*

Philippus etc omnibus iusticiar(iis) et custodibus districtuum et portuum regni nostri ad quos presentes littere peruenerint salutem. Mandamus vobis et vestrum cuilibet quatinus prior ecclesie Cristi Cantuar' ad partes Anglie proficiente cum familia, equis, vessalamentis argenti et aliis rebus suis per loca et districtus nostros permittat(is) saluo et secur(e) ac libere pertransire, nullum ei impedimentum quomodolibet inferentes. Act' apud Arralablenum die mercur(ii) post festum translationis sancti Benedicti anno domini millesimo ccc.^{mo}

86. *Mandate from King Philip (IV) to his prévôt of Paris to release all wine owed to the prior and convent of Christ Church at Poissy and Triel and all possessions at St-Brice-sous-Forêt (Val-d'Oise, cant. Ecouen).* Saint-Ay, 14 July 1300

B = CCA ms. Register A fo.273r (345r), s.xiv, headed *In regno Francie.*

For Philip IV's presence at Saint-Ay (Loiret, cant. Meung-sur-Loire), see *Itinéraire de Philippe IV le Bel (1285–1314)*, ed. E. Lalou, 2 vols (Paris 2007), ii, 175.

Philippus Dei gratia rex Francorum preposito nostro Paris' salutem. Mandamus tibi quatinus priori et conuentui ecclesie Cristi Cantuar' vel eorum mandato omnia vina que ex concessione predecessorum nostrorum regum Franc(ie) apud Pesciacum et Trielum habent et habere consueuerunt et percipere prout in cartis inde confectis videbis plenius contineri necnon ea omnia que habent apud Sanctum Bricium ac quandam domum ipsorum sitam apud Trielum sine dilatione et difficultate et quocumque impedimento ammoto facias liberare et ipsos predictorum possessione gaudere. Act' apud Sanctum Agilum, die Iouis proxima post translationem sancti Benedicti anno domini millesimo ccc.ᵐᵒ

---

87. *Notification from William Thibout, keeper of the prévôté of Paris, to his bailiff at Poissy of his receipt of letters of King Philip (IV), above no.86, ordering the bailiff to comply with the king's orders.*
18 July 1300

B = CCA ms. Register A fo.273r (345r), s.xiv.

For William Thibout inspecting Louis IX's confirmation of the Canterbury wine on the same day as the issue of the present letters, see above no.80 text F.

Gwillelmus Thibout garden de la prevost de Parys au suz bailliff de Pessi salucz. Nous vous fasmus a savoyr k(e) nous avoums receves le lettres nostre seygnur le roy de Fraunce en la furme k(e) seusuyt: Philippus Dei gratia etc, par la vertw des quels lettres desus dites nous vous mandums et comaundums ke vous totes les choses desus dites bailes e diliueres saunz delay au dit priour ou a soun certeyn comaundemen en la fourme e en la maner(e) contenu en dites lettres, car nous sumes certeyns des privileges k(e) il ont de nostr(e) seygnur le roy et de devanciers sur ceo entervoigne de ceo nous avoms mis en cestes lettres le seal de la prevoste de Parys le an de grase mil ccc. le lundi davant la Maudeleyne par le temoygne Huitace Pasee.

---

88. *Notification by King Charles (IV) of France of his confirmation of no.82 above.*
La Tour-du-Grain-en-Valois (Oise, cant. Betz, com. Gondreville),
June 1322

A = BL Additional Charter 15482. Endorsed: *carta Karoli reg(is) Franc(ie) de centum modiis vini et omnibus aliis ad usum conuentus pertinentibus* (s.xiv); *registratur* (s.xiv, perhaps from the French royal chancery); *xiiii.* (s.xiv); *registrata est* (s.xiv).

Acquired at the Dering sale of 13 July 1861 lot 938, with the catalogue recording the sale of this item to the dealer Boone, for 13s. On the front of the plica, at the left hand side contemporary with the writing of the document *facta est collatio soluit v. s(olidos)*, on the right hand side *per dominum regem ad relationem domini Alberti de Roya z. Maillardus*. Approx. 398 × 195 + 45mm. Sealed *sur double queue*, pink and green cords through 2 holes, seal and counterseal impressions in brown wax painted green. B = AN JJ61 (Register of Charles IV) fo.36v no.97, s.xiv in. C = CCA ms. Register E fo.35r, s.xiv in. D = Ibid. Register A fo.271r–v (343r–v), s.xiv. E = Ibid. Register L fo.97r–v (93r–v), s.xiv med. F = Ibid. Chartae Antiquae F112, copy, s.xv/xvi. G = Ibid. F149, in an inspeximus by Nicholas Hyllington, official of the archdeaconry of Canterbury, 15 September 1514, noting a seal on silk cords.

Briefly listed but not recited in the abstracts of French royal charters in CCA mss. F108, F109, F110 and F113 (s.xv/xvi).

Printed (calendar from B) *Registres du Trésor des Chartes: Tome II, part 2, Régne de Charles IV le Bel*, ed. H. Jassemin and A. Vallée (Paris 1999), 24 no.3695.

For the petitioning from which the present charter resulted, see *Lit.Cant.*, i, 62–7 nos 62–71.

Karolus Dei gratia Francorum et Nauarre rex. Notum facimus uniuersis presentibus et futuris nos infrascriptas vidisse litteras in hec verba: (*recites no.82 above*) Nos autem ad beatissimum martyrem predictum pie gerentes deuotionis affectum prenominatorumque predecessorum nostrorum in hac parte vestigiis inherentes, concessiones predictas et omnia suprascripta rata habentes et grata, ea volumus, laudamus, approbamus et tenore presentium auctoritate nostra regia ex certa scientia confirmamus, nostro in aliis et alieno in omnibus iure saluo. Quod ut perpetue stabilitatis robur obtineat, presentes litteras sigilli nostri fecimus impressione muniri. Actum et datum apud Turrem de Gronio in Valesio, anno domini millesimo trecentesimo vicesimo secundo, mense Iunio.

89. *Notification (in French) by Louis (XI) king of France, at the supplication of the prior and convent of St Thomas of Canterbury in England, recording that many of the king's progenitors and predecessors, kings of France, in honour of St Thomas, granted or confirmed 100 measures of wine by the measure of Paris, payable from the châtellenie of Poissy and other places, which gift the prior and convent long enjoyed until war between the kings of France and England disturbed these arrangements, so that the places from which the wine was paid were ruined and no wine could be had from them. Out of devotion for St Thomas of Canterbury, the king hereby reassigns the wine to be paid from his lands of the Bordelais and Gascony ('Bourdelois et Gascongne') payable each year at the time of vintage ('la saison de vandenges'), free from all toll or subsidies, commanding his officials and treasurers to ensure annual payment at Bordeaux and to account for the same in their account to the officers of the king's chamber.* Arras, 14 April 1478

A¹ = Canterbury Cathedral Library ms. Chartae Antiquae F146. Marked on the plica: *par le roy .... M Picot.* Various post medieval endorsements. Approx. 398 × 193 + 77mm. Sealed *sur double queue*; fine double-sided seal impression in natural wax on a parchment tag through a single slit. A² = Canterbury Cathedral Library ms. Chartae Antiquae F145/1. Marked on the plica: *par le roy .... M Picot.* Various post medieval endorsements. Approx. 466 × 185 + 88mm. Sealed *sur double queue*; parts (repaired) of a double-sided seal impression in natural wax on a parchment tag through a single slit. B = Ibid. F108, copy, s.xv. C = Ibid. F109, copy, s.xv. D = Ibid. F110, copy, s.xv. E = Ibid. F113, copy, s.xv. F = Ibid. F125, in an inspeximus by John le Grant, lieutenant general of the seneschal of the Boulonnais, 31 August 1478. G = Ibid. F157, inspeximus as in F, 31 August 1478. H = BL ms. Additional Charter 16369, further copy of the inspeximus as in FG, 31 August 1478. Apparently to be identified as the document sold from the Dering collection at Puttick and Simpson 13 July 1865 lot 43 'Document relative to a grant of Wine by the King of France'. I = CCA ms. Chartae Antiquae F126, in an inspeximus by Jean Courel, keeper of the seal of obligations of the vicomté of Rouen, 1 May 1479. J = Ibid. F127, two single-sheet copies, s.xv. K = Ibid. F147, copy, s.xv. L = Ibid. F149, in a notarial inspeximus, 25 September 1514.

Pd (part only) *Lit. Cant.*, iii, pp.xx-xxi. Deliberately not printed below.

For the petitioning from which the present charter emerged, including the promise of spiritual benefits, see *Lit. Cant.*, iii, 292–4 no.1085; *Christ Church Letters*, ed. Sheppard, 33–4 no.30. Accompanied or followed by further letters (all in French): Chartae Antiquae F145/2, from the king's officers of account at Paris, acknowledging receipt of the king's grant and commanding the Exchequer at Bordeaux to implement the king's command, given at Paris, 24 April 1479 after Easter; Ibid. F145/3, from Louis (XI) ordering his treasurers to implement the order of 1478, given at La Motte d'Égry ('La Motte de Gry') (Loiret, cant. Beaune-la-Rolande, com. Égry), 9 July

1480, sealed *sur simple queue*, seal impression missing; Ibid. F145/4, from the king's treasurers commanding the Exchequer at Bordeaux to implement the king's command, given at Briare ('Briawre prez La Motte de Gry') (Loiret, cant. et com. Briare), 10 July 1480; Ibid. F145/5, from the king's general councillors, consenting to the grant of 1478, 10 July 1480, sealed *en placard* with a small round red seal. The whole now filed together with the original grant by Louis XI (Chartae Antiquae F145/1) and sealed with a round seal impression in white wax, showing a shield with the fleur de lys under a crown. Further mentioned in letters of Edward (IV), at Westminster 21 October 1482, which note Louis' award and allow the prior and convent to bring into England 33 doles of wine from the Bordelais and Gascony free from all custom and subsidy (CCA ms. Chartae Antiquae F148, a fine sealed original letters patent, enrolled as *CPR 1476–85*, 328, and endorsed with a note that it was also enrolled in the Exchequer Memoranda Roll, now TNA E 368/255 (LTR Memoranda Roll 22 Edward IV) Michaelmas records rot.10). I am indebted to Elisabeth Lalou for the identification of various place names here, and to Adrian Jobson for the Memoranda Roll reference.

90. *Notification by Pope Innocent (III) addressed to the prior and convent of Christ Church, confirming the 100 measures of wine granted by the late King Louis (VII) of France.*

Lateran, 3 May 1200

B = CCA ms. Register A fo.271v (343v), headed *confirmatio domini Alexandri pape de c. modiis vini*, s.xiv.

Printed (from B) *The Letters of Pope Innocent III (1198–1216) Concerning England and Wales*, ed. C.R. and M.G. Cheney (Oxford 1967), 37, 216 no.222 (*Cum a nobis petitur*), hence not reprinted here.

For the commemoration of the obit of Pope Innocent III at Canterbury on 16 July each year, see BL ms. Arundel 68 fos.34v–35r.

91. *Notification by King Henry (II) of England of his grant of quittance from any custom payable on the transport of the 100 measures of wine granted by King Louis (VII) of France in honour of St Thomas.*

Marlborough [August 1179 X September 1181, ?August 1179 X April 1180]

A = Canterbury Cathedral Library ms. Chartae Antiquae F138. Endorsed: *Carta H. regis* (*Angl'* s.xiii) *de quitancia vini* (s.xii/xiii); *XXIIII* (s.xii/xiii); various post medieval endorsements. Approx. 145 × 150 + 28mm. Sealed *sur double queue, repli redoublé*, parchment tag through 3 slits, seal impression in natural wax, varnished reddish brown, much perished. B = Ibid. F111, copy s.xv. C = Ibid. Register A fo.272r (344r), s.xiii ex. D = Ibid. Register E fo.38r no.33, s.xiii ex.

Printed (facsimile from A) F. Barlow, *Thomas Becket* (London 1986), plate 41; (calendar from A) *BEC*, lxix (1908), 569 no.97; *Acta of Henry II and Richard I*, ed. J.C. Holt and R. Mortimer, List and Index Society Special Series xxi (1986), 57 no.70. T.A.M. Bishop, *Scriptores Regis* (Oxford 1961), no.132 and plate 35, identifies the writer as chancery scribe XLII.

After Louis' pilgrimage of 22–26 August 1179, during which he was entertained by Henry II, and during which his grant was made: Howden, *Gesta*, i, 241; *Gervase*, i, 293; Gerald of Wales, *Expugnatio Hibernica*, ed. A.B. Scott and F.X. Martin (Dublin 1978), 222–3. Before the nomination of John Cumin as archbp of Dublin (6 September 1181). Probably in the immediate aftermath of Louis' pilgrimage, before the king's departure for France in April 1180. For a quittance of £32 owing from the monks' wine at Rouen for the two years 1178–80, made *per breue regis*, see *MRSN*, i, 71. For the obit celebrations offered at Canterbury for the soul of Henry II on 6 July (the octave of SS Peter and Paul) each year, see BL ms. Arundel 68 fo.33r (31r).

H(enricus) Dei gratia rex Angl(orum) et dux Norm(annorum) et Aquit(anorum) et comes And(egauorum) com(itibus), baronibus, iustic(iis), vic(ecomitibus), prepositis et omnibus ministris et balliuis suis totius terre sue salutem. Sciatis me pro Dei amore et beati Thome martiris concessisse monachis sancte Trinitatis Cantuar' ut habeant quietantiam per totam terram meam ducendi libere et quiete centum modios vini quos dominus L(udouicus) rex Franc' dedit annuatim in perpetuam elemosinam Deo et beato Thome martiri et prefatis monachis, et ideo vobis prohibeo ne ab eis vel eorum seruientibus vinum illud ducentibus ullam inde consuetudinem exigatis vel exigi permittatis nec eos aliquo modo inde disturbetis. T(estibus) Godefr(ido) de Luci, Nicol(ao) capellano, Ioh(ann)e Cumin, Rog(ero) Bigoto, Regin(aldo) de Pauilli apud Merlebergam.

92. *Notification by Richard (I) King of England of his grant of quittance from any custom payable on the transport of the 100 measures of wine granted by King Louis (VII) in honour of St Thomas.* Geddington, 17 September 1189

A = CCA ms Chartae Antiquae F93. Endorsed: *carta regis Ric(ardi) de quietantia* (s.xiii); *xxvi.* (s.xiii); various post medieval endorsements. Approx. 215 × 80 + 22mm. Sealed *sur double queue*, parchment tag through 3 slits, fragment from lower half of seal impression in natural wax varnished reddish brown. Badly damp damaged and illegible on folds and at right hand side, letters in brackets ◇ below supplied from B. B = Ibid. Register E fo.38r, s.xiv in. C = Ibid. Register A fo.272r (344r), s.xiv. D = Ibid. F111, copy, s.xv.

Printed (calendar) Landon, *Itinerary*, no. 45; *Acta of Henry II and Richard I*, ed. J.C. Holt and R. Mortimer, List and Index Society Special Series xxi (1986), 177 no.323.

For the obit celebrations offered at Canterbury for the soul of Richard I on 6 April each year, see BL ms. Arundel 68 fo.23r (21r).

Ric(ardus) Dei gratia rex Angl(orum), dux <Nor>m(annorum) et Aquit(anorum) et com(es) Andeg(auorum) comitibus, baroni<bus, iustic(iis), vicecom(itibus), prepositis et> omnibus ministris et balliuis suis tot<ius terre> sue salutem. Sciatis nos pro Dei amore et beati T<home martyris concessisse> monachis sancte Trinitatis Cant' <ut h>abeant quietantiam per totam terram nostram ducen<di libere et quiete centum modios> vini quos dominus <Lu>do<wycus> rex <Francorum> dedit annuatim in perpetuam elemosinam Deo et <beato Thome martiri et prefatis> monachis, et ideo <vobis> prohibemus ne <ab ei>s vel eorum seruientibus vinum illud ducentibus ul<lam inde consuetudinem exiga>tis vel exigi permittatis nec eos a<liquo> modo inde disturbetis. Test(ibus) Walterio Rothom' <archiepiscopo, Regin(aldo) Bathon'>, Ioh(anne) Norwic', Gileb(erto) Roffen' e<piscopis, Ric(ard)o> London', Godefr(ido) Winton', Hub(erto) Sar' electis, <Roberto comite Leycestr', Willelmo> de Manda<uill'> com(ite) Exessie, Rann(ulfo) de Glanuill'. Dat' per manum Willelmi de Long<o Campo cancellar(ii) nostri, anno> primo regni nostri, xvii. die Septembr(is) apud Gaidinton'.

93. *Notification by King John of England of his grant to the monks of Christ Church Canterbury of perpetual quittance from 'modiatio' and all other customs for the 100 measures of wine given by the king of France.* L'Ile-d'Andely, 21 October 1201

A = CCA ms. Chartae Antiquae F95. Endorsed: *carta regis Ioh(ann)is de c. modiis vini* (s.xiii); *reg(is) Anglie* (s.xiii/xiv); *xxvii.* (s.xiii); *xv* (?s.xvi); various post medieval endorsements. Approx. 227 × 102 + 47mm. Sealed *sur double queue*, green silk cords through 3 holes, seal impression in natural wax varnished reddish brown. B = Ibid. Register E fo.38r–v, s.xiv in. C = Ibid. Register A fo.272r (344r), copy from A[1], s.xiv. D = Ibid. F111, copy, s.xv.

For the obit celebrations offered at Canterbury for the soul of King John on 18 October each year, see BL ms. Cotton Nero C ix fo.14r, whence Fleming, 'Christchurch's Sisters and Brothers', 143.

Iohannes Dei gratia rex Angl(ie), dominus Hybernie, dux Norm(annie), Aquit(anie), com(es) Andeg(auie) archiepiscopis, episcopis, abbatibus, comit(ibus), baron(ibus), iustic(iis), vic(ecomitibus), prepositis, ministris et omnibus ball(iu)is et fidelibus suis salutem. Sciatis nos intuitu Dei et ob reuerentiam beati Thome martyris et pro salute anime nostre et animarum antecessorum et successorum nostrorum concessisse et hac carta nostra confirmasse ecclesie Cristi Cantuar' et monachis ibidem Deo seruientibus quod centum modii vini quos rex Franc(ie) eis dedit sint quieti in perpetuum de modiatione et omni alia consuetudine ad nos pertinente ubicumque deuenerint in potestatem nostram. Testibus Will(elm)o Maresc(allo) comite de Penbroc, Hugon(e) de Gornaco, Roberto de Harecort, Ioh(ann)e de Pratell', Gyrard(o) de Forniuall'. Dat' per manum Sym(onis) archidiaconi Wellen' apud Insulam Andeliac' xxi. die Octobr(is) anno regni nostri tertio.

94. *Notification by Eustace count of Boulogne, and Baldwin his brother, of their grant to Christ Church Canterbury of quittance from toll at Wissant (Pas-de-Calais, cant. Marquise) for all the church's business, so that the monks and their men may freely cross, made for the souls of Eustace and Baldwin and of their father and mother and placed on the altar of Christ.*   [1093 X 1096, ?REWORKED]

A = CCA ms. Chartae Antiquae F130. Endorsed: *carta Eustachii comitis Bolonie de libertate thelonei de Witsando* (s.xiii); *xiiii.* (s.xiii); various post medieval endorsements. Approx. 129 × 78mm. Sealed *sur simple queue*, tongue below wrapping tie, seal impression in natural wax varnished brown, an equestrian figure facing to the left, legend defaced. B = Ibid. Register E fo.37r, s.xiv. C = Ibid. Register A fo.270r (342r), s.xiv. D = Ibid. Chartae Antiquae F111, copy, s.xiv ex.

Printed (briefly noticed from A) H.J. Tanner, *Families, Friends and Allies: Boulogne and Politics in Northern France and England, c.879–1160* (Leiden 2004), 319.

After Eustace's succession as count of Boulogne, but before the departure of Baldwin for the First Crusade, following which he became first king of Jerusalem (1100–1118). Although in theory issued nearly thirty years before no.96 below, written in the same or a very similar book hand, presumably of the Canterbury scriptorium, suggesting that the present charter was remade or recopied at the time that no.96 was issued in confirmation. Note that the text itself is written as a narrative notice in the third person plural, rather than as a charter in the first person singular or plural, as in no.96 below. Nonetheless, the witness list is unobjectionable, and the final clause, guaranteeing the gift whether there be peace or war between the king of England and the count of Boulogne, although rehearsed in the confirmation (no.96), might much better suit a date in the late eleventh than the mid twelfth century.

Eustachius comes Boloniensis et Baldeuinus frater eius dederunt ecclesie Cristi Cantuariensi theloneum de Witsando de omni negotio quod ad ecclesiam pertinet, ita ut monachi eiusdem ecclesie et homines eorum libere et secure transeant et redeant absque omni impedimento omni tempore, et hoc donum dederunt pro anima patris et matris sue et animabus eorum. Quod donum ut stabile esset propriis litteris proprio sigillo sigillatis confirmauerunt et super altare Cristi posuerunt. Teste Haimone dapifero et Gosfredo dap(ifero) de Parentit et Winimero constabul(ari)o et Willelmo nepote eiusdem comitis et Egelbode de Witsando cum multis aliis, et ista donatio rata erit semper siue pax sit siue discordia inter regem Anglie et comitem ipsius terre.

95. *Notification by Robert (II) count of Flanders that the monks of Christ Church have his peace and protection throughout his land in transacting their business, quit from all disturbance or toll.*
[1093 X 1111]

A = CCA ms. Chartae Antiquae F171. Endorsed: *<car>ta comitis Flandrie ......chi ecclesie Cristi et homines eorum .....em ad peragenda negocia sua ....am* (s.xiii); *xix.* (s.xiii); various post medieval endorsements. Approx. 45 × 30mm. Sealed *sur simple queue*, wrapping tie above tongue, tongue cut down vertically rather than horizontally from the bottom of the writing, fine seal impression in natural wax varnished brown, round equestrian, legend within the inner rim of a bowl shaped surface [SIGIL] LU(M) ROBERTI COMITIS [IU]NIORIS, according to Jean-François Nieus, the sole surviving impression of Robert's seal, two other exemplars having been lost since the nineteenth century. Of the text itself, only a few words remain from the left hand side, the entire right hand side of the document having perished. Here supplied from B within brackets <>. B = Ibid. Register E fo.37v, s.xiv. C = Ibid. Register A fo.270v (342r), s.xiv. D = Ibid. Chartae Antiquae F111, copy, s.xv.

During Robert II's years as count. Note that unlike the contemporary exemptions granted by the counts of Boulogne, which are presented as narrative notices in the third person, the present text, although written in a book hand quite possibly of the Canterbury scriptorium, is composed as a dispositive act in the first person singular. Jean-François Nieus assures me that the seal and the vocabulary are entirely consistent with authenticity. For Robert's years as count, and for his absence on Crusade from 1096 to 1100, see *Actes des comtes de Flandre 1071–1128*, ed. F. Vercauteren (Brussels 1938), esp. pp.xvi–xvii, with notes on his seal at pp.cv–cvi.

Robertus comes <Flandrens' omnibus fidelibus et ministris suis salutem. Mando et precipio vobis ut> monachi e<cclesie Cristi Cantuariensis et homines eorum habeant meam pacem et tuitionem per totam meam> terram ad fac<ienda negocia sua de quacunque re indiguerint et quieti et absque perturbatione sint et de> teloneo quantum <ad me pertinet. Valet(e)>.

96. *Notification by Stephen (of Blois), count of Boulogne, and by the countess Matilda, his wife, of their grant of quittance from toll payable at Wissant as in no.94 above.*

[1125 X 1135, ?REWORKED]

A = CCA ms. Chartae Antiquae F129. Endorsed: *carta St(ephani) comitis Bolonie ut homines nostri liberi sint a theloneo de Withsant* (s.xiii); *xv.* (s.xiii); various post medieval endorsements. Approx. 197 × 98mm. Sealed *sur simple queue*, on a tongue cut at right angles to the left hand margin of the document, with step and wrapping tie at left hand of foot. Seal impression, round, natural wax varnished brown, equestrian figure, upper part missing, legend ....OLONIE ET MO..., presumably the seal used by Stephen as count of Boulogne and Mortain, before 1135. Two holes on the front of the document, certain missing letters replaced within brackets below from C. B = Ibid. F102, in an inspeximus by R(oger) abbot of St Augustine's, H(ugh) prior of St Gregory's and R. (rural) dean of Canterbury, damaged and illegible in part, 1264/5. C = Ibid. Register E fo.37r–v, s.xiv. D = Ibid. Register A fo.270r–v (342r), s.xiv. E = Ibid. Chartae Antiquae F111, copy, s.xiv ex.

Printed (briefly noticed from A) H.J. Tanner, *Families, Friends and Allies: Boulogne and Politics in Northern France and England, c.879–1160* (Leiden 2004), 322.

After the succession of Stephen as count of Boulogne, but before his coronation as king of England. Like no.94, which is written in the same or a very similar book hand, a narrative notice in the third person plural, rather than a first person charter text as one would expect. For the obit celebrations for Stephen, as king of England, celebrated at Canterbury on 25 October each year, see BL ms. Cotton Nero C ix fo.14v, whence Fleming, 'Christchurch's Sisters and Brothers', 143.

Stephanus comes Boloniensis et comitissa Mathildis coniunx videlicet eius dederunt ecclesie Cristi Cantuariensi thelon<eum de Wy>tsando de omni negotio quod ad ecclesiam pertinet, ita ut monachi eiusdem ecclesie et homines eorum libere et secure transeant et redeant absque omni impedimento omni tempore, et hoc donum dederunt pro animabus suis et pro animabus patrum et matrum suorum. Quod donum ut stabile esset propriis litteris proprio sigillo sigillatis confirmauerunt et super altare Cristi posuerunt. Donatio autem ista rata semper erit siue pax sit siue discordia inter regem Anglorum et comitem ipsius terre. Test(ibus) Roberto de Creuequur et Willelmo filio Ric(ardi) et Hugone filio Fulb(erti) et mult(is) aliis.

97. *Notification by Matthew count of Boulogne to his ministers at Wissant, Boulogne and Nieulay that in honour of St Thomas and for the souls of himself, his wife and heirs he has granted his brothers of Christ Church quittance from toll taken on their goods at Wissant, Boulogne and Nieulay.* [1171 X 1173]

A¹= CCA ms. Chartae Antiquae F132. Endorsed: *carta Mathei comitis de theloneo <de> Witsando, Bolonia et Niwene* (s.xiii); *xvi.* (s.xiii); various post medieval endorsements. Approx. 170 × 178 + 13mm. Sealed *sur double queue*, tag through single slit, seal impression, round, natural wax varnished brown, an equestrian figure with full helmet facing to the right, a device (?a lion rampant) on the shield held in the figure's left hand, legend: ....COM......... A² = Lost, formerly Cotton Charter Vitellius B.xiii, assumed burned in the Cotton fire of 1731. B = CCA ms. Chartae Antiquae F102, in an inspeximus by R(oger) abbot of St Augustine's, H(ugh) prior of St Gregory's and R. (rural) dean of Canterbury, damaged and illegible in part, 1264/5. C = Ibid. Register E fo.37v, s.xiv. D = Ibid. Register A fo.270v (342r), s.xiv. E = Ibid. Register L fo.97v (93v), s.xiv med. F = Ibid. Chartae Antiquae F111, copy, s.xiv ex.

Pd (from E) *Lit. Cant.*, ii, 483 no.928.

After the martyrdom of Thomas Becket but before the death of Count Matthew, fighting against Henry II in the great rebellion of 1173. Count Matthew is referred to in passing by William of Canterbury as a visitor to the shrine of Becket at Canterbury: *MTB*, i, 264. For the identification of 'Niwene' as Nieulay, the embryonic form of the later port of Calais, now the site of the Fort-Nieulay within the modern port (Pas-de-Calais, cant. et com. Calais), I am indebted to Jean-François Nieus, and cf. F. Lennel, *Calais des origines à la domination anglaise* (Calais 1908), 3, 11. Note the reference to the monks of Canterbury as 'my brothers', suggesting some sort of confraternity agreement.

Math(eu)s comes Bolonie omnibus hominibus et ministris suis de Witsando et Bolonia et Niwene tam presentibus quam postfuturis salutem. Sciatis quod ego comes Math(eu)s pro honore Dei et beati Thome archiepiscopi Cantuariensis et gloriosi martiris et pro salute anime mee et uxoris mee et heredum meorum perdonaui fratribus meis monachis scilicet conuentui ecclesie Cristi Cantuarie in perpetuum theloneum et omnes consuetudines que exigi solent in Witsando vel Bolonia vel Niewene a transeuntibus. Volo (er)go et precipio ut ipsi et nuntii et omnes seruientes eorum liberi sint et quieti a me et ab omnibus heredibus meis in perpetuum a theloneo siue pedagio siue omni alia consuetudine et prohibeo ut nullus hominum vel ministrorum meorum eos pro hac re vexare presumat. T(estibus) Arnulfo de Caio, Rogerio de Gauchin, Gileberto de Munfichet, Henrico de Chaumunt, Ysaac de Estru, Thomas de Aurenches, Alulfo de Boctune, Anselmo de Hesdein et aliis pluribus.

98. *Notification by Philip (of Alsace) count of Flanders and Vermandois to his bailiffs of Wissant, Boulogne and Nieulay of his grant of quittance from toll and pedage for the monks of Canterbury and their goods as granted by Matthew his brother (above no.97).*
[1173 X 1181, ?April 1177 or August 1179]

A = BL ms. Additional Charter 16200. Endorsed: *carta Philippi com(itis) Flandrie de theloneo et padagio* (s.xii/xiii); *xxvii.* (s.xiii); *purchased at Puttick's 17 July 1863 lot 562* (s.xix, Madden). Approx. 133 × 38mm. Sealed *sur simple queue*, tongue torn away. Damaged and illegible in parts, supplied from B below within brackets. Almost certainly the charter of Philip count of Flanders offered in the Dering sale at Puttick and Simpson's, 7 February 1863 lot no.1152, marked in the BL copy of the sale catalogue as sold to 'Darcy' for 3s. Offered for sale again at Puttick and Simpson's 17 July that year, as from 'the collection of manuscripts of a well-known collector in the West of England', lot no.562, sold to Boone for the hardly princely price of 1s. B = CCA ms. Register E fo.37v, s.xiv. C = Ibid. Register A fo.270v (342v), s.xiv. D = Ibid. Chartae Antiquae F111, copy, s.xiv ex.

Pd (from ABC) *De Oorkonden der Graven van Vlaanderen (juli 1128 – september 1191: II. Uitgave – band III. Regering van Filips van de Elzas (Tweede deel: 1178-1191)*, ed. T. de Hemptinne and A. Verhulst, Recueil des actes des princes belges vi (Brussels 2009), 23–4 no.532.

After no.97 above, but during Philip's years as count of Flanders, apparently at a time when Philip had control over the county of Boulogne, so after 1173 and before 1181, perhaps at the time of Count Philip's own pilgrimage to Canterbury, accomplished following a sailing from Wissant in April 1177, prior to the count's departure for crusade, or during Louis VII's pilgrimage in 1179, when the count of Flanders is said to have been in attendance at Canterbury, or in August 1184 when he is said to have conducted the archbishop of Cologne as a pilgrim to Becket's shrine: Howden, *Gesta*, i, 158–9; Gerald of Wales, *Expugnatio Hibernica*, ed. A.B. Scott and F.X. Martin (Dublin 1978), 222–3; *Gervase*, i, 262, 313. For a candle of his own weight vowed by Count Philip to the Premonstratensians of Dommartin (Pas-de-Calais, cant. Hesdin, com. Tortefontaine, *alias* St-Josse-au-Bois), in thanks for a miracle worked by relics of St Thomas there, leading to the count's recovery from a secret illness, see T. Stapleton, *Tres Thomae seu res gestae S. Thomae apostoli, S. Thomae archiepiscopi Cantuariensis et martyris, Thomae Mori Angliae quondam cancellarii* (Douai 1588), 147–8 no.63, whence 2nd ed. (Cologne 1612), 128 no.63, whence *Anecdota Bedae, Lanfranci et aliorum*, ed. J.A. Giles (London 1851), 157–8 no.63. According to Charles du Canda (prior of Dommartin), *La Vie de S. Thomas archevesque de Cantorbie* (St-Omer 1615), 270–1 nos 60–1, supplying a less bowdlerized version in French, the illness was haemorrhoids, and the count's gifts included not just a candle but the count's war horse, sword, lance and harness, and a sum of money, King Philip (Augustus) of France being cured of the same illness through the merits of St Thomas. For Count Philip's role as an ally to the monks of Canterbury during their great dispute with Archbishop Baldwin after 1186, see *Epistolae Cantuarienses*, ed. W. Stubbs, Rolls Series (London 1865), 156–7 no.178, 314 no.328. The present charter is not the only English charter of the count. At some time before his death, Philip also confirmed a grant by Count Matthew, his late brother, to the Fontevraudist nuns at Westwood (Worcestershire), of a chapel dedicated to St Nicholas at Droitwich, also confirmed by Ida countess of Boulogne as Matthew's daughter: BL ms. Cotton Vespasian E ix (Westwood cartulary) fos.5v–6r, whence *Monasticon*, vi, 1006–7 nos 17–19; *De Oorkonden*, ed. De Hemptinne and Verhulst, 55 no.553 (1173 X 1180).

Ph(ilippus) Flandr' et Virom' comes balliuiis suis de Witsando, Bolonia et Niwena salutem. Mando vob(is) et precipio ut monachos et ministros ecclesie sancte Trinitatis Cantuarensis euntes et redeuntes dimmitatis liberos <ab> omni exactione thelonei et pedagii sicut confirmatum est eis si<gillo c>omitis Mathei fratris mei, et sicut vos ipsos diligitis, ultra <hoc nichil> de<ce>tero ab eis exigere presumatis.

99. *Mandate from Philip (of Alsace) count of Flanders and Vermandois to R. Lupus and his other bailiffs at Wissant that they are to take no customs from the bearers of the present letters but are to grant them free passage, promising the count's favour to all who grant or encourage others to grant alms to the church of Canterbury.* [1173 X 1181, ?April 1177 or August 1179]

A = CCA ms. Chartae Antiquae F118. Apparently in the same hand as no.98 above. Endorsed: *breue Phil' com(itis) Fland' de teloneo de Witsand* (s.xiii); *xviii.* (s.xiii); various post medieval endorsements. Approx. 147 × 47mm. Sealed *sur simple queue*, step for tongue, tongue and seal impression torn away. B = Ibid. Register E fo.37v, s.xiv. C = Ibid. Register A fo.270v (342r), s.xiv. D = Ibid. Chartae Antiquae F111, copy, s.xiv/xv.

Pd (from ABC) *De Oorkonden der Graven van Vlaanderen (juli 1128 – september 1191: II. Uitgave – band III. Regering van Filips van de Elzas (Tweede deel: 1178–1191)*, ed. T. de Hemptinne and A. Verhulst, Recueil des actes des princes belges vi (Brussels 2009), 24–5 no.533.

Date as above no.98.

Ph(ilippus) Flandr' et Viromand' com(es) R. Lupo et aliis balliuiis suis de Widsand salutem. Precipio et volo ut a presentium latoribus nich(il) consuetudinis exigatis, sed euntes et redeuntes liberum et quietum transitum inueniant. Sciatis etiam quod plurimum mi(chi) placebit et loco et tempore grates eis referam qui ad opus sancte Trinitatis Cantuar' ecclesie auxilium et consilium impendent vel elemosinas suas illuc mittendo vel alios ad id faciendum salubri ammonitione excitando. Val(et)e.

100. *Notification by Gazo (V) de Poissy of his grant made in the chapter house at Canterbury, for love of God, the Blessed Virgin Mary and St Thomas and for the souls of himself and his wife and sons, of quittance at Mantes (Yvelines) and Maisons-Laffitte (Yvelines) for a boat belonging to St Thomas carrying wine and other purchases, save for the tithe payable to the monks of Notre-Dame de Coulombs (Eure-et-Loire, cant. Nogent-le-Roi), and save for a knife without silver or gold ('knilpulum sine auro et argento') payable to his bailiff at Mantes and another to his bailiff at Maisons.*
[1179 X 1189]

A¹ = CCA ms. Chartae Antiquae F115. In what could be an English hand. Endorsed: *carta Gaze de Peisi de quietantia vini apud Maante et Maisuns* (s.xiii); *iiii.* (s.xiii); *triplex* (s.xv); various post medieval endorsements. Approx. 200 × 63 + 14mm. Sealed *sur double queue*, parchment tag through a single slit, central portion of seal impression in natural wax varnished brown, single sided, equestrian with sword in right hand, facing to the right, legend lost. A² = Ibid. F120. In a French hand, distinct from that of A¹. Endorsed: *Gace de Peissi de transitu vini* (s.xii/xiii); *iiii.* (s.xiii); *triplex* (s.xv); various post medieval endorsements. Approx. 132 × 56 + 25mm. Sealed *sur double queue*, single slit, seal impression missing. A³ = Ibid. F136. Written in the same hand as A². Endorsed: *Gace de Peisi de quietantia vini* (s.xii/xiii); *iiii.* (s.xiii); various post medieval endorsements. Approx. 132 × 65 + 20mm. Sealed *sur double queue*, thin parchment tag through a single slit, seal impression, single sided, round brown wax, equestrian as in A¹, legend: S.............CO. B = Ibid. Register E fo.36r, s.xiv. C = Ibid. Register A fo.269r (341r), s.xiv. D = Ibid. Chartae Antiquae F111, copy, s.xiv ex.

Almost certainly after the grant made by Louis VII in 1179 (above no.77). For Gazo (V) de Poissy fl.1182, lord of Maisons-sur-Seine (now Maisons-Laffitte) and his claims, renounced after investigation by the king of France, to levy tolls at Mantes on the ships of the monks of St-Wandrille as an agent of the count of Meulan 1166 X 1178, who died, apparently on the Third Crusade, in August 1189, see *Cartulaire de l'abbaye de Saint-Martin de Pontoise*, ed. J. Depoin (Pontoise 1895-1901), 436–8; Power, *Norman Frontier*, 96, noting a further renunciation of tolls at Mantes in favour of the monks of Jumièges issued in 1182 before King Philip Augustus by Gazo and Jaqueline his wife, in all probability a daughter of the late vicomte of Mantes. For Gerard de Fournival (Oise, cant. St-Just-en-Chaussée), see *Ibid.*, 358n. For the Benedictine priory of La Madeleine (at Villarceaux, Val-d'Oise, com. Chaussy), founded by William Mauvoisin (father of the donor of no.109 below) as a daughter house of the abbey of Coulombs, see *GC*, viii, instr. 328. The reservation of token payments may suggest a determination on the part of the lords of Poissy to demonstrate their continuing independence of the control of the Capetian kings. According to *Diceto*, ii, 43, Gazo de Poissy had served alongside one of the witnesses to the present charter, Gerard de Fournival, as Henry II's envoy to Philip Augustus in 1186.

Sciant presentes et futuri quod ego Wazo de Peisi[a] pro amore Dei et sancte Marie et gloriosi martyris Thome et pro salute anime mee et uxoris mee et filiorum et omnium predecessorum meorum in capitulo ecclesie

Cristi Cant' dedi et concessi et hac carta mea in [b]elemosinam[b] confirmaui monachis ibidem Deo famulantibus [c]aquietantiam[c] [d]unius nauis sancti Thome[d] cum vino et [e]cum ceteris que fuerint empta ad opus eorumdem monachorum in Maanthe et in Maysuns quantum ad me pertinet[e] preter decimam monachorum sancte Marie de Columps[f]. Cum autem nauis illa cum vino et ceteris que dicta[g] sunt per loca iamdicta, s(cilicet) Maanthe et Maysuns, transierit[h], monachus ecclesie Cristi Cant'[j] vel eius seruiens[k] dabit unum cnipulum sine auro et argento bailiuo meo de Maanthe et alium cnipulum [l]sine auro et argento dabit[l] bailiuo meo de Maisuns si forte nauis illa illuc [m]cum vino et ceteris transsierit[m] pro omni consuetudine in signum et recognitionem prefate quietantie[n] memorate nauis sancti Thome. Testibus his: Gerardo milite de Furniual[p], Willemo de Auberuill', Rob(erto) de Turolt[q], Rob(erto) de Frenis et multis aliis.

[a] Gazo de Peysy A[2], Gazo de Peysi A[3b-b] elemosinam perpetuam A[2], perpetuam elemosinam A[3 c-c] quantum ad me pertinet quietanciam A[2], quantum ad me pertinet aquietantiam A[3] [d-d] in Maanthe et in Maysuns unius nauis sancti Thome A[3 e-e] ceteris que empta fuerint ad opus eorum in Maanthe et in Maysuns A[2], cum ceteris que empta fuerint ad opus eorum A[3 f] Culumps A[3 g] predicta A[2]A[3 h] transsierit A[3 j] A[2]A[3] *insert* si ibi fuerit [k] seruiens eius A[3 l-l] *not in* A[2], sine auro et argento A[3 m-m] transierit A[2], transsierit A[3 n] aquietancie A[2 p] Furniuals A[2 q] Turoltd A[2], Turoldt' A[3]

101. *Notification by Adam de l'Isle-Adam (Val-d'Oise) of his grant to St Thomas for the souls of his father and mother of an annual rent of 10 sous parisis, of which 5 sous are his and 5 sous his brother Manasser's, payable annually at Michaelmas to the envoy of the monks of Canterbury who comes every year to Poissy to collect wine.* [1179 X 1189]

A = CCA ms. Chartae Antiquae C210. Endorsed: *cart(a) Ade de Insula de decem sol(idis) Paris'redditus* (s.xiii); *i.* (s.xiii); various post medieval endorsements. Approx. 160 × 43 + 20mm. Sealed *sur double queue*, single slit, tag and seal impression missing. B = Ibid. Register E fo.36r, s.xiv. C = Ibid. Register A fo.269r (341r), s.xiv.

After Louis VII's grant of wine from Poissy, first made in 1179 (above no.77), and before the death of the grantor. For l'Isle-Adam and its lords, see M. Grimot, 'Histoire de la ville de l'Isle-Adam et notice biographique de ses seigneurs', *Mémoires de la Société Historique du Vexin* (and separately, Pontoise 1884). For Adam IV (fl.1156 X 1162 – d.1189), son of Anseau de l'Isle and of Mabile his wife, daughter of Lancelin de Bulles, recorded as taking the cross for the third time in 1188 and assumed to have died, probably on crusade, by 1189 when his son, Anseau II, was in possession of the lordship, see *Cartulaire de l'abbaye de Saint-Martin de Pontoise*, ed. J. Depoin (Pontoise 1895–1901), 418–21 (where it is erroneously stated that Anseau III *c.*1226 was the first member of the family to take the name 'de l'Isle-Adam' as opposed to 'de l'Isle'), with a useful family tree in N. Civel, *La Fleur de France: les seigneurs d'Ile-*

de-France au XIIe siècle (Turnhout 2006), 422, 439 no.11.

Sciant tam presentes quam postfuturi quod ego Adam de Insula Ade dedi et concessi pro anima patris mei et matris mee et omnium antecessorum meorum singulis annis Deo et beato martiri Thome decem solidos Parisienses, quinque sol(idos) pro me et quinque pro fratre meo Manasse. Hos siquidem sol(idos) reddam ego Adam et heredes mei post me singulis annis ad festum sancti Michael(is) nuncio monachorum ecclesie Cristi Cant' qui veniet pro vino eorumdem monachorum apud Pessi. Val(e)t(e).

102. *Notification by Manasser de l'Isle(-Adam) of his grant to St Thomas and the monks of Canterbury of an annual rent of 5 sous parisis in perpetual alms for the souls of himself and his parents Anseau and Mabilia and Adam (IV) his brother and Anseau, Adam's son, and his other brothers Adam and Lancelin, payable at the octave of the feast of St Denis (16 October) from Hemmarus de l'Isle, Manasser's man, and his heirs at L'Isle-Adam. Confirmed by Manasser's brother Adam (IV), with the assent of Anseau his son.*
[1179 X 1189]

A = CCA ms. Chartae Antiquae C174. Endorsed: *Manaserius de Insula* (s.xii/xiii); *cart(a) Manasserii de Insula de quinque sol(idis) Paris' redditus* (s.xiii); *ii.* (s.xiii); various post medieval endorsements. Approx. 148 × 81 + 16mm. Sealed *sur double queue*, single slit for a tag, tag and seal impression missing. B = Ibid. Register E fo.36r, s.xiv. C = Ibid. Register A fo.269r (341r), s.xiv.

Date apparently as above no.101. For Manasser, brother of Adam IV, lord of Rémérangles (Oise, cant. Clermont), married to Amicia daughter of Robert de Milly, see *Cartulaire de l'abbaye de Saint-Martin de Pontoise*, ed. J. Depoin (Pontoise 1895–1901), 418–21.

Manasserius de Insula omnibus Cristi fidelibus salutem. Uniuersitati vestre notum facio quod ego M(anasserius) de Insula dedi et concessi Deo et beato martyri Th(ome) Cantuarien' et fratribus ibidem Deo seruientibus v. sol(idos) Parisien' monete in perpetuam elemosinam pro salute anime mee et parentum meorum Anselini et Mabilie et fratris mei Adam et filii eius Anselini et aliorum fratrum meorum, Ade videlicet et Lancelin(i), et omnium propinquorum et amicorum meorum, accipiendos singulis annis in octauis sancti Dionisii ab Heremaro de Insula homine meo et heredibus suis apud Insulam. Cui donationi frater meus Adam de Insula consensit et filius eius Anselinus presens assensum prebuit, quam et ego presenti scripto confirmatam sigilli mei appositione roboraui. Val(e)t(e).

103. *Notification by Bernard de St-Valery to all his knights and ministers of the honour of St-Valery(-sur-Somme) (Somme) that for the souls of his father, mother, wife and heirs he has pardoned the prior and monks of Holy Trinity Canterbury and their servants traversing his lands all pedage and customs out of love for St Thomas 'whom in my needs I wish to have (as advocate) with the just judge'.*
[1173 X 1191]

A[1] = CCA ms. Chartae Antiquae F116. Endorsed: *carta Bernardi de Sancto Walerico de pedagio et aliis consuetudinibus* (s.xiii); *viii.* (s.xiii). Approx. 159 × 147 + 18mm. Sealed *sur double queue*, parchment tag through 3 slits, upper half of round seal impression in natural wax varnished brown, equestrian with sword in right hand and shield in left, SIGILLUM..... Counterseal, small round, a lion passant facing to the right, legend illegible. A[2] = Ibid. F119. In a different, possibly English or Canterbury hand, distinct from that of A[1]. Endorsed: *carta Bernardi de Waleri de pedagio* (s.xiii); *viii.* (s.xiii); various post medieval endorsements. Approx. 213 × 52 + 19mm. Sealed *sur double queue*, parchment tag through a single slit, central portion of seal impression as in A, showing the lower part of the horse on the obverse, legend entirely missing, and preserving the entire counterseal. A[3] = Ibid. F140. Apparently in the same hand as A[1], although in format closer to A[2]. Damaged and illegible at the beginning and end. Endorsed: *carta Bernardo de Sancto Walerico de padagio et aliis consuetudinibus* (s.xiii); *viii.* (s.xiii); various post medieval endorsements. Approx. 210 × 58 + 18mm. Sealed *sur double queue*, parchment tag through a single slit, seal impression as above A[1]A[2]. B = Ibid. C1277, in an inspeximus by William Thibout, keeper of the prévoté of Paris, 11 October 1300. C = Ibid. ms. Register E fo.36v, s.xiv. D = Ibid. Register A fo.269v (341v), s.xiv. E = Ibid. Chartae Antiquae F111, copy, s.xiv ex.

After the canonization of Thomas Becket (February 1173), and before the death of Bernard de St-Valery, for which see I.J. Sanders, *English Baronies: A Study of their Origin and Descent 1086–1327* (Oxford 1960), 10.

Bernardus de Sancto Walerico omnibus militibus suis et ministris de honore Sancti Walerici salutem. Sciatis quod ego [a]pro animabus patris et matris mee et[a] pro salute anime mee et uxoris mee et heredum meorum[b] perdonaui priori sancte Trinitatis Cantuar' et omnibus eiusdem ecclesie monachis et eorum seruientibus qui per terram meam transierint pedagium et omnes alias consuetudines que in terra mea a transeuntibus exiguntur siue in terram meam aduenientibus, et ideo volo et firmiter precipio ut pacem meam in terra mea habeant ipsi et omnia sua et omnes sui, et prohibeo ne aliquis aliquam consuetudinem que ad me spectat in terra mea amplius ab eis exigat neque eos propter tales consuetudines vexet vel in placitum ponat. Has libertates specialiter concessi eis propter amorem sancti martyris Thome quem in meis necessitatibus apud [c]iustum iudicem[c] adiutorem habere desidero. His testibus[d]: Ernulfo clerico, Milon(e) capell(ano), Bernardo Tachelu, Anchero de Cheresi, Waltero Mabun, Weremundo[e] Caldel.

[a-a] not in A[3] [b]A[3] *inserts* et pro animabus patris et matris mee [c-c] iu........cem A[2], *letters mostly lost* [d] Testibus his A[3] [e]Weremund A[3]

104. *Notification by John count of Ponthieu that he has quitclaimed to the church and monks of Holy Trinity Canterbury and their servants all pedage and toll out of love for St Thomas, making this gift in the monks' chapter house at the time that the convent granted him the society and benefit of their house.* 					[1171 X 1190]

A[1] = CCA ms. Chartae Antiquae F131. Endorsed: *Ioh(ann)is comitis Pontiui* (s.xii/ xiii); *carta I. com(itis) Pontiui de pedagio et theloneo* (s.xiii); *x.* (s.xiii); various post medieval endorsements. Approx. 165 × 73 + 25mm. Sealed *sur double queue*, parchment tag through 3 slits, round, single-sided seal impression in natural wax varnished brown, an equestrian figure facing to the right with round shield in left hand and long lance with pennant in his right hand, legend: SIGILLUM ..HAN.......PO.....
A[2] = Ibid. F121. Written in the same hand as A[1]. Endorsed: *Iohannis comitis Pontiui de pedagio et teloneo* (s.xiii); *x.* (s.xiii); various post medieval endorsements. Approx. 165 × 72 + 27mm. Sealed *sur double queue*, 3 slits, tag and seal impression missing.
B = Ibid. Register E fo.36v, s.xiv. C = Ibid. Register A fos.269v–270r (341v–342r), s.xiv. D = Ibid. Chartae Antiquae F111, copy, s.xiv ex.

After the martyrdom of Thomas Becket and before the departure of Count John for the Third Crusade, during which he died in June 1191. For the family, see *Recueil des actes des comtes de Ponthieu (1026–1279)*, ed. C. Brunel (Paris 1930), which at pp.v–vi supplies a family tree, and at p.165 no.109 notes a charter of Count John to the men of Abbeville witnessed by Walter Senioratus of St-Riquier (dép. Somme), Ingelram seneschal of Ponthieu and Baldwin de Dorcat in 1184, but which fails to notice the present charter. For miracles reported at Becket's shrine concerning men from the region of Ponthieu, see *MTB*, i, 282, ii, 201. Count William (III Talvas) of Ponthieu (d.1221) is recorded as being cured of evil affections through the grace of St Thomas, and thereafter made offering to the relics of St Thomas preserved at Dommartin, including two mills: Charles du Canda (prior of Dommartin), *La Vie de S. Thomas archevesque de Cantorbie* (St-Omer 1615), 271 no.62, 276, recording this count's anniversary as 5 (*recte* 4) October.

Iohannes comes Pontiui omnibus baronibus, militibus et ministris terre sue salutem. Sciant omnes tam presentes quam futuri quod ego comes Ioh(ann)es clamo quietos et liberos ecclesiam sancte Trinitatis de Cantuar' et eiusdem ecclesie monachos et omnes seruientes et omnes homines[a] suos a pedagio et theloneo et omnibus aliis consuetudinibus terre mee que ad me pertinent, et prohibeo ne aliquis eos vel homines suos in tota terra mea in aliquo vexare presumat. Hec autem omnia concessi prefate ecclesie pro amore Dei et reuerentia beati martyris Thome et pro salute anime mee et uxoris mee et heredum meorum et pro animabus patris et matris mee in capitulo predicte ecclesie quando conuentus mi(chi) concessit societatem suam et eiusdem ecclesie beneficium. Testibus his[b]: Gaulterio Seinurei de Sancto Richero, Yngelramno[c] dapifero de Ponteii[d], Hugone de Beamunt, Baldewino Durcat, Roberto de Beloi.

[a] homines *not in* A[1], *supplied from* A[2] [b] His testibus A[2] [c] Yngelranno A[2] [d] Punteii A[2]

105. *Notification by Robert (II) count of Meulan to his bailiffs at Meulan (Yvelines) that he has granted the monks of St Thomas Canterbury for the soul of his father and ancestors free transit at Meulan for their wine and quittance from customs throughout his land.*
[1173 X 1207, ?1179 X 1190]

A¹ = BL ms. Lord Frederick Campbell Charter XXII.1. Endorsed: *carta comitis Roberti Mellenti de quietancia vini* (s.xiii); *vi.* (s.xiii); various post medieval endorsements including *v. Aspil no.10* (s.xviii). Approx. 174 × 80 + 28mm. Sealed *sur double queue*, seal impression in reddish brown wax on red cords through 3 slits, on the face a mounted figure with drawn sword, legend: SIGILLUM ROBERTI COMITIS M'LL[E]T. On the reverse, a mounted warrior carrying a pennant, legend: SIGILLUM ROBERTI DOMINI BELL[U]M[UNTIS]. A² = CCA ms. Chartae Antiquae F124. Apparently in the same hand and format as A¹. Endorsed: *Rob(erti) comitis de Mellent de pedagio ibidem* (s.xiii); *vi.* (s.xiii, cancelled); various post medieval endorsements. Approx. 170 × 78 + 32mm. Sealed *sur double queue* on red cords through 3 slits, seal impression round dark brown wax as A¹ above. B = Ibid. Register E fo.36r–v, s.xiv. C = Ibid. Register A fo.269v (341v), s.xiv. D = Ibid. Chartae Antiquae F111, copy, s.xiv ex. E = BL ms. Stowe 665 (John Anstis' 'Aspilogia') fo.79r (p.181) no.10, copy with facsimile drawing of the seal made when 'penes Thomas Astle', s.xviii.

After the canonization of Becket and before the death of Count Robert (d. *c.*1207, cf. *CP*, vii, 739–40 appendix I), almost certainly earlier rather than later within this period, probably after the grant of wine by Louis VII. For a scribe (*cursor*) of Count Robert of Meulan, cured of leprosy through St Thomas' intervention, see *MTB*, i, 337. The second witness, Richard 'abbate de Tornai' carries a surname ('Abbas') rather than a title as abbot, and can be identified as Richard L'Abbé 'de Tournay' (?Eure, cant. Beaumont-le-Roger, com. Thibouville), who with Geoffrey his son, before 1162, granted the chapels of Saint-Benoît-des-Ombres (Eure) and Tertu (Orne, cant. Trun, com. Villedieu-lès-Bailleul) to the monks of Ste-Barbe-en-Auge (Calvados, cant. Mézidon, com. Ecajeul): Delisle, *Recueil*, nos 169, 756. He attests a number of acts of Count Robert II before 1166, in the lifetime of Waleran count of Meulan, notably as 'Ricardus abbas de Torn': *Select Documents of the English Lands of the Abbey of Bec*, ed. M. Chibnall, Camden Society 3rd series lxxiii (1951), 16–17 no.30. He also appears as 'Ricardus abbas de Tornai' in the count's foundation charter to his Grandmontine priory near Beaumont-le-Roger: BN ms.Vexin 8 p.820. Howden records him in 1173 as rebelling with his lord, Count Robert: Howden, *Gesta*, i, 46. It is tempting to identify Richard with the 'Ricardus filius Gaufridi abbatis', who appears in the 1165 Pipe Roll owing a relief for his fees of Empingham in Rutland: *PR 11 Henry II*, 55; *PR 12 Henry II*, 52. This Richard was son and heir of Geoffrey L'Abbé, seneschal of Earl Robert II of Leicester, uncle of Count Robert II of Meulan: D. Crouch, *The Beaumont Twins* (Cambridge 1986), 92, 142, 219. The family connection between the Leicesters and the Meulans makes the identification more likely, as does the fact that Richard L'Abbé de Tournay called his son Geoffrey. Amongst the other witnesses, Peregrine the chaplain of Count Robert appears to have been the brother of Ralph de Beaumont, 'medicus' of both Waleran II of Meulan and King Henry II: Paris, Bibliothèque Mazarine ms. 3417 (Beaumont cartulary) fo.8r. I am indebted to David

Crouch for many of these details.

Robertus comes Mellenti bailliuis suis de Mell't et omnibus suis presentibus et futuris salutem. Sciatis me concessisse et in elemosinam confirmasse monachis sancte Trinitatis Cantuarie pro amore Dei et beati Thome martyris et pro anima patris mei et antecessorum meorum et mea apud Mell't transitum vini quietum quod ducent ad proprium usum suum et preter hec consuetudinem in tota terra mea de omnibus que emerint ad usus ipsorum que poterunt iuste facere assecurari sua propria esse. Test(ibus) Willelmo Pipart, Ricardo Abbate de Tornai, Rannulfo de Bigart, Radulfo de Botemont, Rogerio Harpin, Peregrino et Hugone capellanis meis.

106. *Notification by Waleran (III) count of Meulan to his bailiffs at Meulan that he has granted free transit to the monks for their wine at Meulan and confirmed quittance from custom throughout his land for all goods purchased, as previously granted by (Count Robert) his father.* [1179 X 1195, ?AUTHENTIC]

A[1] = BL ms. Lord Frederick Campbell Charter XXII.3. Endorsed: *carta comitis Galeranni Mellenti de transitu vini* (s.xiii); *vii.* (s.xiii); various post medieval endorsements, including *v. Aspil' 331* (s.xviii, referring to the drawing of Waleran's seal, from a Bordesley Abbey charter, in BL ms. Stowe 666 fo.26v no.331, itself taken from BL Harley Charter 45.I.30). Approx. 145 × 74 + 24mm. Sealed *sur double queue*, parchment tag through 3 slits, round equestrian seal impression in natural wax varnished red, legend: [S]IGILLUM VALERANI [DE ...LLENT], the missing letters here being supplied from the drawing in E below. A[2] = CCA ms. Chartae Antiquae F139. Endorsed: *carta Galeranni filii comitis Mellenti de transitu vini sancti Th(ome)* (s.xiii); *vii..* (s.xiii); various post medieval endorsements. Approx. 152 × 84 + 28mm. Sealed *sur double queue*, 3 slits, tag and seal-impression missing. B = CCA ms. Register E fo.36v, copy from A[1], s.xiv. C = Ibid. Register A fo.269v (341v), copy from A[1], s.xiv. D = Ibid. Chartae Antiquae F111, copy, s.xiv ex. E = BL ms. Stowe 666 (John Anstis' 'Aspilogia') fo.69r no.585, copy with facsimile drawing of the seal from A[1] made when 'penes Thomas Astle', s.xviii.

Printed (brief notice from A[2] BCD) D. Crouch, 'Robert of Beaumont, Count of Meulan and Leicester: his Lands, his Acts, and his Self-Image', *Henry I and the Anglo-Norman World. Studies in Memory of C. Warren Hollister*, ed. D.F. Fleming and J.M. Pope, Haskins Society Journal xvii (Woodbridge 2007), 105 no.10, where the grant by Waleran's father is dated 1080 X 1118.

The reference to St Thomas suggests that the present charter can only be of Waleran III of Meulan, son of Count Robert II, rather than (as assumed by Crouch) Waleran II (d.1166) son of Robert I (d.1118). Waleran III predeceased his father, dying at some date after 1195 (see here *CP*, vii, 740–1 appendix I, dating Waleran III's death to 1191–2 and the Third Crusade, contradicted by *Cartulaire de l'église de la Sainte-Trinité de Beaumont-le-Roger*, ed. E. Deville (Paris 1912), 24–5 no.16 (as drawn to my attention by David Crouch), where he attests a charter of his father dated 7 January 1195). Professor Crouch has pointed out to me a parallel charter to this Canterbury act in a cartulary copy of an act by 'G. comes Mellenti filius R. comitis' to the abbey of L'Estrée (Eure, cant. Nonancourt, com. Muzy), transferring to L'Estrée a grant 'quem auus meus G. dedit monachis de Pontiniaco' (i.e. Pontigny, Yonne): Evreux AD Eure H 319 fo.58r–v, and cf. *Cartulaire de l'abbaye royale de Notre-Dame de Bon-Port de l'ordre de Cîteaux au diocèse d'Evreux*, ed. J. Andrieux (Evreux 1862), 10 no.12 (transcribed as 'Galeranus filius Roberti comes Mellentis', as drawn to my attention by Daniel Power). The witnesses to the Estrée charter are familiar from acts of Robert II of Meulan, as is the case with the Canterbury act. The reference in the L'Estrée act to 'G(alerannus)' as the grantor's grandfather makes it certain that Waleran III, son of Robert II and grandson of Waleran II, is intended and that he did in fact use the title 'count' in his father's lifetime. It is worth adding that both acts are addressed to Waleran (III)'s officers in Meulan, where it appears from this that he exerted comital authority. After 1204, however, Meulan was taken into the Capetian royal demesne by Philip Augustus and remained in royal hands until the fifteenth century, with Robert II's heirs surviving merely as minor bannerets at Courseulles-sur-Mer (Calvados, cant. Creully), with the surname 'de Mellento' as the only reminder of their comital past. As Professor Crouch has further suggested to me, the witness list to the present charter supplies the names of three men (John de Bosc-Bénard (Eure, cant. Bourgtheroulde), Walter de Flancourt (Eure, cant. Bourghtheroulde) and Richard del Val) all of whom are known to have been in the service or following of Count Robert II in the 1180s and 90s. In A[2], he suggests, the names of the witnesses have been written subsequent to the writing of the main part of the text, in a different colour ink and ignoring the ruled lines already laid out, but I can see no such disjunction and would certainly attribute the writing of text and witness list to the same occasion. The duplicate original now in the British Library is written throughout in a single hand of the late twelfth century, with no disjunction between text and witness list. The seal impression still attached to A[1] is entirely consistent with a date after 1179, and it is worth noticing that the seal, unlike the preamble to the present charter, significantly fails to credit Waleran, here presumed to be Waleran III (d. after 1195), with his title as count. The seal, despite Astle's supposition (above notes to ms. A[1]), is most definitely not the same as that of Count Waleran II attached to BL ms. Harley Charter 45.I.30, which is double-sided, much larger (85mm. in diameter) than the present seal (a mere 60mm. in diameter), and carries an entirely different legend. For further examples of sons adopting comital titles during their fathers' lifetimes, see D. Crouch, *The Image of Aristocracy in Britain, 1000–1300* (London 1992), 68–70.

Gualeranus[a] comes Mellenti bailiuis suis de Mellent et omnibus suis presentibus et futuris salutem. Sciatis me concessisse et in perpetuam elemosinam confirmasse monachis sancte Trinitatis Cantuarie pro amore Dei et beati Thome martiris et pro anima patris mei et antecessorum meorum et mea apud Mell't transitum vini quietum quod ducent ad proprium usum suum, et preter hec consuetudinem in tota terra mea de omnibus que emerint ad usus ipsorum que poterunt iuste facere assecurari sua propria esse, sicut pater meus eis prius concessit et sua carta confirmauit. Test(ibus) Ioh(ann)e de Bosco Bernardi, Gualterio de Florentcurt[b], Ricardo del Val, Ricardo de Barduuile, Baldewino clerico.

[a] Gualeraninus A[2] [b] Gualtero de Frolentcurt A[2]

107. *Notification by Baldwin (II) count of Guînes to all his men of Guînes (Pas-de-Calais) that from love of God and St Thomas and for the souls of himself and his wife and heirs he has pardoned his brothers, the monks of Christ Church Canterbury, from toll and all customs taken in Guînes from travellers.* [1171 X 1206]

A[1] = CCA ms. Chartae Antiquae F133. Endorsed: *cart(a) Baldewin(i) comit(is) de Gisnes de theloneo ibidem* (s.xiii/xiv); *xii.* (s.xiii); various post medieval endorsements. Approx. 200 × 65 + 15mm. Sealed *sur double queue*, single slit, tag and seal impression missing. A[2] = Ibid. F137. In the same hand as A[1]. Endorsed: *Gines* (s.xii/xiii); *carta Baldewini comitis de theloneo de Gisnes* (s.xiii); *xii.* (s.xiii); various post medieval endorsements. Approx. 181 × 77 + 12mm. Sealed *sur double queue*, parchment tag through a single slit, seal impression in dark brown wax, round, equestrian figure facing to the right, legend: S.......DE.........NSIS B = Ibid. Register E fo.37r, s.xiv. C = Ibid. Register A fo.270r (342r), s.xiv. D = Ibid. Chartae Antiquae F111, copy, s.xiv ex.

After the martyrdom of Thomas Becket and before the death of Count Baldwin II, for whom, and for whose particular devotion to St Thomas, by whom he had been knighted *c.*1157 X 1163, who had been received at Guînes during his progress back into England in 1170, and of whom Count Baldwin had subsequently acquired relics used in the foundation of a chapel at La Montoire (Pas-de-Calais, com. Nielles-lès-Ardres), see *Lambert of Ardres, The History of the Counts of Guînes and Lords of Ardres*, trans. L. Shopkow (Philadelphia 2001), 110–11, 120–2, from *MGH Scriptores*, xxiv, 596, 601–2. The witness named Baldwin 'minister of Newington' (i.e. Newington near Hythe, Kent), implies a date before the loss of the count's English estates, apparently unaffected by the events of 1204, whereafter Baldwin II's son, Count Arnold II, was permitted to do homage to King John for his English lands in April 1206 (*RLC*, i, 68). Newington passed to Hubert de Burgh in somewhat murky circumstances, before 1216: N. Vincent, *Peter des Roches* (Cambridge 1996), 323n.; BL ms. Egerton 3789 fo.22v.

Baldewinus comes Gisnensis omnibus hominibus et ministris suis de Gisnes tam presentibus quam postfuturis salutem. Sciatis quod ego comes Baldewinus pro honore Dei et amore beati Thome archiepiscopi Cantuariensis et pretiosi martyris et pro salute anime mee et uxoris mee et heredum meorum perdonaui fratribus meis monachis scilicet conuentui ecclesie Cristi Cantuarie in perpetuum theloneum et omnes consuetudines que exigi solent in Gisnes a transeuntibus. Volo (er)go et precipio ut ipsi et seruientes eorum liberi sint et quieti a me et ab omnibus heredibus meis in perpetuum a theloneo siue pedagio siue omni alia consuetudine, et prohibeo ut nullus hominum vel ministrorum meorum eos pro hac re vexare presumat. Testibus militibus Simone de Echarde, Alelmo de Gisnes, Eustachio de Balingeham, Willelmo de Freitun, Michaele[a] capellano eiusdem comitis, Oliuiro clerico, Baldewino ministro comitis de Niwetune.

[a] Machaele *underlined for correction* A[1], Michaele A[2]

108. *Notification by Walter (of Coutances), archbishop of Rouen, of his grant, for his lifetime, to the prior and monks of Canterbury, out of devotion to St Thomas, of free passage of the Seine at Les Andelys (Eure) for their wine and all their victuals.* [March 1185 X 1189]

A[1] = CCA ms. Chartae Antiquae F134. Endorsed: *ad vitam concedent valet* (s.xiii); *carta Walterii Rothomag'archiepiscopi de quietantia vini* (s.xiii); various post medieval endorsements. Approx. 129 × 92 + 11mm. Sealed *sur double queue*, pinkish brown cords through 2 holes, double-sided seal impression in light brown wax, an archbishop with mitre and crozier, right hand raised in blessing ........OTHOMAGENSIS ARCH<IEPS>...., counterseal, the Agnus Dei with a cross behind, legend partly illegible: S' WALTERI DE CON<STA>NTIS. A[2] = Ibid. F122. Endorsed: *ad tempus concederunt valet* (s.xiii/xiv); *Walt' Rothom' de transitu vini* (s.xiii); various post medieval endorsements. Approx. 126 × 110 + 14mm. Sealed *sur double queue*, pinkish brown cords through 2 holes, double-sided seal impression in light brown wax. Written in the same hand as A[1]. Rubbed and partially illegible. B = Ibid. Register A fo.270r (342r), copy from A[2], s.xiii/xiv. C = Ibid. fo.274r (346r), copy from A[1], s.xiv in. D = Ibid. Register E fos.36v–37r, copy from A[2], s.xiv.

Printed (brief notice from A[1]A[2]) *HMC 5th Report*, appendix, 461.

After the translation of Walter of Coutances from the see of Lincoln to Rouen (March 1185), and before the election of John of Coutances, *alias* John archdeacon of Oxford, as bp of Worcester (January X June 1196), almost certainly before his promotion as dean of Rouen in 1189 (Spear, *Personnel*, 180, 203). As Walter of Coutances, royal clerk, the archbp had previously played a not entirely blameless role in the Becket conflict, before 1170. To this extent, arguably yet another Canterbury charter prompted by a guilty conscience over Becket. For a similar quittance, issued by Walter as archbp of Rouen to the Augustinian canons of Waltham in Essex, themselves founded as a result of Henry II's penance for Becket's murder, see *The Early Charters of Waltham Abbey, 1062–1230*, ed. R. Ransford (Woodbridge 1989), p.44 no.81, and for attempts by the monks of St Augustine's Canterbury to claim quittance from toll at archbp Walter's port of Dieppe, see above no.44.

Uniuersis sancte matris ecclesie filiis ad quos presentes littere peruenerint Walterus Dei gratia Rothom'[a] archiepiscopus in domino salutem. Ad uniuersitatis vestre noticiam volumus peruenire nos diuino intuitu et ob deuotionem et reuerentiam quam habuimus et habemus erga beatum Thomam matirem concessisse dilectis amicis nostris et fratribus .. priori et conuentui sancte Trinitatis Cant' transitum vini sui per Secanam apud Andeleium manerium nostrum et omnium que seruientes predictorum fratrum nostrorum fide firmauerint ad eorumdem victualia pertinere liberum et quietum quoad vixerimus ab omni consuetudine et passagii exactione, saluo scilicet[b] iure successorum nostrorum et salua post decessum nostrum indempnitate Rothom' ecclesie. Ut autem h(ec) nostra concessio quoad vixerimus rata et firma perseueret, eam presenti scripto et sigilli nostri patrocinio dignum duximus confirmare. Test(ibus) Ioh(ann)e Oxeneford' archid(iacono), Elya et Nichol(ao) capellanis nostris, magistro Roberto de Sancto Paterno, magistro Willelmo de Torintona[c], Willelmo de Brueria[d].

[a] Bathom' D [b] scilicet *not in* A[2] [c] Torint' A[2] [d] Bruer' A[2]

109. *Notification by Guy Mauvoisin of his grant to God, the Blessed Mary, St Thomas and the monks of Christ Church Canterbury of 10 sous parisis each year in his rents at Rosny-sur-Seine and Mantes (Yvelines, cant. Mantes) from the passage money still payable on the monks' wine, made for the soul of William Mauvoisin, Guy's father, and his ancestors, mother and brothers, with this gift being placed on St Thomas' tomb on the day of his passion (29 December), pronouncing anathema on all those who might infringe this grant.*

[1190 X 1200]

A = CCA ms. Chartae Antiquae F135. Endorsed: *cart(a) Guidonis Maleuicini de x. sol' Paris' de pedagio suo de Roeni et Madunte* (s.xiii/xiv); *carta Guid......uicini de x. sol........apud Roeni et ....* (s.xiii); various post medieval endorsements. Approx. 176 × 90 + 25mm. Sealed *sur double queue*, 3 slits, tag and seal impression missing. B = Ibid. Register E fo.36r, s.xiv. C = Ibid. Register A fo.269r–v (341r–v), s.xiv.

For Guy lord of Rosny, son of William Mauvoisin fl.1190-1201 and Adelina his wife, see the family tree supplied by Power, *Norman Frontier*, 507 table 20, and cf. N. Civel, *La Fleur de France: les seigneurs d'Ile-de-France au XIIe siècle* (Turnhout 2006), 441. For a similar renunciation by William de Mauvoisin of rights over the ships of the monks of Fécamp on the Seine, see Power, *Norman Frontier*, 95n. Note that Guy specifically does not exempt the monks from all passage money payable in his lands, but merely reduces by 10 sous the sum that would otherwise have been payable in passage money. The use of the letter 'thorn' in the name of the first witness suggests strongly a charter written by an English rather than a French scribe, and note also the grammatical error, in note 'a' below.

Sciant tam presentes quam futuri quod ego Guido Maleuitinus dedi et concessi Deo et beate Marie et sancto Thome martyris[a] monachis ecclesie Cristi Cantuarie ibidem Deo famulantibus decem solidos Parisienses singulis annis in redditibus meis de Roeni et Madunte in passagiis de vino predictorum monachorum in puram elemosinam, et si plus debent, magis soluent, pro anima patris mei Willelmi Maleuicini et antecessorum meorum et pro salute mea et matris mee et fratrum meorum, et hoc donum super tumbam beati Thome martyris in die passionis sue obtuli et sigillo meo proprio confirmaui, et ideo precipio et prohibeo ne aliquis balliuorum meorum et quicumque eam tenuerit predictos monachos aud nuntios eorum decetero permittatis vexari. Testibus his: Aþline matre mee, Huberto de Rosey, Hugoni Croc, Heymardo capellano meo, Geruasio de Hosprenge, Willelmo de Faueriz et multi alii. Si quis vero successorum meorum vel aliquis alius quicumque fuerit hanc donationem meam aud cartam istam infringere voluerit, in eadem dampnatione cum Iuda traditore qui Cristum tradidit deputatus sit. Amen.

^a *sic* A, *recte* martyris et

110. *Notification by Baldwin count of Flanders and Hainault, that the bearers of the present letters, monks of Canterbury, and their envoys and goods, have been taken under the count's safe conduct throughout his lands, requesting that the addressees of these letters offer similar free passage.*

[1191 X 1204, ?September X November 1197]

A = BL ms. Lord Frederick Campbell Charter XXII.4. Endorsed: *littere Bald(uini) com(itis) Flandr' de protectione* (s.xiii); *xx.* (s.xiii); *v. Aspil' 582* (s.xviii, cf. E below). Approx. 140 × 40 + 20mm. Sealed *sur double queue*, parchment tag through a single slit, central portion of double-sided seal impression in white wax, equestrian side with a sword and shield charged with a lion, legend: SIGI..U........E. Counterseal, small round, equestrian figure, legend: ....T HAI..NOI[E+] B = CCA ms. Register E fo.37v, s.xiv. C = Ibid. Register A fo.270v (342r), s.xiv. D = Ibid. Chartae Antiquae F111, copy, s.xiv ex. E = BL ms. Stowe 666 (John Anstis' 'Aspilogia') fo.68r no.582, copy with facsimile drawing of the seal from A made when 'penes Thomas Astle', s.xviii.

Printed (from A) *De Oorkonden der Graven van Vlaanderen (1191 – aanvang 1206)*, ed. W. Prevenier, 3 vols, Recueil des actes des princes belges v (Brussels 1964–71), ii, 157–8 no.69; (brief notice from A) Landon, *Itinerary*, 122.

The donor could be either Baldwin VIII or Baldwin IX, before the latter's elevation as Emperor of Constantinople. Nonetheless, almost certainly issued by Baldwin IX during his recorded pilgrimage to Canterbury in 1197 (Howden, *Chronica*, iv, 24).

Bald(uinus) Flandr' et Hayn' comes omnibus hominibus et amicis suis salutem. Noueritis quod latores presentium, monachos de Cantuaria et nuntios eorum, cum omnibus rebus suis per totam terram et potestatem meam in conductu meo accepi. Inde vos omnes tanquam amicos meos affectuosius rogo ut eos similiter per totam terram, potestatem vestram cum omnibus rebus suis amoris mei intuitu secure conducatis, quia quicquid ipsis feceritis, michi factum sciatis.

111. *Notification by Reginald count of Boulogne and the countess Ida his wife to their men and ministers at Wissant, Boulogne, Nieulay and Calais of their grant, in honour of God and St Thomas, of pardon to their brothers, the monks of Christ at Canterbury, and their messengers and servants, from all toll and custom payable at the four ports above mentioned, whether there be peace or discord between the king of England and the count of Boulogne.*

[1191 X 1214, ?1197 X 1201]

A = BL ms. Lord Frederick Campbell Charter VII.3. Endorsed: *carta Reginaldi comitis Bolonie de quitancia pegagii et omnibus consuetudinibus de Witsando, de Bolonia, de Nwene et de Caleis* (s.xiii); *xxi.* (s.xiii); various post medieval endorsements, including *Asp. n.4* (s.xviii, cf. F below). Approx. 135 × 112 + 13mm. Sealed *sur double queue*, two double-sided seals on parchment tags, both seal impressions in dark green wax. On the left-hand tag, a round equestrian seal with the mounted figure carrying a shield charged with a shield of arms, a barry of six within a bordure, legend: SIGILL' [REI]NALDI [C]O[MI]TIS BOLO[NIE]. Counterseal a shield of arms as above, legend: SECRETU[M REIN]ALDI [CO]MITIS BOLONIE+. Seal on the right-hand tag, vessica shaped, a female figure standing with a hawk or bird on her left wrist, legend: SIGILL'IDE COMITISSE BOLONIE. Counterseal, two interlinked shields, at the top three torteaux, in the lower shield a barry of six, legend lost. B = CCA ms. Chartae Antiquae F102, in an inspeximus by R(oger) abbot of St Augustine's, H(ugh) prior of St Gregory's and R. (rural) dean of Canterbury, damaged and illegible in part, 1264/5. C = Ibid. Register E fo.37v, s.xiv. D = Ibid. Register A fos.270v–271r (342v–343r), s.xiv. E = Ibid. Chartae Antiquae F111, copy, s.xiv ex. F = BL ms. Stowe 665 (John Anstis' 'Aspilogia') fo.77r (p.177) nos 3–4, partial copy with facsimile drawings of the seals from A, then said to be 'penes Thomas Astle', s.xviii.

For Reginald, count of Boulogne in right of his wife with whom he did homage to Philip Augustus in December 1191, in formal alliance with Richard I of England in 1197–8, and again with King John in 1199–1201 and again 1211–14, thereafter a prisoner after the battle of Bouvines, see H. Malo, *Un Grand feudataire: Renaud de Dammartin et la coalition de Bouvines* (Paris 1898), esp. pp.40–1, 55–6, 137ff., at pp.251, 314 no.26 recording a similar remission of toll at Wissant in favour of the monks of St Bertin's at St-Omer. Various of the witnesses to the present charter, including Baldwin de Doudeauville (Pas-de-Calais, cant. Samer), Daniel de Bethencort, seneschal of the count in 1203, and Peter de Caïeu (Pas-de-Calais) occur elsewhere as witnesses to others of Reginald's charters, with Guy Lieschans and Ralph, the count's brother, serving amongst his pledges in the treaty negotiated with King John at Les Andelys in August 1199: Malo, *Renaud de Dammartin*, 264–7 nos 46–7, 270 no.51; *Rot. Chart.*, 30. Several of them also appear in the witness list of a quittance from toll at Wissant granted, apparently at much the same time, by Reginald and Ida to the monks of Bury St Edmunds: BL ms. Harley 625 (Bury Register) fo.230r–v (203r–v) ('Hiis t(estibus): Radulfo fratre comitis, Roberto filio Walteri, Gwydone Leschans, Galfrido fratre eius, Danielle de Betencurt, Willelmo de Fossa, Baldewyno de Asenuilla etc.'). Note the addition of Calais to the list of ports (not in no.97 above), now clearly emerged from its previous embryonic state as the port of Nieulay, and note also the reference to the monks of Canterbury as 'our brothers', suggesting confraternity.

Reginaldus comes Bolonie et Yda comitissa uxor eius omnibus hominibus et ministris suis de Withsando et Bolonia et de Niwene et Caleis tam presentibus quam futuris salutem. Sciatis quod ego comes Reginaldus et Yda comitissa pro honore Dei et beati Thome archiepiscopi Cantuar' gloriosi martyris et pro salute animarum nostrarum et parentum et heredum nostrorum perdonauimus fratribus nostris monachis scilicet conuentui ecclesie Cristi Cantuar' in perpetuum theloneum et omnes consuetudines que exigi solent in Withsando vel Bolonia vel Niwene vel Caleis a transeuntibus. Volumus (er)go et precipimus ut ipsi et nuntii et omnes seruientes eorum liberi sint et quieti a nob(is) et ab omnibus heredibus nostris in perpetuum a theloneo siue pedagio siue omni alia consuetudine, et prohibemus ne aliquis hominum vel ministrorum nostrorum eos pro hac re vexare presumat. Volumus etiam ut donatio ista rata sit semper siue pax siue discordia sit inter regem Anglie et comitem Bolonie. Hiis testibus: Rad(ulpho) fratre comitis, Guidone Leschans, Baldewino de Dudeuilla, Petro de Caeu, Daniele de Betencurt, Baldewino de Esseuilla, Maneserio de Bolonia tunc capellano, Nicholao clerico et multis aliis.

112. *Notification by Peter (of Nemours) bishop of Paris that in his presence Richoldis de Groslay (Val-d'Oise, cant. Montmorency), for the sake of her soul and the soul of Guy her late husband, has granted the monks of St Thomas at Canterbury 5 measures of wine in perpetuity at St-Brice-sous-Forêt (Val-d'Oise, cant. Ecouen).*
March 1212

A[1] = CCA ms. Chartae Antiquae F96. Endorsed: *cart(a) Petri episcopi Parisiens' de dono Richoldis de Groeles de quinque quart' vinee* (s.xiii); *iii.* (s.xiii); various post medieval endorsements. Approx. 185 × 93 + 25mm. Sealed *sur double queue*, pink silk cords through 2 holes, lower half of vessica-shaped seal impression in green wax, obverse the legs of a bishop dressed in pontificals .....ETRI PARISI...., counterseal defaced and illegible. A[2] = Ibid. F97. Endorsed: *cart(a) episcopi Paris' confirm' donum Richolde de Grolay de quinque quart' vinee* (s.xiii); *iii.* (s.xiii); various post medieval endorsements. Approx. 144 × 73 + 22mm. Sealed *sur double queue*, pink, white and green woven cords through 2 holes, vessica-shaped seal impression in green wax, a bishop with crozier in left hand and right hand raised in blessing, legend: SIGILLU' PETRI PARISIENS' EPI+ Counterseal, small round, apparently a portrait bust in profile looking to the left with elaborate head-dress, no inscription. B = CCA ms. Register E fo.36r, s.xiv. C = Ibid. Register A fo.269r (341r), s.xiv.

Printed (from ?A[1], 'ex archiv(is) eccles(ie) Christi Cantuar') T. Madox, *Formulare Anglicanum* (London 1702), 4 no.9; (calendar from A[1]A[2]) *HMC 5th Report*, appendix, 461.

Dated to the fourth year of Bp Peter, and therefore to 1212 rather than 1211.

Petrus[a] Dei gratia Parisien' episcopus omnibus presentes litteras inspecturis salutem in domino. Uniuersitati vestre notum facimus quod, constituta in nostra presentia Richoldis de Groolai[b], pro anima sua et [c]quondam mariti sui Guidonis[c] dedit et concessit in puram et perpetuam elemosinam monachis sancti Thome Cantuariensis[d] quinque quarterios vinee sitos apud Sanctum Bricium. Nos vero ut hec donatio perpetuo perseueret, ad petitionem dicte Richoldis has litteras fieri fecimus et sigilli nostri impressione muniri. Actum anno domini millesimo ducentesimo[e] undecimo, mense Marcio, pontificatus nostri anno quarto.

[a] P. A[2] [b] Grooles A[2] [c-c] G. quondam mariti sui A[2] [d] Cantuarien' A[2] [e] m°.cc°. A[2]

---

113. *Notification by Thomas de St-Valery that for his own soul and the souls of Edelina his wife and his father, mother and ancestors and successors he has granted to the monks of Christ Church Canterbury out of reverence for St Thomas that the monks and their servants may come and go via his port at St-Valery(-sur-Somme) and throughout his land free from all toll, pedage and custom, save when they trade as merchants when they are to pay custom as other merchants do.*   [1191 X 1219]

A = CCA ms. Chartae Antiquae F117. Endorsed: *Th' de Sancto Wal(er)ico de perdonacione telonei in portu de Sancto Walerico* (s.xiii); *ix.* (s.xiii); various post medieval endorsements. Approx. 164 × 92 + 30mm. Sealed *sur double queue*, parchment tag through 3 slits, seal impression, round, green wax, equestrian figure facing to the right with full helmet and a shield charged with one (or possibly two) lion(s) passant, legend ....LERICO. Counterseal, small round, ? a lion. B = Ibid. Register E fo.36v, s.xiv. C = Ibid. Register A fo.269v (341v), s.xiv. D = Ibid. Chartae Antiquae F111, copy, s.xiv ex.

For Thomas de St-Valery, son of Bernard, and his uneasy relationship with the kings of England after 1204, see Power, *Norman Frontier*, 454–5. As 'frater noster' he was commemorated with an obit at Canterbury Cathedral on 5 December: BL ms. Cotton Nero C ix fo.17r, whence Fleming, 'Christchurch's Sisters and Brothers', 147.

Omnibus Cristi fidelibus ad quos presens scriptum peruenerit Thomas de Sancto Walerico salutem. Nouerit uniuersitas vestra quod ego Thom(as) de Sancto Walerico pro salute mea et Edel(ine) uxoris mee et pro salute patris et matris mee et omnium antecessorum et successorum meorum dedi et concessi et hac presenti carta confirmaui Deo et monachis ecclesie Cristi Cant' ob reuerentiam beati martiris Thome quod ipsi et seruientes eorum veniant et redeant in portum meum de Sancto Walerico et per totam terram meam liberi et quieti ab omni exactione telonei et pedagii et consuetudine ad nos pertinente de omnibus que ad necessaria et ad proprios usus eorum pertinuerint. Si tamen predicti monachi vel seruientes eorum more mercatorum aliquod attulerint de partibus transmarinis, reddant aliorum consuetudines mercatorum. Hiis testibus: magistro Ph(ilippo) le Ver, Ingerr(ano) capellan(o), Roberto de Mostellet milite et multis aliis.

114. *Notification by Baldwin (III) count of Guînes, son of Count Arnold (II), that out of love of God and St Thomas and for the souls of himself and his wife and heirs he has pardoned his brothers, the monks of Christ Church Canterbury, from toll and all customs taken from travellers in Guînes.* February 1233

B = CCA ms. Register E fo.37r, s.xiv. C = Ibid. Register A fo.270r (342r), s.xiv. D = Ibid. Chartae Antiquae F111, copy, s.xiv ex.

Coincides with a visit paid by Count Baldwin to England, during which he briefly recovered possession of his family's manor of Newington near Hythe in Kent, and assisted the king against rebels in the Welsh Marches, for which see *CPR 1232–47*, 2, 25; N. Vincent, *Peter des Roches: An Alien in English Politics 1205–1238* (Cambridge 1996), 323, 395 n.141, 406.

Uniuersis sancte matris ecclesie filiis ad quos presens scriptum peruenerit Baldewynus comes de Gisnes filius Arnulphi[a] comitis de Gisnes salutem eternam in domino. Nouerit uniuersitas vestra quod ego Baldewynus comes filius Arnulphi[a] comitis de Gisnes pro honore Dei et amore gloriosi martiris Thome quondam Cantuariens'[b] ecclesie archiepiscopi et pro salute anime mee et uxoris mee et heredum meorum perdonaui fratribus meis monachis, videlicet Cantuariens'[c] ecclesie[d] conuentui, in perpetuum theloneum et omnes consuetudines que exigi solent in Gisnes a transeuntibus. Volo ergo et precipio ut ipsi monachi ecclesie Cristi Cantuarie[b] et eorum seruientes liberi sint et quieti a me et ab omnibus heredibus meis in perpetuum a theloneo et pedagio et omni alia consuetudine que exigi solent[e] a transeuntibus per totum comitatum de Gisnes[f]. Prohibeo etiam ut nullus hominum vel ministrorum meorum predictos monachos vel eorum seruientes vexare presumat in hac parte. In cuius rei testimonium presenti scripto sigillum meum duxi apponendum. Act' anno domini millesimo ducentesimo tricesimo tercio, mense Februario.

[a] Arnulfi CD [b] Cant' C, Cantuar' D [c] Cantuarien' CD [d] D *inserts* Cristi [e] solet CD [f] Gines D

115. *Notification by Matilda countess of Boulogne to her men at Wissant, Boulogne, Nieulay and Calais of her confirmation out of love for God and St Thomas and for the souls of herself and her parents and heirs of all liberties granted by her father and mother (above no.111), namely quittance from toll and customs at Wissant, Boulogne, Nieulay and Calais.*   La Neuville-en-Hez, June 1234

A = CCA ms. Chartae Antiquae F98. Endorsed: *carta Matildis comitisse Bolon' de theloneo de Hwtesand, Boloyne, Niewene et Caleys* (s.xiii); *xxii.* (s.xiii); various post medieval endorsements. Approx. 167 × 85 + 31mm. Sealed *sur double queue*, parchment tag through 3 slits, three quarters of the lower part of a seal impression in natural wax, vessica-shaped, a standing female figure with left arm outstretched holding a bird, legend: ....U..ALTID....SOR'IS....FIL.....EGIS FR, counterseal, small round, a shield or arms, a bar of five points, six fleurs de lys, within a bordure, no inscription.
B = Ibid. F102, in an inspeximus by R(oger) abbot of St Augustine's, H(ugh) prior of St Gregory's and R. (rural) dean of Canterbury, damaged and illegible in part, 1264/5.
C = Ibid. F103, copy, s.xiv ex. D = Ibid. Register E fo.38r, s.xiv. E = Ibid. Register A fo.271r (343r), s.xiv.

As pointed out to me by Daniel Power, the forest of Hez formed part of Matilda's inheritance from the county of Clermont-en-Beuvaisis, so 'Villam Novam in Hez' is more likely to be La Neuville-en-Hez (Oise, cant. Clermont) than a location such as Villeneuve-d'Ascq (Nord) within the ancient county of Boulogne.

Mathildis comitissa Bolon' omnibus hominibus et ministris suis de Witsando et Bolonia et Niwene et Caleis tam presentibus quam futuris salutem. Noueritis quod nos pro honore Dei et beati Thome archiepiscopi Cant' et gloriosi martiris et pro salute anime nostre et parentum et heredum nostrorum volumus et confirmamus omnes libertates illas quas antecessores et pater et mater nostri dederunt et concesserunt monachis et conuentui ecclesie Cristi Cant', scilicet theloneum et consuetudines que exigi solent in Witsando et Bolonia et Niwene et Caleis a transeuntibus. Volumus igitur et precipimus ut ipsi et nuncii et seruientes eorum liberi sint et quieti a nobis et heredibus nostris in perpetuum a thelonio siue pedagio siue omni alia consuetudine, et prohibemus ne aliquis hominum vel ministrorum nostrorum eos pro hac re vexare presumat. Act' apud Villam Nouam in Hez, anno domini m°.cc°. tricesimo quarto, mense Iunio.

116. *Notification by Robert (V) count of the Auvergne and Boulogne to all the men of Wissant, Boulogne, Nieulay and Calais of his grant of quittance from toll and custom.*
Étaples (Pas-de-Calais), August 1267

B = CCA ms. Register E fo.38r, s.xiv in. C = Ibid. Register A fo.271r (343r) s.xiv in. D = Ibid. ms. Chartae Antiquae F103, copy s.xiv ex.

For Robert V, count of Auvergne from 1247 and of Boulogne 1260–d.1277, see *L'Art de vérifier les dates*, 3rd ed., 3 vols (Paris 1783–7), ii, 364–6. For some idea of the exactions charged at Wissant, see *Lit. Cant.*, iii, 387–8 no.51, where, in 1306, Archbishop Robert Winchelsea was charged 40 marks passage money for a single crossing to and from the port.

Robertus comes Aluernie et Bolonie omnibus hominibus et ministris suis de Wythsando^a, Bolonia, Niewene^b et Caleys tam presentibus quam futuris salutem in domino. Noueritis quod nos pro honore Dei et beati Thome archiepiscopi Cantuarie^c et gloriosi martyris et pro salute anime nostre et parentum et heredum nostrorum volumus et confirmamus omnes libertates illas quas antecessores nostri dederunt et concesserunt monachis et conuentui ecclesie Cristi Cantuarie^d, scilicet theloneum et consuetudines que exigi solent in Wythsando^a, Bolonia, Niewene^b et Caleys a transeuntibus. Volumus ergo et precipimus ut ipsi et nuncii et seruientes eorum liberi sint et quieti a nobis et heredibus nostris in perpetuum a theloneo siue pedagio siue omni alia consuetudine, et prohibemus ne aliquis hominum vel ministrorum nostrorum eos pro hac re vexare presumat. Act'^e apud Stepl'as^f anno domini m°.cc°.lxvii°. mense Augusto.

^a Witsando CD ^b Niwene CD ^c Cantuar' D ^d Cant' C, Cantuar' D ^e Actum D ^f Stopl'as C, Staplas D

117. *Notification by Robert (VII) count of Boulogne and the Auvergne to his men at Wissant, Boulogne, Nieulay and Calais confirming, in honour of St Thomas, all liberties granted to the church of Canterbury by his ancestors.*
6 December 1314

A = CCA ms. Chartae Antiquae F142. Endorsed: *carta Rob(erti) fil(ii) ...com(itis) Bolon' et Aluern' de consuetudinibus in Witsand, Niwene et Caleys* (s.xiv); various post medieval endorsements. Approx. 236 × 67 + 17mm. Sealed *sur double queue*, parchment tag through a single slit, seal impression, lower half only, in dark green wax, round, equestrian with sword in right hand, legend illegible. Counterseal, round, ?a shield of arms, now illegible. Damaged, illegible letters shown within brackets below, restored from B. B = Ibid. Register E fo.35v, s.xiv. C = Ibid. Register L fo.97v (93v), s.xiv med. D = BL ms. Stowe 924 fo.89v (p.184), copy made for Dering from B, s.xvii.

Issued by Robert VII (*c*.1314–*c*.1326) in the year that he succeeded as count.

Robertus comes Bolognie et Aluernie omnibus hominibus et ministris nostris de Wissando, Bolognia, Niwene et Caleis tam presentibus <quam futuris> salutem in domino. Noueritis quod nos pro honore Dei et beati Thome archiepiscopi Cantuarie et gloriosi martiris et pro salute <anime> nostre et parentum et her<edum nostrorum> volumus et confirmamus omnes libertates illas quas antecessores nostri dederunt <et con>cesserunt monachis et <conuentui ecclesie> Cristi Cantuarie, scilicet theloneum et consuetudines que exig<i solent> in Wissando, Bolognia, Niwene et Caleis a transeuntibus. Volumus ergo et precipimus ut ipsi et nuncii et seruientes eorum liberi sint et quieti a nobis et heredibus nostris in perpetuum in dictis locis a theloneo, pedagio et consuetudinibus supradictis, et prohibemus ne aliquis hominum vel ministrorum nostrorum eos pro hac re vexare presumat. In cuius rei testimonium sigillum nostrum presentibus litteris duximus apponendum. Datum anno domini millesimo trecentesimo quatuordecimo, die veneris in festo beati Nicholay hyemal(is).

118. *Notification by Robert (VII) count of Boulogne and the Auvergne in similar terms to no.117.*   8 September 1317

B = CCA ms. Register E fo.35v, s.xiv med. C = Ibid. ms. Register A fo.268v (340v), s.xiv. D = Ibid. Register L fo.97v (93v), s.xiv med. E = Ibid. ms. Chartae Antiquae F103, copy, s.xiv ex.

Apart from the date, identical to above no.117.

Robertus comes Boloignie et Aluernie omnibus hominibus et ministris nostris de Wyssando, Boloignia, Niwene[a] et Caleys[b] tam presentibus quam futuris salutem in domino. Noueritis quod nos pro honore[c] Dei et beati Thome archiepiscopi Cant'[d] et gloriosi martiris et pro salute anime nostre et parentum et heredum nostrorum volumus et confirmamus omnes libertates illas quas antecessores nostri dederunt et concesserunt monachis et conuentui ecclesie Cristi Cant'[d], scilicet theloneum et consuetudines que exigi solent in Wissando[e], Boloignia, Niwene et Caleys[b] a transeuntibus. Volumus ergo et precipimus ut ipsi et nuncii et seruientes eorum liberi sint et quieti a nobis et heredibus nostris imperpetuum in dictis locis a theloneo, pedagio et consuetudinibus supradictis, et prohibemus ne aliquis hominum vel ministrorum nostrorum[f] eos pro hac re vexare presumat. In cuius rei testimonium sigillum nostrum presentibus litteris duximus apponend(um). Dat' anno domini m.ccc. septimodecimo, die Iouis in festo Natiuitat(is) beate Marie virginis.

[a] Niwenene D [b] Kaleys CD [c] honore BD, amore C [d] Cantuar' CD [e] Witsando CD [f] nostrorum *not in* C

119. *Notification by A(maury) (III) count of Evreux that out of love of God and St Thomas he has granted the monks of Christ Church Canterbury an annual rent of one mark to participate in the benefits of the church payable within the octave of St Andrew.*

[1181 X 1193]

A = CCA ms. Chartae Antiquae C172. Endorsed: *de marca comitis d(e) Ebroicarum* (s.xiii); various post medieval endorsements. Approx. 180 × 65 + 23mm. Sealed *sur double queue*, 3 slits, tag and seal impression missing. B = Ibid. Register H fo.34v, s.xiii med.

The present charter must have been issued by Amaury III count of Evreux, rather than his son, Amaury IV, since, following Amaury III's death on the Third Crusade, Amaury IV remained a minor in custody until the fall of Evreux to the French in 1199: Power, *Norman Frontier*, 63–4, 228–31.

<A. comes Ebroi>carum omnibus Cristi fidelibus salutem. Sciatis me pro amore Dei et beati martiris Th(ome) dedisse <monachis> ecclesie Cristi Cant' in perpetuam elemosinam marcam unam argenti annuatim reddendam infra oct(abas) s(ancti) Andree quam mittam eis per seruientem meum pro eiusdem ecclesie beneficiorum participatione et pro salute anime mee et omnium parentum meorum et hoc carta confirmaui. Testibus his: Gisleberto capellano, Gileb(erto) de Landes, Euerard(o) de Tremlega, Guaklino de Aprileo.

120. *Notification by Mabel (of Gloucester) countess of Evreux, and Amaury her son, of their grant to God and St Thomas of an annual rent of one mark from their mill of 'Goseham' at Marlow to pay for a light at St Thomas' tomb.*

[1187 X 1200]

A = CCA ms. Chartae Antiquae M261. Endorsed: *carta Mabilie comitisse de Euereus de marca arg(enti) recipiend'* (s.xiii) *de molendino de Merlaue ad luminar' s(ancti) Thom(e)* (s.xiii/xiv); *diuers'* (s.xiii); various post medieval endorsements. Approx. 204 × 41 + 14mm. Sealed *sur double queue*. Tag through a single slit, vessica-shaped seal impression in natural wax varnished brown: a woman standing in full length with a bird on her left hand and her right hand holding a flower. Legend mostly illegible: ....S... ROICA. Back of the seal repaired with modern plaster of Paris. B = Ibid. Register B fo.402r, s. C = Ibid. Register H fo.34v, s.xiii ex.

Apparently issued by Mabel after the death of Count Amaury III, which occured at some point between 1187 and 1193, during the Third Crusade, whereafter her son, Amaury IV, remained a minor until the fall of Evreux to the French in 1199 (Power, *Norman Frontier*, 63–4, 230). The countess Mabel, as 'Mabilia comitissa Ebroicens' soror et be(nefactrix) nostra', was commemorated at Christ Church Canterbury with an obit on 1 November: BL ms. Cotton Nero C ix fo.15r, whence Fleming, 'Christchurch's

Sisters and Brothers', 144.

Sciant presentes et futuri quod ego Mabilia comitissa de Euereus et Amauricus filius meus dedimus et concessimus et presenti carta confirmauimus in liberam et perpetuam elemosinam Deo et sancto Thome martiri ad inueniendum luminare coram predicto martire unam marcam argenti annuatim de molendino nostro de Goseham in Merlaue pro salute nostra et omnium predecessorum nostrorum, et ut h(ec) nostra donatio rata in posterum et stabilis permaneat eam presenti scripto et sigilli nostri appositione confirmauimus. Hiis testibus: Nicolao de Tokeuill', Iohanne de Wailun, Hug(one) filio Gregorii, Turstano de Crascherne, Hug(one) de Breinmustier, Ric(ardo) de Lintot, Rob(erto) de Beauchamp, Walt(ero) de Boseboc, Rad(ulfo) Angl(ico), Rad(ulfo) pistore et multis aliis.

121. *Notification by A(maury IV) count of Evreux of his grant to God and St Thomas and the church of Canterbury of an annual rent of one mark which A(maury) his father granted and the countess M(abel) his mother confirmed from the mill of 'Goseham' at Marlow (Buckinghamshire) to pay for lights at St Thomas' tomb.*
[1199 X 1213]

B = CCA ms. Register H fo.34v, s.iii med. C = Oxford, Bodleian Library ms. Dodsworth 90 fo.113r, copy by Dodsworth from a lost original, with drawing of a vessica-shaped seal impression charged with a shield, bendy, legend: +SIGILLUM AMERICI COM[ITIS], s.xvii.

After Amaury IV achieved his majority, and before his death in 1213, for all of which period Amaury was effectively exiled from Evreux itself, for a time being recognized as earl of Gloucester by virtue of his descent from his mother, Mabel of Gloucester. Cf. T. Madox, *Formulare Anglicanum* (London 1702), 184 no.303 for a grant by Amaury IV to Jordan Dimidiofranceiso of land in Marlow ('ex autogr(apho) in arch(ivis) S(ancti) Petri Westmon'), noting a green wax seal and witnesses named William de Hesteland 'my steward', G. de Autuil, W. de Wilekers, R. clerico, G. camerario meo, R. Revel, R. de Perepont, R. de Gurneio and eight others.

A(imericus) comes Ebroicarum omnibus hominibus suis tam Normannicis quam Anglicis salutem. Sciatis me concessisse et hac carta mea confirmasse in perpetuam elemosinam Deo et sancto T(home) martyri Cant'ᵃ ecclesie ad inueniendum luminare coram predicto martyre unam marcam argenti annuatim quam A(imericus) comes Ebroicarum pater meus ei dedit et M(abel) comitissa mater mea ei concessit pro salute nostra et omnium predecessorum nostrorum ad diem sancti Michael(is) percipiendam de molendino meo de Goseham apud Marlaue[b], et ut hec nostra concessio et confirmatio rata et stabilis in posterum[c] permaneat, eam presenti scripto et sigilli mei appositione confirmaui[d]. Testibus hiis[e]: Willelmo de Estillant, Reginaldo de Autoil, Willelmo Puintel, Willelmo de Wilekers, Reginaldo de Bayllol, Rogero clerico et multis aliis.

[a] Cantuariensis [b] iuxta Merlaue [c] in posterum B, imperpetuum C [d] roboraui C [e] B *ends here, witnesses supplied from* C

INDEX OF MANUSCRIPT SOURCES

An asterix * denotes an original charter published above.
Numbers in bold italics denote texts published in full above.

Aylesbury, Buckinghamshire Record Office ms. AR. 38/62/1: *71*

Birmingham Central Reference Library ms. Wingfield-Digby A1/6: *38**

Caen, Archives départementales de Calvados 386 Edt 1: *3*; F4068: *66–7*; H322: *66**, *67C**

Cambridge, University Library ms. Hengrave Hall 117: *68**

Canterbury Cathedral Archives mss.

> Chartae Antiquae C172: *119**; C174: *102**; C210: *101**; C1277: *103*; F90: *77**;
> F91: *77**; F92: *78**; F93: *92**; F94: *79**; F95: *93**; F96: *112**; F97: *112**; F98:
> *115**; F99: *80**; F100: *80*; F101: *80*; F102: *96–7, 111, 115*; F103: *115–16, 118*;
> F108: *77–8, 89*; F109: *77–8, 89*; F110: *77–8, 89*; F111: *91–100, 103–7, 110–11,
> 113–14*; F112: *77–82, 88*; F113: *77–8, 89*; F115: *100**; F116: *103**; F117: *113**;
> F118: *99**; F119: *103**; F120: *100**; F121: *104**; F122: *108**; F124: *105**; F125:
> *89*; F126: *89*; F127: *89*; F129: *96**; F130: *94**; F131: *104**; F132: *97**; F133:
> *107**; F134: *108**; F135: *109**; F136: *100**; F137: *107**; F138: *91**; F139: *106**;
> F140: *103**; F142: *117**; F145/1: *89**; F145/2–5: 89n.; F146: *89**; F147: *89*;
> F148: 89n.; F149: *77, 79–82, 88–9*; F157: *89*; F171: *95**; M261: *120**
> Register A: *77–88, 90–106, 108*; Register E: *77–82, 88, 91–108*; Register B: *120*;
> Register H: *119–21*; Register L: *77–8, 80, 88, 97, 117–18*

Dieppe, Bibliothèque Municipale ms. 45: *2*

Eton College Records ECR 18/4: *49**; ECR 27/3: *6**

Evreux, Archives départementales de l'Eure H1418: *58*; H1437: *57, 59*

London, British Library

> Additional Manuscripts 14291: *34*; 22641: *81*; 24319: *49*
> Additional Charters 9810: *31**; 11352: *57*; 11353: *60*; 15278: *65**; 15480: *78**;
> 15481: *82**; 15482: *88**; 16200: *98**; 16355: *81**; 16369: *89*; 17839: *69**;
> 17841: *70**; 19803: *25**; 20236: *43**; 21175: *37**; 47381: *50**; 47382: *51**;
> 47383: *52–3*; 47385: *54**; 47386: *55**; 47387: *56**; 47388: *58**; 47389: *61**;
> 47392: *63**; 47420; *53*; 47998: *60**; 47999: *60*; 48002: *62**; 67578: *73**; 67579:
> *74**; 67582: *75**
> Cotton Manuscripts Julius D ii: *44*; Claudius D xi: *45*; Cleopatra A vii: *46*
> Cotton Charters XI.35: *37**; XVI.47: *81**; Vitellius B.xiii (lost): *97*
> Harley Manuscripts 85: *4, 5*; 1436: *48*; 1756: *48*
> Harley Charter 45.C.9: *42**

Lansdowne Manuscript 203: *41*

Lord Frederick Campbell Charters VII.3: *111**; XXII.1: *105**; XXII.3: *106**; XXII. 4: *110**

Stowe Manuscripts 665: *105, 111*; 666: *106, 110*; 924: *44, 77, 117*

London, College of Arms ms. Vincent 59: *40*

London, The National Archives

    C 47/12/6 no.14: *6*; C 52/1: *4*; C 52/10: *6*; C 52/26: *4, 5*; C 64/3: *57*; C 64/12: *7–9*; C 64/13: *10*; C 64/15: *1–3*

    DL 25/199: *19**; DL 25/200: *21**; DL 25/201: *20**; DL 25/202: *22**; DL 25/532: *24**; DL 25/722: *18**; DL 27/101: *27**; DL 27/254: *15**; DL 27/259: *17**; DL 27/260: *16**; DL 27/296: *23**; DL 36/1/152: *26**; DL 42/2: *17, 26–7*

    E 32/199: *11*; E 40/15643: *12**; E 210/10188: *13**

    PRO 31/8/140B part 2: *64*

    SC 1/11 no.89: *28**; SC 1/20 nos 124–124A: *32*, 33**

Manchester, John Rylands Library Beaumont Charters 4: *72**; 43: *71**

Northampton, Northamptonshire Record Office mss. Brudenell-Bruce D.v.10: *47*; Finch-Hatton 170: *81*

Nottingham University Archives Mi D 3317: *35**; Mi D 4825: *36**; Mi D 4826: *36**

Oxford, Bodleian Library mss. Dodsworth 90: *40, 121*; Dugdale 18: *41*

Paris, Archives nationales

    J461 no.9: 81n.; J461 no.22[15]: 81n.; J655 no.32: *81–2*; JJ46: *2*; JJ155: *2*; JJ61: *88*; S4889[b]: *8*

Paris, Bibliothèque nationale mss.

    Latin 10063: *66*; nouvelles acquisitions latines 1428: *71–6;* françaises 26476: *8;* Bréquigny 76: *78*; Moreau 625: *78*; Moreau 630: *7–9*; Moreau 631: *1, 2, 10*; Moreau 673: *3*

Rouen, Archives départementales de la Seine-Maritime

    G851: *2*; G8685: *30*; 2H464: *2**; 7H1: *40*; 7H51: *14**; J294: *29*, 30**; Untraced: *2*

Rouen, Bibliothèque Municipale ms. 1224: *70*

Saint-Pierre de Semilly, Marquis de Mathan mss. Lenoir 3: *8*; 69: *1, 3, 8, 9, 57*; 73: *3*; 76: *8*

Stafford, Staffordshire Record Office ms. D1744/73: *40*

Taunton, Somerset Record Office DD/WO Box 10 Bundle 3: *39**

Windsor, St George's Chapel Muniments XI.G.28: *26*

INDEX
OF PERSONS AND PLACES

The Introduction to the present edition is indexed below by page (p./pp,) and footnote (n./nn.) number(s). The Latin texts are indexed by piece number(s) (no./nos). As anyone who has ever dealt with French place-names will be aware, there are many pitfalls on the French onomastic highway. Where possible below, and relying here upon a combination of the internet listings of communes and the best of the local dictionnaires topographiques, I have attempted to assign modern equivalents, specifying département, canton (or where a place named is itself a canton, arrondissement), and commune. English place-names are assigned to their pre-1974 counties, even in instances (such as Bristol, not a member of Gloucestershire since 1373) where some degree of localization may be helpful to readers unfamiliar with English topography. Capital letter 'W' signifies appearance as a witness.

INDEX OF SUBJECTS

What follows is a summary list, indexing only the Latin texts above, here listed by item number.

THE

PIPE ROLL SOCIETY

Established 1883

FOR THE PUBLICATION OF THE
GREAT ROLLS OF THE EXCHEQUER

COMMONLY CALLED

THE PIPE ROLLS

Annual Subscription due 1 June

Individual Member £10 $25 €20 Institutional Member £15 $40 €30

President
Professor SIR JAMES HOLT

Chairman of Council
Dr. J. R. MADDICOTT

Council

Professor D. A. CARPENTER
Dr D. CROOK
Dr H. DOHERTY
Dr M. HAGGER
Professor C. HARPER-BILL
Dr A. JOBSON
Dr N. KARN

Professor B. R. KEMP
Dr R. MORTIMER
Dr J. NELSON
Professor W. M. ORMROD
Professor R. C. STACEY
Dr B. L. WILD

Hon. Auditor
J. D. CANTWELL, esq.
The National Archives, Ruskin Avenue, Kew, TW9 4DU

Hon. Treasurer
Professor P. A. BRAND
All Souls College, Oxford, OX1 4AL

Hon. General Editors
Dr P. DRYBURGH
Borthwick Institute for Archives, York
Dr L. WILKINSON
Canterbury, Christ Church University

Hon. Secretary
Professor N. VINCENT
University of East Anglia

Website
www.piperollsociety.co.uk

LIST OF MEMBERS

Members of Council and Officers of the Society are starred

CANADA
Davies, A., Esq., 108 Church Street, PO Box 237, Pugwash, Nova Scotia, Bok ILO.

FRANCE
Dufour, Professeur J., 72 Avenue Anatole France, 92700 Colombes.
Lemaitre, G., Esq., La Gare, 76780, Nolleval.
Moitrel, Ms P., 21 Rue Pierre Renaudel, 76500 Elbeuf.

GERMANY
Jenks, Dr S., Privat, Vacher Str., 252, 90768, Fuerth.

ISRAEL
Rokeah, Dr Z., 2/2 Prof. Pickard Street, Har Homa, Jerusalem, Israel 93126.

JAPAN
Asaji, Professor K., 5-35-14 Senriyama-Nishi, Suita, Osaka 565-0851.
Fukuda, Professor M., Hama 3-8-30-105, Naka-KU, Okayama-shi 703-8256.
Morioka, K., Esq., 3-12-4, Sanno, Ota-ku, Tokyo.

TURKEY
Latimer, Dr P., Department of History, IISBF, Bilkent University, 06533 Bilkent, Ankara.

UNITED KINGDOM
Aird, W., Esq., 255 Dalkeith Road, Edinburgh EH16 5JS.
Aitkenhead, R. M., Esq., 42 Dunkeld Road, Talbots Wood, Bournemouth, Dorset BH3 7EW.
Barratt, Dr N., 34 Revere Way, Epsom, Surrey KY19 9RQ.
Bartlett, Professor R. J., Department of Medieval History, University of St. Andrews, St. Andrews, Fife, Scotland KY16 9AL.
Bates, Professor D., 2, Ivy Court, Sleaford Street, Cambridge CB1 2NX.
Baxter, Dr Stephen., Reader in Medieval History, History Department, Kings College, London WC2R 2LS.
Beacham, M. J. A., Esq., 24 Arle Road, Cheltenham, Gloucestershire GL51 8JX.
Bellamy, D., Esq., Homestead Lodge, Wigsley Road, Harby, Nottinghamshire NG23 7EF.
Bennett, Dr N. H., Esq., Hawthorn House, Main Street, Nocton, Lincoln LN4 2BH.
Berg, Ms. M., 5 Orchard Street, Canterbury, Kent CT2 8AP.
Beun, S., Esq., 24 Ferndale Road, Hove, East Sussex BN3 6EU.
*Brand, Professor P. A., 155 Kennington Road, London SE11.
Britnell, Professor R. H., Department of Economic History, University of Durham, 23–26 Old Elvet, Durham DH1 3HY.
Brocklesby, R., Esq., The Elms, North Eastern Road, Thorne, Doncaster, Yorkshire DN8 4AS.
Brown, Dr G. P. A., St. John's Jerusalem, Main Road, Sutton-at-Hone, Dartford, Kent DA4 9HQ.
Brown, Mrs V., Friar's Lodge, 108 Hardwick Lane, Bury St. Edmunds, Suffolk IP33 2RA.
Burn, N., 20 Egerton Road, Lincoln LN2 4PJ.
Butt, R., Esq., 1 Sawyer's Close, Chilcompton, Bath, BA3 4PB.
*Carpenter, Professor D. A., 101 Langton Way, Blackheath, London SE3.
Carpenter, D., Esq., 40 Grovelands Road, Risinghurst, Oxford OX3 8HZ.
Cassidy, R., Esq., 37, Finsen Road, London SE5 9AX.
Cawley, C., Esq., Flat 44, 73 Upper Richmond Road, London SW15 2SR.
Chambers, A., Esq., 20 Mill View Gardens, Croyden CR0 5HW.
Channer, R., 252 Buckhurst Way, Buckhurst Hill, Essex IG9 6JG.

CHURCH, Professor S. D., School of History, University of East Anglia, Norwich, Norfolk NR4 7TJ.

CLOUGH, G., Esq., Little Beckams, The Green, Chiddingfold, Surrey GU8 4QA.

COCKER, M., Esq., 179 Bredhurst Road, Gillingham, Kent ME8 0QU.

Coss, Professor P. R., 5 Allen Close, College Green, Old St. Mellons, Cardiff CF3 9DH.

Cox, Professor A. D., Wensley Hall, Wensley, Matlock, Derbyshire DE4 2LL.

CROCKFORD, Dr J. E., 39 Chester Court, Lomund Grove, London SE5 7HS.

*CROOK, Dr D., 3 St Andrews, Grantham, Lincolnshire NG31 9PE.

CROOK, Mrs F. R., 3 St Andrews, Grantham, Lincolnshire NG31 9PE.

CROUCH, Professor D. B., Department of History, University of Hull, Hull HU6 7RX.

CURK, J., Esq., Wolfson College, Oxford OX2 6UD.

DAVIDSON, Dr P. J., Stow House, Daisy Green Lane, Wickham Skeith, Eye, Suffolk IP23 8NB.

DEVILLE, Sir Oscar, C.B.E., Bexton Cottage, 18 Pound Lane, Sonning, Berkshire RG4 0XE.

*DOHERTY, Dr H., School of History, University of East Anglia, Norwich NR4 7TJ.

*DRYBURGH, Dr P., Borthwick Institute for Archives, University of York, Heslington, York YO10 5DD.

DYER, Professor C. C., Centre for English Local History, University of Leicester, Marc Fitch House, 5 Salisbury Road, Leicester LE1 7QR.

EALES, Dr R. G., Bourne Lodge, Bridge Hill, Bridge, Canterbury, CT4 5AS.

EVERARD, Dr J., Fitzwilliam College, Cambridge CB3 0DC.

FINN, C., Brownacres, Green Lane, Grantham, NG31 9PP.

FITZGERALD, Ms C., 40 Ringford Road, London SW18 1RR.

FLEMING, F. J., Esq., 4 Vine Court Road, Sevenoaks, Kent TN13 3UU.

FOSTER, A., Esq 26 Alne Terrace, York YO10 5AW.

FRECKNALL HUGHES, Dr J., Professor of Accounting, The Open University Business School, Walton Hall, Milton Keynes MK7 6AA.

GALLAGHER, E. J., Esq., 119 Franklin Road, Harrogate, North Yorkshire HG1 5EN.

GARNETT, Dr G. S., St. Hugh's College, Oxford.

GOACHER, Ms D., The Cottage, Little Buckland Farm, Buckland Lane, Maidstone, Kent ME16 0BH.

GOLOB, Dr P. E., 15 Chepstow Villas, London W11 3DZ.

GREEN, Professor J. A., School of History and Classics, University of Edinburgh, William Robertson Building, 50 George Square, Edinburgh EH8 9JY.

GREER, R., Esq., 4 Kensington Park Gardens, London W11 3HB.

*HAGGER, Dr M., Esq., University of Bangor, Wales.

*HARPER-BILL, Professor C., 16 Cusack Close, Strawberry Hill, Twickenham, Middlesex.

HARRINGTON, D., Esq., Ashton Lodge, Church Road, Lyminge, Folkstone Kent CT18 8JA.

HARTLAND, Dr B., History Department, KCL, Strand, London.

HARVEY, Miss B. F., 6 Richie Court, 380 Banbury Road, Oxford OX2 7PW.

HASKELL, M. A., 168 Broughton Hall Road, Broughton, Nr Cheshire, Flintshire CH4 0QN.

HAWES, T. L. M., Esq., 8 Keswick Road, Cringleford, Norwich, Norfolk NR4 6UG.

HAYWARD, J. M., Esq., 12 Preston Avenue, Highams Park, London E4 9NL.

HEGARTY, His Honour Judge T. B., 18, Clifton Park Road, Davenport Road, Stockport, Cheshire SK2 6LA.

HOLDSWORTH, Professor C. J., University of Exeter, Exeter EX4 4QJ.

*HOLT, Professor Sir James, Fitzwilliam College, Cambridge CB3 0DG.

HORLER-UNDERWOOD, T., Esq., 31 Fennel Drive, Bradleystoke, Bristol BS32 0BX.

HUDSON, Professor J. G. H., Department of Medieval History, University of St. Andrews, St. Andrews, Fife, Scotland KY16 9AL.

HUSCROFT, Dr R., Westminster School, Little Dean's Yard, London SW1P 3PF.

ISPIR, C., Esq., Flat 168, Therese House, 29-30 Glasshouse Yard, London EC1A 4JL.

JENKINS, R., Esq., 16 Eagleswell Road, Boverton, Llantwit Major, Vale of Glamorgan CF61 1UF.

JOHNSON, D. A., Esq., William Salt Library, Eastgate Street, Stafford.

JOHNSON, Dr D., St Peter's College, Oxford OX1 2DL.

*KARN, Dr N., School of Humanities, University of Southampton, Avenue Campus, Southampton SO17 1BF.

KEATS-ROHAN, Dr K. S. B., The Old Plough, 16 St John's Road, Wallingford OX10 9AD.

*KEMP, Professor B. R., Department of History, University of Reading, Whiteknights, Reading RG6 2AA.

KING, Professor E. J., 84 Knowle Lane, Sheffield, Yorkshire S11 9SJ.

KNIGHT, Dr G. A., Woburn House, Holmgate Road, Clay Cross, Chesterfield, Derbys S45 9QE.

LANSLEY, D., 41 Whitecross Street, Barton on Humber, DN18 5EU.

LEWIS, P. N., Esq., 12 Curling Pond Court, Cupar, Fife, Scotland KY15 4UD.

LOUD, Professor G. A., School of History, University of Leeds, Leeds LS2 9JT.

McDONNELL, P., Esq., 23, Babington Road, Dagenham, Essex RM8 2 XP.

McKENNA, Mrs C., 18 Halstead Road, London N21 3EH.

*MADDICOTT, Dr J. R. L., Exeter College, Oxford OX1 3DP.

*MORTIMER, Dr R., 61 Church Road, Gurnard, Cowes, Isle of Wight PO31 8JP.

*NELSON, Dr J., The National Archives, Ruskin Avenue, Kew, Surrey TW9 4DU.

NEWHAM, T. M., Vine Cottage, Chapel Lane, Ludborough, Lincs. DN36 5SJ.

NICOL, Mrs A., Hope Cottage, 14 Wood Lane, London N6 5UB.

NISBET, Mr M., 2 Millground Cottages, St Mary Well Steet, Beaminster, Dorset DT8 3LY.

OGIER, Dr D., Island Record Office, St Barnabus, Cornet Street, St Peter Port, Guernsey GY1 1LF.

*ORMROD, Professor W. M., Centre for Medieval Studies, University of York, King's Manor, York YO1 7EP.

OSBORNE, Miss S., Principal Library Assistant, Acquisitions Services (Serials), Collections and Resource Department, Bodleian Library, Osney One Building, Osney Mead, Oxford OX2 0EW.

PHILLIPS, G. I., Esq., Cairns House, 46 Colegrave Street, Lincoln LN5 8DR.

POTTER, L., Esq., National Trust, East of England Regional Office, Westley Bottom, Bury St Edmunds, Suffolk IP33 3WD.

POWER, Professor D., Department of History, University of Swansea, Singleton Park, Swansea AS2 8PP.

PRESTWICH, Professor M. C., Department of Medieval History, 43/46 North Bailey, Durham DH1 3EX.

RAY, Dr M., Esq., 24 Brangwyn Drive, Brighton, Sussex BN1 8XD.

RIDGEWAY, Dr H. W., History Department, Sherborne School, Abbey Road, Sherborne, Dorset DT9 3AP.

ROFFE, D., Esq., 31 Moody Street, Congleton, Cheshire CW12 4AN.

SABAPATHY, Dr J., Department of History, University College London, Gower Street, London, WC1E 6BT.

SHARPE, Professor R., Faculty of Modern History, George Street, Oxford OX1 2RL.

SIMS, J. J., Esq., 7 Leys Gardens, Newbury, Berkshire RG14 1HX.

SLADE, Mrs M. A., 28 Holmes Road, Reading RG6 7BH.

SMITH, T., Esq., Rowan House, Mayfield House, Rotherfield, East Sussex TN6 3LS.

SPENCER, A., Esq., Flat 2, Leckhampton House, 37 Grange Road, Cambridge CB3 9BJ.

STACEY, Dr N. E., Dyrham Park, near Chippenham, Wiltshire SN14 8ER.

STEWART, Dr S. M., 23 Tweedbank Ley, Inner Leithen, Peeblesshire EN44 6PE.

STEWART PARKER, W., Esq., Timberlee, Lyncombe Vale Road, Bath BA2 4LS.

SUMMERSON, Dr H. R. T., 40B, Compton Road, London N1 2PB.

TALBOT, T. R., Esq., 9 Sadler Road, St Albans, Herts AL1 2BL.

THOMPSON, Dr B. J., Somerville College, Oxford OX2 6HD.

THOMPSON, Ms. K., 43 St Andrew's Road, Brincliffe, Sheffield S11 9AC.

THOMPSON, Professor P. J., 3 Greystoke Close, Berkhamsted, Hertfordshire HP4 3JJ.

THORNTON, Dr C., VCH Essex, Department of History, University of Essex, Wivenhoe Park, Colchester, Essex CO4 3SQ.

TILLEY, C., Esq., 135 Spencer Road, Isleworth, Middlesex TW7 4BW.

VAN HOUTS, E., 7 Water Street, Cambridge, Cambridgeshire CB4 1NZ.

VEACH, C., Esq., Department of History, University of Hull, Hull HU6 7RX.

*VINCENT, Professor N. C., School of History, University of East Anglia, Norwich, Norfolk NR4 7TJ.

WEBB, Mr C., Cold Arbor, Coldharbour Road, Pyrford, Surrey GU22 8SJ.
WEBSTER, P., Esq., 8 Cefn Coed, Cyncoed, Cardiff CF23 6HE.
WHITE, Professor G. J., 58 Cross Green, Upton, Chester CH2 1QR.
WHITTOW, M., Esq., Corpus Christi College, Oxford OX1.
*WILD, Dr B., Leighurst, Idminston Road, Porton, Salisbury, Wiltshire SP4 0LD.
*WILKINSON, Dr L., Canterbury Christ Church University, Canterbury, Kent.
WILL, Miss E. H., 23 St Ruald's Close, Wallingford, Oxfordshire OX10 0XE.
WOOLGAR, Professor C. M., 16 Stinchar Drive, Badgers Copse, Chandlers Ford, Eastleigh, Hampshire SO5 3QH.

UNITED STATES

AMT, Professor E. M., Hood College, 401 Rosemont Avenue, Frederick, Maryland 21701.
ARNOLD, Judge, M. S., PO Box 2060, Little Rock, Arkansas 72203.
BISSON, Professor T. N., 708 Widener Library, Harvard University, Cambridge, Massachusetts 02138.
BRUTHER, Ms B. J., 3008 B Ela Lago North Drive, Indianapolis, IN 46227-4008.
BURDEN, C., Esq., 473 West End Avenue, Apartment 14-C, New York 10024.
DEMPSEY, J. G., Esq., 3325 Lamarque Drive, Cincinnati, Ohio 45236.
GREENE, D., PO Box 398, Demorest GA 30535-0398, USA.
HELMHOLZ, Professor R. H., University of Chicago Law School, 1111 East 60th Street, Chicago, Illinois 60637.
HILL, K. D., Esq., 1505 Burnett Avenue, Ames, Indiana 50010.
*JOBSON, Dr A., 1012 Everglades Drive, Pacifica, California 94044.
LIGHTFOOT, Esq., K., 56 W. Ferry Street, New Hope, PA 18938
LOENGARD, Dr J. S., 75 Old Army Road, Bernardsville, New Jersey 07924.
MASSCHAELE, J., Esq., Department of History, Rutgers University, 16 Seminary Place, New Brunswick, New Jersey 08903-1108.
MORTORFF, Ms D., 7910 Balboa Road, Atascadero, California 93422.
PATTERSON, Professor R. B., History Department, University of South Carolina, Columbia, South Carolina 29208.
POINDEXTER, Ms J. D., 1413 Winslow Lane, Madison, Wisconsin 53711-3739.
SMITH, N., 1232 Villa Lane, Unit C, Charlottesville, VA 22903, USA.
*STACEY, Professor R. C., Esq., Department of History, University of Washington, Seattle, Washington 98195.
TATE, J., 3315 Daniel Avenue, Dallas, TX 75205, USA.
TURNER, Professor R. V., 842 Santa Rosa Drive, Tallahassee, Florida 32301-5641.
WAUGH, Professor S. L., Department of History, University of California, 405 Highland Avenue, Los Angeles, California 90024.

LIBRARIES AND INSTITUTIONS

AUSTRALIA
The Institute of Advanced Studies, Australian National University, Canberra
State University of Victoria, Melbourne

CANADA
The Main Library, University of British Columbia, Vancouver
The University of Toronto Library, Toronto

EIRE
University College Library, Cork
King's Inns Library, Dublin
Trinity College Library, Dublin
University College Dublin Library, Dublin

FRANCE
École Nationale des Chartes, Paris
Bibliothèque Nationale et Universitaire, Strasbourg

GERMANY
Niedersachsische Staats-und-Universitätsbibliothek, Göttingen
Universitätsbibliothek, Würzburg

ITALY
Biblioteca Apostolicia Vaticana, Citta del Vaticano, Rome

NEW ZEALAND
University of Auckland Library, Auckland

NORWAY
Universitetsbiblioteket, Oslo

SWITZERLAND
Universitatbibliothek, Basel
Zentralbibliothek Zurich, Zurich

UNITED KINGDOM
Aberdeen University Queen Mother Library, Aberdeen
The National Library of Wales, Aberystwyth
The University College of Wales Library, Aberystwyth
University College of North Wales Library, Bangor
Queen's University of Belfast Library, Belfast
The Berkshire Record Office, Reading
Central Libraries, Birmingham
University of Birmingham Library, Birmingham
The University Library, Bristol
The Bristol and Gloucestershire Archaeological Society, Bristol
St. John's College Library, Cambridge
The Seeley Historical Library, Faculty of History, Cambridge
Trinity College Library, Cambridge
The University Library, Cambridge
University Library, Cardiff
Royal Institute of Cornwall, Truro
Downside Abbey Library, Stratton on the Fosse, Bath
Durham Cathedral Library, Durham
The University Library, Edinburgh
The Essex Record Office, Chelmsford
University of Exeter, Exeter
The Main Library, Glasgow University, Glasgow
The Island Archives, Guernsey
The Hereford and Worcester County Public Library, Hereford
The Brynmor Jones Library, The University, Hull
The Kent Archaeological Society, c/o Maidstone Museum, Kent
The Brotherton Library, University of Leeds, Leeds
University of Leicester Library, Leicester
The Athenaeum, Liverpool
The University Library, Liverpool
HM College of Arms, London
The Guildhall Library, London
The Honourable Society of the Inner Temple, London
Institute of Historical Research, London
King's College Library, London
Lambeth Palace Library, London
The Honourable Society of Lincoln's Inn, London

The London Library, London
London School of Economics and Political Science Library, London
The Honourable Society of the Middle Temple, London
The National Archives, London
Royal Holloway and Bedford New College Library, Egham
The Royal Historical Society, London
The Society of Antiquaries of London, London
The John Rylands University Library of Manchester, Manchester
Chetham's Library, Manchester
The Central Library, Manchester
The University Library, Newcastle upon Tyne
Newport Central Library, Newport
Norfolk County Library, Norwich
Nottinghamshire Archives Office, Nottingham
University of Nottingham Library, Nottingham
The Codrington Library, All Souls College, Oxford
The Bodleian Library, Oxford
Brasenose College Library, Oxford
Corpus Christi College Library, Oxford
Dictionary of Medieval Latin from British Sources, The Classics Centre, Oxford
The Exeter College Library, Oxford
The History Faculty Library, Oxford
Jesus College Library, Oxford
Lady Margaret Hall Library, Oxford
Magdalen College Library, Oxford
St. John's College Library, Oxford
Somerville College Library, Oxford
Surrey Heritage, Surrey History Centre, Woking
The Library of Christ Church, Oxford
Reading University Library, Reading
The University Library, St. Andrew's, Fife
University of Sheffield Library, Sheffield
The Somerset Studies Library, Taunton
University of Southampton Library, Southampton
University College Library, Swansea
University of York Library, Heslington, York
Yorkshire Archaeological Society, Leeds

UNITED STATES
The Boston Public Library, Boston, Massachusetts
Bryn Mawr College Library, Bryn Mawr, Pennsylvania
Young Research Library, University of California, Los Angeles, California
University of California Library, Berkeley, California
University of California Library, Santa Barbara, California
The Joseph Regenstein Library, University of Chicago, Chicago, Illinois
Main Campus Library, University of Cincinnati, Cincinnati, Ohio
Homer Babbidge Library, University of Connecticut, Storrs, Connecticut
Cornell University Library, Ithaca, New York
Duke University Library, Durham, North Carolina
Robert W. Woodruff Library, Emory University, Atlanta, Georgia
Public Library of Allen County, Fort Wayne, Indiana
The Genealogical Society Library, Salt Lake City, Utah
Harvard College Library, Cambridge, Massachusetts
Harvard Law School Library, Cambridge, Massachusetts
University of Notre Dame Library, Notre Dame, Indiana
Parks Library, Iowa State University of Science and Technology, Ames, Iowa
The Milton S. Eisenhower Library, Johns Hopkins University, Baltimore, Maryland
University of Kansas Library, Lawrence, Kansas
University of Michigan Library, Ann Arbor, Michigan

University of Michigan Law Library, Ann Arbor, Michigan
University of Minnesota Library, Minneapolis, Minnesota
Columbia Library, University of Missouri, Columbia, Missouri 65201-5149
The Newberry Library, Chicago, Illinois
New England Historic Genealogical Society, Boston, Massachusetts
Columbia University Libraries, New York City, New York
New York Public Library, New York
The Library, State University of New York at Binghamton, Binghamton, New York
New York University, Elmer Homes Bobst Library, New York City, New York
Northwestern University Library, Evanston, Illinois
The Ohio State University Library, Columbus, Ohio
Pattee Library, Pennsylvania State University, Pennsylvania
University of Rochester Library, Rochester, New York
Rutgers – The State University Library, New Brunswick, New Jersey
University of Washington, Seattle, Washington
The Law Library, Southern Methodist University, Dallas, Texas
Henry E. Huntington Library, San Marino, California
Stanford University Library, Stanford, California
University of Illinois, Urbana, Illinois
Wake Forest College Library, Winston-Salem, North Carolina
Memorial Library, University of Wisconsin, Madison, Wisconsin
Yale University Library, New Haven, Connecticut